DESIGNING
THE
FUTURE

How Ford, Toyota, and other
world-class organizations use
lean product development to
drive innovation and transform
their business

JAMES M. MORGAN
JEFFREY K. LIKER

New York   Chicago   San Francisco   Athens   London
Madrid   Mexico City   Milan   New Delhi
Singapore   Sydney   Toronto

1 2 3 4 5 6 7 8 9   LCR   23 22 21 20 19 18

ISBN   978-1-260-12878-9
MHID   1-260-12878-4

ISBN   978-1-260-12879-6
MHID   1-260-12879-2

Library of Congress Cataloging-in-Publication Data

Names: Morgan, James M., author. | Liker, Jeffrey K., author.
Title: Designing the future : how Ford, Toyota, and other world-class
   organizations use lean product development to drive innovation and
   transform their business / James Morgan and Jeffrey K. Liker.
Description: New York : McGraw-Hill, 2019.
Identifiers: LCCN 2018020164| ISBN 9781260128789 (alk. paper) | ISBN
   1260128784
Subjects: LCSH: Product design—Case studies. | New products—Case studies. |
   Lean manufacturing—Case studies. | Technological innovations—Case studies.
Classification: LCC TS171 .M665 2019 | DDC 658.5/752—dc23
LC record available at https://lccn.loc.gov/2018020164

For my wife, Mary; my partner and my love

For my son, Greg, who has made me prouder
than he will ever know

For Christopher Morgan, who taught us
what it means to be "all in all the time"

—Jim Morgan

27
#ALLIN

A Personal Note

Adapt what is useful, reject what is useless and add
what is specifically your own.

—Bruce Lee

If as Socrates supposedly once said, "True knowledge exists in knowing that you know nothing," then I think I've arrived. After nearly 40 years working in numerous and diverse roles in and around product development, the only thing I am sure of is how much more there is to learn.

Yet I have had the privilege to work with some extraordinary people and to live in what the ancient Chinese curse refers to as "interesting times." So there is much to share. But that doesn't answer the fundamental question of "Why write another book?" I write out of a feeling of profound and compelling obligation (義理) to the many, many people who have helped me over the years. It is my small way to give back by sharing experiences with those who find themselves in similar circumstances and who perhaps do not have the benefit of such mentors. And I am particularly inspired by the example of one of those mentors. "To serve is to live," Alan always says . . .

So it is in that spirit that I offer this book for your consideration to adapt, reject, or add to as you see fit. Good luck on your journey and hold fast to that which matters most.

Jim Morgan
Old Mission Peninsula
Traverse City, Michigan

Contents

Foreword

I have been fortunate throughout my career to have the opportunity to contribute to truly important endeavors, help to create great products, and serve alongside exceptionally talented people. While at Boeing I had the opportunity to contribute to the design of all of Boeing's commercial airplanes and to lead the development of the game-changing Boeing 777 airplane; the integration of Boeing, McDonnell Douglas, and Rockwell; and the turnaround of Boeing Commercial Airplanes in its battle against European government–subsidized Airbus. As my responsibilities grew from an engineer to a chief engineer to a senior executive, it became ever clearer that the keys to a sustainable competitive advantage were great products and great people. Nothing else mattered if we did not get that right. Designing and building exceptional airplanes with the Boeing team and extended enterprise was my passion. So it was an extremely difficult decision to leave Boeing, my home for more than 37 years, and to take the helm as president and CEO of Ford in 2006. But I realized that I was once again being given the chance to contribute to the restoration of another American and global iconic company and have a positive impact on many lives.

The Ford situation was indeed dire—far worse than it had appeared from the outside. A $17 billion loss in 2006, a 20-year share decline, supplier bankruptcies, and the looming great recession were just the obvious issues. Inside I found an uncompetitive portfolio of products and a chaotic collection of brands that were sucking the life out of the company. Worse, warring regional fiefdoms and insular functional organizations were inhibiting the creation of a unified plan to get the company righted. But even with all this, I knew that the path to success would lie in the people—and Ford had no shortage of talented and hardworking people. What was needed was a plan. A plan, and a method to laser-focus the efforts of all those amazing people.

I had been employing and refining my "working-together management system" since my early days at Boeing and knew that it would be effective at Ford. The principles and practices of this management system not only provide a system for governance and decision making, but also outline expected leadership behaviors focused on respect, inclusion, and accountability. It enabled me to focus the entire global enterprise on a single plan and create an environment and culture of collaboration, transparency, and accountability that allowed the people of Ford and all Ford's stakeholders to work together to flourish and excel.

One of the people whom I came to know well during this time was Jim Morgan. He was a key senior leader important to our efforts to transform both our products and our product development capability. This work enabled us to create the industry-leading products that our customers valued and bought, and were central to our Ford revitalization plan. Even in the most difficult times we continued to invest in our products and our people, because a single hit product does not create a successful business. It is the ability to deliver great products over and over again and create profitable growth for all stakeholders, your people, customers, dealers, unions, and communities, that defines a successful enterprise.

In this book, Morgan and Liker leverage their considerable knowledge and experience to provide a blueprint to build this capability in any organization. It is a must-read for any leader who wants to create lasting value by building not just a great product, but a turbocharged product-creating machine. The authors provide both the theoretical underpinnings and real-world examples of how great companies are employing these ideas and methods every day to transform their organizations and create a better future for their people, their customers, and their communities.

I now have the honor to serve several more iconic organizations as a board member at Google, the Mayo Clinic, and Carbon 3D. And while the industries may be different, the fundamental working-together principles of management and leadership are the same. It's still about the people, and respecting and appreciating their talent and contributions. There is nothing more powerful than talented people working together to deliver a compelling vision, using a comprehensive strategy and a relentless implementation plan; and I know of no better way to accomplish this than our working-together principles and practices. The aim of all our work is to create products and services of unprecedented value for our customers and deliver profitable growth for all our stakeholders. This is the purpose of any business. And reading this book is a critical first step toward that goal. But don't stop there. Take action and put these ideas to work in your organization.

Good luck on your journey. I wish you the greatest success and fun along the way. But most of all I wish for you the opportunity to contribute to something that truly matters.

Alan R. Mulally

Acknowledgments

So many people have helped us on this book, and we have learned from so many others over the years. We are grateful to all of them. And we would like to list them all—but that list would be at least in the hundreds. You know who you are—we sincerely thank you. There are some people we would like to thank by name who directly helped with this book. In fact, we could not have done it without them.

We would like to start by thanking Mr. Alan Mulally for his guidance, feedback, and hours of discussion time that he provided us on this project—incredible! He was one of Jim's most important mentors at Ford and continues to remain a friend and confidant.

This project was a bit of an experiment. It was the first ever, three-way partnership between McGraw-Hill, the Lean Enterprise Institute (LEI), and us. This provided us with tremendous support. In addition to the excellent editorial assistance at McGraw-Hill by Noah Schwartzberg, we also received assistance from James Womack, founder of LEI, and John Shook, chairman of LEI. John has been teaching us about the Toyota Way for decades. He was Jeff's initial contact at Toyota where he was assistant general manager. He later left Toyota to join the University of Michigan and became a mentor to both of us, sharing his deep knowledge about Toyota's history, philosophy, and methods. Jim continues to learn from him as they work together at LEI. John read each chapter, providing priceless edits and challenging questions. Jim Womack, as we expected, provided high-quality feedback and asked questions that made us say, "Oh yeah, right!"

Two editors who read, edited, and provided feedback were Tim Ogden and George Taninecz. George was with us chapter by chapter, rewriting and turning our rough prose into a readable story. We are grateful to editors who can help engineers write.

Others who read and provided direct feedback on early versions of this manuscript were Ms. Mary Morgan, Mr. Andy Houk, and Mr. Charlie Baker. Your insights have proved invaluable on this project.

Mary is Jim's wife. She spent her career at General Motors where she was an engineering manager and lean coach. Mary not only provided valuable insights but also helped to keep this project organized. She as much as anyone else is the reason this book actually got written.

Thank you to Jim's friends and colleagues at Ford who shared an experience that would be difficult for anyone else to understand. People who taught him about much more than just product development include, Mr. Joe Sammut, Mr. Dave Pericak, Mr. Terry Henning, Dr. Derrick Kuzak, Mr. Joe Hinrichs, Mr. John Fleming, Mr. Jesse Jou, Mr. John Davis, Mr. Eric Frevik, Mr. Hiro Sugiura, Mr. Randy Frank, Ms. Susan DeSandre, Mr. Art Hyde, Mr. George Bernwanger, Mr. Scott Tobin, Ms. Marcy Fisher, Mr. Frank DelAsandro, Ms. Jennifer Palsgrove, Ms. Debra Keller, Dr. Bruno Barthelemy, Mr. Matt DeMars, Mr. Bob Trecapelli, Ms. Jeri Ford, Mr. Steve Crosby, and so many more.

Jim and TDM grew up together: from a small prototype shop to a major engineering, stamping, and build resource, eventually purchased by Ford. Thank you to Jim's TDM friends who were his lean learning partners before he knew what that meant: Mr. John Lowery, Mr. Steve Guido, Mr. Ned Oliver, Mr. Bill Anglin, Mr. Steve Mortens, Mr. Tim Jagoda, Mr. Scott Baker, Mr. Bill Roberts, Mr. Bill Morrison, Mr. Gerry Potvin, and so many more.

Once again Toyota was a remarkable partner and teacher to us. When we asked to return to do interviews about the company's latest in product development practices for this book, the team at Toyota graciously agreed. They set up whatever interviews and site visits we asked for. They spent many hours in interviews teaching and answering questions, driving cars, and walking the gemba. We visited the Toyota Technical Center in Ann Arbor many times and interviewed all the American chief engineers. We visited Japan twice and hammered the people there with questions about the Toyota New Global Architecture (TNGA). We learned about the development of Toyota's hybrid, electric, and hydrogen fuel cell cars. And the folks were marvelous hosts and fun to be around. We are incredibly grateful for the time, access, and attention we received.

Mr. Maki Niimi of Toyota's Global Communications Department was our chief point of contact and was responsive, patient, and on top of things and always helped us with a smile. Thank you very much for your support for nearly three years.

We have both learned so much from our friends at Toyota over the years, it is impossible to name them all. Still, our research at Toyota over the past couple of years for this project requires that we specifically thank the following people for their extensive support:

In Japan

Prius Development
Kouji Toyoshima (chief engineer)
Shinsuke Sugano (project manager)
Osamu Sawanobori (assistant manager)
Shoichi Kaneko (project general manager)

TNGA Development
Kazuhiko Asakura (general manager)
Kentaro Masuda (group manager)
Kiyohito Morimoto (executive general manager)
Masashige Ono (general manager)
Motoo Kamiya (project general manager)
Keiichi Yoneda (project general manager)

Mirai Production Line
Hirokazu Ishimaru (LFA factory manager, Motomachi plant)
Yasuhiro Kutsuki (department general manager, Motomachi plant)
Takao Minami (project manager)

Mirai Development
Yoshikazu Tanaka (chief engineer)
Mikio Kisaki (chief professional engineer)

Hydrogen Society Promotion
Taiyou Kawai (project general manager)

Lexus International
Yoshihiro Sawa (managing officer)

C-HR Development
Hiroyuki Koba (project general manager)

Production Engineering
Hirofumi Muta (senior managing officer)
Tatsuya Ishikawa (executive general manager)
Toshio Niimi (general manager)
Tadashi Kitadai (group manager)
Shinichi Inoue

Manufacturing (Kamigo Engine Plant)
Mitsuru Kawai (executive vice president)
Tomihisa Saito (general manager)
Hisashi Tsuchiya (department general manager)

Production Engineering (Body Engineering Division, Tsutsumi Plant)
Harutsugu Yoshida (general manager)
Tetsuya Obata (department general manager)

Public Affairs
Shigeru Hayakawa (senior managing officer)
Hiroshi Hashimoto (general manager)
Ryo Sakai (department general manager)
Katsuhiko Koganei (group manager)
Takashi Ogawa
Rika Nomura
Masahiro Yamaoka (general manager)
Jean-Yves Jault (group manager)
Riho Kakuta
Brian Lyons (group manager, Global Communications)

Toyota Technical Center, USA
Monte Kaehr (chief engineer, Camry)
Randy Stephens (chief engineer, Avalon)
Greg Bernas (chief engineer, Highlander)
Mike Sweers (chief engineer, Tundra)
Andy Lund (chief engineer, Sienna)
Don Federico (general manager, Vehicle Evaluation)
Masato Katsumata (chief engineer, Global Camry)
Seija Nakao (president)

• • •

One person who went beyond being interviewed to give us guidance and help with the book is Toyota chief engineer Randy Stephens.

We wrote about many cases in this book. The people in these stories are friends and colleagues we have been working with and learning from for many years. To our learning partner companies, which have challenged, experimented, and persevered with us, it has been an honor to work with you. Thanks for sharing your hard-earned learning. We are truly blessed to know you:

- **Herman Miller:** Mr. Matt Long, Mr. Beau Seaver, Mr. Jeff Faber, Mr. John Aldrich, Mr. Tom Niergarth, Mr. John Miller, Ms. Linda Milanowski, Mr. Ted Larned, and Mr. Scott Bacon

- **TechnipFMC:** Mr. Paulo Couto, Mr. David McFarlane, Mr. Mike Tierney, Mr. Alan Labes, Mr. John Calder, and Mr. Kerry Stout

- **Schilling Robotics:** Mr. Tyler Schilling, Mr. Andy Houk, Mr. Scott Fulenwider, Ms. Valerie Cole, Mr. Garry Everett, Mr. David Furmidge, and Ms. Hannah Waldenberger

- **Michigan Medicine:** Dr. Jack Billi, Dr. Steven Bernstein, Dr. Larry Marentette, Mr. Paul Paliani, Ms. Jean Lakin, and Ms. Jeanne Kin

- **GE Appliances:** Mr. Kevin Nolan, Mr. Sam DuPlessis, Mr. Al Hamad, Ms. Marcia Brey, Mr. Derrick Little, Mr. Daryl Williams, and Ms. Kyran Hoff

- **Embraer:** Mr. Manoel Santos, Mr. Waldir Conçalves, and Mr. Humberto Pereira

- **Solar Turbines:** Mr. Howard Kinkade, Mr. William Watkins, and Mr. Mike Fitzpatrick

- **Bose:** Mr. Sean Garrett, Mr. Robert Mullett, Ms. Karen Mills, Mr. Mark Heinz, and Mr. Mark Sellers

- **The Lean Enterprise Institute:** Dr. John Drogosz, Dr. Katrina Appell, Mr. Eric Ethington, Mr. Matt Zayko, Dr. José Ferro, and Dr. Boaz Tamir

- **Menlo Innovations:** Mr. Rich Sheridan

Introduction

The Power of Product Development Excellence to Compete and Prosper

The best way to predict the future is to create it.
—PETER DRUCKER

Designing the Future

"Insanely great" products can revolutionize an industry or even create one. Think of Apple's iPod and iPhone, Google's search engine, Facebook's original friend-to-friend software, or Amazon's product fulfillment service. These wildly successful start-ups led by visionary geniuses began with a new idea embodied in a new product and made their founders billionaires. It seems a great idea is hatched and an industry is magically transformed.

Then there's the rest of us.

Revolutionary products that get the lion's share of press are only the tip of the product development iceberg. The vast majority of new products and services will be innovations on a previous theme that attract far less attention but are no less important to the firms that create them or to their customers. The good news: there is an "insanely great" way to create them by employing the principles of lean product and process development (LPPD).

1

These principles are being applied and validated in firms in industries ranging from aerospace to healthcare to office furniture to robotics. The common feature of these early adopters is that they refuse to accept the status quo and understand that creating a steady stream of new products and services that surpass the competition is still the surest path to sustainable growth. These companies know that "the best way to predict the future is to create it" and recognize that the best way to do that is by redesigning their product development system so they can consistently design the best products. While brand-new start-ups may get away with missing deadlines and releasing buggy products, established businesses can't. They need a reliable way to produce the next great product or service that will continue to generate revenue and grow their business in order to ensure a bright future for their people, their customers, and their community.

In this book we aim to get inside the "black box" of development to help you realize your product and service dreams with speed, precision, and quality—and at an affordable cost. To that end we will go beyond broad generalizations on how to "be innovative," and dig deeper into concrete practices that are leading to exceptional results in LPPD pioneers we have worked with. We want to demonstrate how any organization can create and deliver great products and services, some breakthrough and some incremental, at a steady pace to continually renew their enterprise. Just a warning: no magic happens except the collective efforts of many people who work with passion to achieve something great.

Building the Capability to Design the Future

This book is for you if you strive for product greatness but aren't willing to gamble on a lightning strike of inspiration. It is for you if you're willing to take the harder path that requires more disciplined effort, continuous learning and improvement but far less luck. If you are, the best way we know to sustained greatness is by methodically and intentionally building your *capability* to create excellent products and services over and over again.

This book provides a reality-based approach to creating your future through new products and services that will bring joy to your customers— products and services that surpass their expectations, work as intended, and launch on time. The secret is enabling skilled and talented people to work together persistently and collaboratively to achieve the seemingly impossible, and then do it again. And who knows, had some of those "wildly successful start-ups" employed this system, perhaps their products would have been less buggy and their customers happier from the start.

Lean Development:
The Engine for Consistent Innovation

The concept of "lean" was first introduced in the bestseller *The Machine That Changed the World*. Lean production does more with less: build the best-quality products, delivered on time, in the quantity ordered by customers, with less inventory, lead time, space, and labor hours. The main model for this new paradigm of manufacturing was Toyota. Other auto companies had to adopt this new manufacturing method as best they could because the benefits were just too large to ignore. Manufacturing in other industry sectors quickly followed suit. Who does not want more for less?

Most people who read *The Machine That Changed the World* focused primarily on operational excellence and the Toyota Production System; however, there was one important chapter about lean in product development, based on the research of Taka Fujimoto and his dissertation chair at Harvard, Kim Clark, who in a subsequent book provided more detail about how Japanese auto companies were producing higher-quality product designs faster with fewer engineering hours and lower material costs. And because it cost these companies less people, time, and money to develop new products, they could update their products more frequently. Their product designs also integrated well with their lean manufacturing systems, so they quickly launched the product in the factory without creating a crisis of quality problems and redesign that was so common in the West (aka the "production Hell" Elon Musk talks about in regard to Tesla's Model 3 launch).[1]

Some of the key characteristics of lean product development that Clark and Fujimoto documented were:[2]

- A clear understanding of the customer that was front and center in every stage of the development process
- A single, powerful individual, the chief engineer, who was the architect of the overall development program and was responsible for everything from the identification of customer needs, to concept design, through to production preparation and launch

- Simultaneous product and process design that both sped up the development process and made it relatively easy to build in quality efficiently
- A high degree of teamwork among well-trained engineering specialists with deep knowledge of their components and systems
- Tight integration of key suppliers that design products and processes collaboratively with the team

Nearly concurrent with this work at Harvard, a series of research studies were undertaken at the University of Michigan resulting in a deeper understanding of specific practices and tools that were being employed at Toyota. In addition to our own work, research and writing by our colleagues Allen Ward and Durward Sobek contributed significantly to our understanding of Toyota product development. It is Al who actually coined the awkward but descriptive term *lean product and process development*.

Based on our U of M research, we published *The Toyota Product Development System* in 2006 and provided still greater detail in the form of 13 principles to define lean in development at Toyota. The model was organized around people, processes, and tools. We explained that lean development is a system—meaning that you cannot cherry-pick parts of it, but need to build an integrated system of people, processes, and tools to get Toyota's exceptional results.

Our Continuing Education

Since we wrote our previous book, we have continued to learn—a lot. We have, of course, continued to learn from Toyota, but also from a very broad set of experiences in many different industries. Our learning outside Toyota has been from our work with a wide range of firms and, in Jim's case, from personal experience as an engineering executive in the product-led transformation of Ford from 2004 to 2014, all of which provided examples from which we will draw throughout this book. Through these experiences, we have continued to flesh out the model in our previous book and have learned a great deal about the transformation process for companies that are not Toyota.

One thing we learned for sure: copying Toyota isn't the right way to go. Cutting and pasting does not work! Lean transformation is a journey of experimenting and learning and building your own system and culture.

But there are many ideas to help you on the journey from Toyota, Ford, and numerous other companies that are well on their way in the transformation to lean product and process development.

This book shares what we have learned since *The Toyota Product Development System*. We have discovered additional tools and methods, but perhaps even more important we have learned a great deal about leading major product-centered change and driving toward a true culture of continuous improvement and innovation. We are excited to share with you our models, our stories, and our experiences to help you on your journey.

Inspired to Change

There seems to be a natural attraction to improvement activities that focus on current operations, mostly in manufacturing and labor reductions. Quite frankly we are a bit confused by this. Certainly reducing operating costs and improving how products and services are delivered is of great value. However, there are far greater opportunities to do this in the development stage of products and processes. Successful new products can increase revenue, margin, and market share and create a halo effect that can change the way your organization is perceived. And the decisions you make during the product and process development period will in large part determine your operating costs and product quality for years to come. In addition to the immediate business benefits, product-process development is a unique opportunity to bring the enterprise together. Your product or core service is the one thing all your people have in common. By bringing your entire organization together in support of your products, you can help to create a collaborative, customer-focused culture that will prove a competitive advantage in its own right. This is why we think of product and process development as an opportunity to quite literally design your future.

Fortunately, a number of companies, often inspired by the benefits of lean on the shop floor, decided to move upstream looking for additional benefits. In the more than 10 years since the publication of *The Toyota Product Development System*, we have had the opportunity to lead, advise, and learn from many forward-thinking companies that have applied LPPD to their development operations. Through this work we have learned invaluable lessons from companies including Ford, Mazda, Menlo Innovations, Caterpillar, Solar Turbines, GE Appliances, University of Michigan Medicine, Herman Miller, TechnipFMC, Honda, Bose, and

Embraer. Working across such a wide variety of companies in disparate industries has required that we return to basics, to "first principles," to be effective in each of these environments. While this has required a great deal of experimentation and learning, it has led to the most exciting news of all: lean product and process development has been effective not only in automotive but in every industry where it has been tried. We share these stories in this book, and it is to these companies that we owe a profound debt. This work changed both the companies and our thinking about LPPD.

Through this work in transforming development capability in widely diverse industries, we have evolved our views on high-performing product development systems and have a far better understanding of what is required to transform an organization's development capability. In our last book we did our best to describe and contrast Toyota's system with traditional product development thinking. We had limited experience at that time with transforming organizations or adapting this model to different industries.

A Model of Lean Product-Process Development

The LPPD system has numerous unique and powerful practices, tools, and methods that we will discuss throughout this book. Perhaps the most critical point to understand is that LPPD is indeed a system. Successful product and process development capability relies on multiple interdependent elements that interact to create a complex whole. The best results are achieved by understanding and addressing an organization's people and social systems, as well as its processes, tools, and technical systems in order to understand and affect the way the whole functions. What's more, this system is dynamic—it must react effectively to changes in the internal and external environment over time. Our LPPD approach directly addresses each of these elements and also allows for the creation of a "living development system" that can evolve and improve. Figure I.1 provides a snapshot of the model and chapter guide detailed below.

Figure I.1 Lean PPD model and guide to chapters

UNDERSTAND CUSTOMERS AND CONTEXT

Chapter 1: Creating the Right Product. It starts and ends with creating value for the customer.

Product and process development success is determined by the specific and real value delivered to individual customers. To accomplish this you have to start with a deep understanding of both the customer and the context in which your product will operate. It requires a visceral understanding that can only be gained by observing customers at the *gemba* (the actual place where customers use the product). In addition to observation, this understanding is enhanced through targeted experimentation, set-based engineering, and rapid learning cycles at the front end of the development process. In Chapter 1 we will share techniques and tools used by companies to deeply understand their customer, close other critical knowledge gaps, align the team, and dramatically improve the chances for development success.

PROCESS EXCELLENCE

Chapter 2: Delivering with Speed and Precision. Use transparency, collaboration, and cadenced concurrent engineering to create flow in the development process.

The old waterfall model of product development was widely criticized as far back as the 1980s. Lean product-process development shows us how to create a far more integrated and simultaneous process. Product specialists, manufacturing system specialists, suppliers specializing in their components, and even people who will eventually build the product are collaborating from the earliest possible point in the program. A lean development process leverages a deep understanding of how the work actually gets done to identify key interdependencies in order to effectively integrate work across functions and achieve an exceptional degree of concurrency. Keeping it tight and on track, with ideas and testing and prototyping flowing smoothly from stage to stage, is a monumental task and requires high levels of competence, transparency, and collaboration at all levels in all specialties. However, the velocity and precision achieved is a significant competitive advantage.

The traditional approach of working on a new product in isolation is not enough to deliver maximum value to your customer or to create the best possible future for your organization. To do this you must examine and impact the entire value stream required to deliver value. Concept development, engineering, manufacturing, sales, installation, and serviceability are just some of the steps that make up the value delivery system. In addition, organizations must consider how this specific product fits within their overall goals and values. In Chapter 2 we provide tools, techniques, and examples from companies that have made powerful changes in how they execute product programs.

PROCESS EXCELLENCE

Chapter 3: Fixed and Flexible: The Yin and Yang of Lean Product Development. Standardize what is common across products for high quality and low cost, and to free up time for engineers to innovate on what makes the offering unique.

What might sound like a contradiction is actually two faces of the whole. LPPD shows that the harmonious integration of what we call the yin and yang of product development results in both creativity and efficiency. In the West we tend to see differences as opposites—choose one or the other, for example, standardized designs or innovation. Eastern philosophy often embraces opposites as harmonious, producing something new and beautiful. Anyone who has been taught by a Toyota Production System expert is tired of hearing "without standards there can be no *kaizen*." What is meant is that "standards clarify the best we know now, and we will build on that to create a new and better standard through kaizen" (continuous improvement).

Toyota's rule of thumb when developing the next new version of an existing model, for example, is to keep about 70 percent the same and focus on changing what will differentiate the product and deliver more value to the customer. There are many parts of the vehicle the customer never sees, and it makes sense to use the best design standards to date. This allows for maximum creativity in the areas that will differentiate the product. It also speeds up the design process, supports quality, reduces costly tool changes, and supports mixed model production in the same factory. In Chapter 3 we give examples from several companies on maintaining this balance.

EXCEPTIONAL PEOPLE

Chapter 4: Building High-Performance Teams and Team Members. High-performance teams and team members are the heart of a sustainable development system.

People are the single most important element of great product development systems. They provide the skills, energy, and creativity to drive your system and provide continuity over time. It is their ability to learn and grow that enables the system to evolve and improve. This is so important to the leaders at Toyota that they purposely "develop people and products simultaneously." At LPPD companies people development is not an extracurricular activity delegated to HR. It is integrated into how they do their work every day. In Chapter 4 we share examples of how successful companies hire, develop, and enable their teams.

EXCEPTIONAL PEOPLE

*Chapter 5: Leading Development. People need strong
leadership with strong customer vision.*

In our last book, we wrote about the role of the chief engineer at Toyota. That continues to be one of the topics that garner the most interest from other companies and rightfully so. It seems old-timers can recall the days when they had someone in that role, but over time this devolved into a program manager role. Many organizations have a technical lead of some type plus a more powerful program manager who administers timing and budget. And marketing acts as the voice of the customer. But we believe that breaking up leadership roles into pieces is simply not as effective as having one powerful chief architect with business responsibility, technical capability, and a deep understanding of the customer for each individual product. The chief engineer ties together the enterprise, like the conductor of an orchestra.

However, the chief engineer is not an island and cannot be successful on his or her own. The chief engineer relies heavily on leaders in different roles across the enterprise. The LPPD system requires all leaders, from the office of the CEO down to the various functional leaders, to be focused on making the chief engineer and the product successful. And an effective operating system combined with the right leadership behaviors creates the management system required to pull this all together and consistently deliver great products. In Chapter 5 we discuss the various roles of leaders in product development and the importance of establishing strong management systems.

CAPTURE AND APPLY KNOW-HOW

*Chapter 6: Creating and Applying Knowledge as a Learning
Organization. A learning organization creates and applies
knowledge to create new value in its products and services.*

Modern engineering organizations have powerful computer systems to capture knowledge, and many have created "books of knowledge" (both physical and virtual) and different types of checklists to aid in knowledge capture and dissemination. That's because the majority of development organizations think of learning as a tool problem. They want to know the latest technology or tool they can employ to improve their ability to learn and apply knowledge. However, we find that a new tool is rarely what's needed. More often we see that organizational cultural issues are at the heart of the problem. People who fear admitting to problems, undervalue or do not understand learning, and treat learning as an extracurricular activity are the primary inhibitors of effective organizational learning. True learning organizations look for problems, respond quickly to contain them, and then deeply reflect to learn for the next time. Sharing problems and solutions is what takes individual know-how and turns it into organizational knowledge. While tools and technologies are useful, working on the human side of learning most often yields the greatest benefit. In Chapter 6 we address both the social and technical elements of creating a learning organization.

PRODUCT EXCELLENCE

The Pursuit of Product Perfection. Act as masters of your craft, continuously improving how you create true value for each customer.

Even with all these pieces in place, product excellence is not guaranteed. Both the design and delivery of the actual product need to be executed with a high level of quality. Okay, but what does that mean? First and foremost it means that the product provides true value to the customer. But this value can take many forms. Styling, usability, reliability, workmanship, and efficiency of design all directly impact the quality and competitiveness of your product. Increasingly, companies like Apple, Toyota, and Ford integrate design, workmanship, and manufacturing excellence into a single seamless attribute called craftsmanship that not only differentiates their products but is at the core of their product excellence philosophy. Craftsmanship is much more than a set of technical criteria. The best products create an emotional connection with the customer. That may sound esoteric, but it can be simple. Products that are easy to use, are reliable, and work as intended every time often yield the strongest emotional connections. In Chapter 7 we share practices designed to improve design, reliability, and design efficiency.

TURNING CONCEPTS TO ACTION

Of course, just reading this book will do nothing to help your organization. You have to do something. At the end of each chapter, we provide questions for you to reflect on and suggest some challenges you might accept to help move your organization forward in your own way. In the final chapter we discuss our experiences with LPPD transformations, provide additional examples of organizations that have followed different transformation paths in a variety of industries, and present an emerging model of product-led transformation support.

The Purpose of This Book

Through this book our goal is to instruct, inspire, challenge, and provide you with actionable methods and tools to get great product ideas to the market fast and efficiently and with delivered quality. Even more, we want to help you develop a powerful and sustainable system of product and process development, not just one successful product program. But lean product and process development is not a software update where you just click through a menu to update your system. You will need to commit to the transformation and do the hard work that is always required to make meaningful change.

In fact, hard work, resilience, and commitment are the common denominators across all our transformation stories. Nowhere was this more evident than during the historic, product-led transformation of Ford Motor Company under CEO Alan Mulally. Before taking you through the details of LPPD, in the next chapter we will give an overview of Ford's historic success in transforming its products—and the fate of the company—leveraging many of the tools and methods you will read about in more detail later in the book. We are not necessarily holding Ford up as a global benchmark for lean excellence. Ford, like most automakers, is in the midst of a difficult struggle with the future of autonomous vehicles, ride share, and electric vehicles (EVs) and is continuing to evolve. However, the Ford story will set the stage for discussing LPPD in action and sharing stories from many other organizations on a similar journey in later chapters of the book.

From Concepts to Action

We do not assume that we know what is most important to you in each chapter, and therefore, we decided not to provide a table of "key take-aways." Instead we would like to turn that over to you. We often find ourselves reading the words of a book without taking the time to deeply reflect on their meaning. So we will conclude each chapter by asking you to reflect on what you read and how it might relate to your organization. Starting with Chapter 1, we will have a standard format for these reflections:

1. **Creating a vision.** We will summarize the LPPD vision that the chapter is suggesting. A vision is long term, 5 to 10 years out or more. Then it is your turn: What makes sense, and what would you modify as a vision for your organization?

2. **Your current condition.** Where is your organization now as it relates to the vision? If the answer is "We are there," then the vision is not ambitious enough. Go back to 1. If the answer is "The gap is huge in these areas, we have gotten started in these areas, and we are doing well in these other areas," you are on the right track.

3. **Taking action.** What first steps can you take right now? We do not expect that you will read a chapter, make a major organizational transformation, come back and read another chapter, and so on. But taking some action will both clarify the message of the chapter and get you started. After all, the first step is often the hardest. We also recognize that you may not be the top person in charge. What can you do within your span of influence? It may be convening a group of associates and asking them to read the chapter and discuss possible actions. It may be trying to implement on a rudimentary basis one or more of the concepts in the chapter. It may be sketching out a rough plan for how to approach a development project you are working on now or soon to begin.

Your Current Condition

This being the Introduction, we did not get into detail about any of the guiding principles, but it is still worth reflecting on the strengths and weaknesses of your organization to embark on a journey like the one we are suggesting:

1. Does your organization focus the right resources on the development of your products and services given how much impact they have on your future?

2. Do your leaders think of the development of your products and services as a capability that must be *continuously* improved?

3. Do your leaders think deeply about your future, the organization's strategy, and the types of new products and services you need to stand out to your customers?

4. Do your leaders treat people with the respect they deserve and invest in developing people at all levels?

Taking Action

1. Take the time to understand the network of influence in your organization that influences how product and process development are prioritized.

2. Get a copy of your organization's strategy and study how clearly it lays out a future vision for your products and services.

3. Reflect on the principles of LPPD in this chapter and how you are doing in your organization measured against these principles.

Ford's Historical Turnaround

How Ford Connected a Bold Strategy to Product-Process Excellence

When I got to Ford I found that the problems were not as bad as I thought. They were much, much worse.

—ALAN MULALLY, FORMER PRESIDENT
AND CEO, FORD MOTOR COMPANY

Setting the Stage

Can product development really make a difference to a business? People often learn best through stories, so we thought we would start with a pretty amazing one. The Ford story will provide a context and preview for the lean development model explained in the rest of this book. In a sense we are starting with the conclusion—what does a product-led transformation look like? We are not holding Ford Motor Company up as a perfect example of a lean enterprise; rather we are sharing invaluable lessons learned from the dramatic, product-led transformation of an iconic global company—perhaps one of the greatest business turnarounds in U.S. history.

One of us, Jim, was fortunate to be part of this most interesting period at Ford, first as one of the leaders of the global product development system (GPDS) creation (two years) and then as the global director of body and stamping engineering (eight years). He joined Ford shortly before former president and CEO Alan Mulally arrived. The other of us, Jeff, meanwhile, had been studying Ford from the outside. We have combined these different vantage points in an effort to provide you with an example of the power of new product development from which you might draw insight and inspiration. Ford's transformation helps to illustrate many of our principles, which we will examine in more detail throughout this book. But first, let's take an insider's look at this turnaround story.

Finding the Right Leader

On April 30, 2009, Chrysler filed for chapter 11 bankruptcy. On June 1, 2009, General Motors followed suit. Could Ford be far behind? To the surprise of many, Ford, also on the verge of total collapse, decided to brave its own deep financial crisis and take on the challenge without court protection or taxpayer support. All three companies, with so many iconic vehicles creating so many cherished memories for customers, simply were no longer making products customers wanted. This was far from the remarkable product innovation that characterized the early days of Ford and helped create the auto industry.

In 1925, Henry Ford took out an extraordinary ad in the *Saturday Evening Post*. In it he articulated the driving vision behind all the company's efforts. It read in part, "The whole-hearted belief that riding on the people's highway should be within easy reach of all the people." Ford wanted nothing less than to open the highway to everyone. Democratizing the automobile was the simple but powerful idea behind Ford's hugely successful Model T. This breakthrough product, which was within the means of most working people, was the manifestation of game-changing innovations in design, manufacturing, and supply-chain management.

While most people recall Ford's assembly-line innovations as his most important contribution to industry, we would argue that it was Henry's drive to deliver his unique and compelling product vision that changed how most people lived and spawned one of the most important industries in the world.

Ford Motor Company continued to improve on this unique product proposition by continually working on product evolution and manufacturing efficiency. In 1912 the Model T retailed for about $525. By the time Henry ran the ad in 1925, the same vehicle cost just $265. Henry's company was amply rewarded for its efforts with unparalleled profitable growth for many years, capturing a phenomenal 54 percent global market share with the Model T; an incredible 15 million vehicles sold over the Model T's life.

His relentless focus on this revolutionary product enabled Henry to change the world and build a high-performing automotive juggernaut that was far ahead of its competitors and seemingly unstoppable. From its humble beginnings in Henry's garage, Ford had become, in the words of the ad, "an industrial organization, which is the greatest the world has ever known."

OPENING THE HIGHWAYS TO ALL MANKIND

Source: https://media.ford.com/content/fordmedia/fna/us/en/features/opening-the-highways.html#

This was hardly the company that Alan Mulally found when he arrived on September 5, 2006. On that Tuesday when he pulled into the executive garage under the company's world headquarters in Dearborn, Michigan, he was joining a company that was deeply and profoundly troubled. Ford was no longer revolutionizing the world with its products, and not even enormous financial incentives could keep consumers from turning away from Ford's products in record numbers. Alan surely considered this as he rolled past executive parking spaces filled with Jaguars, Land Rovers, and Volvos, luxury nameplates owned by Ford. Not even Ford's leaders were driving Fords. This was more than a little disturbing to a longtime product guy like Alan, and presented a pretty good clue about the underlying problem of this once iconic American company. One thing was clear: no matter what other problems it might have, Ford had a serious product problem.

In fact, due largely to its nearly total lack of competitive products, Ford would lose a record $17 billion in 2006, continue a more-than-a-decade-long market share decline, face critical supplier bankruptcies, and watch employee morale tank. The stock price also continued its precipitous drop, eventually bottoming out at a pathetic $1.01 per share. The financial result was a total market capitalization of only $5.5 billion (the same as that of a decent tech start-up) and a junk bond credit rating.

Internally, Alan found well-intentioned functional and regional organizations with a lot of very talented people—the good news. However, they acted as independent companies, each focused on their own plans to improve the company, which created confusion and robbed the organization of crucial resources and energy—the bad news. He also found a chaotic collection of brands, each with an uncompetitive portfolio of products that few people wanted to buy—the worst news.

Couple these "self-inflicted wounds" with a U.S. economy that was about to enter the greatest financial crisis since the Great Depression, now known as the Great Recession, and the outlook for Ford was dire. This was in fact an unprecedented time in the American auto industry, during which both GM and Chrysler failed as independent enterprises, taking many key suppliers with them. It was clear that Ford's problems were, indeed, much, much worse than Alan had previously thought. In fact, the general view around the auto industry was that Ford was caught in a high-velocity death spiral and the last thing the company needed was an "airplane guy."

It is difficult to pinpoint the start of Ford's troubles, but there were some clear signs as far back as the late 1990s.

By 2000 Ford was suffering an organizational identity crisis. Ford executive leadership seemed like it wanted the company to be almost anything but an auto company. But most of all, it seemed like it wanted the company to be General Electric. The executives decided to broadly diversify the business, fragmenting leadership attention and energy. They diverted crucial product investment in order to finance a colossal spending spree on a multitude of companies, from junkyards to Hertz rental cars to Jaguar. Consequently, they were forced to settle on a "fast-follower" product strategy that resulted in new product introductions that barely kept pace with the industry.

They stripped out critical internal technical capability, often outsourcing fundamental design responsibility to suppliers that they pitted against each other in a scheme to get the lowest-possible pricing. Senior leadership also promoted a level of internal cross-organization competition that drove local optimization at the expense of any collaboration. Coupled with the adoption of GE's zero-sum performance evaluation system— which graded A, B, and outcast C players on a forced distribution—they created a noxious level of internal competition.

Ford had become a dangerous environment of "palace intrigue" and excess executive privilege. But perhaps worst of all, Ford abandoned the early product- and customer-value focus of its founder in favor of shareholder value and growth at any cost. The results were predictable, and when the bottom fell out, Ford reacted the way large companies often do, by letting go of people and making bone-deep cost cuts.

In 2002 alone, Ford laid off more than 20,000 people and announced the closing of five plants. Reductions continued into the next year, cutting ever deeper and more broadly, eventually affecting every corner of the company. The layoffs and cost cutting served to intensify internal strife and choked off any remaining product investment.

William Clay (Bill) Ford Jr., great-grandson of Henry, who had finally wrested back control of the company, recognized that this time the cost cutting, no matter how deep, would not be enough to save the company. So in 2006 he pulled out all the stops to recruit a proven leader who had successfully turned around another huge, iconic American company— Boeing.[1] Bill Ford saw recruiting Alan as perhaps the only path to the survival of his company. Alan was not the best of the short list. He was the short list. Bill Ford would spare no effort or expense to get his man.

The Ford team was incredibly persistent, and after saying no several times, Alan finally agreed to join the company. Alan's suspicions about the paucity of competitive new products at Ford were confirmed when Ford leaders shared both current model vehicles and new product prototypes. In fact, it became clear that the product situation was even worse than he thought. It was clear that while he needed to continue to cut costs, it would be even more important to raise capital and get the global Ford team working together to create products that customers would truly value.

If the solution to Ford's problems was to create fully competitive products that delivered exceptional value to customers, then the company would need money—and a lot of it. So he and CFO Don Leclair headed to Wall Street to take out what Alan later described as "the largest home-improvement loan in history." Together in November of 2006 they raised about $24 billion to fund these product programs just before the recession caused funds to dry up and access to capital became nearly impossible.[2] The assets held against this loan were nothing less than the entire company, including the blue oval.

During the previous regime, the company had fallen woefully behind the industry in almost every area of capital spending—the price paid for the prior leadership's acquisition spree. Most of Ford's manufacturing plants and equipment were old, engineering technology and facilities were out of date, marketing spend had been drastically reduced, and many other needs had been left unfunded. In a sense the "easy thing to do" would have been to equally divide the capital across all these needs. But Alan concluded that this would just delay Ford's inevitable demise. Ford needed to both change the way it developed products and completely reinvent its global product portfolio, so the majority of the money was earmarked for new product. This bold decision illustrated both Alan's courage as a leader and his absolute certainty that great products were central to this turnaround. "We have to create product our customers will value and buy" became Alan's call to arms.

However, it would take more than just money to accomplish this product-centered revolution. Alan had to figure out how to bring his far-flung enterprise together in order to fully leverage its capability. So Alan's next step was to develop a strategy to bring the extended enterprise together through his "One Ford" blueprint. This plan clearly communicated how Ford and its extended enterprise must act as a single, aligned team in order to successfully compete and "create profitable growth for all."

To deliver on this audacious plan, he needed a way to connect deeply with the people throughout Ford. Despite Ford's current difficulties, he knew Ford employees were proud of the company's heritage, and he was confident that they had the ability to return it to those heady days. That's when Alan found the *Saturday Evening Post* advertisement from 1925. Not only was the ad steeped in Ford tradition, but it also communicated a powerful mission of delivering differentiating, customer-defined value in a compelling, inclusive, and product-centric way. What's more, by utilizing a part of Ford's proud history, it was the perfect way to connect with and reenergize the depleted but talented Ford team he had inherited.

Having secured the capital and energized the global team around his vision rooted in the urgent need to create compelling products, Alan sought to more deeply understand the causes of Ford's current situation. Despite the relentless pressure to act, he knew he first had to understand the reasons behind the lack of product and the fundamental problems that lay beneath Ford's dreadful performance.

Start by Deeply Understanding the Current Reality

The transformation at Ford would have to start with an unflinching and unvarnished examination of its current reality, both acute and chronic issues. Alan committed to personally leading this effort. The deeper his examination went, the worse Ford's situation looked. What Alan saw in his early days had to be depressing, but he remained philosophical, saying that Ford was an opportunity-rich environment and that he would be more concerned if Ford was in all this trouble and everything was operating well.

Understanding—Macro Level

Alan is still proud to say he is a student of Toyota. He learned a great deal during executive learning missions to Toyota while he was with Boeing and is a longtime student of lean. So he knew that to truly understand, he had to go to the source (to the *gemba*) to see, hear, and feel for himself what was really happening. He held town halls, he visited assembly plants, he joined in design meetings, and he set up one-to-one meetings with key people throughout the company. In fact, this is how Jim's relationship with Alan started. He received a short note from Alan asking him to stop by to talk. Alan had worked with renowned lean coach James Womack at Boeing, and when Alan joined Ford, Womack had made him aware of Jim and his background. This first meeting led to a strong friendship, many one-on-one discussions, and Alan's unwavering support for the work of Jim's team over the next seven years.

Alan did not stop by just looking inside Ford. He also held meetings with auto dealers and key suppliers, which were crucial partners in the extended enterprise. His level of visibility, availability, and unfiltered communication was unprecedented at Ford—exactly what he wanted and Ford needed.

Alan also set out to better understand the industry and Ford's place in it. He was amazed to find that Ford had very few competitor vehicles available, and staff access to them was limited to specialist vehicle evaluators, who provided "politically correct" reports to senior leaders. In other words, Ford products were almost always better. He wanted to drive the competitor vehicles, he wanted his leadership team to drive them, and most of all, he wanted the product engineers to drive them. So he directed the product development group to make a fleet of competitor vehicles available.

He searched broadly to understand different perspectives on Ford, including visits to third-party industry organizations like JD Powers, the Center for Automotive Research, automotive safety organizations, local newspapers, and various financial organizations, and he even sought out experienced automotive beat reporters. In many of these visits he had key Ford leaders in tow with orders to listen, reflect, and not rationalize away the criticisms they heard.

But most important of all, he knew he needed to better understand the customer (further discussed in Chapter 1, "Creating the Right Product"). Here especially he wanted unfiltered access to what the customers had to say. Consequently, he spent several full days in dealerships—selling cars, talking directly to customers, and learning directly about their buying considerations. He also began a regular practice of cold-calling customers who had purchased a Ford in the past 90 days to get their direct feedback on the product and their experience with Ford Motor Company.

His *gemba* immersion was personally compelling and led to profound insights, both large and small, that informed his plan every step of the way. However, as important as this was, a successful transformation would require this type of investigative work throughout the company at all levels.

Transformation from the Macro to the Micro Level

At this point many stories about Ford's turnaround would stop. The single hero rode into town, identified the problems, and single-handedly saved the day. But what saved Ford went well beyond a single leader, no matter how good, and the "heroes" in this turnaround story were legion. Alan certainly had a great influence on the *context* for galvanizing the right leaders and team members focused on the right priorities; however, much of the actual work that saved the company happened in the trenches, at the micro level. These were the actions of thousands of dedicated women and men, whose names may not end up in the business press, but whose contributions were crucial to Ford's success. So we will also share a portion of that story by describing the transformation experience within one engineering organization: body and stamping engineering.

Understanding—Micro Level

Body and Stamping Engineering Jim's team, the body and stamping engineering (B&SE) organization, was one of several global engineering organizations within Ford (along with electrical, chassis, etc.). B&SE was responsible for the product engineering, process development, tooling, testing (including safety), and launch of vehicle body structure, closures, and exterior systems (e.g., lamps, fascias, glass, trim) as well as all related performance attributes for Ford globally. In essence, the B&SE team is responsible for everything the customer can see on the outside of the vehicle except for the tires and wheels. Team members represented a wide variety of engineering disciplines, as well as toolmakers, machinists, and technicians in Dearborn, Michigan; Cologne, Germany; Bahia, Brazil; Mexico City; Nanjing, China; and Melbourne, Australia.

This is a unique organization. Historically in Ford, as in most companies, body engineering was part of the product development organization, while stamping engineering and tooling were part of manufacturing. However, the communication and collaboration between product development and manufacturing was broken. Their interactions were more like a series of skirmishes than a cooperative endeavor. Derrick Kuzak and Joe Hinrichs (EVP of global manufacturing at the time) realized they did not have the time to work on harmonizing these very different cultures and made the bold decision to combine them into a single organization and asked Jim to lead it. Jim was at first a bit skeptical of this move. However, primarily because of the talented, dedicated, and very outspoken team he had, he soon became a passionate believer in the strategy.

Like Mulally, Jim and his team also needed to deeply understand their current reality. Many of the practices they put in place to do this proved so valuable and such effective learning tools that the team made them part of its regular cadence long after the initial current-state evaluations were complete.

The B&SE leadership team began by holding informal skip-level meetings in which they skipped levels of management to talk directly with engineers at all levels in the organization. These meetings led to candid discussions about the issues that working-level engineers were experiencing as well as ideas to improve the situation. In addition to skip levels, "all-hands" meetings were held across various locations around the world in order to get direct feedback from engineers, technicians, and managers and share the One Ford product-driven strategy face-to-face. Initial discussions were sometimes emotionally charged, but it was important to start the candid dialogue, and the honesty helped to build trust.

Weekly design and quality reviews often moved out of insular conference rooms and to the factory floor, dealerships, suppliers, and test tracks. "Go and see," understand, and work together became the normal expectation, and this dramatically increased shared understanding, teamwork, and performance.

B&SE team members also began to meet with both their upstream and downstream partners in the product and process development value stream. They talked with operators, technicians, and supervisors in assembly plants, stamping plants, prototype shops, and tool shops, and they saw firsthand the difficulties their designs had created and discussed how they could make them better. This provided valuable insight in how work was done throughout the value stream, identified specific areas where coordination was needed, and helped the team to see how they could improve their overall performance and the resulting products.

They drove competitor vehicles from the new fleet Alan had brought in and held team design "walk-arounds," during which Ford vehicles and comparable competitor vehicle were placed side by side and gone through with a fine-tooth comb. They attended auto shows as a team and evaluated both current and future models.

The B&SE team also pored over quality "verbatims" directly from customers—actual customer comments explaining in their own words what their issues were with Ford products. Verbatims that were relatively straightforward and understandable were assigned directly to quality leads or managers to develop countermeasures, review, and update standards as required and to share findings with the team. In cases where verbatims were not fully understood, engineers traveled to the location and worked through local dealers to talk directly with customers to more fully understand the specific issue and design effective countermeasures. In addition, engineering teams worked with dealerships and their mechanics to lower repair costs through design changes that would enable more efficient repairs when required.

Engineers and managers attended customer events for products like Mustang (shows, track events, etc.) and F150 (off-road events and races, other sporting events) to study firsthand how customers interacted with their vehicles and to get direct feedback. (Engineers are often enthusiastic participants in these events in any case!) They talked with customers, studied competitive offerings, and came back to share their insights and develop strategy with the broader team.

B&SE also held a series of detailed benchmarking events where they examined both Ford and competitor products by tearing them down and studying subsystems and components. These events included people from key suppliers, manufacturing, and product development working closely together in order to provide a broad perspective on how to deliver ever-greater value to their customer.

Coming Together to Create "Profitable Growth for All"

The company's goal was as elegantly simple as it would be incredibly difficult to achieve: "to become a lean global enterprise building the best cars and trucks in the world to create profitable growth for all." One thing was certain; it was the people of Ford who would be key to accomplishing this tremendous task. Alan and his executive team needed to tap into that capability. That being said, they would have to find a completely new way of working together if they were going to save the company they loved.

Coming Together—Macro Level

When Alan arrived, people both inside and outside Ford waited for the axe to fall on Ford's top leadership team. Isn't that what always happens in a good turnaround story? But it never did. Despite expectations that Alan would "clean house" and bring in his own team, he largely stayed with the leadership group he inherited. There were two early exceptions: Steve Hamp, chief of staff and brother-in-law to Bill Ford, and Mark Schultz. Alan simply felt that Steve created an unnecessary extra layer between himself and his team. Mark self-selected out. While Alan did not replace senior leaders, he did do a bit of reshuffling to make sure the right people were in the right seats and ready to work together.

Assembling the Team   Getting the team right is a major part of how senior leaders create a context for success, and Alan went about this in a very methodical and thoughtful manner. He selected proven, results-oriented leaders who also knew how to build a team. For a product-led turnaround to succeed, there was one executive position he had to get right—global VP of product development. He selected Derrick Kuzak.

While Ford products were for the most part marginally competitive, there was one bright spot in Ford's relatively small European market. As vice president of product development for Ford's European operations, Derrick sparked a renaissance of kinetic design-driven products that embodied the best performance attributes and competed successfully with tough European competitors. He already had a deep understanding of LPPD from his earlier assignment as leader at Mazda in Japan. Quiet, strong-willed, and unassuming, Derrick had the technical acumen and a clear vision for both Ford's future products and its product development organization. And for the first time in decades, Ford truly had a single global leader of product development.

One Team, One Plan, One Goal   Alan acted quickly to create sharper focus in the organization. His One Ford campaign was much more than just a pocket card. From his first day, Alan worked with his senior executive team to develop the One Ford product-led revitalization plan to align the entire enterprise. He initiated global functional organizations to better leverage capability around the world, he divested brands (e.g., Volvo, Jaguar, Land Rover) to increase leadership focus, and he worked to enroll each and every employee in the plan through an effective strategy deployment process and tireless communication. He also implemented his powerful "working together management system" that breathed life into the One Ford plan, leveraged the talent, changed the culture, and moved the enterprise collectively forward.

Creating a Leadership Cadence   The heart of Alan's management system was his business plan review (BPR). It was one of the first things he put in place to align his leadership team and help create the focus he envisioned across the enterprise. Every Thursday, Alan brought together all functional and regional leaders to review the business environment, the progress to the plan, and the status of key objectives. Only new issues and changes from the previous week were reviewed. This event became the management "pacemaker," driving management activities throughout the organization. Disciplined cadence was key. Alan would quip, "The neatest thing about this process is that we are going to get back together next week, and I *know* you will make progress by then."

Pleased to Hold Ourselves Accountable   When Alan walked into his first BPR he was happy to see his senior executive team seated eagerly around the large, round mahogany table. However he also noticed that the chairs around the periphery of the room were filled with people holding laptops, binders, and books—people he had not seen before. When he inquired about them, he was told that they had the reference data and other information that the execs might require for the meeting. Alan commented that he was quite certain these folks had more important things to do, unless of course some of the executives didn't know what was happening with their business. They showed up the next week sans support staff.

You Can't Manage a Secret   The next major organizational problems to emerge from the BPR was that Ford had no problems. None. Alan was stunned. Despite the fact that Ford was losing billions of dollars, company stock was in free fall, and market share continued to decline, slide after slide presented at the BPR meeting was as green as his home state of Washington. After a couple of weeks of this, it became clear that the real problem at Ford was fear of admitting problems—rather than getting help. In the past, people who surfaced problems often found their careers limited. One crucial lesson that Alan learned from his experience at Boeing was the need for transparency and the ability to discuss problems openly. The senior leadership team would need a level of transparency and candor not seen at this level of the organization in decades. Alan called the team out on this behavior and made clear his expectations going forward.

Finally, Mark Fields, president of the Americas, presented a red issue on vehicle launch. All eyes were on Alan while the room held its collective breath, many of them thinking about how they would miss Mark. Alan began to applaud, and then went around the room asking who might be able to help resolve this issue. This story went through the organization like wildfire. Many of the old Ford hands remained skeptical that you could actually raise a problem and get help; however, over time and through consistent leadership behavior, surfacing issues became common practice in most of the organization. Alan continually reminded the organization that we may "have" a problem, but that "you" are not the problem. "You" are part of the solution.

Going Global   Before joining Ford, Alan assumed it was a global company. He quickly came to realize that it was really a collection of regional companies that just happened to be carrying around the same business cards. In addition to implementing the BPR, he moved quickly to globalize organizations (product development, manufacturing, marketing, etc.) and identified single global leaders for each. This move was crucial in Ford leveraging its global talent base and its scale (and critical for its standardization and platform strategy discussed in Chapter 3, "Fixed and Flexible").

Product Development Organization   Ford had experimented with numerous product development organization structures in the past. However, the company eventually settled on a matrix organization structure that leveraged the strong functional organizations for deep learning, but focused attention on the chief engineers (CEs) and their product programs (discussed further in Chapter 4, "Building High-Performance Teams and Team Members"). The functional groups worried about the development of great people, while the CEs worried about the development of great products. The CEs determined *what* the product needed to be, while the functional groups worked on *how* that vision was to be achieved, with the CEs pulling it all together. The greatest difference was actually in the organizational software. The matrix looked similar to many functional organizations, but at Ford the functional groups knew it was their job to make the programs successful—that's how they would be judged. This matrix-supported product focus permeated the entire organization, daily behaviors, the decisions people made, and the way they were rewarded.

The level of collaboration under this matrix had been all too rare in the functional organizations of old.

Coming Together—Micro Level

Body and Stamping Engineering: Aligning the Global Organization Through a Product Focus   We have already discussed the unique structure of the BS&E organization. At first, globalization added yet another layer of organizational complexity. The key to bringing this diverse, global engineering team together was a relentless focus on the product. Engineering is a highly specialized field, and it is easy for engineers to get caught up in the details of their own specialty and lose sight of how they are contributing to the overall product. This changed. The team had to literally reframe the purpose of the organization and its highly skilled engineers and technicians around creating the best possible products instead of prioritizing the completion of their specialized functional work. The design studio became the immediate customer, rather than the enemy. It meant moving from a mentality of downstream engineering writing feasibility rejections and vetoing interesting design features, to one of collaborating across functions to deliver the most compelling designs in Ford's history. It meant working with the vehicle's chief engineer to understand and deliver the team's vision for a specific product. Working this way was difficult and often quite contentious. But it was also rewarding in a way the old way of working could never be. As people began to take pride in the products, it created a strong bond across functional organizations. One small example was how the cross-functional team worked on the new Fusion.

Part of the chief engineer's goal for the all-new Fusion was to bring exciting styling to the midsize sedan category. This was a major task for the design studio. There were many challenges, but one that was particularly vexing was the character line (a sharp crease) that ran down the entire side of the vehicle exterior. The crispness and continuity of the line was crucial. This new styling line created serious technical challenges for manufacturing and in the past would have certainly been rejected as not feasible. Instead, stamping engineering redesigned the dies to get it just right, and together with the studio designers, it reviewed early painted panels in the shop that made the stamping dies (Dearborn Tool and Die). This team worked long hours to get the details just right. Not only was it the first time that designers had been in that plant; several did not even realize Ford had a tool shop. The Fusion went on to redefine midsize car styling and was widely copied.

The Extended Enterprise—Matched Pairs and Repairing Supplier Relationships Product and process development does not stop at the four walls of the company. In automotive, as in most industries, suppliers play a critical role in developing new products, and by 2007, Ford ranked dead last in the annual Supplier-OEM Relationship Survey. Ford was the auto company with which suppliers least liked to work. Ford's decades-long confrontational relationship with suppliers, missing program volumes, and disrespect of suppliers' technologies and capabilities had led to an unhealthy, antagonistic relationship. To make matters worse, suppliers were often confused about how to work with Ford. It seemed like engineering and purchasing were delivering two different messages, which led to incredible frustration and waste. Engineers were focused on breakthrough technical innovations, while purchasing came along with a singular focus on cost.

Leaders of engineering and purchasing met off-site to discuss possible countermeasures. They came up with an innovative *matched-pair* process. This process matched up professionals from each organization based on their specialty. It started by matching the global engineering directors with the global purchasing directors and worked down the organization so that the leaders for each subsystem in each organization were matched up with each other. The pairs were responsible for delivering programs, developing long-term strategies, and delivering annual cost-reduction targets. They also spoke to suppliers with one voice. Directors cochaired a weekly matched-pair meeting in which the combined leadership teams worked through program cost issues and supplier-performance issues and developed business plans for each commodity.

The matched-pair strategy not only improved Ford's relationships with its suppliers, moving the company from last to first among U.S. carmakers in the annual survey, but also allowed Ford to improve costs by working on both technical and commercial aspects and improve supplier performance. And it was a tremendous education process for both engineering and purchasing. We will discuss the matched-pair process further in Chapter 4.

Creating a More Effective Management Cadence in B&SE There has been a great deal of attention paid to Alan's BPR and rightfully so. However, to stop at that level of the organization is to see only the tip of the iceberg. The system was not limited to a small circle of the most senior executives; it permeated the entire enterprise, cascading from Alan to the EVPs to directors to CEs to managers and engineers across the company and around the world. They had the same plan, focused on aligned priorities, and utilized the same format and interdependent metrics. Most importantly, they insisted on the same level of transparency and candor among the B&SE team. They organized a B&SE *obeya* (big room) where they covered the walls with important data on their initiatives and performance levels that were reviewed each week (discussed further in Chapters 1 and 2). When tightly coupled with other key mechanisms, such as design reviews, development milestone reviews, and matched-pair meetings, they created a powerful, cadenced management system that enabled the B&SE team to move the business forward.

Creating Great Products and People Simultaneously The global engineering organization recognized that it needed to redouble its efforts on developing technical excellence. The previous leadership regime made it clear that it valued individual "entrepreneurs" far more than people's technical capability, even outsourcing many critical technical tasks. Engineers also had believed that the fastest way to get promoted was to change jobs in a race to management positions. The outsourcing mindset coupled with engineers' career strategies and major organizational changes under way led to a serious lack of technical capability in a number of important areas.

In some cases, engineering had to hire needed skills from the outside. But it was clear that this was not a long-term solution. Individual engineering discipline leaders worked closely with their HR partners to develop a technical skill acquisition model for each of the engineering disciplines. They assigned technical mentors who met with team members on a regular basis. They went even further and halted the seemingly random position hopping of engineers trying to get promoted. While this might seem like a strategy to frustrate engineers, it was a breath of fresh air for most who strove to master their technical disciplines.

Creating a Single, Competitive, Global Development Process for a Globally Competitive Organization

Not only were Ford's products different across regions as previously discussed, but so was its product development process. This combination of geographical product independence and lack of a common global development process left Ford unable to truly leverage its global scale to match its best competitors. Consequently, the creation of a fully competitive, global development process became a priority.

Creating the Global Product Development Process—Macro Level

The Ford Product Development System (FPDS) was originally intended as a global system. Unfortunately, it evolved very differently in each region. It was not very effective in any of the regions and had eventually become a bloated bureaucratic labyrinth that program teams struggled to understand let alone navigate successfully. The results were missed milestones, late engineering changes, frustrated development teams, and late, troubled launches.

The weakness of FPDS was a result of the process of creating it and the mindset behind it. In an earnest attempt to improve Ford's product development performance, the various staff groups created a lot of rigid rules and audited programs against those rules. They built a stage-gate model since it seemed an effective way of exerting control (a better approach to milestones and design reviews is presented in Chapter 2, "Delivering with Speed and Precision"). Teams would need to pass through the gate reviews (called toll gates by some companies), and the corporate groups could define the review criteria to force specific practices. Over the years the various groups in charge of FPDS had repeatedly piled "best practices" onto the gate reviews to the point where it became exceedingly complex and onerous to pass a gate—or even understand gate requirements. While well intentioned, the complexity made problems difficult to identify, and they frequently remained hidden until quite late in the process.

Ford decided to completely redesign the development system, starting with a clean sheet of paper—with the goal of creating a truly global product development system. Over several months Jim assembled a strong cross-functional team. He sought out opinion leaders from each major function of product development, open-minded people, and ideally people who already had some experience with world-class systems. For example, two of the members had relocated to Japan for several years to work on Mazda programs. But most importantly, each one was an expert in a particular discipline and understood what it took to develop a new vehicle.

The first step for the team was to learn together and build a common vision of what the process needed to be. The GPDS team visited and benchmarked all the Ford brands and regions, from Volvo to Jaguar and across the globe. At that time Ford owned a large stake in Mazda, so it was able to benchmark Mazda's process in detail. The team also met with many third-party product development experts and studied product development across multiple industries in order to fully understand the art of the possible in product development. The team eventually chose Mazda's lean development process as a foundation for GPDS, while integrating best practices like Volvo's Virtual Series. Ford modified the Volvo approach and, working with key technology suppliers, developed a suite of highly customized virtual-reality and solids-based design tools to support the process from beginning to end.

The overall development system of a vehicle was divided into major "work streams" required to bring a new vehicle to market: body development, electrical and electronics development, chassis development, prototyping, vehicle testing, manufacturing engineering, and launch.

The leaders selected became "work-stream leaders" to develop the LPPD process for their specialty area as well as gain the commitment of their home functions. The team organized an obeya (visual meeting room) in order to share its work across work streams and encourage collaboration. (Obeya is discussed in various chapters, starting in Chapter 1, as a key to "developing with speed and precision.") An obeya enabled the team to visually lay out the process on the walls of the room to allow the team to focus on key issues, anticipate problems before they grew serious, and better integrate its work. The walls were populated with benchmarking information organized by work stream. As the walls became populated with information, team members grew surprised and a bit disappointed by the large gaps between Ford and Mazda. But it also showed them where to focus their efforts.

The obeya was originally set up to help the team visualize the process and help to develop the global product development system, but it had some unexpected benefits as well. The GPDS obeya also became a favorite destination for Ford leaders who wanted to know what was going on in product development. The gaps were clearly displayed, and countermeasures were being defined. Individual work-stream leaders led discussions on the work they were doing. The room resonated with rigorous debate and many tough questions, and while everyone may not have agreed, all were clearly engaged. It also served as a model for obeya later used to manage actual development programs as well as global functional organizations.

Considerable time was also spent piloting the ideas on a small scale in various areas, in parallel with the mainstream product development projects. Through this experimentation on "in-flight" programs, the team learned what did and did not work and made adjustments to GPDS accordingly. The pilots also served to demonstrate results that could later be used as part of the change process while simultaneously spreading the word that changes were afoot.

Creating the Global Product Development Process—Micro Level

Setting up the corporate-level GPDS process was necessary, but it was far from sufficient to change how actual development programs were run. There was much more detailed work that had to be done within each of the functional organizations on how they supported the delivery of the GPDS requirements. There was a significant learning curve of new capabilities needed to support more demanding lead times, cost targets, and quality requirements. (The approach used here became the foundation for the method successfully used with other companies, discussed in Chapter 9, "Designing Your Future.")

As a starting point, each functional group had to develop a plan to deliver to cost, quality, and timing targets. Each function needed to understand its starting point, and so each work team created detailed current-state value-stream maps of its portion of the product and process development processes. These were typically three-day events in which teams used sticky notes and large sheets of plotter paper to map out the key process steps and information flows in a typical product development project. They also conducted detailed benchmarking of engineering, prototyping, and tooling operations from around the world, both inside and outside the auto industry. The gap analyses highlighted numerous opportunities for improvement.

Because the B&SE teams identified so many opportunities, they prioritized them using a prioritization chart and set about understanding the issues more deeply. This led to developing countermeasures and discussing them with colleagues. They used this as an opportunity to teach the lean practice of creating the A3 problem-solving report—a report on one side of A3-sized paper that included only the key points needed to understand the flow of reasoning. The A3 reports always ended with time-bound implementation plans. The reason for confining team members to A3 reports was to make their thinking crisp and to enable communication with other groups. The A3 was carried around by the lead person creating it in order to get input and consensus among stakeholders.

One fairly typical insight from the value-stream mapping exercises was that an engineering group or individual engineers completed and froze their designs prematurely, leading to a large amount of rework waste later as they discovered issues with the designs. Too often engineers would settle on a design concept, analyze the design at a detailed level, and produce detailed CAD models, only to find out some time later that the design would be incompatible with the designs of interfacing subsystems or with existing manufacturing capability. So the team embraced a principle it referred to as "compatibility before completion" (CbC) to fight this tendency. It is a way of considering the product from many perspectives before prematurely freezing the design. (This is discussed in more detail in Chapter 2.) The result of this extra work in the front end of design was elimination of a great deal of waste downstream and faster speed to market.

The team openly shared GPDS requirements and supporting best practices with suppliers. The team also worked to a principle of not asking suppliers to do anything they could or would not do. This principle led to a transformation of Ford's internal tool and die shop, discussed in detail in Chapter 4. While a few suppliers self-selected out of Ford business, most valued the opportunity and what they learned to help them improve their own processes, and the collaboration strengthened relationships with Ford.

Results—Ford's Future State

Looking back at the Mulally era, we can conclude that Ford's turnaround results were impressive by nearly any measure. Several authors even called it "one of the greatest corporate turnarounds in U.S. business history."[3] However, many outside analysts also incorrectly attributed Ford's success solely to strategic decisions made by Mulally. They failed to recognize that it was a product-led revitalization that require committed people at all levels of the organization. As a result, the turnaround not only saved an American icon; it returned it to a thriving global competitor. For example, Ford was the highest-ranked North American motor vehicle company on *Fortune's* list of the World's Most Admired Companies in 2017.[4]

Results—Macro Level

Development Capability   By 2010 the GPDS process had already helped to reduce late engineering changes by 50 percent, reduce total program lead time by more than 25 percent, and decrease total development costs by 60 percent,[5] and the process powered the development of a record number of some of the most exciting and awarded products in Ford's history.

In support of this performance was the improvement in Ford's platform engineering capability. For example, Ford reduced the number of vehicle platforms from 27 in 2005 to 12 in 2014 and then to 9 by 2016, all while supporting more individual product nameplates and making significant improvements to the efficiency and performance attributes of each of the products.

Financial Results   The financial results were remarkable:

- Profit grew from a $17 billion loss in 2006 to an $8.6 billion profit in 2013.[6]
- Gross margins increased from 2 percent in 2006 to 13 percent in 2013.[7]
- Sales per employee increased from $533,743 in 2006 to $811,656 in 2013.[8]
- Stock prices increased from $6.65 the month before Alan arrived in 2006 to $17.00 in December of 2013.[9]
- Ford's credit rating went from junk in 2006 to investment grade in 2013.[10]

Perhaps most important, Ford's profit per vehicle (transaction price indicator) went from a loss on each vehicle to second only to Toyota and 66 percent more per vehicle than General Motors' profit per vehicle.[11]

Results—Micro Level

The results from lean practices were equally impressive at the micro level:

- Tool design and engineering lead time was reduced by 50 percent.
- Tool cost per die was reduced by 55 percent.
- Internal tool and die quality issues decreased by 80 percent.
- Engineering productivity increased by 20 percent.
- Stamping material utilization improved 10 percent.

Product quality and craftsmanship improved:

- Body craftsmanship (fit and finish) and perceived quality improved dramatically.
- Repairs per thousand opportunities for body exterior parts were reduced by 53 percent.
- "Things gone wrong" (TGWs) were reduced more than 30 percent.

These small but critical quality factors also contributed to Ford's rise in customer satisfaction:

- Ford received the most five-star ratings for safety by the National Highway Transportation Safety Association of any carmaker.[12]
- In 2013 Fusion won the Automotive Excellence Award for design and manufacturing excellence for the body-in-white/closures and was a five-star top safety pick.
- The BS&E team helped to deliver segment-leading products like the 2015 Mustang and 2015 all-aluminum F150.
- The Ford body exterior team won a Premier Automotive Suppliers' Contribution to Excellence Award[13] for demonstrating its commitment to strong supplier partnerships.

On top of these achievements and over approximately the same time period, the Employee Satisfaction Index improved by 26 percentage points within B&SE, as measured by a Ford corporate survey. The business and engineering practices put in place not only resulted in better products and improved efficiency; they actually helped make Ford BS&E a better place to work.

LOOKING AHEAD

The inspiring Ford story helps to demonstrate the potential of a product-focused turnaround. It also shows that such a turnaround is not simply the result of a prescribed cookie-cutter set of bureaucratic rules. It is a difficult and complex undertaking that requires hard work and tremendous discipline and engages the entire enterprise—but one that is well worth the effort.

While the magnitude may differ, we believe that any company in any industry can accomplish the same product-led transformation achieved by Ford, even without the threat of bankruptcy. We have included examples of many other organizations from a variety of industries throughout this book.

Any product-led transformation must begin with an unflinching examination of the organization's current state, and that starts with a deep understanding of the customer and the product. In Chapter 1 we will share how several practicing LPPD organizations are accomplishing just that.

Your Reflection

We will begin our standard format for reflecting on chapters, and taking action, in Chapter 1 that follows—but any good case study deserves some reflection:

1. List three to five takeaways from the Ford case about successful product-led transformation.

2. Do you have a CEO like Alan Mulally—passionate about product development and skillful at building a winning team?

3. If not, who is the highest-level executive who can or does lead the transformation to product development excellence?

4. What types of initiatives have you started to improve product-process development excellence, and are those initiatives mostly bureaucratic, making it harder for teams, or do they support product development excellence?

1

Creating the Right Product

By now lists like this are well known: Ford Edsel, Pontiac Aztek, New
Coke, Crystal Pepsi, HP TouchPad, Apple Newton, and Microsoft Zune,
and we could go on—and on. Billions of dollars and countless hours of
human effort have been squandered on product disasters that not only did

not sell, but in some cases did serious damage to the brand that required years to recover.

But these examples were in the "stone age." Surely today, in our high-tech, information-intensive environment, where companies know truly invasive levels of detail about their customers, such colossal flops are not possible, right? Well, maybe a little possible:

- Samsung Galaxy Note 7 exploded due to faulty batteries, leading to massive recalls and a $2.3 billion write-down.[1]

- Amazon's Fire Phone (2014) had its price slashed from $199 to $0.99 and still took a $170 million write-down; the phone was discontinued in 2015.[2]

- Google Glass (2013) was cool, but few wanted the computerized eyeglasses.[3]

- Lululemon Astro Pants (2013) were so sheer that some were recalled because they were virtually see-through.[4]

- Burger King Satisfries (2013) had fewer calories than regular fries and fewer fans as well.[5]

- Google Nexus Q (2013), an overpriced spherical media player, was pulled almost as soon as it started shipping.[6]

- Nike FuelBand (2014) could not compete in the crowded fitness-device field.[7]

- Government projects, like the *F-35* joint strike fighters or the aircraft carrier *USS Gerald Ford*, despite cost overruns into the hundreds of millions and multiyear delays, have not come close to meeting expectations.[8]

And these are just the high-profile commercial failures. For every public product embarrassment, there are thousands more we never hear about.

In fact, while not necessarily failures, the majority of new products seldom come close to meeting expectations, despite unprecedented attention from senior executives. A McKinsey & Co. poll found that "84% of global executives reported that innovation was extremely important to their company's growth strategies, but a staggering 94% were dissatisfied with their organization's innovation performance."[9]

So how does this happen? More resources and attention than ever are being paid to innovation. We have access to an unprecedented amount of customer information to fuel sophisticated sales and marketing strategies. Yet products seldom meet expectations. We think it is because more information, more sophistication, and more resources are not necessarily better and, by themselves, insufficient. Our experience indicates that most organizations do not dedicate nearly enough time up front to truly understand their customers, and not nearly enough time experimenting to close other critical knowledge gaps before beginning detailed development.

Front-End Loading

One of our principles from *The Toyota Product Development System*[10] is "front loading," and the first step in that process is what Toyota calls the *kentou*, or study period. At the time of our research for the book, Toyota stood out from other companies in the amount of time it religiously devoted to deeply understanding the customer and context in which each and every product would be used. This was a very intense period led by a small, knowledgeable team of senior engineers, who solicited information broadly and generated many potential designs before converging.

The study phase precedes detailed engineering design and asks fundamental questions like:

- What problem is this product intended to solve?
- What features are most critical or valued?
- How will this product deliver unique value to the customer?
- What overall context does the product operate within?
- How will it exceed anything our competitors might create in the next cycle?
- What are our knowledge gaps and areas of significant risk?
- What is our plan to deliver?

The study period, we argued, was perhaps the most important part of the Toyota product development system: creating the wrong product is, after all, the worst possible form of waste. It is a waste of product development time, money, and talent from across the enterprise.

At the center of Toyota's front end is a single, responsible leader for each product called the *chief engineer* (CE). We shared stories in our previous book about how CEs led their teams in deeply understanding the customer and how they develop a vision for the product to deliver unique value to that customer. One famous story in *Toyota* is when the Sienna minivan CE personally drove existing Toyota models through every state in the United States, every state in Mexico, and every province in Canada. He studied customers outside Home Depot as they struggled to fit plywood sheets into rear openings that were slightly too narrow. He experienced firsthand the buffeting wind on the high-profile van as he drove across the Plains. He saw the need for cup holders for each passenger on long trips (he also witnessed the importance of keeping children occupied on those long rides). Toyota had fallen behind Honda Odyssey as the top-selling minivan in the United States, but that decline led to many innovations and a bestselling minivan that, eventually, surpassed sales of the Odyssey.

For many companies, engineering works to the design concepts of sales and marketing people who go through large amounts of data to try to understand what their customers want. In Toyota, sales and marketing serve their most important customer—the chief engineer. Data is useful, but chief engineers want to also get a personal feeling for the customers and product through direct observation. The chief engineer understands the technology and what is possible, gets a feel for the customer, understands the drivers of cost, and develops a vision for the product.

We also shared the practice of developing early study drawings, or *kentouzu*. Generally, these were hand-drawn sketches. The engineering team used these early drawings to capture and communicate multiple potential design proposals during the study period. The team members also engaged in simple, rapid prototyping and experimentation to help them understand higher-risk areas of the project.

The point of all this work is to identify and close important gaps in knowledge that the product team has early in the development process, before large amounts of human and financial resources are invested in the product. While the team may have identified an opportunity for a new product or service, there is still a great deal it does not know. The study period is intended to enable the team members to better understand the customer, the environment, and the product, as well as the significant risks and challenges that they are likely to face and sets the stage to create a plan to deliver a successful product. This does not mean that they will have all the answers—far from it. Learning will continue throughout the program. But it does mean that they will have at least a strong conceptual understanding of how their product will successfully deliver unique customer value and a reasonable plan to deliver.

Since our earlier research, we have had the opportunity to work with many companies across numerous industries. This allowed us to build upon what we knew and refine our thinking about closing critical knowledge gaps during the study period. This ongoing work has led us to identify four broad categories of activities that successful companies employ at the front end of new product development programs:

1. Work to deeply understand.

2. Generate sets of potential solutions.

3. Experiment to learn.

4. Compile, align, and enroll before you execute.

Work to Deeply Understand

In the early stage of developing a new product or service, we offer one simple piece of advice: don't assume you know. Do the work to deeply understand what your new product needs to be. As Steve Jobs observed in the opening quote, this includes going beyond what customers ask for to understand their needs better than they do and what is possible to satisfy those unmet needs. And the best place to answer those questions is at the *gemba*, or the place where your customer is. Immerse yourself in your customer's environment in order to gain critical insights into just how the product or service can deliver the best customer experience, optimally solve your customer's problem, or complete your customer's task better than any competitors' products.

Go and See

When Charles (Charlie) Baker was appointed as the first American CE (called "Large Project Leader") for a full model change for Honda, he was sent to Japan for training. Charlie expected he would be spending time in the company's technical center learning the latest systems and technologies for designing and developing new cars. Instead, a very experienced

CE assigned to mentor Charlie took him to Tokyo. As they walked the streets of Tokyo, his instructor asked him what he saw. Charlie described all the cars around him and their characteristics. The teacher said, "No, no, what do you see? Do not tell me about cars." Charlie eventually got it, and he began describing the people and how they handled traffic patterns, admired certain cars, and got in and out of cars. He was learning to see what really matters to customers. Then his mentor encouraged Charlie to look beyond cars and really study people and the other aspects of their lives. What are their values, their choices, and how can this deeper under-standing be leveraged to create a compelling product? "The emphasis," Baker says, "was on understanding the people, your customers, and their values and decisions. Everything else was trivial."

Go and see at the source is classic lean advice, and it is just as powerful in product development as on the plant floor. Don't only rely on market reports or focus-group summaries; go experience for yourself. Understand customer needs as well as the context in which a product will be used.

Go and see is more than looking around and taking notes. Be sure to sharpen your observation skills and how you interact with those you meet. It's not just about asking your customers what they want—it's not their job to know; it's yours. Immerse yourself in your customer's world. The visceral experience is far more powerful and contains nearly unlim-ited potential to generate innovative insights to differentiate your product and provide unique value to your customers. In our previous book, we described how Toyota CEs used "go and see" to better understand how products solved their customers' problems or helped them accomplish tasks, as was the case with the Sienna minivan. But what about when your product objective is to deliver an emotional experience?

Immersion to Deliver an Emotional Customer Experience

Willie Davidson, former senior vice president and chief styling officer of Harley Davidson, once said, "Form follows function, but both form and function report to emotion."[11] There is no doubt that emotional connection plays an important role in customers' buying decisions and their product experiences. However, capturing this elusive characteristic—like catching lightning in a bottle—has proved incredibly difficult for many products.

The Ford Mustang is all about emotional connection. There is no log-ical reason to buy a Ford Mustang. There are many more rational transportation choices available to consumers. Owning and driving a Mustang is an experience the customer wants that is extremely difficult to describe, much less precisely quantify. For example, it can be a visible statement to the world of the customer's individualism. So, just how do you go about understanding the visceral experience and personal identity that customers expect to get from Mustang? While we do not have a stepwise formula, we believe that there is a great deal we can learn from Dave Pericak's experience in gaining a deep understanding of, creating a compelling vision for, and delivering the very successful 2015 Mustang.

When Pericak first took on the role of CE and the responsibility for developing the next model of the Mustang, the brand was running a distant second to the Camaro in sales and had been trailing the Chevrolet product for the previous five years. Mustang had clearly lost its emotional connection with its customer base, and Pericak had to figure out how to get it back.

"The Mustang following is cult-like," Pericak says,[12] "and a very unforgiving cult at that. If you don't get it right, they [the customers] know it immediately, and they are not shy about letting you know." There are more than 250 Mustang clubs around the world, whose members take Mustang ownership seriously. Mustang had lost its "mojo," and customers were definitely letting Ford know.

Pericak had been a "Mustang guy" as long as he could remember. He had owned several, worked on more than a few, and even proposed to his wife in a Mustang. Mustang was, in fact, part of the reason he had joined Ford. He lived and breathed Mustang. Even though he grew up with Mustang, he realized he needed to take the time to study and think deeply about the emotional connection between Mustang and its customers. He needed to understand where Mustang had gone wrong. How had it broken faith with its core? He needed to go and see and to talk with customers of all kinds.

He started by attending Mustang events across the country, listening to all the exuberant stories of multigeneration ownership and how Mustang was intricately and inseparably woven into the stories of customers' lives. He studied the people. He experienced owners' pride and passion as they detailed their Mustangs with a toothbrush. He shared their ear-to-ear smiles as they started engines and heard that rumble. He saw the Mustang tattoos. He found elaborate airbrushing, literally one-of-a-kind artwork, tucked under the hood. He witnessed customers' transformation as they got behind the wheel.

From Pericak's observations, he began to understand what Mustang meant to these people. It was a form of individual expression. Customers were flexing their muscles, flexing their individuality. He knew that every detail of the *next* Mustang had to be about this raw, emotional expression. He also knew that anything that did not enhance this experience did not belong on a Mustang. He would constantly challenge the product team on decisions: Is it personally expressive? Does it look strong? Is it bold and edgy? Does it say Mustang? If the answer is no, get rid of it.

Then Pericak did something else that is fairly rare for this type of car. He met with groups of women. Dave felt that they had been overlooked in the past, both as customers and as influencers, and that this was a big mistake. He wanted to understand their perspective. Why did some sports cars resonate with women while others seemed to almost offend them? At the end of one of the discussions, Dave tried to summarize what he heard: "So what you're saying is you like bad boys, but you don't like assholes." After they were done laughing, they responded, "That's it exactly."

Through these discussions Dave came to understand that if the vehicle's styling says angry and aggressive, it did not resonate with women at all. But if the car looks intriguing, a bit edgy, strong, and confident, that gets their attention. These sessions had a big influence on styling. Pericak and his team would review concepts and ask, "Is this angry, or is it confident and strong?" He and his team engaged many of those same women in early reviews of the Mustang's styling. These sessions fundamentally changed the design language for the program.

Pericak and his small team began to sift through everything they had learned, trying to understand where Mustang had lost its way and, more importantly, where it could find the way back. Based on their collective experiences, it was clear that Mustang had to be far more strong, unique, and bold. At the same time, developers were cautious of creating something that looked ticked off or cartoonish. It had to stand out in a way only Mustang could—authentic, true to its roots, and not pretending to be something it was not. It must push limits and be a source of personal expression for its owner. Every inch must be uniquely Mustang.

Rebuilding the emotional Mustang experience would clearly need to begin with artistic styling. He had to get this right, so Pericak headed right to Kemal Curic, chief designer for Mustang, where they began poring over concept sketches and scale models. They selected the Joe Lewis Fist monument in downtown Detroit as a symbol of fearlessness, strength, and power that Mustang would embody. This was a symbol that represented the path-breaking independence of both the fighter and the original Mustang launched in 1965. Success in delivering this experience lay in the details of hundreds of decisions by Pericak, Curic, and their team. We will share three from the program:

1. **Designing the right look.** A large part of portraying the appearance of latent power in the exterior design comes from the Mustang's "haunches." It makes the car look like it's poised and ready to pounce. Strong "hips" are essential to this design cue. That is the area of the rear quarter above the rear wheels. The design team modeled countless versions of this area until finally landing on a look that was just right.

   Of course, design is not the only element in bringing a car to market; it must be built, and unfortunately, some of the best styling created impossible manufacturing conditions. The rear quarter panel design was particularly challenging for stamping. Not willing to compromise, Pericak reached out directly to the members of the body and stamping engineering team to ask for their help. In the past they might have simply marked the styling infeasible and vetoed the design. Instead, a small team was assigned to collaboratively develop several significant innovations in the stamping process in order to deliver this critical design characteristic. The team delivered—the Mustang looks like it's in motion when it's just sitting there.

2. **No-compromise fighting for critical customer features.** Pericak knew that sequential rear turn signals are another iconic part of Mustang design DNA. "It can be pitch black out and you flip on the turn signal and instantly you know this is a Mustang." The problem was that those signals put the program about $20 over budget, and he was under tremendous pressure to remove them from the program. As he feared, senior leadership finally directed him to remove them from the car. He refused, saying, "You have the authority to remove me from this job, but you put me here for a reason. I am representing the customer, and I know these tail lamps are critical. I am not going to remove them." After an awkward silence, the leader said, "Okay, keep the lamps, but you owe me $20 by the next meeting." Dave worked with Jim's body team and other engineering groups to offset the cost elsewhere and delivered the lamps. He was willing to

put his job on the line to deliver what he knew was right. (We will talk more about this type of courage in Chapter 5 on leadership.)

3. **Delivering emotion in the car's functioning.** Sit in a Mustang and push the start button. Feel that throaty rumble? Now step down on the accelerator. The deep growl quickens your pulse and gives you goose bumps. This is what power feels and sounds like, pure and simple. This is no accident. Pericak worked with powertrain engineering to tune more than 50 different exhaust systems to arrive at just this sound. It is all part of the Mustang experience. It makes us think of the Harley-Davidson sound that was actually patented.

According to Pericak, "It has to be a design that calls to you—a product you have to have; a design that is unmistakably pure Mustang and not trying to be anything else. It is an emotional experience that channels Steve McQueen in *Bullet*, iconic American muscle, and Joe Lewis's fist."

Pericak lived and breathed Mustang culture. He really *knew* his customers and knew what was most important to his customer. Armed with this knowledge, he battled, pushed, and took total ownership for his product. He fought hard against tremendous organization pressures to compromise, even to the point of risking his job. This is very different from bringing the voice of the customer into the conversation through a tool like quality function deployment, a market survey, or focus-group data. Data and these tools can certainly be useful, but they do not replace deep understanding, vision, and leadership.

All of Pericak's efforts paid big dividends, starting with a 2015 Mustang sales improvement of 49 percent over the previous year. The Mustang also:

- Outsold the Camaro in 2015 by 37 percent[13]
- Continues to outsell both the Camaro and Challenger up to the time of this writing[14]
- Remains the bestselling sports car in the world at the time of this writing[15]
- Was named No. 1 "dream car," finishing one place above the Tesla Model S and five spots above the Camaro[16]

The Mustang is a great success story, but sometimes the customer experience you are trying to create does not come from metal and glass.

Sometimes it is bits and bytes. So how can you use "go and see" to achieve this same understanding and produce an excellent customer experience in the world of software?

Think Like an Anthropologist

Menlo Innovations is a small, custom software company that has a big mission—"end human suffering in the world as it relates to technology." To do this, the company has had to "change everything" in the way software is developed, resulting in High-Tech Anthropology, paired programming, and an open and collaborative working environment.

Deeply understanding the customer at Menlo is done by pairs of professionals, each with the job title of High-Tech Anthropologist (HTA). Together they visit and methodically study the environments and the people who will use their products. HTAs focus on the end user as the "customer" for this work, rather than their point of contact from the client company who is usually in IT. They spend many days at the workplaces where their product will be used (i.e., the gemba), observing and interviewing target users in the users' native environment in order to grasp the complete context of product performance. They watch carefully for what they call "the pain points"—problems the users are having that may provide the greatest opportunities to add value.

Empathy is a requirement for the HTA role. HTAs create "mind maps" in which they capture critical aspects of their interviews with potential users and graphically illustrate the users' thinking about both the current situation and the desired future state. Doing all this at the actual workplace is crucial. As CEO Richard Sheridan says, "Design is contextual, and we have to study users in their native environment."[17] Next they have to transform their new knowledge into specific design solutions.

Generate Sets of Potential Solutions

At Menlo Innovations, their HTAs do much more than identify customer needs. They are the thread of customer focus that runs through the entire development project. After initial visits with users, the development process starts with HTAs crafting a clear problem statement and the start of a future state vision. This brief, handwritten summary describes what HTAs are setting out to accomplish. The easy-to-understand document, albeit not easy to create, is shared with clients to be sure they have a strong and shared understanding of exactly what Menlo is trying to accomplish. Was HTA empathy work accurate? This early collaborative process creates alignment with the client and the rest of the Menlo team.

Once alignment is understood, the lead HTAs will use the statement to call on other HTAs to help brainstorm ideas. They engage as many fresh perspectives as necessary in these lightning-fast sessions, generating quick sketches of potential design solutions for the user interfaces. This is followed by an HTA debrief in which the lead pair sorts through all the sketches and discusses and develops more focused solutions. The lead HTAs also utilize the mind maps (Figure 1.1) created from their inter-views to further clarify their thinking and communicate their vision for the customized product.

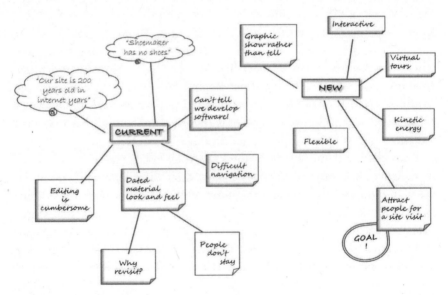

Figure 1.1   Interview mind map to convey essential points (website design example)

Persona Convergence

Building on observations, idea generation, and evaluations, the pair of HTAs creates 10 to 30 "personas." Each persona is a detailed composite story of a potential target user, captured on a handwritten persona card with a fictitious name and photo. The cards are brought to a persona map that looks like a target, and then the fun starts. The pairs challenge the customer to select the key persona as the target user. There is discussion and debate, but in the end, the customer must settle on a single target.[18]

As difficult and exhausting as it may be, the HTAs force their customer to pick just one key persona out of the group so that they can focus their actual development work on a very specific customer, referring to him or her by name. That persona is taped to the center of the target. (The imagery of a target is also instructive: it conveys the team's aim, but with room to make trade-offs as more knowledge is acquired, such as choosing to exclude or scale back a feature in order to achieve a faster ship date.) The HTAs will ask the client to select two secondary personas, and they are taped on the outer rings of the target. They insist that this is a critical priority, because "if you try to create a product for everyone, it will not work well for anyone, and you will get killed in the market."

Design Assessments

The next step in the development process is for the HTAs to create simple, low-fidelity, hand-drawn screen mock-ups of their vision for the product based on all their research and client dialogue. They share these mock-ups with "persona"-type targeted users at the gemba and make quick changes as feedback is digested. This is where a "make mistakes faster" philosophy and spirit of rapid experimentation really comes into its own. The HTAs do not attempt to hit the target center with a single shot, but rather develop multiple potential design solutions in order to create the best possible product for the target user.

Most Menlo projects require three or four major design assessments with end users, along with many more minor, incremental reviews. At a typical design assessment, the HTA pair shows the prototype interface to the end users in their native environment with little or no explanation, describes the user scenario, and asks the users to perform the target task. The HTAs write down everything the users do or say during the review. If the interface is not totally intuitive to the user, the HTAs start to ask questions to understand what must be changed. They frequently utilize multiple prototypes in order to assess a range of attributes across design alternatives, taking copious notes and returning to debrief from each experience.

All these actions occur during software planning before any code is written. The mock-ups of screenshots are turned into story cards (on

index cards) describing one feature per card. Pairs of programmers esti-
mate the time required to create the code for each card. The customers
then play a planning game to identify the story cards they want to include
in the scope of work organized in weekly sheets of work with the number
of hours multiplied by 2 for a pair of programmers multiplied by the daily
rate. They are still planning and can add and remove cards to prioritize
and stay within their budget.

Finally, in the execution state the story cards are "played" by the customer to identify the week-by-week project scope. The played cards are
prioritized each week as the customer authorizes the workload for the coming week. The cards are laid out visually on a "work authorization board"
on the wall to give a day by day work schedule for programmers, and the
customer comes back each week for a hands-on design review, resulting in
playing the next week's cards. This cycle of learning, or PDCA (plan-do-
check-act), continues week by week, ushered by the HTAs representing the
voice of the user. Perhaps it is no surprise that there is very little rework and
that it typically results in almost 100 percent customer satisfaction.

Data Will Set You Free

Up to this point we have emphasized direct observation. Where are the
marketing surveys? Where are the reams of quantitative data? Don't ignore
the data. It is useful. There is value in understanding population statistics
and how the project will compare with competitive offerings.

We view larger-scale data as necessary input, just not sufficient. The
data can help identify trends, central tendencies, and variations in needs,
and developing charts and graphs to visualize the data is critical. There is
now more data available than ever before, sometimes too much. But it is
the interpretation of the information that determines its value.

One interesting example of how different kinds of data can be produc-
tively used was by the CE of the first Lexus, as described in *The Toyota
Way*.[19] The CE, Ichiro Suzuki, reviewed market research as a context,
but then personally interviewed owners of competitive vehicles in focus
groups. He identified patterns in preferences among owners of Mercedes,
BMW, Volvo, Jaguar, and Cadillac. He then developed trade-off curves.
The competitors neatly lined up as being strong on one factor, such as
refined appearance, and weak on another, such as aerodynamics. He then
set a "no-compromise" condition. For example, one target was refined

styling *yet* aerodynamic. These design challenges then directed the major innovations that made this first Lexus the bestselling luxury car in America in its first year.

Monozukuri Innovation

The literal translation of *monozukuri* is "making things of value"—*mono* (object of value) and *zukuri* (to make or build)—but it has a far more profound meaning. It captures the passion of the artisan—a fresh spirit of excellence, innovation, and pride in making something especially well. Jim learned by working with Mazda that it is for them also a specific method for cross-functional teams to work together on delivering greater value to the customer. It is a highly effective way to generate innovative ideas in support of new development programs.

Small, cross-functional teams—typically made up of people from product engineering, manufacturing, purchasing, and key suppliers—are at the center of the monozukuri process. The teams are challenged to rethink how the value of a particular vehicle subsystem is created. The starting point is to study the current condition, which means existing vehicles. It's a focused learning and innovation forum in which these teams study targeted subsystems, from both internal products and competitor vehicles. The teams "tear down," study, and contrast different versions of the subsystem from their various functional perspectives to determine the best design and manufacturing strategies to enable maximum performance at minimum total cost.

The teams initially work independently, and once a team fully understands the best currently available, it proposes new and better ways to design and execute the subsystems. One could say it is competitive benchmarking, but with far more creativity than we normally see from this technical exercise.

The participants have learned both from tearing down different systems and from each other's perspectives, and are then prepared to utilize a total value-stream perspective (all the steps required) in order to generate fresh, innovative ideas to improve the total value delivered to the customer.

Parts of the subsystem, along with sketches and ideas, are mounted on *karakuri* (mechanism) boards, and the various teams visit each other, share ideas, and provide feedback. The output is captured and proposed to the individual program teams for potential incorporation into their next-generation product. These ideas lead to significant improvements in quality, attribute performance, and cost. The functional participants on the teams also work on multiple programs, which establishes an effective way to share learning across projects and drive commonality where appropriate.

When facilitating monozukuri events with companies these days, we encourage them to broaden their learning search and include examples from other types of business. The resulting sketches, diagrams, and mockups are evaluated against specific product-focused criteria (performance, cost, supply chain, etc.) by project teams, and a subset is selected to move forward into higher-fidelity testing and experimentation.

Start with Broad Sets of Alternatives and Converge Thoughtfully

Conceptually, front loading is about generating lots of alternatives and then carefully converging on multiple aspects of the design simultaneously. Our friend and colleague Allen Ward called this "set-based concurrent engineering," and observed that Toyota was the best at it in the automotive industry. In an article, "The Second Toyota Paradox: How Delaying Decisions Can Make Better Cars Faster," Ward and coauthors argued that this was as great a paradox as the just-in-time irony that holding less inventory can lead to more reliable, on-time delivery.[20]

The more traditional approach to development is point based: to quickly converge on a single solution and then iterate to make it feasible from multiple perspectives, for example, trying to make a product achieve a function and then later modifying it to make it more manufacturable (Figure 1.2). The outcome is usually suboptimal from every perspective—including that of the customer—and results in a product that kind of works, is not very innovative, and takes more time and cost to develop. This approach also leads to a lot of rework, as evidenced by all the redesign for new vehicles, with various functions, such as manufacturing, tossing designs back because they cannot be efficiently accommodated. This is often in effect a veto, instead of the thoughtful collaboration that allowed Dave Pericak to work with stamping engineering and realize the complex styling that made the Mustang distinctive.

The irony of a set-based approach is that a lot more time and effort at the front end, which can delay decisions, actually leads to a better design faster—from all perspectives, including the customer's. By thoroughly exploring the solution space when there are few constraints and little capital invested, cross-functional teams come to deeply understand the customer, the context of use, and the way a design fits with the manufacturing process (Figure 1.2). This early in the process you often don't have all the answers you need to reduce sets of solutions or make required decisions. So how do you make decisions? Do an experiment.

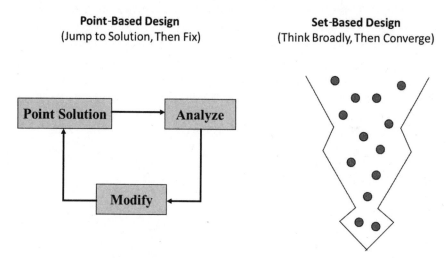

Figure 1.2   Point-based versus set-based design

Experiment to Learn

At various points in the front end of product development, different people will have interesting ideas, and often each of them will be convinced that his or her idea is the best. This can lead to some pretty interesting debates. This is a good thing. But even the most intense debate is not usually sufficient to arrive at the best alternative. While honest debate among a diverse group of pros is a crucial part of product development, it can only get you so far.

Instead of discourse, the best engineers think like scientists and prefer to immediately take action and test ideas to understand their strengths and weaknesses. Your knowledge is limited and your ability to predict imperfect. It is much better to ask, "How can we test this idea?"

Mike Rother in *Toyota Kata* presents a model of scientific thinking very similar to the process described here, along with practice routines (kata) to help build the scientific mindset (discussed later in this book in Chapter 6).[21] At the center are rapid PDCA loops to learn the way to the challenge step by step. The challenge is clear, and it is big, in this case the CE vision. But the way to get there is not clear and requires an iterative learning process toward a series of nearer-term objectives, referred to by Rother as "target conditions." Unfortunately, neuroscience research finds that people do not naturally think scientifically. There is internal pressure in our brains to make assumptions and jump to solutions before deeply understanding the solution space. Point-based thinking seems natural, and set-based thinking requires an unusual degree of patience. In the words of Nobel Prize winner Daniel Kahneman, we are more naturally "fast thinkers" than we are "slow thinkers." The improvement kata is a way for learners to practice slow thinking until it becomes natural. A great tool for iterative learning is rapid prototyping.

Targeted-Fidelity Prototypes

The idea of testing prototypes in product development probably goes back earlier than when the first wheel was affixed to a platform and rolled out. But it seems that over time prototyping has been a continuous march toward increasing cost, formality, complexity, and time—with decreasing focus on learning. In many companies there are separate departments and specialists to create and test elaborate prototypes. They get really good at prototyping, but have limited understanding of the reason for the prototypes and what needs to be learned from them. This has led many companies to conclude that physical prototyping is an unaffordable luxury to be replaced, if possible, with computer models and simulations.

Virtual prototypes can be powerful and help to streamline the testing process, but a blanket elimination of physical prototypes in the development of physical products is usually a bad idea. The purpose of prototypes is learning, for closing those critical knowledge gaps in performance, design interfaces, manufacturability, and even safety. There is something very powerful in the ability to touch, study, and share physical prototypes—to engage all your senses. Simple physical prototypes can definitely speed learning and enhance collaboration.

One reason virtual prototyping seems attractive is because of the time and expense to design and create physical versions. We do recognize that increasingly sophisticated physical prototypes not only are very expensive and time consuming, but often require highly specialized technicians to create, which often removes engineers and developers from the process and, consequently, dramatically reduces learning potential. But instead of eliminating physical prototypes, let's figure out how to learn even more from prototypes that are faster and cheaper to create.

We think companies should creatively pursue the lowest-possible-fidelity prototype required to learn what is needed at a given point in a project. Overly complex and elaborate prototypes are another example of point-based design: You rapidly converge on the best solution. You make it as complex as the actual product. You ignore that which you specifically are trying to learn. Teams are not sure of the needed knowledge or what or how to test, so they compensate by creating an expensive duplicate of the product. At this point they feel committed to the design solutions embedded in the prototype, and only extreme issues will lead to a design change. To avoid this trap, use prototyping as part of the set-based convergence process and think deeply about the purpose. What are the specific hypotheses you are trying to test at this point in design? What is a simple, inexpensive, and fast way to test your hypothesis? Now you are thinking like scientists. Very rarely do prototypes tested in a scientist's laboratory remotely look like a saleable product.

Schilling Robotics and Prototyping   Low-fidelity prototyping is a message Tyler Schilling, founder of Schilling Robotics Company, has been delivering for years. Schilling builds incredibly complex ROVs (remotely operated vehicles) that are capable of completing very difficult and detailed tasks at 4,000 meters (13,123 feet) below sea level. His ROVs are so successful that they represent more than a 40 percent market share and growing fast, and the company's manipulator arms, perhaps the most difficult and important part of the product, control more than 95 percent of the market.

But Schilling observed a disturbing trend. He had noticed that over the years engineers were requesting ever more elaborate and expensive prototypes to test their ideas. Rather than jump to computer models and drop physical prototyping, he challenged his engineers and program leads with a simple question:

> "How would you prototype this if a meteor was about to strike earth tomorrow morning and all of civilization was going to be wiped out, unless you are able to build this prototype today? So engineers

quickly forget about catalogues, machine shops, and outsourcing. Instead they looked to metal, fittings and fasteners that are lying in stock, welders, small pieces of wood, and glue guns. And virtually every time we are very quickly able to create a functional prototype to help resolve the issue."

While some may find such prototypes "ugly," Schilling knows that "having this knowledge now—instead of four to six weeks from now—is far more valuable than the fancy version would have been. We will make it beautiful later," he explains.

Prototyping on the Atlas Actuator Arm   Scott Fulenwider, a 12-year veteran at Schilling, has used the hands-on, "minimalist" approach many times and believes it not only speeds learning but also serves to deepen learning for engineers. Schilling leverages a full suite of sophisticated, state-of-the-art CAD and simulation tools, which are excellent for certain aspects of development. However, experience has shown that it is not as good for other aspects, such as maintenance access for humans or highly flexible parts of the product (e.g., hoses and wires).

While developing a product named Atlas, Fulenwider and his team were challenged to design and build an actuator arm that would be much stronger than anything currently available, with increased levels of precision and flexibility. He knew that one of the most difficult technical problems to solve on this arm was the "pitch-yaw joint," which required the last three joints to be as closely coupled as possible and still achieve strength requirements. Linear actuators were required to move the joints, and these hydraulic actuators required hoses running through the center of the arm to provide power. The design challenge was to weave these hoses around the actuators and other mechanisms so that they never kinked or became bound up under any circumstances.

Fulenwider remembers walking out of a design review, during which the team reviewed the design in CAD, and feeling like he had "nailed it." Still, he could not help but wonder why Willie Klassen, one of the brightest guys in the company, had been skeptical about the design during the team dialogue. Fulenwider respected Klassen and his experience, so decided to test his own assumptions.

With Schilling's hypothetical meteor story ringing in his ears, he headed down to the prototyping area and set out to build a low-fidelity model that would prove out his design. He printed out some screenshots of the design; drew them out on pieces of wood; and sawed, glued, and fastened together a rough working model of the critical aspects of the arm. He realized almost instantly that the arm would not work. Fulenwider immediately called the people on his team together, and they studied the issues. They continued to think through alternatives and rapidly built prototypes by hand, increasing fidelity to better represent system operating context, and within three weeks the team was able to come up with a design that met or exceeded all requirements.

Had the team proceeded in development without the simple, cobbled-together prototypes, the problem would not have been discovered until much later in the development process. Consequently, time would have severely limited the design options, and the team likely would have had to settle for a much larger, heavier, and more expensive arm in order to meet the strength requirements—and one with less operating precision. Exploring the solution space with simple prototypes built by the design team enhanced creativity and provided a far better design.

Schilling Prototyping for Software Development   Schilling Robotics also applies this same principle of targeted-fidelity prototypes to software development and user interfaces. On a program called Gemini, the company combined this strategy with the Menlo HTA process. Existing ROV user interfaces (UIs) were complex and required very experienced operators, who were both high-priced talent and in very scarce supply. An HTA pair consisting of Valerie Cole, Schilling's software lead on the program, and Garry Everett, customer liaison, was determined to change this. The objective was to make controlling the breakthrough Gemini ROV completely intuitive so that less-experienced operators could become proficient in a relatively short period of time.

"I would look at some of the existing UIs, and they were so complex my brain would shut down," said Cole. "They were designed by engineers, who felt compelled to make every possible bit of information available to the operator." This resulted in numerous complaints about how difficult the UI was even for experienced users. The two partners faced a big task.

As a software development veteran, Cole was familiar with the persona process and storyboarding. However, the process that had been used by Schilling Robotics required tons of programing work and fairly long lead times just to produce a minimum viable product. This significant investment made it very unlikely that the engineers would make major changes to a UI even when they found issues. They were far more likely to create overlays to solve the problem, and, consequently, prone to add complexity.

Cole and colleagues were looking for an alternative approach, and they were intrigued when they learned about Menlo's process of hand-drawing various UI designs and working directly with potential users to get feedback, make fast and easy updates, and converge on a potential solution. Cole explained, "We saw our lean coach working with the hardware guys on set-based, low-fidelity prototypes and getting good results, so we thought the Menlo process would give us an opportunity to apply this same thinking to our software world."

First, the team members worked on identifying their target persona. Because they were trying something very different for their industry, persona development would be critical. They spent significant time meeting with experienced people both inside and outside Schilling Robotics. They visited sites to observe different people in their roles. They spent a great deal of time debating, updating, switching, and refining their targets, and they even brought in some Menlo experts to help.

They ended up with "Chet" at the center of their persona target. Chet was young, bright, a bit brash, and very familiar with game consoles and smartphones (a natural and integral part of his life). He also has worked several years in the industry. A secondary target was "Hank," who is Chet's supervisor. Hank is more experienced, has a strong skill set, and is good at mentoring. Hank protects his knowledge, however, in order to create scarcity and increase demand for his skills. He is not the user for whom the UI is intended.

Then the team members brainstormed ways to design an ultra-simple UI, and they hand-drew hundreds of potential screens. They eventually selected three "design kits" (series of UI screens) for user testing:

- A "hand-holding" version, nicknamed "The Baby Sitter," led the user through every little step.
- A "Don't Know, Don't Care" kit did not show any information that was not currently required.
- A version that was closer to their more traditional approach, "Control Freak," was not as complex as screens currently in the field, but it still provided a great deal of feedback to the operator.

They then packed up their design kits and went to work at the customer site. The only problem was that they could not find any "Chets" because they were all working out in the field. In fact, the people who had been tagged by their customers to review the design kits were closer to being Hanks (supervisors) than Chets (field users). Cole and Everett agreed to try the review process with the available Hanks since they were the only people available. This was a big mistake.

In one round, Cole acted as the "CPU," changing paper UIs based on participant input, while Everett took copious notes. The participant became extremely frustrated and angry because Cole would not tell him what to do when he struggled with the UI. He was used to having all the answers and was very uncomfortable. In fact, as they worked their way through the participants, it became clear that the persona mapping would not be successful without the right person. They explained what they were looking for in more detail to their customer, and finally they found a guy whose flight out to a rig had been canceled and who was still hanging around the offices. He was perfect, and, indeed, he was Chet. From there it was easy to find more Chets, and the learning came fast and furious for Cole and Everett.

While working with the users, Cole and Everett were surprised by a number of discoveries they made. For example, the Baby Sitter design kit took you through the process step by step, "wizard style." It had a breadcrumb trail at the bottom showing your progress as you went along, and the team was particularly proud of this feature. Not one user even noticed it. In another design kit the UI was split in half so that the user could minimize one-half of the screen while focusing on the other. The designer placed huge arrows right in the center of the screen. Not one person understood what the arrows did, and several did not notice them.

When Cole and Everett returned to Schilling Robotics, they excitedly gathered the team around to share what they had learned. They placed sticky notes next to specific design features with feedback from the trials, like "this button never used," or added a smiley face for successful features. They worked through the information, looked for patterns, and developed hypotheses about what was going on that they could test during the next round. They organized these into a "hypothesis grid" (Figure 1.3), which helped them to capture the insights and incorporate them into the next set of design kits—then they debated some more.

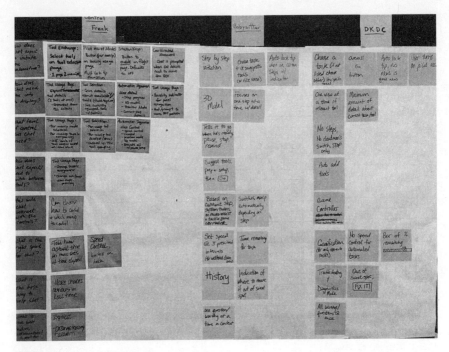

Figure 1.3 Hypothesis grid

In the subsequent round with users, they combined their updated design kits with a bit more fidelity, adding a video and improved controls to their pencil-and-paper UIs. The hardware guys had developed working prototypes of the actuator arm, and in the next round Cole and Everett plan to incorporate videos of the arm at work along with new design kits to better represent the user experience and refine their designs again.

This combination of building low-fidelity prototypes, using a set-based approach, and working directly with users on experiments proved so successful in saving time and money and creating a superior UI that Schilling Robotics is working toward making it standard on software projects.

The point, of course, is not to reduce all prototypes to cardboard, wood, and paper. The point is to get out of debate mode, identify the most effective, easiest way to test ideas or solve problems, and go do it. Surprisingly, even for highly sophisticated products, the answer may be lower fidelity, cost, and time than you may think necessary.

Testing Product Ideas Through Experimentation at FirstBuild

We have seen how thorny problems can be solved, hypotheses tested, and designs optimized early in the program through targeted-fidelity prototyping. But what if your challenge is to understand if a completely new technology will sell? The idea of creating a minimum viable product (MVP) was popularized by Eric Ries in his bestselling book, *The Lean Startup*.[22] While we have heard from companies that they have been doing this for many years with concept testing, Ries encouraged companies to go further, put their concepts to the ultimate test, and see if customers would actually pay money for those products.

While *The Lean Startup* community focused primarily on software applications for small start-up companies, Kevin Nolan, chief executive officer at GE Appliances (now owned by Chinese company Haier), was determined to adapt this idea to relatively complex consumer products hardware. He wanted a fast, low-cost way to put GE Appliances's product ideas to the ultimate test. What's more, he wanted a way to engage a broader community to generate new product ideas.

As with all good lean practitioners, Nolan started by understanding what problem he was trying to solve. The GE Appliances "hit rate" on new technologies was about average for the industry, but it was lower than some of the newer competitors. He wanted a way to increase his new technology success rate. After benchmarking companies around the world and conducting numerous internal experiments, Nolan decided he had to turn the traditional technology development process on its head. Instead of developing products in secret, he wanted to find a way to more directly link innovation with his customers—to codevelop new technologies in the open and make speed his competitive advantage. This was the birth of FirstBuild.

FirstBuild is a 35,000-square-foot design/engineering space and microfactory located adjacent to the University of Louisville campus in Kentucky, about eight miles away from GE's famous Appliance Park, where GE Appliances annually manufactures millions of appliances. FirstBuild has the capability to do most kinds of small-scale manufacturing and assembly of wood, sheet metal, and plastic. Laser cutting, forging, welding, forming, pressing, multiple types of 3D printing, and even an extremely flexible assembly line are available. The workspace also has CAD-capable computers, manual and electronic whiteboards, hand tools of every type, various raw materials, and a selection of printers. Directly outside the glass-walled workspace are a demonstration area and a new product showroom, where new products are available for anyone to examine and test. But facility capability is just the tip of the iceberg.

When entering FirstBuild, the creative energy is palpable. As you look past people examining the new product displays, you see several small groups huddled around mock-ups, whiteboards, and renderings. Staff members work on large wood tables in the design space, while makers and artists wearing safety glasses are scattered throughout the shop area, operating equipment both high tech and ancient, while others evaluate an assembly process in minute detail.

Jim had the opportunity to work with the FirstBuild team, and Nolan explained to him, "We encourage the collision of ideas." Engineers—on both their own time and the company's—mix with students, faculty from the university, and people "off the street," working on technologies both simple and complex, all under the watchful eye of expert technicians who are available to guide and assist. It is this energy and enthusiasm Nolan works hardest to protect: "It's passion that drives this place. We love it and want to protect it at all costs. It's the first place I have experienced where at the end of the workday, people will want to start working on their projects."

But, of course, creative energy does not necessarily translate into product success. GE Appliances solicits and accepts input from a large community, both online and in person. But all ideas must be subjected to rapid, real-world validation testing. The leaders of FirstBuild are highly skeptical of market research, and like opinions even less. They believe the true test is if people are willing to pay money. This often makes engineers and designers—who are usually convinced that they have the next great idea—uneasy. Sometimes FirstBuild will test ideas by "crowd funding" online, not for the cash to develop the idea, but for the opportunity to test idea validity. Then the staff might quickly build a small number of "good-enough" concept products that will be available for sale online and through FirstBuild's new product display area. This work has led to both technology successes and failures, and the staff members learn from both.

One success story is chewable ice. This is an idea that was kicking around GE Appliances for some time but could not get any interest from program teams. Team leaders thought it was a stupid idea that would never sell, and consequently, it never got traction in GE's traditional development system. One of the FirstBuild teams picked up the idea, got crowd funding on Indigogo, and built both countertop- and in-refrigerator versions. The product was a big hit and is generating millions of dollars in profit.

As the team members reflected on the sales data from the chewable ice program, they discovered that the vast majority of sales were from the U.S. Southwest, especially Texas, and that they had very few sales in the Northeast. Interestingly, the team leaders who had previously rejected this idea were all from the Northeast.

Another success story is home pizza ovens. These are high-end specialty ovens with huge margins, but equally large development and build costs, at least in a traditional development system. With these constraints, the idea could never really get started within GE. However, broad-based FirstBuild community response and rapid concept sales provided evidence that there was a very passionate customer base. By working on both design and manufacturing process costs and leveraging the unique capability of FirstBuild to create low-volume, highly customized products in its microfactory, GE Appliances was able to introduce a highly successful, high-margin-generating product that likely would not have been possible in the traditional way.

One of the ways that FirstBuild kept fresh ideas flowing was to borrow another idea from the software community—"hackathons." Hackathons started off as software people coming together and coding. They tried to hack into things and create things that hadn't been done before with the existing code sets.

In this case, hackathons "morphed into a 'hack together appliances and ideas,'" says Sam DuPlessis, manager and one of FirstBuild's founding members: "It's not just coding, it's electronics, it's physical, putting together some idea that you have in a weekend and try to make an event out of it and give it a challenge. [We] create prizes for the best concepts so that the best ideas can also win some money. GE Appliances gets hundreds of excellent ideas, some of which actually become products."

"Hackathons are a unique way to just drive creativity." adds DuPlessis. "There are people that are very passionate that want to come in, and we [do that] over the weekend. Sometimes, they bring their own team in. They're doing that potentially for prize money, but mainly it's an atmosphere of creativity that drives people to come in and do that. At [the] Appliance Park Engineering Center, they are constrained on what they can do on big programs by requirements for high-volume production. The engineers can come back here and really play and develop the stuff that they don't have the ability to do in their day-to-day job. That really intrigues some people."

Hackathons have produced some great ideas for GE Appliances. Some hackathons are themed, such as "The Future of Cooking," but that tends to constrain individuals to the topic, such as things found in a kitchen, according to DuPlessis. Others, like "Mega Hackathon," have no theme. The first Mega Hackathon brought together 250 people, many who were then assigned to teams. Teams often arrive already formed, but as just noted, FirstBuild also will facilitate teaming. DuPlessis notes, "They come in with their skill set usually on a badge, and we'll tell them, 'Hey, if you're a design engineer, maybe you want an industrial designer on your team so that not only would you have a good functional product, but it'll also have good usability and appearance as well. You can really have a nice-looking idea at the end of the weekend.'"

FirstBuild will also feed ideas to teams. "We'll have a board full of things that FirstBuild wants to work on," says DuPlessis. "We just hadn't had time to do it. If they like that idea, they can go pull it off the board, and that could be their project, or they could have their own idea. From there, we're really just facilitating them creating. We're giving them the materials and the space to whiteboard stuff out, to brainstorm, to go get samples, to do group prototypes. . . . We bring in appliances. We have a cool graveyard of old appliances, and let them just pull parts or create something out of one of the old appliances."

Suppliers also participate in the hackathons. "We probably had 20 suppliers that brought up the level of hacking by bringing their materials and teaching people how to use it," recalls DuPlessis. "For example, 3M came with a large engineering support team. They're there to train you on two-part adhesives, adhesive tapes, or whatever products they had." Suppliers frequently work with GE Appliances engineers to use technologies that would be difficult to introduce at Appliance Park, where people are hesitant to try new stuff on high-volume products. At FirstBuild, the technologies can be trialed and even put into low-volume production and tested.

FirstBuild philosophy and hackathons go beyond commercialization of successful products. In one instance the FirstBuild team and Louisville Water came together in support of a local charity called WaterStep. WaterStep's mission is to provide clean water to underserved areas of the world. The charity has responded to many natural disasters, the latest being the 2017 hurricane in Puerto Rico.

WaterStep had been buying chlorine gas generators for purifying water. These units run off car batteries and had a very high cost. They're pretty versatile devices, easy to use, and rugged, but they're quite expensive, and the price tag was severely limiting WaterStep's ability to help communities. It also had no control over availability. When a disaster struck and WaterStep tried to buy the devices, it could never get enough.

FirstBuild formed a team with the Louisville Water Company and engineers from GE, which set out to design a new chlorine generator that the charity could make itself. "One of the points was [that] we wanted to design it so they could be built by anybody looking at the normally available tools," says DuPlessis. "The team followed the lean principle that first you look at your manufacturing capability and design for that. We wanted a readily available part, so we built it all out of plumbing parts, with very simple machining operations. With that in mind, we got a solution for them that reduced the cost by 80%."

The FirstBuild units had the same capabilities of the more expensive generators, if not actually enhanced, and the new generator was five times more effective for WaterStep's donation dollars. Thousands have been distributed all over the world.

In the spirit of continuous improvement through experimentation, FirstBuild recently held a hackathon dedicated to further improving these devices. About 18 teams of engineers and designers showed up to answer the challenge and compete for prize money. One of the winning ideas was a solar-powered chlorine generator, developed by a team that included two of DuPlessis's sons.

Of course, not every FirstBuild product is a success. In fact, most fail. But the goal is to fail fast and inexpensively and learn from the experience. One such example is cold-brew coffee. Many people inside GE Appliances were passionate about technology that enabled the brewing of cold coffee in less than 10 minutes, while retaining the same taste and quality of beverages that required 24 hours of cold brew. GE Appliances staff were so positive that it would be successful that they were set to introduce it into the traditional GE development process. Someone suggested they first test it through the FirstBuild process, and to their surprise, it failed to generate any reasonable support. Now the team is working to learn from this experience and understand exactly why this product failed. By dissecting this very inexpensive and fast failure, the team hopes to deeply understand the root cause of the failure. Through this learning, perhaps the product will reemerge in a modified form and go back through the process again.

While there is still work to do at FirstBuild, like connecting its work more effectively to GE Appliances's product planning and large-scale program teams, it is obvious that FirstBuild is having a significant impact on the way the company thinks about developing new technologies. Based on the successes in Kentucky, GE Appliances is expanding the FirstBuild factory and opening a new one in Shanghai.

We think FirstBuild provides a strong example of how to quit arguing over ideas and find creative ways to test hypotheses. It has allowed GE Appliances to accelerate its innovation process and put product concepts to the ultimate test: Will customers buy the product?

The Concept Paper to Align and Enroll

Let's assume your development team has done a great deal of work going to the gemba, prototyping, experimenting, and testing with an aim to close critical knowledge gaps about the customer, the environment, the product, and risks. That's great. But it is not enough to merely answer questions and gather information about the product and the customer. That information must be turned into a clear and compelling vision for the product, prioritized performance characteristics, and a delivery plan that is shared with those who will help to deliver the program. The concept paper is developed and evolved during the study period, not just written at the end, and it is, in a sense, the "product" of the study period.

We described in our previous book how the concept paper, also known as the chief engineer's vision inside Toyota, can be the culmination of many months of research, experimentation, and debate between the CE and key members of the team. The document rarely exceeds 25 pages and includes detailed quantitative and qualitative goals and objectives for the product's performance, as well as system-level targets for cost and quality. It also includes project scope and schedule and provides a high-level financial justification for the project. But perhaps most importantly, it provides a compelling vision of what this product must be and what must be accomplished in order to deliver that vision. It should both inform and inspire the development team.

There are three primary steps when developing a concept paper: compile data and information, align with key stakeholders, and enroll the extended team.

Compile

The first step in writing the concept paper is to synthesize the enormous amount of information that has been learned during the study period. During a highly interactive process, the CE and the core team work through all the information, synthesize it, and integrate it into a single, coherent description of the product—a vision of what the product needs to be and how it will deliver unique value to the customer.

Deciding what to leave out is as important as what to put in. Just because we can, does not mean we should. It is about focusing on the customer and context that is key here. What problem will this product solve for the target customer? What does the customer value? What is the experience we are trying to create? What are the key risks? What knowledge gaps need to be addressed in the development process?

Too many companies rely heavily on customer and marketing studies and rationalize bad decisions by saying, "That's what they asked for." The best CEs make the product their own and take full responsibility for any failures in the program. The CE adds value at this point by knowing the product potential better than anyone else and synthesizing that with the intimate customer and context knowledge into a compelling vision of a successful product. Anyone can create a list of customer desires. That is not what the CE does. It is his or her responsibility to prioritize, adapt, and add value to the information in order to create a product that will be truly successful.

In our work with companies, we have found that just the exercise of writing the concept paper helps the CE check his or her own thinking. It helps CEs refine their vision, prioritize product attributes, identify high-priority risks, and check their own logic. CEs report that when they start to create a concept paper their thinking is surprisingly fuzzy, that their priorities are conflicted, and that their vision is not sufficiently compelling. The process of creating the concept paper forces them to resolve these issues.

Compiling a concept paper is a challenging process that helps to develop a detailed product vision. The next step is to build organizational buy-in—align—and truly put that vision to the test.

Align

While the CE is the undisputed leader of the project, his vision must be understood and endorsed by the larger organization, and the organization has to begin the process of developing plans to support the program. It is important to involve key leaders and other critical stakeholders in the program early on when the concept can still be revised. To that end, the CE visits with key decision makers and shares the concept paper as it is being created, to both explain the vision and get input from these experts and leaders. This is the beginning of building support and enthusiasm for the project. The best CEs know that this is the time to begin creating excitement. This is also the kickoff for each group to generate its own vision and requirements for its subsystems that will align with the CE's overall concept and plan.

A general guideline for these discussions is that while the CE owns "what the product needs to be," functional leaders own "how the product vision can best be achieved." As the experts on their disciplines, functional leaders are responsible to find the best path forward to deliver the critical attributes of the CE's product vision while meeting targets on cost, quality, and timing. The CE will push and stretch functional groups to maximize customer value, while the functional expert—also pushing the art of the possible—must keep the discussion grounded in reality. Supporting the CE does not mean always saying yes, but it does mean working alongside the CE and experimenting often as alignment is sought. Multiple visits to key leaders are often required, as the CE must make required trade-offs between disciplines, and suppliers, in the best possible way to deliver the overarching product vision.

By the end of this process there should be a solid multilevel plan to deliver the product, with critical characteristics clearly prioritized, major risks and mitigation plans identified, and at least a high-level plan of who will do what by when in order to deliver the product. The CE is obliged to make sure that the vision for the program is clearly understood, and functional leaders and other key decision makers must take full ownership of their commitments. Going forward, the concept paper will serve as the contract between the program team and functions, and it will provide guidance for the thousands of decisions that will have to be made as the project progresses.

We asked several successful CEs how they would escalate issues where they had difficulty aligning with engineering leaders, many of whom outrank them organizationally. They had essentially the same response (paraphrased): "If we have to force them to comply by appealing to more senior leadership, we have already failed. Yes, we could go to the top of the organization, but we want the power of our ideas to enroll them in the program. We want those ideas to excite and drive them to want to be a part of the program. If they do not, perhaps we do not have the right vision." We think this provides an important insight into both the nature of successful CEs and the nature of the alignment period.

We discussed the CE of the first Lexus model, Ichiro Suzuki, and his no-compromise goals. We want this *and* that. That was easy to say, but there is a reason there were trade-offs. It was not yet known how to achieve both simultaneously. For example, he wanted powerful engines that were quieter than any automotive engine on the market. That was traced back to the need for tighter tolerances for machined parts. The vice president of powertrain, who outranked the CE, at first simply laughed at the request. It would require reducing variation in the parts below the variation of machine tools, and Toyota already had the best machine tools in the world. Impossible!

Suzuki was arguably working on the most important product in the company at the time. Yet he did not rush to see the president, nor did he compromise. Instead he asked the vice president to humor him and hand-build one engine that met the specifications. "We can build one of anything. The problem is mass-producing it," replied the VP. Still he had his best people build the engine and then try it out in a vehicle at the test track. One by one the engineers came out of the car exclaiming they had to find a way to mass-produce an engine like that. And they did!

Enroll

After gaining agreement on plans with the senior leaders, the broader team must learn what product it is developing and why—why it matters, how it will compete, and how it will differentiate itself in the market. A CE needs to be sure that all the members of the team are working to create the *same* product, that they understand their role in creating it, and that they are excited about the program. The starting point for this process is sharing the concept paper broadly with everyone who will be working on the project.

At Toyota, for example, about 100 copies of a concept paper are distributed to the critical members of the development team. The distribution in Toyota is limited to a fraction of the total personnel working on the project for security reasons. However, those 100 people are in key positions from which they can provide needed information as required to other members working on the program. For smaller teams, we recommend sharing the concept paper with the entire team. The information from the concept paper then becomes the starting information on the obeya walls—the center of all future program discussions. Pictures, graphs, sketches, schedules, and targets spell out the purpose of the team. In the obeya, the people on the team track their progress against the timing, goals, and objectives of the program over time, never losing sight of what it is they are trying to create.

Another way to reach out to a broad team is with a program kickoff event, structured around the concept paper. This is often an undervalued part of the process and is frequently viewed as compliance to a process requirement. Yet when properly executed, these events can be an important step in engaging the team members, getting them excited, making sure they truly understand the value proposition, and helping them to understand their role in delivering it. Remember, "enrolling" your team in the project is a very different thing from directing the team or just communicating to the people on the team about the project. You are trying to get them to internalize the value proposition—to make delivery of the project a personal priority. Consequently, these events are very interactive with many questions and even challenges. This actually gives the CE an excellent opportunity to share what everyone has learned through the long study process. Effective kickoff events often incorporate elements from the concept paper and communicate renderings, early prototypes, or other aids to bring the team up to speed.

Another tool that helps to communicate the product vision is storyboarding. Humans are visual by nature, and engineers seem to be even more visual than average. Borrowing a common practice in creating movies or software and one that is routinely used by companies like Pixar, Schilling Robotics uses visual images on storyboards to communicate its futuristic vision of advanced underwater vehicles. Such was the case for its Gemini program in which tool change and sophisticated task capabilities were communicated in a kickoff meeting through a series of storyboards. One of the key new attributes of the Gemini ROV is its ability to change tools under water and accomplish multiple tasks without needing to surface—a significant competitive advantage. In the Gemini storyboard (Figure 1.4) the leader used a series of simple sketches to communicate the vision for this capability. These simple sketches generated a great deal of debate and discussion and, ultimately, resulted in a far more aligned team.

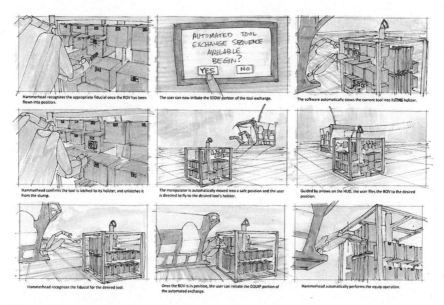

Figure 1.4 Storyboarding Gemini's path-breaking capabilities

Program leaders engaged the team in discussion around storyboards, making updates and modifications as they reviewed the renderings. The storyboards and the collaborative way in which they were shared in the kickoff meeting helped to promote robust dialogue among team members. Leaders credit the storyboards with engendering a deeper understanding of the future product, which otherwise would not have been possible. Use of storyboards during the kickoff meeting also identified critical knowledge gaps and high-risk areas and helped to generate potential countermeasures and even some initial experiments for the program. The storyboards remained up in the obeya as a visceral reminder to the team members of the vision for the product and their intent to once again revolutionize their industry.

In Summary

Successful development starts with fleshing out a strong product concept and identifying critical knowledge gaps to be closed. This seems obvious, but for some reason it seems to be a weak point of many development programs. We often hear that "senior management" is in a rush and does not want to take the time or allocate sufficient resources up front—the most critical part of the development process. We included a good deal of advice about how to do front-end loading the right way in this chapter. We can think of it as a four-step convergence process (see Figure 1.5):

1. **Deep understanding of customers.** Data is useful to get a sense of the population characteristics of the customer base, but true understanding requires deep immersion at the gemba, that is, where customers are. It requires an emotional connection and empathy in addition to direct observation to create great designs.

2. **Set-based design.** Instead of jumping to a point solution and trying to make it work through iteration, in set-based design we broadly explore the solution space before committing to a particular solution. Different functions should explore the solution space concurrently while working together to find connection points.

3. **Experiment to learn (PDCA).** Think like a scientist with a healthy skepticism. What appear to be "great ideas" should be tested. Don't waste time just arguing about it. Each experiment is an opportunity to learn to inform the next experiment. Targeted prototyping is a great tool for rapid PDCA learning.

4. **Concept paper.** The chief engineer's concept paper is a culmination of the broad exploration and then convergence in what some call the "fuzzy front end." Ideas are intentionally fuzzy when we start the conceptual design phase so that we can explore broadly, but the concept paper is very concrete. It is more than a report. It is a culmination of a great deal of learning and a great deal of internal debate and discussion aimed at aligning and enrolling key stakeholders to commit to the vision. It serves as a launching point for all the engineering work that will discover ways to achieve the vision.

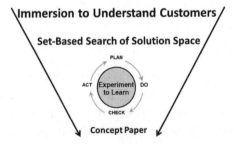

Figure 1.5 Front-end loading to narrow and focus development

LOOKING AHEAD

In the next chapter we will examine the execution phase of detailed engineering, tool, and process development. We will share examples of practices and techniques that speed the time to market and ensure precise execution.

Your Reflection

Creating a Vision

We cannot pretend that it is possible to predict the future of your new products and services with 100 percent accuracy if you do these things. We are confident that you will get in the ballpark more often and even hit some home runs. The vision we laid out for how to get the product right the first time is:

- The development program is headed by a visionary leader who has the technical, business, and social skills to develop and sell a compelling vision for the program.
- Sales and marketing support the visionary leader with market research data and facilitate visits to the gemba to deeply understand the customers and context of use.
- Direct observations of customers and the context lead to a feeling for what will emotionally connect with customers.
- Your best people are part of a cross-functional team in the "fuzzy front end" who take the time in a defined study period to broadly explore the solution space.
- The project team (or subgroups for large projects) explores alternatives through sketches, mock-ups, targeted-fidelity prototypes, and rapid experiments.
- Broad input from downstream groups, like manufacturing, and from customers testing models and prototypes continually informs the convergence process.
- The senior leader (CE) develops a concept paper and broadly circulates it to get feedback and to build consensus.

Does this vision fit what you think is needed in your company? How would you revise this vision to better fit your company's situation?

Your Current Condition

1. Are your products meeting expectations? What are the key issues or opportunities to improve?

2. How do you use your time on the front end to understand the customer, environment, and risks early in a product program? How can you improve?

3. Do you generate sets of potential solutions and converge or iterate on a single solution?

4. How do you use sketches, models, and prototypes to close your knowledge gaps at the front end of the program?

5. How do you communicate and enroll the team in the product vision?

6. What are some areas of high concern that would be worth working on right away?

Taking Action

Pick one of the high-concern areas and write down some ideas for how to get started working on it. Some possible directions might include:

1. Ways to deeply understand the customer and the context in which a product is used and to determine what the product must be. Try doing it through direct experience of the developers so that they can experience firsthand, viscerally, what the product needs to be—not filtered and published by another organization, such as marketing.

2. How to learn through experiments and targeted-fidelity prototypes— hands-on learning and direct experience.

3. What would go into a concept paper.

4. An approach to align and enroll the team in delivering the vision represented in the concept paper.

2
Delivering with Speed and Precision

Conventional project management attempts to
[determine what to do and when] by defining a
detailed plan and trying to stick to it. . . . This almost
never works. Lean companies create a web of small,
constantly operating, rapid, cadenced cycles.

— ALLEN WARD AND DURWARD SOBEK,
LEAN PRODUCT AND PROCESS DEVELOPMENT

Execution Excellence

You've done your homework; you understand the unique value proposition of your product or service. You've created and shared a compelling vision. The team understands and is on board with the concept paper. Everyone understands the risks and has identified initial knowledge gaps. Now it's time to transform a great idea into a game-changing product and to catch the market at the right time. It's time for detailed engineering, testing, tool-up, and launch—it's time to execute. Creating great products involves much more than innovative ideation. No matter how good your idea is, you still have to execute well. You have to deliver.

Companies that can execute with speed and precision during this phase possess a formidable competitive advantage. Execution excellence is about attending to the details of the work, minimizing waste, and operating precisely and predictably in order to get the right product to the customer on time. Reducing rework, waiting time, and poor communication not only enables more effective development, but also engenders a far more respectful environment in which to work. And as you will see, this approach provides a foundation for creating successful value streams instead of isolated products.

Speed is powerful. Time is the most limited resource we have. Reducing management cycle time, working more concurrently, and creating transparency can have a dramatic effect on your product development lead time. If you can deliver faster than your competitors, you can be first to market and get more "kicks at the can."

To be sure, moving from the study phase to execution is not a switch flip. It is not so much a handoff as it is a baton exchange. During execution there are still things to figure out, problems to solve, and the bulk of product and process engineering work yet to be done. Detailed execution, however, does have a character distinct from the study phase: there is a solid understanding of true north and an increased urgency about the work. This sets the stage for teams to leverage some concepts, practices, and tools that have been shown to improve nearly any company's ability to deliver products on time, at cost, and with quality.

To an unfortunate degree, legacy product development systems in most companies we see are based on the twentieth-century assumption that organizations are like machines. As machines, the mandate is command and control from the top. One approach to control is to put people into boxes based on their functional specialty. Input the right information in the engineering analysis box and out pops analysis results. Input specifications in a component group box and out comes a component design. Input the designs in the process engineers box and out will come a manufacturing process. Then you control the boxes through standard procedures and reviews at gateways. What you get is the "waterfall" model of development (see Figure 2.1). In fact, what happens is that the information inputs are not sufficient, and without feedback from other functions, each "box" produces a lot of defects—analysis that does not answer the right questions, designs that are not manufacturable, components that do not fit together. This leads to rework and churn, especially as the program nears launch and every function is called into action to fix all the problems under duress.

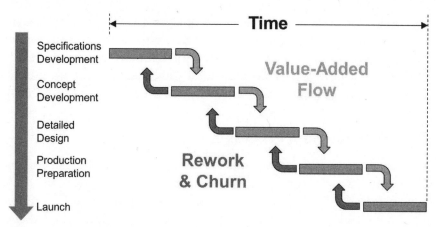

Figure 2.1   Waterfall model of product-process development.
(*Source: Bob Kucner, Caterpillar*)

The desired process is parallel and flowing streams of thought and activity (see Figure 2.2). The idea of simultaneous engineering may not be new, but establishing it as the routine operating pattern and excelling at it requires a lot of work. The result is a much smoother, more leveled flow of work, instead of fits and starts of defining something and then later reworking it when the problems suddenly become clear.

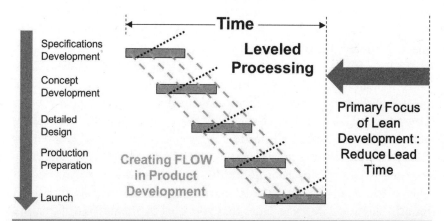

Figure 2.2   Simultaneous product-process development.
(*Source: Bob Kucner, Caterpillar*)

Standard operating systems and clear milestones can never replace people in product development. People are the very epicenter of successful development—period. (This is a topic we will return to later in this book.) However, supporting your people with a lean process, a proven framework, and just *enough* structure will give them the best chance to succeed.

Lean Development Process

A lean process in product development is *not* the Toyota Production System (TPS) applied to the engineering department. After experiencing the benefits of TPS on the shop floor, many companies are often keen to move "upstream" and directly apply the tools and techniques that helped them so much in manufacturing. It is a mistake. Toyota does not think this way, Ford did not use this approach, and neither have any of the other successful companies we have worked with. Don't go down this rabbit hole.

Now that we have that out of the way, there are some foundational elements of lean process thinking that can be quite helpful. It is the manifestation of that thinking, the actual tools and practices, that is quite different. For example, the ability to create flow across functional organizations and build in quality is greatly enhanced with the proper use of milestones and the practice of compatibility before completion. Another example is making the work visible in order to determine normal from abnormal conditions, signal for help, and provide timely help that can be enabled through the obeya management system.

We have found a powerful tool for getting started is value-stream mapping. Jim successfully adapted this tool to the unique product development environment, and we discussed it in detail in *The Toyota Product Development System* and in Chapter 9 of this book go through an example of how it was used at Solar Turbine. The simplest approach, which we have found very powerful, is to roll out a large piece of paper and hang it on the wall. Across the top column headings write the timing of your development program from start to launch of the product, usually month by month. The rows are swim lanes that you label by the different functions working on the program. Within the swim lanes use Post-its to write in the tasks of each function at points in time in the process. Connect the Post-its with arrows and showing rework loops. Start by mapping the way you ran a recent project using your current process. Then identify bottlenecks, rework loops, and other evidence of poor coordination. Next develop a future state map for how you want information and the work to flow using LPPD principles. This will not only give you a high-level plan for your development process, but is also a great team-building activity for your cross-functional team that will turn the picture into reality. The most powerful part of this process is often the coming together that occurs among the cross-functional teams as they truly "see" the work and the issues, understand the interdependencies, and create countermeasures together.

The future state value-stream map becomes a high-level plan that will change as you encounter the realities of development. The obeya, discussed later in this chapter, provides a daily or weekly cadence for creating flow, building in quality, and recognizing and dealing with abnormal conditions. One of the key mechanisms for doing this is the proper design and use of milestones.

Using Milestones to Improve Flow and Enhance Learning

The work of product and process development can seem chaotic and rife with problems. In fact, one perspective of development is that it is the business of solving problems and progressively closing gaps between the knowledge you need and what you currently know that you discover as you work on the design. Clearly a level of uncertainty is a natural part of any development program, but that does not mean the members have to flail around in the dark hoping to achieve something. Providing teams with a flexible operating framework will aid them in navigating through this uncertainty without imposing unnecessary bureaucracy. This is challenging, to be sure, but not impossible. Redefining milestones and how they were used was fundamental to the work at Ford to improve the global product development system (GPDS), and it has been the same for all the companies with which we have worked.

Herman Miller's Venture into Lean Product and Process Development

Herman Miller, a manufacturer of office furniture, equipment, and home furnishings, is an extraordinary organization. Companies from around the world travel to Zeeland, Michigan, to benchmark the company's culture. Herman Miller is world renowned for its design excellence and innovation, with an incredible decades-long run of prestigious design awards and several iconic products ensconced in art museums.[1]

Perhaps less well known is that Herman Miller is an outstanding practitioner of lean *manufacturing*. In fact, the company's teacher, Toyota, directs companies to Herman Miller to see what is possible, and refers to it as one of its best students in applying lean manufacturing outside of automotive.

While Herman Miller had made great progress in lean manufacturing, and despite the company's brilliance in the artistic design of furniture, it had not spent time on lean product-process development. In fact, more than 70 percent of development projects failed to hit their timing requirements. This is particularly problematic in an industry that is driven by an annual event (NeoCon), at which furniture makers put their latest products on display for customers, and the cost of late products that are not available for the show can be a major loss of sales.

By analyzing program performance data, conducting structured interviews, and mapping the current process, teams were able to identify variability in program execution as an important underlying cause in project delays. Herman Miller already had a high-level product development process that was well accepted. Instead of overhauling that system, teams initially decided to experiment with component development plans. A component development plan, which we will describe more fully later in this chapter, is a highly effective tool for creating an individual part or subsystem development plan that is, among other things, synchronized with the larger milestones of the program.

The process of trying to create a component development plan turned out to be an insightful experience. As the members of the team worked through an example plan, they discovered significant disconnects across functional organizations in understanding expectations and coordination for the higher-level development system. The team realized that it needed to back up a step and get the higher-level, cross-organizational problems addressed before it could proceed with the creation of an individual component plan. In other words the team needed to turn a disconnected set of processes into a connected set of processes across functional organizations. Defined agreements on who should deliver what to whom and when were sorely needed before work on individual plans could be done.

Leaders of supply chain, engineering, manufacturing, design, and marketing gathered as a cross-functional steering team and began the critical work of redesigning their product development process. These leaders focused on creating better cross-functional coordination and a common understanding of the overall product development process. They recognized that this work would need to begin by creating more effective integration mechanisms—the transformation began by looking to improve the effectiveness of milestones as integration mechanisms.

To transform from a "traditional" use of milestones as mere activity checkpoints into one based on lean principles, Herman Miller created a large map of key milestones and functional "swim lanes," which run horizontally below the main program and its milestones. With the swim-lane/subsystem milestones as process anchors, each function used sticky notes to re-create its understanding of the purpose, work, and deliverables for each event. Not surprisingly, understanding and expectations varied wildly—functions needed to come to a common agreement on the purpose of each milestone and what they expected to learn from each milestone review.

Work began on the milestones one at a time, starting with a clear and agreed-to purpose statement and including deliverables and the specific criteria that would define quality for each milestone activity. The cross-functional leadership team set up a cadence of regular cross-functional meetings, with most detailed work done as "homework" between meetings.

Beau Seaver, vice president of manufacturing engineering, orchestrated the large steering-team meetings, but each functional team spoke for itself as the teams aligned on purpose and committed to inputs, outputs, and quality of event criteria.

After this experience, Seaver said, "Product development at Herman Miller is a company-wide effort. The old adage of 'it takes a village' is truly fitting here. The focus of our milestone work was initially targeted at improving development quality and predictability. Bringing together the various stakeholders (functional disciplines) to gain insight and empathy for the required and associated timing started to unlock new doors. Gaining clarity of who owns what at each phase of the development and launch process was vital. While we have definitely experienced an increase in development stability, one of the unplanned benefits of this work is a significant increase in professional trust and a deeper understanding of the functional needs across the business."

Beau's team went on to create Manufacturing Readiness Levels (MRL) that mirrored product design maturity and were integrated into milestone QEC to provide a model for a "normal" standard for manufacturing process and tooling maturity levels at each milestone.

Herman Miller's work on redefining and aligning around milestones provided the foundation for many other lean development initiatives. This effort was a key factor in a dramatic improvement in program delivery, and at the time of this writing, more than 90 percent of all programs are on time.

The Problem with Milestones as Coercive Bureaucracy

Effective milestones are an important but often misunderstood part of a company's development process. Their effectiveness often suffers from one of two extremes—hallmarks of a rigid bureaucracy or mere suggestions for unmanaged teams that have been anointed as "self-directed." On the one hand, in what Paul Adler names "coercive bureaucracy," they become part of a system of control.[2] They become an external mechanism for managers and specialists on development processes to *audit* product development processes based on predetermined checklists. We have seen companies referencing several-inch-thick binders of criteria at each gate review or milestone, scoring each criterion as green, yellow, or red with little substantive discussion of problems and how to address them. This checklist mentality seldom leads to better actual performance.

On the other hand, companies that prefer free-floating, bottom-up teamwork find that separate teams (i.e., functional teams) rarely coordinate well and are prone to miss details and deadlines. They struggle to understand normal from abnormal conditions and wait far too long to react to issues. And even worse, there usually is little to no learning that takes place across program teams.

One of Adler's great insights came when he was studying Toyota's joint venture with General Motors, NUMMI, and he discovered many plans and standard work and standard operating procedures that actually helped team members to do their work. He called this "enabling bureaucracy" because, when properly designed and utilized, standards helped teams to coordinate and to learn together, while providing a constructive role for senior management.

Milestones can and should be like sheet music that, along with a skilled conductor, aligns and guides your development orchestra. To that end, we'll share some thoughts on the purpose of milestones, suggest ways to create useful ones, and offer a few tips on holding effective milestone reviews.

The Purpose of Milestones

Milestones, as the word implies, are guideposts on the development journey:

- **Reference points to determine normal from abnormal.** Milestones tell the team members if they are on track so that they can decide how best to proceed. They should define a "normal" condition for that point in the development process. This is not a "go or no-go" gate, but a key indicator to enable the team to take appropriate action to course-correct as required. The idea is similar to Sakichi Toyoda's loom or the lines on the floor of an assembly-line workstation, indicating the percentage of work to be completed at that point in the station. If a worker is at the 50 percent line, and only 25 percent of the work is complete, he or she can pull the *andon* to signal for help. The team leader can then come over to help fix the issue in the station without disrupting the rest of the line. Of course, this system is worse than useless if the team identifies abnormal conditions but has no signaling mechanism, or if leadership does not provide real help to the team. The obeya management system is key here. The goal is ultimately to identify and resolve issues early and effectively— to shorten management cycle time and keep the project on course.

- **Key integration points.** Milestones are an important part of synchronizing work across functional groups. They should be designed to recognize key interdependencies between disciplines—like software and hardware or design and manufacturing—and provide common reconciliation points. To do this effectively teams must understand both the tasks and the sequence of tasks within each functional discipline. This detailed knowledge allows them to sync work across the functions because they recognize what's needed or being delivered by each. This allows for maximum use of incomplete but *stable* data, necessary to optimize concurrent work. The better the companies get at this, the faster they can go. In fact, this synchronization is far more effective in shortening lead time than attempting to reduce individual task time.

- **Critical component of a development operating system.** Senior development leaders typically have many different programs to manage simultaneously. They must have the ability to recognize issues, respond quickly and effectively to struggling project needs, and make adjustments as required in the rest of the development factory. A project-health dashboard built from the feedback of properly designed milestones can be a powerful tool to enable this work.

Creating Useful Milestones

Our experience is that milestones, like most things in life, are as effective as you make them. We've found that useful milestones share these qualities:

- **A real purpose.** Start by asking yourself, "Why do we have this milestone?" You need to be able to create a clear, concise, product-oriented purpose statement. If you can't, you should question the need for the milestone. Another way to think about this is, "What problem are you trying to solve with this milestone?"

    Milestone purpose statements should optimally be linked to the chief engineer concept paper and reviewed in the program kickoff event. It is also crucial that you align cross-functionally on the milestone purpose statement.

- **Clear quality of event criteria (QEC).** Many companies create milestones based on activities or events. While this may be necessary, it is not usually sufficient. Just completing an activity does not tell you very much about the program status or health. For example, you may complete an early prototype-build event, but have done so with component parts that are not the correct pedigree for the design or manufacturing process level, thus rendering subsequent testing and learning spurious. You have not closed the required knowledge gap or reduced risk to a sufficient degree. However, because the team members completed the prescribed activity, they and their leadership might be lulled into a false sense of security.

    By establishing QEC for the milestone, the team gets a more realistic picture of where it really is in the development journey. Four things we like to think about in evaluating QEC: (1) The QEC should be the critical few predictors of project success, not a wish list of every possible failure mode you can brainstorm. (2) Is the requirement binary? (3) If it can't be binary, is there a quantitative range that can be established and measured? (4) If it can't be binary or quantitative, is there clarity about who decides if criteria have been met?

- **Scalability.** Not all programs are alike. Levels of content, complexity, and risk can vary significantly across projects. Well-designed milestones can be reconfigured to best fit the program without losing the basic intent or effectiveness.

Milestone Reviews

At many companies, milestone reviews can be universally dreaded events in which teams try to convince senior leadership that everything is okay, and senior leadership plays a game of "stump the chump," grilling the team in an attempt to ferret out what's really going on. Milestone reviews should and can be so much better.

There are several types of milestone reviews, most of which should be handled within the team (we will discuss these in the obeya section of this chapter). However, this section is primarily about major milestones that may require critical "outside" participation by senior leadership or other stakeholders. The following principles help to get the most value from a major milestone:

- **Support the team.** Updating leadership is important, but the primary intent should be to provide help and guidance as required.

- **It's okay to be red, but it's not okay to stay red.** "What's your plan to green?" was a philosophy Jim practiced while he was at Ford. While you want to drive fear out of these reviews, you don't want to eliminate accountability. The team eventually must deliver on commitments.

- **Define who should attend each milestone review.** Some reviews will require senior leaders, functional representation, or particular specialists—others will not. Consider the milestone purpose for guidance here.

- **Milestones are an opportunity for the team to regroup, align, and sync up on the way forward.** Milestones should energize the team, not demoralize it. Even a difficult review should end with the team still standing and motivated to continue. Leaders should look at milestones as a chance to "turbocharge" the team like the old Hot Wheels spin stations. The cars come out with much more energy than they came in with, and so should your teams.

- **Hold the reviews at the gemba whenever possible.** There is no replacement for actually seeing for yourself, both to truly see and understand the issues and to build excitement in the team. This is also the reason that many companies move the location of their obeya over the course of the program—to be near the action.

Leading Indicators

As powerful as milestones are as integration points and for identifying and resolving significant problems, it is a mistake to wait to discover all your problems at milestones. At the next level down, we need to establish leading indicators to predict problems as early as possible. This requires identifying truly predictive indicators and reviewing them on a more frequent cadence. These might form the basis of daily meeting discussions within an individual team.

Consider the following example. If "tool release" is a milestone, then a particular level of design maturity will be required in order to do the tooling work, and the progressive timing indicators for the required level of design maturity become a leading indicator. If tools are to be built by suppliers, then supplier selection could be an early indicator (i.e., if the supplier has not been selected, then on-time tool release is unlikely). The better you understand the work of product development, the better you will become at identifying these early indicators and the sooner you can surface potential issues or abnormal conditions. You may also find an opportunity to standardize certain aspects of this work even further.

Commodity Development Plans

Planning should not stay at the level of the overall development program, and needs to be supported by nested, specific plans for systems and even components. Complex products generally have complex multicomponent structures, sometimes numbering into the hundreds. These components have to be designed in parallel so they are on time and functional and fit together. Too often those developing these components—frequently suppliers—do not understand how their individual part fits into the big picture and thus how the failure to deliver on just a few critical components can bring down an entire program. One tool that can be particularly helpful for this is the commodity development plan (CDP).

A CDP is a standard development plan for an individual part or subsystem that can be modified by the developer to fit specific program needs. These plans are developed and maintained by part type and owned by the group responsible for the development of that part. They are particularly useful for standard components used across different products, such as a chair base, a valve, or a car fender. They begin with a generic template, and information is input for part-specific design maturity progression, performance and test requirements, standard interfaces, and timing of various inputs and outputs. Because specific requirements may vary across programs, the developer will download the generic plan, modify it to fit the specific program, and have it approved.

Commodity development plans are maintained by the group responsible for developing that part and are an excellent tool for coordinating individual part development to the larger program, providing a foundation for standard work, a training medium for new developers, and a basis for continuous improvement.

Creating Profitable Value Streams

Creating a successful product on time is certainly a major accomplishment. But what if there were something even better? What if there were a system of thinking and a framework that supported the creation of entirely new value streams? And what if the path-breaking innovation were not limited to the product but encompassed all the steps required to bring value to your customer, even how it impacted the world? Just think of the potential.

This idea, of course, is one of the foundational elements of lean product and process development (LPPD). It is an important part of what differentiates LPPD from traditional ways of thinking about product development. "Creating profitable value streams" via LPPD was the insight of our late friend and colleague Allen Ward. Instead of thinking about a product in isolation, the developer considers design, manufacturing, serviceability, installation, and any other value-creating activity required.

How can individuals and organizations see beyond one product and instead think through the creation of profitable value streams? We have two principles to suggest: The first, compatibility before completion, focuses on understanding each part's system compatibility before finalizing the part. The second principle, synchronize work across functions,

requires a deep understanding of the product to identify critical integration points across functions, which leads to value-stream thinking and has
the added benefit of significant reductions in lead time.

Compatibility Before Completion

One of the most useful concepts developed by the GPDS team at Ford
during its turnaround was compatibility before completion (CbC). Ford
had developed an unhealthy obsession with racing out of the gate of new
product development to get components developed as quickly as possible,
and then deal later with big spikes in engineering changes. The CbC principle was a countermeasure to force a more thoughtful approach in the
front end. Engineers had to demonstrate that designs were compatible with
all system and value-stream requirements before they were completed and
released. It served that purpose well, but it turned out to be so much more!

Feasibility checkpoints are a type of milestone designed to drive design
convergence and promote the practice of compatibility before completion. They are most often used early in the development process and frequently span both the study phase and execution phases of development.
They focus on the progressive closing of knowledge gaps, particularly with
regard to compliance to or compatibility with requirements for critical
value-stream attributes (e.g., manufacturing, craftsmanship and quality,
serviceability, installation, or safety).

Ford identified critical compatibility checks throughout the development process. This progressive series of checks contained demonstrable
requirements timed to match the maturity level of the design along with
scheduled feasibility checkpoints. It is, of course, important not to waste
time evaluating premature and unstable data too soon—it's just going
to change. But neither should you wait until after designs are complete.
That will just drive rework. Progressive, cross-functional inputs and outputs should make up a set of JIT delivery requirements for development
work.

Each area that benefits from this work—manufacturing requirements,
product serviceability, product installation, product and process environmental footprint implications, quality, safety, etc.—has its own series
of common, progressive check requirements. It is a powerful, customer-
centered, systems way of thinking that encourages the team members to
collaborate as they think through the entire value stream.

Many companies, such as Toyota and Ford, employ this concept in their value-stream creation efforts. At Ford a central part of this process is digital pre-assembly, or DPA. Both Ford and Toyota make extensive use of virtual reality, simulation, rapid prototyping, and standards to drive alignment to help ensure product quality and manufacturing efficiency. Their efforts start very early in the process by examining master sections and standard locators and then progress simultaneously with product design maturity all the way to part transportation, presentation, and sequencing—with many virtual "JIT checks" along the way.

The following example of material utilization at Ford illustrates this concept in practice. Much of the steel required to make the stampings that are assembled into a car body is wasted. And like most companies, Ford sets targets for material utilization in order to minimize wasted material. But most of the work of achieving utilization targets was done only by stamping engineering relatively late in the development process— during the processing and tool tryout phase of development. By then the design of the body parts and even die design were done and the degrees of freedom for improvement were severely limited. By building material-utilization checks into the development process through feasibility checkpoints and making *both* body engineering and stamping engineering responsible for the material-utilization targets, Ford was able to increase average utilization by nearly 10 percent per program. When you consider the average steel spend at an automaker, 10 percent per program is a dramatic reduction in cost and would not have been possible without building this work early into the development process.

We now have everything from stunning virtual reality environments, to incredibly powerful simulators, to the numerous additive-manufacturing technologies that aid in rapid prototyping. But none of these is as important as the organizational drive to create a truly excellent, total customer experience and an enabling, foundational infrastructure to promote value-stream collaboration. This upstream collaborative work is far more powerful than anything you can do after the product and process are launched.

Synchronize Work Across Functions for Speed to Market

Doing compatibility before completion well has another potential advantage: speed. By understanding the work of development deeply and identifying key cross-functional integration points, you are able to work more concurrently. This can dramatically reduce time to market in the execution phase. Concurrent engineering is not a new concept; however, very few companies seem to do it well. Their processes either are fraught with rework loops from poorly executed simultaneous engineering or have evolved into a long and linear process as a result of failed attempts at concurrent engineering. Yet simultaneous development remains one of the most potent ways to reduce lead time. Why don't more companies take advantage of this opportunity? We think that it is at least partially because they do not truly understand the work of development.

Too often, well-intended efforts to increase speed to market are reduced to arbitrary directives to shorten large chunks of "block timing" without any enabling countermeasures. Consequently, these types of efforts often focus on rushing individual task completion without a thorough understanding of the larger system implications. Once again this results in lots of late changes, rework, and delays.

Achieving excellence in concurrent engineering begins with having a value-stream creation consciousness and truly understanding how the work is done in each function, identifying key interdependencies, and learning how to work with incomplete but stable data. The key here is stability of data. Downstream functions working with data that is unstable and still subject to change will dramatically increase the chances of rework. You must understand the design maturity progression of each function to allow you to maximize the utility of incomplete but stable data as an input to the work of the downstream function.

One way Ford learned to develop this understanding was through a series of "gives and gets" meetings between interdependent functions, such as design studio, body exterior engineering, and stamping engineering. These forums usually went something like this:

1. The cross-functional team began by discussing current-state data delivery assumptions.

2. In this process they discovered a number of major disconnects between delivery expectations of one group and the way in which an upstream group (which expects to receive the data) worked.

3. The team learned that some of the development processes were built on incorrect assumptions; in other words, failure modes were built into the development process.

4. The team worked to understand the detail of how each group worked.

5. The team then reorganized development work processes to directly address the interdependencies and data-maturation progression instead of fighting them.

Synchronizing development work across functions is a key underpinning of the successful execution of simultaneous engineering and thus helps to reduce lead time and create great products. However, it is not easy. It requires a value-stream mindset as well as a significant level of organizational collaboration and technical capability. We recommend starting this work with relatively small overlaps of concurrent tasks until you deepen your understanding and sharpen your capabilities. The best organizations continually work to increase overlap and, consequently, speed to market.

Bringing the Process Together—the Obeya System

All of the technical tools in the product development world will be wasted if communication is poor. This is especially true for cross-functional work where individuals naturally think in the language of their own specialty. One paradox of great communication is that more is not necessarily better. The focus and quality of that communication as well as transparency and ongoing collaboration are often more important than quantity. That is the contribution of the obeya system.

The Beginnings of Obeya

Takeshi Uchiyamada had a problem. He had just been named chief engineer for arguably the most revolutionary product in Toyota's history—what would become the Prius. The original goal for this program, initially identified as Global 21 (G21), was to develop—on an extremely compressed timeline—a car for the twenty-first century and achieve nothing less than 1.5 times the fuel economy of Toyota's best small cars. To make matters more difficult, Uchiyamada had never been a chief engineer before. He earned his position, and respect within the company, by being a leader in advanced R&D and leading the largest reorganization of R&D in Toyota's history. However, he lacked the technical depth and experience to develop and commercialize the advanced hybrid technology that would be required. In fact, no single person at Toyota had the necessary expertise. He quickly realized that he would need an unprecedented level of collaboration, transparency, and speed of decision making to make this program a success. In his humble words: "chief engineers are expected to know everything and I knew nothing."

Consequently, his first path-breaking innovation had nothing to do with engine technology. Since he felt like he knew so little, he decided to surround himself with people who knew a lot—from all key functions—sitting in one room. He created a fundamental innovation in product and process development that came to be known as the *obeya management system*.

Obeya was a "big room" that Uchiyamada holed up in with a senior leadership team so that he could effectively use the team members' expertise and authority to make high-quality, rapid decisions. In this system, he met every two to three days with all required technical experts, with all pertinent information posted on the room's walls. This information was available to everyone on the team at any time. The Prius went on to revolutionize the auto industry, dramatically raising the bar for fuel economy and leaving competitors years behind. And the obeya system, credited with making a major contribution to the Prius success, became a development staple at Toyota.

We first heard this story nearly 18 years ago while meeting with Uchiyamada during the research for our previous book. At the time he was working with a team of Toyota engineers, who were tasked with standardizing and teaching obeya throughout the Toyota development community.

Toyota is a learning organization. The company tries to minimize detailed prescriptive methodologies and maximize kaizen. This includes continuous improvement of processes like the obeya. Uchiyamada was not interested in rolling out a prescribed obeya system. There were certain underlying principles that he believed in and wanted to pass on, but then he wanted to encourage the chief engineers to experiment and learn from each other.

Toyota had not adopted the approach of collocated project development teams that became popular as part of simultaneous engineering. Engineers still reported into their functions, such as body engineering, and dotted-line-reported to the chief engineer when they worked on a specific project. Initially for Uchiyamada, the obeya was for intensive meetings with the senior leadership team. Other chief engineers decided to use the obeya less frequently (often weekly) with a larger group of engineering managers to collaborate and to provide transparency in situations where they could not collocate all program teams. Later, other chief engineers chose to have a really big room, where many engineers worked full time in the obeya. We know of one chief engineer who invited general managers of engineering functions to move their offices into the obeya. Another used a good deal more computerization than we had seen before. Experimentation and learning have been rampant.

Principles of Obeya

We have helped organizations establish an obeya system in many industries, including consumer electronics, automotive, appliances, heavy equipment, and healthcare. The main thing to understand about obeya is that it is much more than hanging stuff on the wall. It is a powerful, team-centric management system that creates elevated levels of transparency, communication, decision making, and accountability. Below are six important points to consider as you think about applying the obeya system to your organization:

- **Engineers are not necessarily collocated.** The team may be collocated or use the obeya as a meeting place. This includes both program cadence meetings and smaller huddles of subgroups working on assignments and utilizing the latest information available in the space. Even with a collocated team, there will still be many people, such as suppliers, which will work from their own sites and come to select meetings as needed. Whether or not teams are collocated, the obeya becomes the communication hub of the development program.

- **Paper-based visual management is the key to effective communication.** The walls are plastered with important program information that typically has been derived from the chief engineer concept paper, which now serves as a combination true north and contract for the team. Design data—including information on alternatives communicated through CAD drawings, recent test results, alternative evaluation status, decision criteria, and status—is displayed with trade-off curves. Plan and status to achieve attribute performance and cost targets are shown with glide path charts. It is also important to visually display program status in relation to schedules, including supplier readiness levels, in a way that is flexible, interactive, and easy to use. We have also seen teams fill the obeya with early versions of the product. These prototypes are often among the most powerful of communication aids.

Teams using the obeya often say they are "walking the walls" with each responsible party reporting on their portion of the room. These are stand-up meetings, and subteams meet there often between meetings. The paper documents can be supplemented with online communication. In some cases participants will call in to meetings and participate virtually, perhaps using cameras for visuals. We have even worked with companies that have two identical obeya, with the same documents on the walls, in different parts of the world (e.g., China and the United States).

- **Clear standards are displayed, and deviations from the standard are highlighted leading to corrective action.** The process of preparing and updating information and visuals in the obeya forces the team to think clearly about expectations, targets, and standards for program management. What should be happening? What is happening? How can we close gaps? There are many rapid PDCA cycles closing gaps within the meeting or shortly after instead of letting these issues drag on for months.

- **Meetings are dynamic, are energizing, and evolve to fit the program.** Meeting cadence varies across teams. Some teams meet daily, others weekly, but most vary their meeting cadence with the activity intensity of the program. The content of the meeting may also change as the program matures. The important thing is that the meetings be germane, highly interactive, and crisp. It is not just a "status meeting" in the traditional sense. The meetings should encourage debate and collaboration, provide aid in identifying issues early, and promote transparency and a "one-team" approach to delivering the program. On the other hand, the meetings are not intended to spend a lot of time solving complex problems that involve a few individuals while others become spectators. At Caterpillar, the policy became only discuss broad cross-functional issues in the obeya. Then assign issues involving one or a few functions in the room to a team to work on outside the meeting and then report back in the next obeya meeting. At Schilling Robotics, the VP of engineering, Andy Houk, talks about "communication density or efficiency" and claims that "we get more done now by using obeya in 30 minutes than we ever did in our old 1.5 hour status reviews." In short, the meetings should simultaneously identify issues and turbocharge the team.

- **The obeya location often moves with the program.** The actual location of the room typically starts in design engineering and then moves to prototype and finally to the plant for launch. Teams definitely benefit by being located near the gemba so they can quickly go and see. We realize that this is not always possible. The most important point is to provide the team with a dedicated space that can serve as a gathering place as well as control central for the program.

- **The obeya is a central planning and communication site for milestone and other reviews.** The companies we have worked with usually have some type of structured development process that includes phases and gates as part of their formal review processes. These are typically longer-cycle reviews (several months) compared with the rapid decision making that occurs within the obeya. We have found that rather than spend an inordinate amount of time preparing lengthy PowerPoint presentations to review program status, we can use the obeya as a logical and effective alternative medium. It's common to hear, "We should have our milestone reviews in the obeya. We already have all the program status information on the walls." These reviews then become a value-added part of the overall process of learning and PDCA, rather than stand-alone events filled with waste.

During research visits to Toyota, we saw how obeya at Toyota has continued to evolve through careful PDCA. There were innovations such as adding CAD and simulation capability in order to facilitate real-time design discussions. But the heart of the system remains active visual management and the intent to improve communication, transparency, and cross-functional integration in order to quickly identify and solve problems.

Transparency and collaboration were also the essence of Alan Mulally's message at Ford when he said, "You can't manage a secret" (and we would add, "and you can't solve a problem you're not aware of"). He challenged everyone to increase honest, fact-based communication and improve cross-functional transparency and collaboration across the enterprise. One of the ways the development groups responded was with an obeya system. Obeya was used not only to manage program performance, but also to integrate cross-functional teams in the creation of the GPDS and to manage a global engineering function.

Obeya in Action at Schilling Robotics

We were reminded of the benefits of obeya when the Lean Enterprise Institute LPPD Learning Partner companies came together in Davis, California, in June 2017. This is a learning group founded by Jim that consists of a wide variety of companies focused on improving their development capability and willing to share the results as they learn (discussed in detail in Chapter 9). While experience levels and specific practices varied across the companies attending the June meeting, each was experimenting with obeya, and all reported performance improvements. Several teams reported "best-ever" product development results that they attributed to obeya. In our subsequent discussions, we learned many nuances of how they were each leveraging the power of obeya. However, all of them found that the real benefits of obeya were in transparency, speed of problem resolution, and team engagement. One of those stories comes from Schilling Robotics.

David Furmidge is a highly experienced and very capable project engineer. He worked 7 years in the aerospace industry on satellite development at Lockheed and then 10 years leading development projects at Hewlett Packard and Schilling Robotics, where he heads up the company's most complex and difficult ROV (remotely operated vehicle) programs. It was no surprise when Andy Houk, VP of engineering, asked him to lead the Gemini program (the user interface design was discussed in Chapter 1). The vision of Gemini was to develop a robot that could travel to the worksite as far down as 13,000 feet below sea level on the ocean floor and carry out complex tasks, including changing tools, without having to return to the surface. This in and of itself would be a huge advance and save Schilling's customers millions of dollars and days of time. But the company also aimed to make Gemini much simpler to operate, giving its customers increased flexibility in operator selection. In short, Gemini would be a game changer—and the most advanced and complex product ever developed by Schilling.

Even with all his experience, David knew this would be the toughest program he ever led. And as if that weren't challenging enough, Andy asked him to use an all-new method to develop it. According to David,

"Of course, I said, 'Yes, we will do it,' but I was thinking, 'Holy cow, we have got this huge project we're doing, and now we are going to change our development practices!' It just seemed like a lot of added work on an already difficult task."

Despite being a skeptic, David had an open mind about learning. He and Andy were inspired by what they had read about obeya and a visit they had made to Herman Miller to see how project teams were using the obeya system to great benefit in their development work. Although David and Andy were impressed by what they saw at Herman Miller, they both wondered if the process would scale to something as complex and sophisticated as Gemini. David, in particular, remained quite doubtful and even kept a separate, detailed schedule in Microsoft Project on his laptop in anticipation of when "this obeya thing would all fall apart."

Schilling has a vital experimentation culture in which people are very willing to try new things; however, those same people are also exceptionally bright and opinionated. David heard initial grumblings about what some saw as just another status meeting where they had to waste time that they could have spent actually "doing their jobs."

"People didn't say much in our first few obeya meetings," recalled David. "I think it was a combination of speaking in front of 40 or 50 people and the fact that they did not really understand or trust the process at first. So I invested some time taking small groups of people through the room and explaining the purpose. I assured them it wasn't a status meeting; it was an issue identification and problem-solving meeting, [and] that our goal was to work together to deliver this incredible product and to support each other in the process. Within a few weeks people started to see how powerful this system was [and] that we had a level of transparency and collaboration we had not had before. That's when things started to change dramatically—and I even ditched my secret MS Project schedule for good."

On one side of Schilling's obeya room was a giant schedule. It was anchored at the top with the overall project-critical milestones serving as column headings. Beneath the milestones were horizontal swim lanes for each of the subsystem project teams, such as manipulator, tether management, controls, as well as functions like software and safety. In each swim lane were placed sticky notes that identified critical tasks in support of the milestone timeline.

"At first, we only had really good fidelity for about an eight-week period; after that, tasks were identified at a higher level," said David. "And we would add detail as we progressed from left to right on the project. In the meeting, though, we really kept our focus on the upcoming week. We noted upcoming events, but we really wanted to work on what had to be done this week."

In the meetings, individuals responsible for tasks would speak to the status of their tasks: issues they were experiencing and where they needed help. They had a movable red line that was located on today's meeting date, and everything to the left of that line should have been completed. As a task was completed, the sticky note on which the task was written was crossed off with a green pen. "By getting the group together around the schedule board, it made it much easier to identify disconnects and conflicts—especially in areas where we had struggled historically, like hardware and software integration," noted David. "As a leadership team, we never attacked or criticized a team for being behind; we just asked what help was needed. But there was a ton of peer pressure in that meeting. No one wanted to let the team down. We seldom, if ever, had someone be late a second week." The meetings were held weekly for most of the project, but occurred daily as the project moved into the test phase and work moved faster. As the team got better, the schedule discussion only took up about 10 minutes of the meeting, and the rest of the time was spent on the product side of the room.

On the product side of the obeya room was a set of posters for each of the various project subsystems. The posters showed the latest design information, notes on the latest thinking, decisions that had to be made, and concerns or issues in a particular area. Eventually the posters were expanded to include a rich assortment of operations, safety, and supply posters. As this process matured, the team was encouraged to write questions, suggestions, or issues on sticky notes and put them on the posters. The owners of a poster were typically given until the next week to respond to the comments. "This really helped to streamline decision making," said David.

Issues were not allowed to fester in the obeya, and the team members supported each other as they faced challenges. Because of the obeya process, "I really felt like part of the development team," said Hannah Waldenberger, a manufacturing engineering manager at Schilling. "We weren't design people or operations people; we were one development team. We owned the issues and the product together."

As time went on, Andy spotted more and more small groups huddled around some part of the obeya between meetings, working through issues or discussing plans. "That helped convince me that this was really getting traction," said Andy.

David turned from a leading skeptic to a leading proponent. "I think the obeya management system enabled us to eliminate a lot of large issues and the associated drama that usually accompanies this type of project." He believes that not only was it successful from a program delivery perspective, but it was instrumental in bringing the team closer together and relieving him of a great deal of stress as project leader. "I think the obeya system was the greatest contributor to our success. It helped us integrate engineering and operations into one team, and built in transparency and accountability. I could definitely see this working in [the] aerospace industry. We finished the first project phase two weeks early with no open issues—and that's a first for us."

Tyler Schilling, the founder, is no less enthusiastic about the obeya system. The company had experienced incredible growth over the years, but one downside of that was more and more electronic communication. He explained, "Over the last how many years, there has been a constant wind that has been blowing, a trend to do all your communicating with Microsoft tools, even with people a few feet away. I have nightmares of my most critical resources around here, inside of a PowerPoint program resizing circles, changing fonts, and just wasting their time. I thought, 'Holy cow! I can't have that kind of thing going on.' And then I saw what you guys were doing with obeya. The paper charts, the Post-its—it was a wonderful expression of spending time on substance and as little as possible on form."

"I love attending the obeya meetings," added Tyler. "It is a frictionless flow of information that happens in a truly efficient manner. Once a week a group of 50 people or so get a super-charged dose of what's going on. Decisions are made and the team moves on. It's brought back the synchronization and rich communication we had in the old days. We are advancing Gemini in a much more predictable manner than recent projects. It really reminds me of the early days at Schilling when we were just a small start-up."

And Tyler sees another advantage to the obeya management system. "It seemed like the success of any given subproject within our larger development programs was mostly correlated with the leadership capability of whoever was in charge of it. If you had a superstar leader you would get great results; if not, well, you had to redo a lot of work—it was crippling. Our bandwidth, our ability to do projects, was being limited by the number of talented leaders we had. So we had to change what we were doing. We turned down projects. It was painful.

"The obeya techniques have increased our leadership bandwidth," he continued. "It brings everyone together and synchronizes all these sub-projects. It's much easier for a less experienced leader when they see the right leadership behaviors modeled each week. They are part of a team. It's been really exciting to see our competency tier and our people grow." Tyler sees this as a major people-development opportunity going forward as the use of obeya is expanded across the company.

For now, however, Tyler has been focused on Gemini: "Our biggest overarching story [on obeya management] is that this is one of the first times in 30 years where such a large-scale program has met all of its development objectives and been within budget."

The obeya system was a great fit with Schilling's existing culture, which enabled the company to make fast progress. It clearly promoted values that the company already held dear, such as collaboration, creativity, transparency, and a passion to create great products. But obeya can also be a way to stimulate the development and growth of those values. As our friend John Shook, Lean Enterprise Institute chairman and CEO, has said, "sometimes it's better to act your way to a new way of thinking than to think your way to a new way of acting." At Schilling simply seeing and hearing about obeya was not enough. They had to experience it and act their way to a new way of thinking.

Decreasing Lead Time Through Visual Workflow Management at Solar Turbines

Solar Turbines, a wholly-owned subsidiary of Caterpillar based in San Diego, is a global energy solutions company that designs and manufactures industrial gas turbines and compressors and provides life cycle product support. Primary applications include electric power generation, oil and natural gas production, and natural gas transmission.

Solar started its LPPD journey with help from Jeff and our colleague John Drogosz after reading *The Toyota Product Development System*. Leaders began by value-stream mapping and establishing an obeya management system. The deeper level of understanding and increased transparency created by this work led to significant improvements in product quality and reduced time-to-market. We will discuss how they got started further in Chapter 9.

However, because of the success of this initial work in value-stream mapping and obeya, Howard Kinkade was asked to expand LPPD to an entire product line. His supervisor, Bill Watkins, director of Gas Compressors, saw that there was a need to increase the development pipeline for new products in the coming years. And while the previous LPPD work had led to local improvements, there were still departments that were struggling to meet their timeline commitments. The overall development performance for the gas compressor line needed to be improved if the team was going to meet the goals set by the organization and the future needs of customers. But where should they start?

They decided to build on the work they had already done and create an even greater level of transparency in the work. There were several perspectives about what was causing the flow issues ranging from not having enough resources to unrealistic timelines. However, before jumping to solutions, they decided that each functional team should start by making all their work visible. They posted all their activities on individual boards so everyone could see what work was in progress as well as all the work that was still in queue. The boards were all posted in one area where everyone could see what each person in each organization was currently working on and the backlogs in each department. Once all the work was there for all to see, the teams could start to both quantify and prioritize all the workflow issues and attack them one by one.

This level of transparency also enabled the team to step back and analyze the overall process of gas compressor development. Several consistent challenges quickly emerged:

- Prioritization of work
- Work scope
- Too much work in the system
- Resource constraints

Prioritization of Work   Looking at the work on the wall, it became clear that while priorities may have been established, not everyone was executing to them. The question was, why? The team discovered that priorities in departments often changed based on new requests from various different groups. In fact, they discovered that work requests found their way into Gas Compressors though 15 different channels! Team members were, of course, trying to be helpful and responsive to all the requests, and this caused the associates to frequently drop one task/project and move on to another.

It was clear that while there were existing meetings to discuss priorities, there was really no process to consistently and effectively prioritize the work from their various customers. The team set up a standard process to receive, evaluate, and prioritize incoming work. Standard criteria of customer value, safety, quality, and financial performance along with budget considerations were applied. The queue of requests and the evaluation process was also made visible so the prioritization was transparent to all. Most importantly, this process provided a consistent structure for the management team to discuss and align on priorities for the entire product line. This process was the start of creating their workflow management system.

Work Scope   Another issue troubling team members was the lack of clarity in the work requests submitted by upstream customers. Requests were either unclear, lacking the correct information to complete the tasks, and/or the scope of work would change midway through the project. Often under deadline pressure associates would start work without the information they needed only to have to stop and redo much of what they had accomplished. This stop-and-go waste was a source of frustration for many of the associates and both time-consuming and expensive for Solar.

The project and department managers worked together to define a standard for a minimum information threshold required to begin each type of work. This removed the ambiguity between the requester and associate. Work requests now stayed in queue and could not be released to an associate until standard information became available. The work queues were displayed visually and showed what was ready for work versus what was still waiting on data. The practice of not passing on incomplete work requests had a dramatic impact on reducing rework and churn between departments.

Too Much Work in the System   Another issue that became apparent as the Solar team began utilizing the workflow boards was the large amount of work-in-process that was in the system. Some of this was a natural outcome of changing priorities and scope and the associated rework. However, another major issue was the lack of process for managing the release of work into the system. In the course of any given year, more work would enter the system than would exit. Work was assigned to a department and then a person(s) as soon as it was authorized or budgeted without regard to existing workload. This practice resulted in some departments being overloaded and becoming a bottleneck while others had nothing to do.

As the team stepped back to reflect, they realized that there was really no process in place to measure the capacity of any given department. At best it was an educated guess based on past experience. So the department leads worked with their teams to determine an effective maximum WIPCAP (maximum work-in-process capacity) for their departments and associates. Once the standard was established for each department, no work beyond this threshold was released until such time that departments fell below their WIPCAP.

Resource Constraints Many team members felt that there were significant resource constraints in the system, but it was hard to pinpoint exactly where and by how much. As the team addressed the challenges with priorities, scope, and work-in-process, the true resource-driven bottlenecks became visible on the workflow boards. By making the work visible in this way the team was better able to see that the problem was not so much that they needed more people, but rather that they needed to expand the skill sets of associates. This would allow them to flex with the changing mix of work and reduce the burden on a handful of key people who had specialized skills.

Building in Learning and Continuous Improvement As the team found and resolved issues in the workflow management system, they also gained a deeper understanding of their work. This led teams to create better work standards. As improvements are made, they are updated in their standard work and shared with their team members. The standards have also helped to accelerate the growth in skills sets of the associates.

Results The implementation of the visual workflow management system resulted in a more leveled and cadenced workflow through the overall value stream. In the first year of implementation:

- Workflow stoppages were reduced by 60 percent.
- Backlog of work was down 29 percent.
- The number of designs successfully generated by the system increased by 41 percent.

- Work capacity increased by 30 percent without adding any additional resources.

- Alignment and collaboration improved greatly between departments and projects.

Conclusion   Adding the workflow management process to the obeya management system has helped the Gas Compressor team to improve its performance significantly. It also helped to build in a process for continuous improvement to meet their ever-changing business and customer needs. Managers and associates now feel they have the knowledge, ownership, and tools to continue to improve their development system.

What most impressed us about this example from Solar was the approach to solving problems. By the time Howard and his team got started, Solar already had experience with different software solutions for workflow management. The team could have simply implemented these. Instead they stepped back and decided to highlight problems and systematically identify the blockages to flow and experiment with different possible countermeasures. They took a learning approach and experimented. In this way they developed solutions that fit their situation, and felt the passion that comes when a team works together to achieve something great.

From Rote to Value-Adding Routines

Compelling visions require great execution in order to truly create breakthrough innovations. Innovation is an inherently unpredictable process. We cannot predict exactly what we will learn and discover or when it will happen. Structured development processes have proved beneficial in bringing some order to the chaos and significantly improving development performance. On the other hand, as these structured development processes evolved, they often became part of a coercive bureaucracy. Large staff organizations were responsible for the corporate development process, and they continued to add gate review items. Voluminous notebooks led to voluminous PowerPoint presentations and countless meetings in which increasing numbers of weary participants rated hundreds of items red, yellow, or green. Productive, substantive discussion was replaced with mind-numbing habits to check progress.

Lest we throw the baby out with the bathwater, we covered a few types of reviews that can add great value and structure to the product development program. To create a context for ongoing discussion and problem solving, marked by periodic reviews, we introduced the concept of the obeya. The founder of Schilling Robotics lamented the product development energy and excitement that was lost as his company grew in size and complexity, and was delighted by what the obeya system brought back.

In the end, excellence in development execution requires that you achieve the right level of balance in your development process between structure and creative flexibility. Remember, the point of the framework is to help the development team, and by extension the product, be successful. It is not meant to be a command and control mechanism for auditing organizations.

LOOKING AHEAD

This chapter focused on how the right level of structure can bring order to what is inherently a somewhat chaotic process of developing something new. Too much structure through coercive bureaucracy will stifle creativity, and too little will cause long lead times, a great deal of rework, and products not meeting their objectives. We suggested that the right level of bureaucracy can enable and support innovation.

We continue this theme in Chapter 3. We will wade into the age-old battle between those who view standards for the product or service being designed as stifling and those who see them as enabling. We will argue, as in this chapter, that it will depend on the standards and how they are used. We use as one example how Toyota has created a new global architecture for its vehicle platforms that is allowing design teams to use their creativity for more stylish designs, with far better performance. In fact, we believe that standards and flexibility are like the yin and yang of product development, complementing each other, creating some tension, and pushing the design team to develop great designs.

Your Reflection

Creating a Vision

The focus in this chapter is excellence in the process of delivering a product or service with speed and precision. The key characteristics of the vision portrayed are:

- Work flows smoothly across functional specialists who synchronize their work from the start, identifying interdependencies and learning how to work even with incomplete but stable data.
- The work is made visible to distinguish normal from abnormal conditions to signal for rapid corrective action.
- Milestone reviews are used to assess progress to plan, check interdependencies, take corrective action, and learn.
- Leading indicators are developed and used to anticipate problems before there is a crisis.
- Feasibility checkpoints are used drive "compatibility before completion."
- The obeya management system is used as a central planning, communication, and collaboration site for the cross-functional team to meet (at least weekly) and rapidly identify and resolve cross-functional issues as they arise.
- The development process is well understood by all participants.
- The development process itself is studied with regular reflections to learn and continuously improve.

Does this vision fit what is needed in your company? How would you revise this vision to better fit your company's situation?

Your Current Condition

How good are you at product and process development execution?

1. Is development execution a competitive advantage for your organization? In what ways yes and in what ways no?
2. Is your current formal system of project management, gate reviews, and design reviews supporting your development teams in continuously improving to create smooth, parallel flow?
3. Consider the vision you agreed to for your organization. How would you rate each item (1—Weak, 2—Pretty Good, 3—Excellent)?

Taking Action

Pick one of the areas where you are weak and write down some ideas for how to get started working on it. Some possible directions might include:

- Get a cross-functional, multilevel group together to map out and discuss your current development process and its capability to establish clear agreement on purpose, deliverables, and quality of event criteria at each milestone.

- Bring a group of development team leaders together to discuss how they currently operate and how an obeya management system or changes to the development process itself could help them be more effective in delivering products.

- Make a plan to pilot an obeya management system on one of your programs.

3

Fixed and Flexible

The Yin and Yang of Lean Product Development

Yin and Yang in themselves are of course opposites, so we use Yin and Yang to generalize opposing elements such as up and down or day and night. But Yin and Yang do not exist in separated and independent forms. Yin and Yang are two faces of the whole, or, it may be said, Yin and Yang join together and combine into the whole.

—JINGHAN HE, *BAGUA DAOYIN: A UNIQUE BRANCH OF DOAIST LEARNING, A SECRET SKILL OF THE PALACE*

Creating Balance in Your Development Strategy

Far too many product developers take sides in the (alas, unnecessary) conflict between the unlimited potential of human innovation and the incredible power of good standards. In one camp, the "free spirits" fear that lean standards limit creativity and lead to painfully boring products.

In the other, the "technocrats" are haunted by visions of cost overruns and operational chaos that result from unconstrained imagination run amok.

This binary thinking can be quite limiting. It is much more effective to embrace this "conflict" as a source of innovation. We find that an effective way to think about this dilemma is to see it not as an "either-or" problem, but as an "and" opportunity. Instead of conflict, this is the "yin and yang" of product development: opposite yet complementary forces that make up the whole. The yin and yang symbol, of course, is a well-known part of Chinese Taoist philosophy. It reflects balance of what appears to be two opposing forces, in this case the fixed and flexible influences of lean product development (Figure 3.1).

Figure 3.1   Fixed and flexible—the yin and yang of LPPD

The fixed and flexible philosophy emerged out of work that the Ford team did with its colleagues at Mazda more than a decade ago, which led to significant benefits to both companies. By building a fixed and flexible strategy around shared best-in-class components across vehicles, the companies were able to achieve both improved quality and scale. The standard designs and components removed some of the more routine design work, which allowed them to focus on the challenging problems that truly needed to be customized. We believe this seemingly simple concept can have profound implications for your development capability.

Fixed elements in product development are often expressed through standards that are experience-based solutions for typical and recurring problems. They are usually applied where new solutions will not add to customer value. These standards are a powerful mechanism for applying the learning from one project to the next. Over time, experience and knowledge accumulate, standards are updated, and developers are able to make decisions faster and with better quality. These clear criteria (which are captured and communicated to the team) make the ability to learn and apply new knowledge a true competitive advantage. Developers do not have to waste time and resources learning things over again. Aligning on the fixed portion of the project is also crucial in understanding and managing the program's risk profile and energy, guiding a product team to focus primarily on the flexible elements.

Flexible aspects of product development are those in which innovation and creativity add customer value and differentiate the product. They are the very heart of the product's unique value proposition—often the reason "why" we are doing this project. In this case, the high-level vision of "what" we are trying to do may be understood, but the "how" is not. Consequently, the risk profile and gaps in knowledge are significant during this part of the project and will require substantive innovation.

Differentiating the fixed from the flexible requires a deep understanding of how the product will deliver value coupled with a compelling vision for the product. It is equally important that the organization is aligned around this vision and that each team member understands how he or she will contribute to achieving success. The chief engineer concept paper and related activities are incredibly helpful in establishing this delineation—identifying a vision for the most creative parts that matter most to the customer and specifying many of the fixed elements.

The yin and yang of fixed and flexible offer a powerful way to think about how your standardization strategy will help you ensure quality, eliminate waste, and deliver maximum value to your customer. When defining the fixed and allocating time and energy to the flexible, it is useful to think of two broad categories: design standards and manufacturing process standards.

Design Standards

Engineers could begin every single project with an open mind and a blank sheet of paper—the ultimate in open innovation and a monumental waste of time and energy. Instead, the yin and yang of fixed and flexible emerge from design standards in the form of platforms, design rules and specifications, and standard architectures, bringing faster and more efficient development and freeing engineers' time for value-adding innovation and creativity.

Platforms

A product platform is a common set of underlying or foundational technologies and components that support multiple products. This can be different from modularity, which brings to mind plug-and-play elements. A standard product platform will specify design standards and architecture for a class of products, but the platforms still may need a degree of customization, or "tuning," for each specific product, which is the case for many products, including an automobile.

In the auto industry, while individual companies have slightly different definitions, platforms can generally be thought of as the base, or lower half, on which new vehicles, or "top hats," are developed. The top hat is what customers see and touch: the body and interior of the vehicle. The platform may be less visible, but it has a major impact on such attributes as ride and handling, turning radii, noise, vibration, weight, safety, and even styling. It is a critical part of the overall product and the driver experience.

In the best companies, many distinct vehicle models can be developed based on the same platform. In fact, companies should be able to get several generations of multiple products from a single platform. Platform engineering presents some considerable engineering challenges, such as providing the capability to interface effectively with different product configurations, building in the ability to tune the platform to match a variety of product performance requirements, and anticipating the rate of change of the underlying technologies. Most companies are accustomed to having a schedule laid out over years for updating existing products and developing new products. Platforms also need to be updated with their own schedule, typically about half as often as the product life cycle; e.g., if products are updated every four years, then platforms might be redesigned every eight years or so. Planning and executing a platform strategy improves quality and performance, reduces development costs, and increases speed to market. An effective platform strategy may not appear to apply to every industry, but we find that most companies can benefit from a platform strategy, often in ways not immediately obvious.

In 2007 Ford was utilizing 27 different platforms for all its vehicles; Ford was expending far too many engineering resources just to maintain this large number of platforms around the globe. Because there were so many, Ford also struggled to update the critical underlying technologies, resulting in less competitive vehicles. This snowballed into individual product programs "tweaking" platform technologies in order to make their vehicle better—which further decreased commonality and exacerbated the problem.

Ford decided to make a major effort to consolidate and then dramatically improve its platforms by:

1. Evaluating the current state of platforms at Ford and rigorously benchmarking competitors.

2. Identifying the platforms that would continue and organizing them into cross-functional platform teams with representatives from across engineering

3. Having teams work to "future" performance targets for all aspects of the platforms

4. Having teams implement platform changes based only on product cycle plan requirements

Ten years later Ford was able to create more individual models than existed in 2007 from just eight global platforms.[1] This consolidation process occurred between 2007 and 2016, with most of the engineering completed by 2013. More significant than the reduction in platforms, the work simultaneously reduced the time to market for individual products, vehicle development costs, and ongoing engineering support requirements; freed up invaluable engineering resources to work on more new products; and improved vehicle performance around the world. The savings were in the hundreds of millions, and Ford's products became far more competitive.

Ford's investment in revamping its platform strategy paid big dividends, but it should not have gotten to the state it was in. Ford had to relearn the importance of updating and maintaining its platform strategy. Ironically, this was a difficult lesson a pioneer of common platforms, Toyota, would also learn, as you will see later in this chapter.

Design Rules and Specifications

We previously wrote extensively about design rules and checklists in *The Toyota Product Development System*.[2] At Toyota, these design rules were literally embedded in checklists, originally paper and pencil. The checklists were in notebooks, maintained by the most senior-level engineers for each technical area, who had final say on any additions or subtractions. The checklists represented accumulated learning and were treated as top-secret intellectual property. Engineers literally checked off their compliance with each standard as they designed the product, and their supervisor also signed off on each item. (Eventually, Toyota checklists migrated electronically to an engineering database.)

Toyota engineers did not view the checklists as confining nor as the core of their engineering work. As one senior engineer explained, "Using a checklist does not make you a great engineer." If you think about an airplane pilot's preflight checklist, it can be critical to safety, but it will not substitute for the skill and experience of the pilot in actual flight.

Toyota engineers could, in fact, violate standards on the checklist, but when doing so, they needed to defend their rationale with data. For example, there may be a range on the radii of a body part beyond which a steel part will crack in the stamping process. If a new, more aggressive body style required a more severe radius, an engineer could knowingly violate the standard but had to prove the design will be manufacturable with high quality. Often violating the standards led to new innovations that formed the basis for new standards.

Ford also had developed design standards that provided a strong foundation for engineering work. For example, individual part-interface standards for components that are part of a larger system are good places for the application of design rules. Craftsmanship, manufacturability, and durability are other examples where design rules can be very useful. Ford's strategic application of proven standards allowed for maximum creativity and flexibility on the majority of the component designs, while simultaneously safeguarding critical system performance with a few fixed design attributes. Ford made the rules more effective and increased their use by:

- Organizing design rules into "bite-sized chunks"
- Making them available JIT and right at the point in the design process in which they were needed
- Building them directly into CAD design tool software

Standard Architecture

We first heard about standard architecture at Toyota during our research more than 20 years ago. Toyota makes it very clear that it "develops standard architectures, not modular designs."[3] While the image of plug-and-play modules in industries like consumer electronics is quite popular, Toyota executives feel that plug and play has somewhat limited application in complex structural applications like automotive.

Standard architecture seems to have various meanings across different industries. For the purposes of this discussion, we mean the physical manifestation of the part function—the physical geometry, pattern, or form required to accomplish the intent of the part or group of parts. It can also refer to the basic arrangement or fundamental elements of any product or service.

One of Jim's body engineering managers, Randy Frank, who led a portion of the standard architecture initiative at Ford, came up with what we think is both a clever and useful analogy of the role of standard architecture (Figure 3.2): At the basic level, engineering lessons learned are like autopsies, which provide a potentially valuable learning opportunity to help future patients; of course, the patient autopsied does not benefit. The next level consists of engineering disciplines, such as design rules and failure mode effects analysis, which are like preventative medicine, such as inoculations or an improved diet. These antidotes are potentially lifesaving, provided you actually use them. Standard architecture and knowledge-based engineering work occur at the genetic level and build the solution right into the DNA of the part. Standard architecture is extremely powerful, but it can be risky if applied incorrectly. It requires caution, thoughtfulness in application, a deep understanding of part function, and a robust fixed and flexible strategy in order to avoid unintended consequences.

The Ford body and stamping engineering (BSE) journey into standard architecture started with a fairly straightforward benchmarking exercise for a front-hood assembly. The study found that Toyota hood assemblies were quite similar across products, but the Ford hoods were all unique. This study was the subject of one of Jim's first meetings with CEO Alan Mulally, who, as a former chief engineer at Boeing, immediately recognized the implications. A picture was worth a thousand words, and he became an ardent supporter of standard architectures.

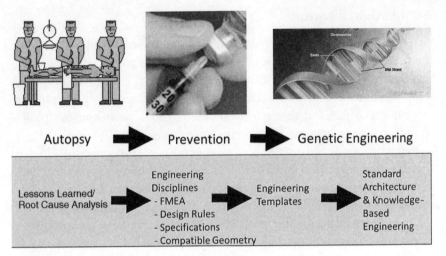

Autopsy ➡ Prevention ➡ Genetic Engineering

| Lessons Learned/ Root Cause Analysis | ➡ | Engineering Disciplines - FMEA - Design Rules - Specifications - Compatible Geometry | ➡ | Engineering Templates | ➡ | Standard Architecture & Knowledge-Based Engineering |

Figure 3.2 Medical analogy—standard architecture strategy

The hood assembly is made up of a hood outer (the styled part of the hood you see on the outside of the car), a hood inner (the part that provides strength and stiffness to the assembly), and an assortment of reinforcement and mechanical parts. Our teardowns revealed that each Ford hood inner design was different. It appeared as if each engineering group had started its hood design with a "clean sheet of paper," and consequently, all were required to relearn many of the same lessons each time.

By contrast, Toyota's inner hoods all had a very consistent and identifiable basic geometry that had been adapted to fit different car models. Whether it was a Lexus or a base Toyota model, the architecture was the same. The commonality allowed Toyota to apply a proven, high-quality solution to its products while simultaneously reducing engineering hours, test time, and manufacturing process development requirements for each program. And surprisingly, this standardization only affects what is invisible to the customer and takes nothing away from styling.

As the BSE team members learned more about the multiple Ford programs and faced new design challenges, such as pedestrian protection or crash regulatory requirements, they updated the geometry. Unlike in the past, though, all Ford programs worked from the same foundation and evolved geometry in a coordinated way across programs in order to maintain the advantages.

In this example of fixed and flexible standard architecture, the inner hood, whose function goes largely unnoticed by customers, is created from standard geometry and only modified to fit the specific shape and size application (fixed). The outer hood, however, is crucial to vehicle styling, and appeal is left largely to the creative direction of the designer (flexible).

Even outer skins, which are styling-intensive parts, are subject to fixed and flexible thinking. A fender is a visible exterior part that is, among other things, crucial to the styling of the vehicle. Of course, safety comes first, but then design trumps any other engineering concerns on a part like this. The unexposed, functional portions of the fender, such as locating features, mounting surfaces, and stiffening geometry—all of which are critical to fender function in forming, assembly, and crash performance—can benefit significantly from standard architectures. The key is to maximize design space while simultaneously standardizing those attributes that contribute to other aspects of a part's performance.

An additional benefit of this approach is an ability of product engineers to leverage powerful design tools. "Smart CAD" with embedded engineering knowledge and parametric part templates can guide engineers, optimizing their time and improving design effectiveness—if the technology has been based on a well-thought-out standard architecture strategy. In our experience, the tools are impressive, but they are only as good as the strategy and engineering thinking behind them.

Standard architecture can be a widely applicable and powerful way to improve quality, reduce costs, and focus resources on areas of the product that benefit most from differentiation. In establishing your architecture, you will have to work your way through many trade-offs. You then need to consider the implications of a new architecture for quality, attribute performances like weight or strength, manufacturability, development and investment costs, and piece price. To do this well, first understand how this component or subsystem contributes to customer-defined value, which helps you set what to fix and what to leave flexible.

Manufacturing Process Standards

Manufacturing standards can reduce development and manufacturing costs, improve quality, increase development predictability, and provide greater manufacturing flexibility (i.e., produce multiple products on the same production line)—as long as you keep in mind how your product delivers value to your customer and let that guide your decisions on fixed and flexible. Manufacturing capability can be a source of singular competitive advantage, both for high-quality, efficient production and for the ability to deliver eye-catching design and craftsmanship. Applying the fixed and flexible concept to manufacturing standards helps to make that happen.

Standard Assembly Process

Frankly, the value of establishing a robust, standard assembly process seemed so fundamental that we nearly did not include it in this book. Our work across industries, however, reveals that many still don't understand its benefits. The idea of one best way to assemble products and to guide design and development efforts is still a sufficiently foreign concept to enough companies that it is worth a short description.

A standard assembly process can bring many benefits, including improved quality, reduced investment and variable cost, and increased manufacturing flexibility. To accrue these benefits, however, essential information about the assembly process must be communicated and adhered to during the development process. This is efficiently done through a standard assembly process document, frequently referred to as a bill of process (BOP), which includes three major elements:

- **Part assembly sequence** is the order in which you put the parts together (e.g., inside out, outside in, from the bottom up). There are many implications for these decisions, such as access and visibility for people or machines, ergonomic and safety considerations, repeatability, and work efficiency. The implications of the order in which you build should be known and tracked during the development process.

- **Organization of assembly lines** determines what will be assembled on the main line and which subassemblies are best handled on support or feeder lines. Organization also covers the relative location of lines for the best flow of parts.

- **Standard part locator strategy** determines how best to locate parts at assembly. This can be done by identifying locating holes to accommodate the pinning of parts together or by designating locating surfaces or other means as a part of the geometric tolerance and dimensioning.

The dimensional quality implications of these decisions are important but are far beyond the scope of this book.

By standardizing a high-level assembly sequence, line organization, and locating strategy, you can often build many products on the same assembly line with minimal or no alteration of the line. This significantly lowers your investment costs and creates an improved ability to quickly match up with variations in product demand. A proven, best assembly methodology is also key to quality and predictability, in both manufacturing and development.

In the automotive industry, aligning manufacturing and product design around the fixed (common part locating strategies and basic standard assembly sequences contained in a BOP) and the flexible (keeping the majority of a vehicle's design open to deliver its unique value proposition) has paid big dividends. It has allowed the best companies to build six or more very different vehicles on the same assembly line, which creates incredible efficiencies and manufacturing flexibility with a high degree of quality. Those that have done this well deliver distinctive vehicles from the same line and not merely a "badge differentiation" across the products.

Process-Driven Product Design for Stamping

Stamping may seem too arcane and specialized an area of engineering to warrant much of your attention (unless, of course, that is your business). However, we think that the yin and yang lessons of process-driven product design (PDPD) transcend any particular engineering discipline or industry.

Hiro Sugiura had spent more than 30 years in key stamping engineering roles at Toyota, finishing up his Toyota career by leading production engineering efforts in the United States. Jim first met Sugiura-san, who was by then retired from Toyota, when he was in a full-time advisory role at Ford. Unfortunately, despite his knowledge and experience, he was having little impact, having been brought into Ford by the previous senior leaders, who weren't sure what to do with him. They seemed to only value the fact that he was from Toyota. The stamping engineering team was buried under a staggering day-to-day workload and had little time to spend on Sugiura-san's "strategic" concepts. It wasn't until the team freed up a couple of key resources to work directly with him that stamping could finally take full advantage of his deep knowledge.

One of the key initiatives led by Sugiura-san and his small team was PDPD. Based on detailed benchmarking, PDPD defined world-class stamping processes, including the number of allowable dies (or stamping hits) for each of the major stamped parts. Furthermore, it communicated the part design characteristics that were crucial to enabling this best-in-industry manufacturing process while simultaneously allowing maximum freedom in all other areas of the part design.

For example, PDPD would define the high-level standard process for stamping a fender in four dies (draw, trim, flange, and finish) and set the important attributes to accomplish this. Considering that Ford had previously required as many as seven or more dies to stamp fenders and that the team was working on all Ford internally stamped parts, the potential cost savings were immense.

There were some legitimate concerns with PDPD: some felt that the only way to accomplish this task was to sacrifice other part attributes, like styling or craftsmanship—this was unacceptable. Ford was leveraging enhanced craftsmanship as a central part of its product-led turnaround. The team was skeptical it could deliver both world-class design and manufacturing efficiency, but the team agreed to "try the experiment."

This initiative drove an extremely high level of collaboration between body and stamping engineers as the teams worked together to deliver both design and efficiency solutions. These seemingly impossible and contradictory challenges brought out the best in a talented engineering crew and actually enabled a level of innovation and invention that likely would not have happened without the pressure of the opposing constraints—the forces of yin and yang.

The team was successful in delivering both imperatives with significant benefit to Ford products. This work also helped to destroy several long-held beliefs, one of which was that more dies made better parts. It was nearly axiomatic that stamping quality was positively correlated with the number of dies used to stamp them. It turns out, if processed correctly, the less you move the stamping during the process and less often you relocate it on another die, the better its dimensional accuracy. Go figure.

PDPD requirements became a critical input to part standard architecture (discussed earlier). It became the new standard practice for development of both product and process for all of Ford's internal parts. Exceptions can be granted, and they are typically discussed in design reviews, but they are few and far between.

Complexity Reduction

Complexity seems a necessary evil in many of today's sophisticated products, such as cars, airplanes, medical devices, and heavy equipment. It is often considered a part of the increasingly competitive environment in which companies exist. "We can't get rid of that; it's *essential* to our customer." But at what point does all this complexity stop adding value for the customer and just become another drain on precious engineering resources? As customization approaches the extreme of designing a different product for each customer, where can engineers draw the line?

Meaningful answers to these questions may be a function of the specific industry in which you operate, but we have visited enough companies to believe that most—and most kinds—have long ago passed this point. In fact, one of the reasons it is sometimes so difficult to eliminate complexity is because it is so ubiquitous. Taking on complexity reduction can be a daunting challenge and will clearly differ across industries. The following simple examples provide fodder for your thinking about this topic.

One fairly straightforward way to start this journey is to begin with fasteners. Fasteners are a seemingly trivial but often vital part of many products. Because they represent a relatively minor cost on a per-product basis, companies sometimes miss the big picture and dismiss this as an inconsequential activity. But the proliferation of unique fasteners—each engineer calls up a favorite catalog on the internet and finds a unique fastening solution to his or her current challenge—can have a negative impact on cost, quality, and manufacturing operations.

By creating a company standard list of fasteners and their approved applications, you can take a small step toward faster decision making, reduced costs, and manufacturing efficiency. Part material selection can be similarly enhanced by creating a part-by-part material "first-pick list" that recommends the best material for a particular application. Exceptions, of course, will be needed, so include an exception process. We have found that companies often have a number of these small opportunities to get complexity-reduction efforts started.

Another way to address complexity is to look beyond fasteners and materials to actual part reuse or part commonality (i.e., use the same underlying functional parts across product lines). When knowledge is effectively shared across product programs, engineers are able to utilize the same parts to meet design challenges. Of course it is important to first work from a product performance and quality perspective; otherwise your "cost-saving" efforts may negatively affect sales and prove to be very expensive.

Offering different product options and optional configurations can provide a clear source of competitive advantage and increased profitability. But they also can add cost disproportionate to their relative value in both development and manufacturing operations. This can be a fairly controversial topic in some companies, especially between the marketing and engineering departments. But it doesn't need to be if you let the "data set you free."

Start by looking at your "take rate" for certain options. If sales of an option don't cover the cost of providing it, that could be your first clue. There are, of course, other reasons for making certain options available that you will have to consider. But if your customers are not voting for the option with their wallets, then it may be time to drop it. And while you are analyzing the data, talk to your customers. More choices do not always equate to greater value in the eyes of your customers—the complexity just confuses them, especially when they feel that you are pushing decisions off on them that you already should have made. In the 1980s Honda and Toyota offered standard option packages at a discount and limited the number of paint colors, and sales grew. Meanwhile, American auto companies seemed to provide endless options and choices often confusing and frustrating their customers.

Putting It All Together—Toyota's New Global Architecture

We think one of the best and most recent examples of fixed and flexible thinking comes from Toyota's New Global Architecture (TNGA). In response to aging and increasingly uncompetitive platforms, as well as a massive proliferation of unique part numbers, Toyota not only reenergized its platforms, but in keeping with the best Toyota lean tradition, used this as an opportunity to create a potentially powerful competitive advantage in both its product development system and its products.

The thinking that led to TNGA started shortly before Akio Toyoda become president in February 2009. The most senior executives from across the company came together to form the "Committee to Regenerate Toyota, with a mission to identify Toyota's most important challenges as a company."[4] One of the top challenges that they identified was the need to radically update all of Toyota's vehicle platforms and powertrains. Platforms, as we discussed earlier in this chapter, are the foundation for individual vehicle performance and a central element in an automotive product development strategy. This news fit perfectly with Akio Toyoda's already strong belief that the key to Toyota's future was to focus the entire organization on improving products. As a result, platform revitalization became a major component of Toyoda's "Ever better cars" proclamation. In 2010 the Vehicle Structure Business Reform team was born, made up of high-level executives who had both the experience and clout to rethink the platform strategy.

Toyota's platform issues began during the heady growth period from 2000 to 2010, when global sales skyrocketed from 5 million to 10 million vehicles sold each year. To say this was a staggering level of growth may even be an understatement when you consider the technical, logistical, organizational, and financial implications of such incredible expansion. What does it mean to produce a full lineup of 10 million cars and trucks every year, with variations across nations globally? For comparison and a sense of scale, the 15-year-old "start-up" company Tesla was struggling to deliver 100,000 total vehicles in 2017 with just three models.

The strain at Toyota during this time was particularly difficult on its most experienced people—especially seasoned technical leaders who were spread extremely thin. In fact, Toyota product engineers were kept so busy on new product support that they did not have sufficient resources to update their platforms. For example, prior to 2000, Toyota usually developed a new platform approximately every two full model cycles. However, the Camry had been allowed to go through four full cycles without a significant platform redesign. In response, an individual product chief engineer (CE), like the one for the Camry, would make platform-level changes in an attempt to improve product performance and meet regulatory requirements. Yet the results of this approach were disappointing to customers and Toyota. The lack of major platform updates limited the ability of the individual vehicles to compete with best-in-industry companies, especially with regard to ride, handling, and styling.

To make matters worse, the CE's tweaks actually worsened the platform management problem because they resulted in a proliferation of "sub-platforms" across Toyota. Toyota's total platform and subplatform count ballooned to nearly 100. This in turn exploded unique platform-related part counts to nearly 1,000. The proliferation of different engines had gotten equally bad, rising from 16 basic engine types to 800 variations. This, in turn, sent Toyota development costs skyrocketing because it had to account for the increased part numbers on each new program.

Component parts for platforms also ballooned, from 72 per platform to about 1,000 per platform, much of it due to all the variations in different countries. Over 70 percent of the platform cost was in supplier parts, and suppliers' R&D costs also shot up. One study showed Toyota's supplier development costs to be as much as seven times that of its best competitors. Worse yet, customers were starting to find Toyota designs boring due to the limitations of the platforms. For the first time ever, Toyota was beginning to see its appeal numbers dropping. These problems were particularly vexing to Toyota leadership—Toyota had previously been the industry leader in part commonality and the ability to derive many different vehicles from a small number of common platforms.

Interestingly, Toyota's profitability was also skyrocketing at this time. The period of 2004 to 2008 saw one record year after another in operating income. But further analysis showed that much of the increase in profitability was due to a weakening yen exchange rate. Without this, profits would have been flat over this period.

Toyota was determined to use this problem as an opportunity to reinvent its platforms, its fundamental thinking about overall platform and architecture strategy, and the relationship between platforms and the products they served. Toyota would transform a challenging situation into a potential competitive advantage. The company created a strategy of "fixed and flexible" in order to deliver an "and" solution that would enable more aggressive styling, dramatically improve vehicle performance, simplify development, and reduce cost.

As we evaluated vehicles, studied subsystems, and spent several days in discussion with people from across Toyota, we found that TNGA was challenging for them to define. It is a bit like the old story about the blind men touching a different part of an elephant—it depends on your perspective (Figure 3.3). It may be more useful to talk about the major elements of the TNGA strategy: platform reduction and revitalization, part sharing/commonality strategy, powertrain reduction and optimization, and new development philosophy.

Figure 3.3 What exactly is TNGA? It depends on your perspective.

Platform Revitalization

Toyota engineers started this process by tearing down both Toyota and competitor vehicles across each platform category for rigorous evaluation. They combed through systems, subsystems, and individual components to more deeply understand the design impacts on performance. Based on the benchmarking, they set aggressive future targets for both vehicle and subsystem performance that they forecast would be best-in-class for the next 5 to 10 years. They also thought about how they could design the platforms to be more "tunable," enabling individual products to get the very most out of a platform's performance capability.

They established two primary pillars for the TNGA platform redesign strategy: product appeal and smart development. Kazuhiko Asakura, general manager of the Corporate Strategy Division, told us this relationship is "a cycle that reinvests the savings from smart development into creating more value for the customer." Engineers who previously worked on components that are now standard and shared "can be freed up to work in areas that add greater perceived quality to our customer on individual products," said Asakura-san.

Product Appeal   Central to the plan to improve platforms were a lower center of gravity and a wider stance. This would improve ride and handling by increasing stability and reducing vehicle roll, as well as help to enable more modern, exciting styling of the individual products. For example, a lower front hood opens up appealing design possibilities. Toyota also wanted to design platforms that could be more easily tuned to the specific needs of individual products. It became clear that this was more than an exercise in developing next-generation platforms; it was a rethinking of the car as a system. All parts are connected, and this led to changes in much of what a driver touched and experienced.

Improving the customer experience was paramount, so all platform development started by exhaustively reviewing all aspects of the driving position, from the placement of the driver's hip point, to the fitting of the seat, to the positioning of the steering. Toyota's "golden ratio of adjustments" created a driving position that keeps the driver's body firmly on the seat and eyes fixed on the road, even when cornering, which makes driving easier for long distances as well.

Another of the goals for TNGA platform development was realizing a lower hood. This would provide greater visibility for the driver and contribute to styling goals. While the hood is not part of the platform, the ability to position it lower requires major changes to the platform. Many skeptics in Toyota engineering did not believe it was possible to achieve a hood that was roughly 100 mm lower than that of current models. TNGA developers strongly believed this was an essential element of the design, and so they persuaded the relevant departments to see their point of view. Thinking that just words and diagrams wouldn't effectively convey their message, they built a prototype of an actual car. If a picture is worth a thousand words, a prototype is worth a million—they got the hood they wanted.

Putting this into practice on a production vehicle was easier said than done; it involved reducing the area in the engine compartment and improving and refining the hundreds of parts inside that area. Many of these were supplier parts, which required drawing on the engineering resources of highly committed suppliers. The result was a substantial boost in driving performance by creating a lower center of gravity while also allowing for more freedom in design.

TNGA developers set an extremely high hurdle for themselves. They were, nonetheless, able to realize this tremendous transformation of Toyota vehicles, which drastically improved driving performance and opportunities for improved styling.

Smarter Development   This is the essence of fixed and flexible and is a key to defining what you should fix. Smarter development creates a working fixed and flexible strategy that both provides the best possible foundation for new vehicles and enables CEs to focus on optimizing the unique aspects of their products. At Toyota, the breakthroughs in standardization through TNGA created a development process that consumes about 20 percent fewer resources and requires less time, while simultaneously providing the customer greater value.

Part Sharing/Commonality Strategy

We asked, "107 parts?"

"Yes, 107," responded Masashige Ono, general manager of the TNGA parts planning department, who led the part commonality effort for TNGA.

Ono-san was so adamant about the number, we had to ask: "Why 107?"

He explained that this was the number of platform parts that could be standardized (fixed) to create a foundation for product performance while leaving opportunity for the CE to tune (flexible) other parts. While some companies focus their part commonality efforts on cost savings through scale and efficiency gains and search out similar parts across product lines, Toyota took a different path. It started from a vehicle performance perspective and derived standard part designs directly from the architecture requirements necessary to deliver system-level performance.

Toyota engineers also did something else unusual in the industry. They recognized that previous platform work focused primarily on internally made subsystems and parts. This turned out to be a severe constraint because nearly 70 percent of platform parts were made by suppliers. If they wanted to maximize the impact of this initiative, supplier parts must be included. Consequently, they worked closely with their suppliers to optimize and standardize 107 critical parts. Their close relationships with suppliers forged over decades allowed for high levels of engineering to achieve the overall enterprise purpose.

The standard platform strategy also enabled standardization of supplier parts which benefited the suppliers. For example, when designing the seat-ing position of the driver, they standardized the ideal hip point. The number of different knee airbag designs then went from 50 to 10 types or fewer.

In working with supplier engineers, Toyota engineers practiced the spirit of "go and see." They went to the gemba to work directly with the supplier engineers at their sites in order to see for themselves how they might refine designs to make manufacture and assembly of the target parts more efficient and reliable. In one case, engineers studied a process at the Tokai Rika line in the Otowa plant. The previous process required 4 workers, 10.6 meters of assembly-line space, and a cycle time of 1.7 minutes; with the help of the Toyota engineers, the number of required workers was reduced to just 1, assembly-line space was reduced to 2.7 meters, and the cycle time remained at 1.7 minutes.

Once a new part process is agreed to and established, Toyota quality engineers periodically audit the process to ensure ongoing quality, and they use this as an opportunity to further improve. Eventually, each of the 107 parts had its own "Part Scenario" that identified critical part characteristics that would enable maximum performance and design efficiency and manufacturability. Each Part Scenario illustrates detailed manufacturing processes and specific critical design characteristics. If engineers feel that they must make a change to one of the 107 parts, they need to attend the monthly Part Scenario meetings to plead their case.

Powertrain Reduction and Optimization

Powertrain refers to all the technology required to generate power and deliver it to the wheels of the car. Toyota found itself in a similar situation with its powertrains as with its platforms. Different regulatory requirements across the many regions of the world in which Toyota operates combined with the tinkering of CEs to improve vehicle performance led to approximately 800 engine combinations. Toyota decided to rethink its powertrain strategy in order to provide better performance, increase span of application, and reduce costs.

Powertrain engineers reviewed the powertrain requirements of each vehicle covered by each platform and designed engines for maximum model coverage. Consequently, each individual engine design was challenged to achieve new levels of performance, efficiency, and versatility. This obviously was and is a major undertaking, and the plan to migrate to a new, consolidated engine lineup was based on the product cycle plan.

As of this writing, specific numbers of planned engines were not available, but it is anticipated that the strategy will result in major improvements. For example, the number of transmissions is likely to be cut in half. Previous engine designs had exhaust pipes located in many different positions, and the new engine design will standardize the location and mounting. This also will be true for oil and water passage. The new design has also commonized the mounting shape and pitch for an alternator, allowing Toyota to reduce the number of unique alternator models from 14 to 6.

New Development Philosophy

TNGA is more than a redesign of product platforms. It is more than a part commonality initiative. It is more than a powertrain revamp. It is a truly "lean" response to a problem. Surface the problem transparently, deeply understand, engage the right resources, and turn it into an opportunity to move your performance to a new level.

Toyota can be faulted for growing so fast that it failed to put the resources into platform development and found itself behind its best competitors. The company did right the ship, however, based on long-term thinking and the practice of putting customers first.

This effort also helped to revitalize development engineering in Toyota. The CEs and their teams got to do something many had never experienced: work on a new vehicle program from scratch and innovate in every part of the vehicle. They could now work out of a platform that excited them—exciting styling, improved ride, and excellent fuel economy. The "standard platform" did not replace the work of these teams. The TNGA group provided standards and certain constraints, but each vehicle designed on that platform had to be engineered to meet performance and styling requirements. One lead vehicle for each vehicle program took a lot of engineering work and as much time as programs before TNGA. Subsequent teams working on vehicles from the new platforms did not design from scratch, and were significantly faster, but they still had the excitement of developing a car of which they were proud. Toyoda's motto was "ever better cars," and you could sense the enthusiasm in developing the next one better than the last.

The TNGA team had developed many interesting design concepts, but it was the development teams who had to put them into practice. They needed to work within the constraints of the platform, yet deliver exciting cars that were the best in their class. This reinvigorated the customer-first design philosophy of Toyota and brought fixed and flexible to a new level. We did not talk to a single CE who felt constrained by the standard platforms and parts. In fact, they spoke glowingly of their new freedom to focus on exciting styling and improve the driver experience.

At the time of our interviews in Japan, the Prius, Camry, and CHR had been beneficiaries of the TNGA work. We were able to evaluate new and old versions of the Prius and the Camry, and we could feel the dramatic difference in ride and handling. Will TNGA-improved products translate into sales? At the launch of the 2018 Camry in the United States, in November of 2017, sales rose by 24% over the same month in 2017. In December sales were up 35%. Sales increases continued into early 2018 at a time when overall passenger car sales were way down.

And Toyota experienced benefits in other ways. Vehicle development costs are expected to drop by 20 percent, and per-vehicle costs for the fixed portion of the vehicle will be reduced. The savings in engineering hours will allow Toyota to either add more content on the product-specific portion or increase its already industry-leading profit per vehicle.

Embrace the Tension

Fixed and flexible may appear to be opposing forces, but understanding how to harness their respective powers can be a boost to your product development capability and your products. Like the yin and yang, what appear to be forces in conflict can actually be complementary and provide balance. There is a clear competitive advantage for those who are able to embrace this tension.

In this chapter we offered a number of examples to help you think about where you may want to employ the fixed and flexible development strategy. Application may extend beyond your products. For example, what aspects of your product service strategy can be fixed, and what parts can be variations of a common platform? The real secret of making the concept work for you lies in understanding what and how value is delivered to your customers and development teams. Ignorance is expensive and wasteful; deep knowledge is key. Creative tension is a necessary part of development—conflict can, indeed, be a tremendous opportunity if you know how to leverage it to get the most out of your development system.

LOOKING FORWARD

Standard processes, design standards, and computer tools are powerful mechanisms for improving your product development capability. But the real key to creating great products is great people. While many companies are quick to reorganize processes and the way they operate (perhaps too quick) as a response to product development challenges, only the best ones are willing to do the detailed work required to build a talented, aligned team for the long term. In the next chapter, we will discuss how the best companies organize, develop, and engage the entire enterprise to build excellence in product and process development capability.

Your Reflection

Creating a Vision

The focus in this chapter is finding the right balance between standardizing some aspects of the product or service to provide a framework for customizing it to fit future customer expectations and needs. The key characteristics of the fixed and flexible vision are:

- The way of thinking is no longer either fixed standards or flexible clean-sheet designs, but finding the right balance to maximize customer value and to harmonize "the yin and the yang."

- Standards can be an effective way to store and apply knowledge. They should be a powerful competitive advantage.

- Products and services are deeply studied to identify the attributes that add customer value and differentiate each product for a particular context of use. The generic attributes that the customer does not directly see or experience are candidates for a level of standardization.

- The benefits of standardization are not only useful for the product but also for the development process—shortening development lead time, reducing manufacturing and supply-chain costs, and improving product quality.

- The enterprise is fully engaged in decisions on standardization from suppliers to upstream and downstream functional groups.

- Standard components of the design are thought of as systems, or "platforms" to build from. The platform does not have to be like a fixed module that gets plugged in, but can more broadly be standard requirements, design rules, standard architecture, standard manufacturing and assembly processes, and some common parts.

How does this model of fixed and flexible fit what you think is needed for your products and services offered by your company? How would you revise the vision to better fit your company's situation?

Your Current Condition

To get you started on grasping the yin and yang of your current development processes, consider the following questions:

1. Do you understand how each of your products or services deliver value to your customer? Can you translate that understanding into the performance characteristics for the various parts of your products and aspects of service?

2. Are you currently building on past knowledge to efficiently utilize your people to deliver the most value to your customers through your products or services? Do you have to relearn the same lessons across product or service offerings?

3. In what ways are you designing based on standard parts, platforms, architecture, and manufacturing processes?

4. Evaluate your tendencies to either overdo standards that are too rigid or allow too much flexibility at great cost.

5. To what degree are you engaging the enterprise in developing standard designs and processes?

Taking Action

To begin to put the concept of fixed and flexible into action, conduct a quick and dirty study. Identify opportunities for application of a fixed and flexible strategy based on what you have learned in this chapter:

- Standard architectures

- Standard platforms
- Standard parts
- Design rules
- Standard manufacturing processes or delivery mechanisms

4
Building High-Performance Teams and Team Members

The strength of the pack is the wolf, and the strength
of the wolf is the pack.

— RUDYARD KIPLING

People Drive Product Development Excellence

Your people provide the creativity, energy, and drive that power your product and process development system. Your team is far more important to achieving excellence than any new technology and likely more important than brilliant product ideas. We agree with Ed Catmull, computer scientist and president of Pixar and Walt Disney Animation Studios, when he wrote, "If you give a great idea to a mediocre team, they'll screw it up. But if you give a mediocre idea to a great team, they'll make it work."[1]

What makes a great team in product and process development? Having very talented people and continually increasing talent density is important. But collecting talented people is not nearly enough. Just hiring the "best brains" and letting them loose can be like a sports team of the "best athletes" whose egos drive them to compete more with each other than with their competitors. Besides, as you will see, there are characteristics that are far more important than a towering IQ.

We think the best teams more closely resemble Kipling's wolf pack, where the strength of the individual feeds the team and the team makes each individual better, driving ever-greater levels of performance for both. The bidirectional responsibility in a wolf pack—or an organization—is key. An organization must nurture a person's growth, amplify a person's abilities, and earn an individual's contribution. At the same time, each person must contribute to the success of the group and the success of others in the group or risk losing his or her place in the group. Leaders must carefully select and develop people and find ways in which each individual can best contribute. It may even be necessary from time to time to remove an individual for the greater benefit of the team.

While nearly every organization declares, "People are our most important asset," or some other shopworn platitude, few seem to actually do the hard work required to recruit, develop, enable, and retain talented people. While organizations will aggressively pursue the latest additive manufacturing technology or cloud-based collaboration tool, they seem willing to leave organization development to HR or even to chance. What's more, the recent start-up craze and rapid pace of mergers and acquisitions seem to have exacerbated this problem. Companies appear to be increasingly less inclined to make long-term investments in people—and that's a troubling trend.

People are the heart of a truly lean organization. You can feel it when you are part of one and often when you visit one. The people-centric nature of the lean community is what continues to attract new people from every industry, even after more than three decades of practice.

In fact, the characteristic that most attracted us to the lean community was the value placed on people. Early in our own lean journey more than two decades ago two comments about the role of people in lean really resonated. The first was when John Shook, then general manager at the Toyota Technical Center in Ann Arbor, Michigan, and now executive chairman of the Lean Enterprise Institute, said, "Lean is not people-agnostic—people are the center of lean and the reason for it." Jim saw this first hand at Ford when Alan Mulally brought his "people first" leadership style to the automaker. The second was when Mike Masaki, president of the Toyota Technical Center, explained that at Toyota, "We develop people and products simultaneously."

What Masaki meant was that at Toyota, people development was not an extracurricular activity delegated to HR. And it was not learning in conference rooms. It is through developing new products at the gemba that there is an opportunity to develop exceptional people and vice versa. To take that opportunity required more experienced people acting as coaches, challenging each engineer and providing daily feedback through on-the-job development. Developing people was at the very center of everything every leader did. It was part of how people did their work every day. And throughout many years of research and study, we have continued to see how Toyota leaders coach, mentor, and consciously develop some of the best engineers in the industry and turn that development into a lasting competitive advantage.

There is a great deal of talk these days about organizational culture. Unfortunately, it is rarely more than talk and hope. There is scant evidence that companies seriously perform the necessary development of the human system—hiring, developing, challenging, and engaging people—to establish a high-performing product development culture.

Hiring the Right People

Every hiring decision will influence your culture. Credentials and previous experience are certainly helpful in initial screening. But there are characteristics more crucial to the future success of both the person and the organization, starting with fit. Fit is about work ethic, values, outlook, and expectations—it is a disposition. There is no single best organizational culture or one best individual personality. A wide variety of cultures and dispositions can lead to success, including what our friend Rich Sheridan calls "joy" in the workplace.[2] To strengthen both culture and disposition requires finding the right fit.

But, of course, this is easier said than done. One of the reasons that companies rely on test scores, degrees, and documented previous experience is because they are quantifiable and can be easily compared across candidates. But in our experience, very little about building an unstoppable team is easy—nor should it be. While we do not advocate the complete abolition of measurable criteria, we do think that there are more important things you should do when making hiring decisions. Product organizations with strong cultures take their time on hiring decisions:

- **Toyota.** Different leaders at Toyota have their own favorite method of hiring people. One leader says his acid test question is, "If you could have any car, what would it be and why?" Another leader asks, "If you worked late some night and noticed some janitor's work had not been done, would you clean up?" Of course, even the best questions will not be enough. Ultimately you will only be able to judge performance best when you see the engineers in action. The Toyota Technical Center discovered an effective approach through cooperative education programs with local universities. They invest significant time and energy into each and every person. Students work on and off at the center for several years with mentors, and at graduation it is clear who should be offered a full-time job. As a general rule, Toyota does not hire senior people from the outside, but prefers to grow them from within.

- **Apple.** The high-tech icon mostly develops from within, but will, on occasion, hire senior people from the outside. When that occurs, the company obsesses about getting the right fit. For example, Apple explored a possible fit with Jim as an engineering director. Over several months, Jim met with more than a dozen people, even Jony Ive, chief design officer, as well as vice presidents and several other engineering leaders. It was only after three separate visits that Apple offered Jim the job. The dialogue ranged from the highly technical to quite personal and included a number of "How would you handle this?"–type challenges. And because fit works both ways, there were candid two-way discussions in which both sides attempted to determine how well matched they were. For personal reasons Jim decided not to accept the job, but it was tempting.

- **Menlo Innovations.** The technology innovator takes fit in hiring even further. According to CEO Sheridan, "Résumés are pretty useless for the all-important, culture-fit imperative, so we don't read much of them. And most interviews are two parties lying to each other." Menlo prefers to discover who a recruit is as a human being and how he or she will fit the culture based on teamwork and people working in pairs—a requirement for all work at Menlo. To do this it employs "extreme interviewing events" about three times per year. In these events, 30 to

50 candidates pair off, with one current Menlonian observing each pair. The pairs are given a paper-based assignment to work on. The point of the exercise is not to demonstrate technical skill, but to see how people work together. Candidates are told in advance not to try to dominate and in fact to try to make their partner, and competitor, look good.

After the event the Menlonians get together to discuss what they saw. As they review each interviewee, they ask if they would like to pair with that candidate. The washout rate is about 60 percent. Successful candidates are invited to a second interview, where each is paired with two different Menlonians and given a one-day paid contract to work on a real client's project. At the end of the day, the Menlonians meet with Menlo's factory-floor manager to discuss the candidate. About half of these candidates are successful, and they are awarded a three-week contract. At the end of the three weeks, about 50 percent of these people go on to become Menlonians.

Developing People

Hiring the right person is just the beginning of your investment. Actively supporting and guiding the person's professional development is a fundamental part of building your team. And it is important that leaders see this task as a primary responsibility. We think that about an 80–20 split of on-the-job mentoring to training seems to be the right mix, but there is no magic ratio.

It is difficult to beat the traditional "master-apprentice" model for the acquisition of critical tacit skills that lead to the most capable team members. "Action learning" at the gemba—solving real problems, working closely with a more experienced person, and a bit of formal training introduced just as it is required—is a powerful and proven method for developing incredibly skilled people that has been employed by the best artisans and engineers for decades. Unfortunately, this practice seems to have gone out of fashion at many companies we visit, and they are certainly the worse for it. This is not the case at Toyota, which still builds on its traditional Japanese roots.

Toyota People Development

Mentoring was the original philosophy at Toyota Motor Company going back to the days of inventing new kinds of looms. Sakichi Toyoda grew up the son of a poor carpenter and leveraged what his dad taught him to invent semiautomated, wooden looms. This led to a lifetime of hands-on inventions, ultimately leading to one of the world's first fully automated looms.

Sakichi taught his son Kiichiro, who later started Toyota Motor Company. His son learned from his dad's passion for hands-on creating and teaching. Sakichi told him, "No engineer is worthy of the name who doesn't have to wash his hands at least three times a day." One day while walking the shop floor, Kiichiro noticed a worker looking confused about how to fix a grinding machine that had broken down. "Kiichiro took one look at the man, then rolled up his own sleeves and plunged his hands into the oil pan. He came up with two handfuls of sludge. Throwing the sludge on the floor, he said: 'How can you expect to do your job without getting your hands dirty?'"[3] (This was a demonstration from the company president that he would get his hands dirty, and also that studying the metal shavings can provide a clue about the cause of the problem.) The master-apprentice mode of developing people has always been part of Toyota, so it did not need to be reintroduced as a program; the details of how to do it, however, have changed over time.

Learning TPS Basics in an Automated Environment

We can start with the most traditional Toyota training, which is teaching people to think and do kaizen on the shop floor. Most readers are probably familiar with TPS (the Toyota Production System) as it is applied to a manual assembly process: wasted motion is removed from the operator's job, work is balanced to takt, and the work is standardized. But what do you do when it is an automated process with long lines of equipment and the operations themselves are hidden from view? That did not stop Mitsuru Kawai from finding ways to develop team members. He was concerned that the young people, who had been hired after the company's machining and forging operations had become automated lacked an understanding of what happened behind the cabinets that separated them from the equipment.

Kawai is unique, even in Toyota—the only former production worker who earned his way to one of the top executive positions at Toyota, including membership on the board of directors. He had the rare opportunity of being trained by Taiichi Ohno back in the early 1960s. He deeply internalized the way of thinking of the master and has used this to accomplish amazing feats throughout his career. Over several years, we had opportunities to visit plants where he has worked, marvel at his creations, and learn as he explained his thinking.

For 50 years he worked in Toyota's Honsha (headquarters) plant that made machined and forged engine and transmission parts, and he had a standing order to increase productivity by 2 percent every *month*. Each month he went back to zero. If one month he achieved 4 percent, he still needed to get 2 percent the next month. He started when the processes were mostly manual, and five decades later the processes were almost completely automated.

Much of TPS focuses on reducing waste in the work of humans, but to Kawai the same principles applied whether it was a person or machine doing the work. "Materials will be flowing while changing shape at the speed we can sell the product. All else is waste," he explained. "Operators need to learn how to use the machine and the materials and their five senses to create a good part at a reasonable price. Then intelligent automation can be developed to reduce as much as possible any transportation or movement that does not change the shape or form." This meant getting inside the equipment and redesigning it to eliminate waste.

This is something he became quite expert at doing, but there was a problem. He would not be around forever, and younger engineers and managers did not have his unique experience with manual machines. He was deeply concerned by the mentality that "you push a red button and a part comes out." He needed engineers, managers, and production team members to get inside the machine and learn how to see waste even inside an automated process. Toward that end, he decided that all junior people, even engineers, needed to develop the following four skills:

- Visualize production.
- Develop explicit knowledge of the process.
- Standardize the knowledge.
- Develop intelligent automation through kaizen.

Based on Ohno's teaching method, he believed these four skills could only be learned at the gemba, and even engineers had to learn to do the actual processes manually.

He did a number of things over the years to develop people. First, engineers and managers had to get their hands dirty. He required all engineers and managers to perform the forging and machining jobs manually.

Second, he created a manual assembly line so that engineers and managers could experience a traditional application of TPS and improve upon it. Kawai was not satisfied with Lego simulations; he wanted a real production line. He saw an opportunity when the decision was made to close a plant in Brazil that had assembled transmissions for 75 years. It was a manual assembly operation, and early in its life Toyota questioned whether it was economical to make low-volume assemblies at the Brazil plant. Ohno insisted it had to be possible to profitably make the transmission in Brazil, even with low volume and high variety, so he personally went to the plant and taught the workers TPS. The plant became profitable and produced parts for decades, but finally it was too outmoded to continue. Kawai asked to have the transmission assembly line boxed up and moved to his plant in Japan. He reasoned that he could use a manual assembly operation to make low-volume models efficiently, models that would not be economical to mass-produce using automation.

The task assigned to engineers, managers, and production team members was to work on the line and manually assemble a high variety of low-volume models economically, and to do it without electricity. He called it the "TPS basic learning line." The students got specific challenging assignments for kaizen, learned on this manual line, and then went to the forging and machining lines to improve the automated processes. Over time they cut the floor space of what was already an efficient transmission assembly cell in half, and made it flexible enough to be run with only a single person or at higher volumes with a few people.

There were many innovations born of the challenging objectives on the TPS line with the constraints of using simple, mechanical devices at almost no cost. For example, one of the challenges was to find a way to accurately pick the right parts for a transmission among a large variety of choices. With today's technology, this would be done electronically with light curtains, bar codes, and computers. The bin of the next part to pick would light up, and if a worker tried to pick the wrong part, sirens would go off and lights would blink. How could this be done without computers or electricity?

The students came up with an ingenious device that performed two functions: it acted as a kanban and enabled them to replenish parts at low volume, and it acted as a mistake-proof device. They called it the "key kanban." A small number of each part was kept on the assembly line. When the production operators used enough parts that they reached a point to trigger replenishment, a rectangular metal key kanban (unique for that part) would be brought to the store of inventory. The kanban was color coded and had identifying information that corresponded to a specific bin where those parts were stored. A plastic see-through cover had a picture of the part and the identifying information. You put the key kanban into a slot and pulled down, and it would lift one and only one bin cover—the one for that part (Figure 4.1).

Figure 4.1   A manual key kanban opens the right parts cover.

For learning to kaizen the automated processes, Kawai assigned to each equipment operator one piece of equipment, called "my machine." The job of each operator was to hand-draw in detail everything that happened to the part, second by second, as it was moved, oriented, and transformed. The managers and engineers needed to get up to speed to answer the tough questions asked by equipment operators who expected them to be mentors. The learning curve was steep, and the improvement curve for quality was equally steep. Defects were reduced exponentially over time to almost zero.

Toyota Senior Workers Do Kaizen and Transfer Knowledge

When Kawai was promoted by Akio Toyoda to become an executive vice president and board member, his scope shifted to teaching how to develop people globally. He returned to the idea of learning lines, and these began to be developed in Toyota plants globally.

He led the creation of a second skill-development line in an engine assembly plant in Japan to act as another model. This time the challenge came from the demographics of an aging workforce. For decades in Japan, the workforce has been aging rapidly, birth rates have declined, and immigration has been low. The result is a labor shortage that only promises to get worse over time.

Kawaii had an idea that senior workers could help close that gap. They have vast experience in manufacturing and in TPS, but often they are physically unable to do the demanding task of manual work for entire workdays. He wanted to change that and tap into the ingenuity of senior workers. He set up a "super-skill line" with a four-part mission:

- Return to the fundamentals of manual work; then aim for ultimate automation.
- Create an elite group of high-skilled workers; then evolve.
- Utilize this line as an ideal for skill transfer for members at large.
- Create a line that is friendly to post-retirement members.

The workers assigned to develop this line either were retired or were late in their Toyota careers. They worked with engineering to set up the initial line, which manually assembles engines for the Lexus LC. The super-skill line hand-builds a small percentage of actual engines for Lexus LC vehicles (most of which are built on larger and more automated lines), but its main purpose is for skill development. Every process, including final inspection, is manual, with only a few lights connected to sensors to indicate problems. There are no jigs to aid in building, but only hand tools. Even the final test bench, which usually is computerized, is 100 percent manual—testing for performance, sound, and leakage. The challenge is not simply building an engine, but developing super-operators who can efficiently build and test perfect engines.

Why manual? Kawai explained, "If there is a defect at the end or something breaks down, you will be disassembling with your hands and replacing the parts. If you cannot do this, you cannot [be called] a high-skilled person. When you think of a high-skilled person, he has to know everything. If he is going to do a manual operation, he has to know for every part what will be the most appropriate strength to tighten the bolts for this location and that location. He needs to know everything."

Kawai's goal is to enhance the workers' skill so that "even with their eyes closed they can assemble an engine by themselves." At the same time, he wants them to develop the skill to do studies and analysis and improve upon the process.

The super-skill line would make any fan of Rube Goldberg gadgets applaud with delight. Parts slide in and out, are raised and lowered, and are moved by sliding on roller bearings. Bolts are placed into slots, and if one is missed, a red light comes on as a mistake proofing device. To tighten the bolts operators simply reach up and pull a lever to bring down a tool that tightens to the correct torque. There is only a minimum of electricity and a minimum of physical exertion required by the operators. Yet they are building by hand a sophisticated Lexus engine out of heavy parts.

One problem is moving the finished engine off the super-skill line. This would be an obvious place to use an electrical transfer system, but instead the workers invented a mechanical method: The engine is on a cart on wheels, and when the operator pushes a lever with his foot, a spring is released and the cart moves about 10 feet on its own. As the cart moves, it rewinds a spring for further power.

The types of mechanisms used in the super-skill line are called *karakuri,* which has spread across all Toyota plants. The term *karakuri* originally referred to paper dolls that could move without electricity.[4] At Toyota, these simple devices are custom-designed for each application to allow for movement of materials without electricity. For example, a RAV4 plant in Canada had large parts that had to get from an operation on one side of the aisle to an operation on the other side without interrupting material delivery in the aisle. The solution: a small motor raises the containers of parts that then move across the aisle and are lowered into place for assembly through mechanical mechanisms and gravity. There is a karakuri training area in each plant that contains standard building blocks. These can be stretched, shaped, and adapted in endless combinations to address many material movement conditions. In addition to saving some money on motors and electricity, this has become a fun way to unleash the creativity of operators, who delight in watching their creations at work.

Kawaii's super-skill line has become a tool for continual training on how to build engines, use all your senses, and develop the skills and mindset of kaizen. Two to three students at a time are taken off their current job for three months and go to work as a team member building engines. They are given a seemingly impossible goal that they need to reach through kaizen: reduce defects, reduce the level of physical effort, and increase productivity. Day by day they analyze the line, develop hypotheses, test them, and get continual feedback from skilled coaches. They experience failed experiments and are praised for trying and learning. They also experience successes and, ultimately, achieve the goal. They are changed people at the end of three months and bring these new higher-level skills to their regular job.

The purpose of the super-skill line is not to replace automation. In fact it is to make automation better. It acts as a pilot line for creating a smooth flow of work, which then informs automation. Think about the discussion of prototypes in Chapter 1. The goal was to identify the simplest prototype possible to rapidly test ideas, later building more elaborate production prototypes. The super-skill line is a way to rapidly test ideas without purchasing inflexible, expensive automation. From the manual line it becomes clear where automation can help so that simple automation and people can work in harmony. Ideas from the manual line are in the high speed automated lines throughout the plant.

Developing Toyota Engineers Over a Career

The intense devotion to developing people in Toyota factories also applies to all engineers. To Toyota a technical project manager is not an engineer. An engineer designs things. An engineer creates something new, grounded in engineering science and hands-on experience.

There is a very clear pattern to developing product development engineers, and the training is laid out over an entire career. Most of this occurs at the gemba using the master-apprentice model, but there also is classroom training.

Toyota does not believe that engineers come out of college fully baked, even if they have top grades from top universities. New hires are carefully selected, but are viewed as raw material to be molded into real engineers.

Toyota's engineering training curriculum has evolved over decades. It is summarized in the sidebar and timeline ("Toyota's Engineering

Curriculum") in this chapter. Within Toyota this information is simplified and formatted in a large matrix on four pieces of 11-by-17-inch paper. Our version is not complete, but it offers examples of the different types of knowledge and skills that the engineers at Toyota need to have.[5]

We have broken down the engineer requirements into five categories: fundamental skills, core job-specific knowledge, ancillary task knowledge, policies and judgment, and accumulated know-how. Toyota does not use this terminology internally, but these titles are reflective of Toyota's categories. For example, what we refer to as core job-specific knowledge was found in Toyota's matrix under "technical division" classes. The engineer is assigned to a technical division that is the "functional specialty" of the engineer (e.g., body exterior, body interiors, chassis, engine, materials, controls engineering, electrical engineering, etc.), and there is detailed technical training for each specialty. Most of what we refer to as ancillary skills are described as "business techniques" and "intellectual property" in the Toyota matrix.

TOYOTA'S ENGINEERING CURRICULUM

Year 1: General Knowledge About the Company and an Appreciation of Key Customers of Engineering

In Japan, hundreds of "freshman engineers" are annually hired out of a top university, start on the same day, and gather in a big auditorium. At this point the engineers have not been assigned to a division, so it is not certain in what specialty field they will work.

The first year of general training includes three to four months of working on the shop floor, building cars as a freshman team associate. The engineers are taught jobs by production workers. They do not necessarily work in the same area in which they will later specialize. The point is to get a general understanding of the Toyota Production System, recognize the demands of a routine manual job, and gain an appreciation for one of the key customers of the product development engineer—the shop-floor worker who will be building what the engineer designs. When it comes to design for assembly and manufacturability, the engineer will have a very different perspective after this experience.

Engineers also spend several months in sales, working at a dealership and selling cars. Part of this time is spent in door-to-door sales in Japan. It is common in Japan for automotive dealers to have extensive databases of customers and to send out a salesman when, for example, a child is about to get a driver's license. New engineers get an appreciation for what customers look for in a car as well as the challenge of making a sale.

One of the fundamental skills of all engineers at Toyota is sketching by hand, without a computer. There is some native ability in sketching, and engineering recruits are asked to sketch something as part of the new-hire evaluation process. It is said in Toyota that manual sketching creates a more powerful connection between the body and mind than using computers and an engineer who cannot manually sketch cannot engineer a vehicle. Even today it's believed that an engineer that cannot sketch by hand cannot adequately create computer-aided drawings.

In the Toyota Technical Center in Ann Arbor, Michigan, there is a weekly sketching class for 30 minutes led by an experienced engineer. Students are given something to sketch, and the teacher then critiques the sketches and grades them. The students must continue to go to this class every week until their level of sketching is acceptable. Even after the first year in Japan, there is an advanced set of classes that focuses on geometric sketches.

Ed Mantey, when he was vice president of engineering at the Toyota Technical Center, explained, "Sometimes I look over the young engineers' shoulders at their computer-aided design (CAD) screen, and I know the design will not work. I ask, 'Did you sketch this out? Did you manually draw the relationship to other parts?' Of course, the answer is 'No.'"

The "ancillary tasks" learned in the first year include planning basics and report writing. This is where Toyota engineers learn how to write one-page A3 reports, described in Chapter 6. Toyota engineers also have to understand the various design support systems, like prototyping; basic personnel policies of the company; and data security and intellectual property policies.

In the first year, engineers are beginning to learn critical know-how that they will build upon over their careers. The most profound learning is gained from experiential learning in the factory and at the dealership. Ask Toyota engineers who have worked for 20 years at Toyota, and they can vividly recount experiences they had on the factory floor and their struggles when selling cars. Through these experiences, as well as those to come in the design room, they also learn to respect the people who do every manner of work in the organization.

Years 2 to 10: Becoming a Real Engineer

As we mentioned, Toyota does not view a university graduate as an engineer. The company knows that top universities in Japan select the best students from high school, and it also knows that engineering students get a broad background of basic education (e.g., reading, writing, math), fundamental engineering sciences (e.g., thermodynamics, structural mechanics), and computer training. These skills will accelerate their learning process at Toyota, but as yet they do not know how to be an engineer and certainly not a Toyota engineer.

As Toyota engineers develop, they are continually expected to draw manually and do their own computer work; CAD drawing is a fundamental skill for a Toyota engineer. The company does not believe in a model whereby engineers lead technical projects and leave the actual drawing to CAD specialists (although it does have CAD specialists acting as technicians). In Japan, engineers spend their second year assigned to a drawing department and learn to use CAD from CAD specialists.

Engineers are assigned to their technical division by year 2, and the CAD work will be included in their engineering specialty. They also get assigned a "freshman project" within that specialty, which is a real and challenging engineering task done under the supervision of a highly critical mentor. For many it is the first time they have actually engineered something real. The freshman project is another one of their lifelong memories.

After the second year, the young engineers are working full time within their specialty. They are part of a work team led by a more experienced engineer acting as a team leader (a team consists of four to six engineers). The work team is just one of a number of work groups to which the engineers belong. Some are cross-functional module development teams that perform simultaneous engineering (between styling, other engineering specialties, and manufacturing, for example). But the specialty team is within a function, and the team leader's job is to teach the young engineers how to be a Toyota engineer for that specialty. Team leaders know that one of their primary jobs is to be a teacher, and their performance appraisal will evaluate how well the students are performing.

Engineers attend many classes, which are frequently taught by senior engineers and focus on technical topics within a specialty (e.g., injection molding, polymer characteristics). A lot of the new knowledge is from on-the-job development under the team leader. Toyota's policy is that it takes two vehicle-program cycles for someone to be considered a "full engineer." Mantey explained, "It takes an engineer a four- to five-year time frame to go through two programs and be equal as a full engineer wherever you are in the world to design a part, negotiate with suppliers, negotiate with styling, work with purchasing—an engineer who can do all those things, including [designing] functionality of the part." Mantey was responsible for body engineering, and in this area alone there are about 60 classes that engineers must take, all taught internally.

Beyond 10 Years: Learning to Be a Senior Specialist or General Manager

Beyond 10 years it is expected that engineers have developed deep technical knowledge in their specialty, and they usually are assigned a second, related specialty. The engineers need to continue to hone their knowledge and skills and become real experts. A key part of becoming a real expert is teaching others—learning how to be a team leader and how to develop the next generation of engineers. Some expert engineers will develop patents and can get funding from Toyota to spin off as a subsidiary or third-party business.

Dual tracks are available to experienced engineers: Some stay on a "technical track," become a "senior engineer," and focus on the craft of engineering—getting better and better and teaching others—without taking on a lot of administrative responsibilities. Others shift to an administrative track and become assistant general managers of a department and perhaps a general manager. They attend professional study classes that are taught by general managers and senior executives. Again, we see the strong value Toyota places on learning on the job with experienced mentors guiding the way.

It is important to note that at Toyota the most important job of any manager is to teach. It was drilled into Mantey's head that "the biggest success of any manager is the success of the people they have taught." And he required all his general managers to teach formal classes to more junior engineers in addition to their day-to-day mentoring responsibility.

Toyota sometimes refers to these career paths as inverted Ts. It also uses the metaphor of a tree developing a strong trunk before branching out. The lower portion of the inverted T is the initial breadth of education and experience that the engineers get in their first two years, like the roots of a tree. Then it is depth within a technical discipline, building the trunk. It is even narrower than one might imagine. Let's say a young engineer is assigned to a body engineering team and in the first development project is assigned to design the front bumper integrated with supplier parts. It is likely that this engineer will do the same task for the second development project before branching out. This may sound redundant, but these young engineers are learning a lot more than the technical details of developing the bumper. They are learning the entire development process and how to work with others, including manufacturing and suppliers. Keeping the part they are designing constant helps them to focus on learning the entire development process.

Design Reviews as People Development

Toyota and other "people-centric" organizations are always looking for opportunities to develop people as part of their everyday work. Design reviews, which we will consider in more detail in Chapter 6, are an excellent opportunity for developing technical talent. Jim and his leadership team at Ford made them a central part of their people development strategy. Because they are focused on solving difficult problems, it is an excellent time to mentor, guide, and demonstrate behaviors, such as collaboration, that are important to a high-performing organization. It is also a great opportunity to learn how your engineers are thinking about problems and the challenges of their work in general. Asking thoughtful questions during reviews is one of the best ways to do this—giving them "the answer" is probably the worst.

There is an interesting side effect of increasing expectations for design reviews. As key participants begin to up their game, it puts pressure on others to follow suit. This is especially true for members of the leadership team, who are trying to stay a step ahead of the team. This becomes a virtuous cycle of increasing expectations and continuous improvement that impacts the culture in a very positive way. It is not a competition so much as it is an effort to maintain momentum and not be the "weak link" in the process. It is a tremendous opportunity for leaders to model targeted behaviors, such as preparation, collaboration, and attention to detail.

Creating a Framework to Support People Development

The best way to develop people is through their work, and providing a supporting framework can be very useful, particularly for larger, global organizations that distribute development work to multiple locations around the world. A framework can provide a common mechanism with which to understand and align on current technical capability and expectations at various locations across a far-flung enterprise.

We talked to several companies that have created a technical maturity framework for each technical specialty that is important to their products, such as electrical, mechanical, or manufacturing engineering. Human resources specialists and technical experts from each discipline work together to create a skills-acquisition pathway along which engineers advance by demonstrating increasingly difficult technical skills on the job. Those capabilities are tied to their level and pay. The pathway starts fairly narrow and then branches out into potential areas of specialty.

To shepherd the process, each engineer is formally assigned a mentor, usually his or her supervisor, who takes responsibility for his or her technical growth. Engineers and engineering managers throughout the organization will complete an individual technical development plan that outlines their specific technical aspirations. Progress toward these goals is typically reviewed two to three times per year. On the basis of these reviews, individuals are given more challenging assignments and targeted training to help achieve their objectives. For these types of frameworks to be successful, developing people must be a priority for leaders. Otherwise the process becomes just one more form that must be filled out. While it is often difficult to find the time, given all the other demands that leaders face, making time to coach, mentor, and give ongoing feedback to your people will pay big dividends in the long run.

Ongoing Dialogue and Performance Feedback   While providing "formal" performance feedback to people a few times a year may be necessary, especially in large organizations, the content of those discussions should never be a surprise. When managers truly take an interest in the development of their people, the feedback will be constant and the dialogue will flow in both directions. Remember, there is a reciprocal performance responsibility in effective organizations.

Here are five characteristics of a performance discussion for you to consider:

- **Be *candid*.** You are not going to accomplish anything by lying to each other. Be respectful by providing an honest assessment of strengths and opportunities.

- **Make it a *conversation*.** Ask questions. Actually listen to the answers. Engage your people in their development process.

- **Provide real *content*.** Give specific examples to support the discussion. Don't make the person guess. And create an agreed-to plan, including follow-up for going forward.

- **Be *constructive*.** People should leave the discussion feeling better about themselves and the organization. If not, you have missed a great opportunity. Mulally was a master of constructive discussion.

- **Engage in a *continuous* dialogue.** Be sure to hold up your side of the relationship before you question the actions of others.

Remember that each person is different and contributes in a unique way, but contribute he or she must. It is the leader's responsibility to work with that individual to identify the best course forward. One of the most destructive practices we have encountered is "forced-ranking" people of similar salary levels. It reinforces the very negative, noncollaborative behaviors you should be trying to weed out of a product development organization and provides an easy excuse for poor managers ("What do you expect? I am stuck with C players"). And it is unnecessary "branding" of individuals that rarely motivates collaborative behavior. You can differentiate contribution through pay, promotion, and other forms of recognition; there is no reason to actively promote negative internal competition.

Personal Pursuit of Mastery Development of people is a dual responsibility. While the company should provide the opportunity for learning and growth, each individual needs to take personal responsibility for his or her professional growth. Individual engineers should continually seek to raise their own "standard," and they should witness those around them doing the same. It is virtually impossible for the company to "develop you" if you have no passion for learning. The pursuit of mastery should be a foundational value for every person in your organization, and it starts in the employee-selection phase.

We believe there is an innate desire in most people to excel in their work. This is the spirit of mastery. It is universal, and it connects people to their work in a very personal way by conferring pride and meaning to their work. Whether it's the precise movements of a surgeon who has mastered her craft, the meticulous attention to detail of a highly skilled machinist, or black-belt Marcelo Garcia's exacting execution of Brazilian jiujitsu, they all leave an observer wide-eyed. Consequently, the achievement of mastery in one's work brings an internal joy only possible by accomplishing something incredibly difficult—and personal. To be sure, this arduous journey has a lasting impact on those who choose to follow this path.

But a word of warning: In a world of "shortcuts to the top," "instant acclaim," and "pivoting," this journey will require a great deal of hard work and loads of perseverance. And some people looking for the fast track will leave. Yet as lean thinkers, value creation and the pursuit of perfection are, after all, what we are about. The spirit of mastery is a key component to creating something of lasting value, and the pursuit will change the character of both the work and the worker.

Professional Education   We think that many of the problems with "people development" in organizations actually begin long before those people get to the company. It often starts with their fundamental education.

In a *Fast Company* article, Alan Webber relayed a telling question raised by Jeffrey Pfeffer, professor at the Stanford Graduate Business School: "Would you undergo heart surgery if the surgeon had been trained the same way business school students are trained? Imagine that the surgeon had sat around in medical school discussing heart-surgery cases, watching heart-surgery videos, and listening to great heart surgeons talk about what they did—and now you are lying on the operating table, that surgeon's first real patient. Would you actually let that surgeon cut into you?"[6]

But business schools are not the only ones with this problem. Robert McMahan, the president of Kettering University, says, "If we taught musicians the way we teach engineers, they would get 12 years of music theory before ever touching an instrument." This focus on application is what separates a handful of engineering schools, like Kettering, which insists on engineering internships, from ivory tower competitors. Every other semester Kettering students work at a sponsoring company applying what they have learned in their classes. The next semester they return to school as full-time students to continue to add to their knowledge.[7]

Another school that is breaking the mold and stressing the application of knowledge in real-world environments is MIT. In the D Labs at MIT, students work and learn together in teams in order to take on real-world product development projects for underserved markets. The "D" in D Lab stands for Development through Discovery, Design and Dissemination, and that is how the students pursue their objective. Whether it is the challenge of providing clean drinking water, improving the backbreaking work of coffee farmers in Tanzania, or making charcoal briquettes from agricultural waste in Haiti, D Lab students create products that solve real problems and sometimes even spawn businesses. The real skill and deep knowledge gained throughout the development process, from understanding the customer and their context, through scaling up production, are invaluable to the students and help to make the world a bit better.

Excellent product companies engage with and build long-term partnerships with schools like Kettering and MIT in order to influence the development of engineers and other technical professionals early on. They make sure that students are getting the hands-on experience that is so important. We believe that if more schools and businesses would emulate this in their education strategies, engineers would enter the workplace much better prepared to contribute to their organization's ability to learn. However, even with engineers coming from exceptional education programs, companies must continue to focus on developing their people. Even the best students are not truly engineers until they are developed through working on real programs under the tutelage of mentor engineers who know how to teach. We have emphasized that even with Toyota's careful hiring process for demonstrated abilities and "fit," they view engineering graduates as excellent raw material to be developed.

Engaging People as One Team

In 1987, Kiyoshi Suzaki wrote *The New Manufacturing Challenge*.[8] Affectionately known within the lean community as "the red book," it is chock-full of wonderful stick-figure images and demonstrates the key constructs of what was then a new science of customer-focused organizational performance.

You've probably seen the now-ubiquitous diagram of people rowing a boat to illustrate teamwork—we first saw this in Suzaki's book. He also drew another boat prior to that, in which a group of people row and bail water from a boat surrounded by sharks, with the caption, "We are all in the same boat." His point was that successful organizations must develop a

sense of "co-destiny." A key leadership responsibility is to establish a sense
of common purpose and enroll the enterprise in its pursuit. Although
individual talents and capabilities may be different, all are united in a
larger purpose to which they all can and must contribute.

As previously discussed, when Mulally arrived at Ford, he found
a deeply divided, fractious, and internally competitive organization.
Organizational fissures were expanding everywhere. And the external environmental pressure was acting to broaden and deepen those divides. Ford
was rich with extremely talented, hardworking people. But they urgently
needed a unifying vision and a way in which they could engage together
to move forward.

On Friday, October 13, 2006, just a few weeks into the job, Mulally
sent a masterful e-mail to the entire company that read, in part:

> It wouldn't take very long for anyone to recognize that Ford people
> are winners by nature. The sense of pride in the value Ford has always
> created in more than a century is obvious and justified. And it is
> encouraging that there are so many areas of excellence we can point
> to within our company right now. But pockets of success are not
> enough. Not today. Not in this competitive environment. We need
> success across our entire enterprise. To get there we need to have a
> universally agreed to and understood plan. It needs to be a single
> plan and it needs to work for the whole company. Competitors may
> try to "divide and conquer" us; I am determined that we are not
> going to do that to ourselves.

Mulally went on to describe the specifics of the weekly business plan
review in which every top senior regional and functional leader in the
company would participate. He noted how all the leaders would work on
the same plan from the same data and said that they would cascade that
single plan throughout the organization. He closed the e-mail with the
following:

> I know that the people of Ford have been through some tough times
> in the past few years. . . . I can tell you from previous experience that
> as demoralizing as a slide down may be, the ride back up is infinitely
> more exhilarating. And there is no better feeling than knowing that

your personal contribution is helping to move this great enterprise forward again.

Everyone loves a comeback story. Let's work together to write the best one ever.

Thank you!

This was the beginning of his "One Ford" vision and tireless effort to bring the organization together and harness its full potential. His vision was as simple as it was difficult:

- **One Team.** People working together as a lean global enterprise for automotive leadership as measured by customers, employees, dealers, suppliers, investors, and community satisfaction.
- **One Plan.** Aggressively restructure to operate profitably at current demand. Accelerate the development of products that customers want and value. Finance our plan and improve the balance sheet. Work together effectively as one team.
- **One Goal.** An exciting, viable Ford delivering profitable growth for all.

Mulally continued to deliver his message in every venue possible across the company. He joined Jim for visits to crash safety labs, new vehicle craftsmanship walk-arounds, and tours of Dearborn Tool and Die, and he personally attended nearly every one of Jim's global "All Hands" meetings. He joined Jim on stage and would start out these talks by thanking the team for inviting him to "Body and Stamping Engineering, the center of the universe as we know it." Then he would update the team on the company's progress to the plan, thank people for specific initiatives he knew they were working on in support of the plan, and spend an hour answering questions from across the globe. His message was the same: it's our Ford, it's our plan, and together we will do this. "After all," he would say with a wink, "engineers are the source of all wealth creation, right?" The reaction of the team, most of whom had never seen any Ford CEO in person, was phenomenal. Even though there were thousands of people that attended those meetings either in person or via video, most felt a personal connection with both Mulally and the plan.

Mulally also conducted his own global "town halls," supplier and dealer visits, and media events. His message was basically the same outside the company as it was internally. Once when asked at a press conference if Ford was considering a merger, Mulally replied, "Yes, we are going to merge with ourselves." Point taken.

The rest of Ford's leaders, including B&SE, took the cue from Mulally and worked to bring their diverse team together by focusing on their role in delivering the One Ford plan. They needed to act as one global team, aligned around creating great products that customers would truly value, and there was no reason to complicate the message any further. They leveraged an annual strategic A3 process to develop and execute a plan in support of the company strategy.

Each year a part of this plan was to improve engineers' engagement. Like many companies, Ford had an annual engagement survey that gave people a chance to communicate how they were feeling about the company and where things could be improved. The BS&E leadership team utilized this information along with input from biweekly skip-level meetings and biannual global town halls to develop specific countermeasures for improvement that became part of the annual A3 and organizational performance objectives.

Challenging People

When Akio Toyoda became president of Toyota in 2009, he quickly had a full plate. He had to deal with the largest recall and public image crisis in Toyota history. In his second year, he dealt with the largest earthquake-tsunami in Japan's history—and the severe part shortages it caused. The third year was no joy either, with the worst flooding in the history of Thailand, where Toyota makes many vehicles and parts. Yet his most lasting legacy from this time may be his challenge to the organization to make "ever better cars."

In Chapter 3 we discussed Toyota's New Global Architecture (TNGA) countermeasure to its poor state of platform design after a decade of doubling global sales. Though Toyota never suffered near-bankruptcy like Ford, it had its own rebuilding project. What reenergized both products and processes at Toyota has been the battle cry of "ever better cars" and President Toyoda's passion for exciting cars that are fun to drive.

Now a global challenge like this is not sufficient unless it gets translated into local challenges for each organization unit. We saw that the TNGA team's challenge was to develop attractive vehicles on platforms that could provide a 5- to 10-year advantage in the sensation of driving and handling. In the meantime, production engineering had the challenge of radically remaking manufacturing technologies with a mantra of simple, slim, and flexible. These high-level challenges then had to be translated into specific challenges for even more specialized units. For example, one TNGA challenge was to lower the center of gravity from the driver's perspective to be best in the world, which translated into a whole host of challenges for different functional groups and the redesign of hundreds of Toyota parts and supplier parts.

There is a famous saying, "You get what you measure." It may be more appropriate to say, "You get what you challenge." Teams will respond to challenges if they are well developed, are supported, and can be meaningfully translated for each team's tasks.

Organizing Your Team

Reorganization seems to be the "go-to" strategy to fix everything in so many companies. Some companies become addicted to it—a sort of panacea for all organizational ills—and you can see it in their people. Even in the best cases, reorganization drains energy, creates confusion, and dilutes focus during the transition, which always takes longer than imagined.

That being said, the way in which you are organized—and the way teams are organized—does matter. It can have a significant impact on a team's performance, especially over the long term. While it is crucial to organize in a way that focuses on creating value for the customer, you must also enable cross-program learning and continuous improvement.

Toyota Structure

Toyota's organizational structure has changed over time at the senior level. For example, the organization of vehicle centers has shifted a number of times in an attempt to become more responsive to customer segments. But deeper in the organization, the structure has been remarkably stable. Toyota uses various forms of a matrix organization. From the perspective of most development engineers, they are on the functional side of the matrix. Engineers report within their technical specialty up to a super-engineer, who grew up in the specialty. For example, the general manager of body engineering in any vehicle center has learned body engineering over his career from multiple masters. Even as a general manager, he or she continues to teach fundamental principles of body structures.

The other side of the matrix consists of vehicle programs, which are headed by chief engineers, or CEs (discussed in detail in Chapter 5). Toyota may reshuffle assignments of CEs—e.g., a higher-level CE for the global Toyota Camry may support Camry CEs in different regions of the world—but the role of the CE has not changed fundamentally since the role was created in the 1950s.

In our interviews we learned that Toyota was working to improve speed of decision-making and further deepen customer understanding through what they call an "in-house company" management structure. These businesses within the business are organized around specific product areas or initiatives and provide greater individual customer focus and agility while maintaining the integrity and balance of their original matrix.

Ford's Organizational Journey

Ford has experimented with several different organizational structures in product development over the years. Ford had long been known for strong and capable functional organizations, and the people in them took great pride in being part of their respective teams. Each discipline strove for excellence in its area, and most were quite successful. However, this did not always translate into better products, it often created impenetrable walls between functions, and a "zero-sum" mentality dominated the organization.

In an attempt to remedy the pitfalls of a functional organization, Ford became more product focused, and it reorganized into product-based clusters. These clusters were organized around specific vehicle types, such as trucks, small cars, SUVs, etc., and each was an independent and self-contained operating unit. The problem here, of course, was a decreased ability to learn across programs and maximize functional capabilities. This structure also was quite costly, inhibited standardization of any kind, and provided highly variable inputs to the manufacturing plants that still had to build vehicles from across the clusters. In short, a product focus created silos of a different kind and continued to hinder progress.

Ford decided to return to a matrix organization. This enabled them to balance horizontal value streams to deliver specific products with strong engineering functional capability and maximize the opportunity to learn and continuously improve. The matrix also had an organization-wide focus on product success. The functional groups were now measured primarily on their contribution to great products, not functional excellence in and of itself. In other words, functional capability was valued to the extent that it contributed to great products. The next step was to globalize the engineering functions to further increase benefits. What brought the enterprise together was the relentless focus on creating great products, and it started with leadership.

Product Creation Is an Enterprise Activity

Lean product and process development is not just an engineering or design activity. It should never be something that the design people "inflict" on the organization. Success requires you to engage the broader enterprise in product and process development. Consequently, when you think about your high-performance product development team, you must include talented people from manufacturing and from across your supply chain—not as an afterthought, but as fully contributing and accountable members of the development team.

Manufacturing Know-How in Product Development

As powerful as modern computer technology is for analysis and visualization, knowing how to make things matters. The knowledge and ability to make things well is a significant competitive advantage in product and process development. Knowing how to make things that your competitors cannot is a game changer. For some time we've seen a crucial gap between, on the one hand, product ideation and innovation and, on the other, the process and toolmaking. The application of manufacturing know-how and creativity to the development of great products has not received nearly the attention it deserves. It bears repeating: knowing how to make things well and fully integrating that knowledge into the development stream is a huge competitive advantage. The following examples demonstrate the importance of manufacturing know-how in product development.

Apple Stretches the Boundaries of Manufacturing You may not think of Apple as a manufacturing company, especially since it outsources much of its manufacturing to companies like Foxconn. When you examine Apple products closely and marvel at the physical product excellence, you have to ask yourself, "How do they make this, especially in the volumes they do?" Apple's iconic design, world-class craftsmanship, and success are highly dependent on understanding and advancing the art of manufacturing. Consequently, executives care deeply about making things. Jony Ive, Apple's iconic design leader, is constantly learning more and pushing boundaries in the art of the possible in manufacturing, and his designers continue to stretch their own capability, working directly with the most knowledgeable people in their field, both inside and outside Apple.

Apple once again demonstrated its commitment to advancing manufacturing capability for its products when in May 2017, CEO Tim Cook announced a $1 billion Advanced Manufacturing Fund and awarded a $200 million investment to Corning to "support R&D, capital equipment needs, and state-of-the-art glass processing."[9] The funding demonstrates that Apple understands how important manufacturing is to maintain the company's competitive edge.

Partnering Throughout the Ford Value Stream   Putting an aluminum body on the F-150 pickup was one of the biggest gambles in Ford's history: the F-Series had been the bestselling trucks for the previous 37 years, and no one had ever produced all-aluminum vehicle bodies in high volume. But the team knew that the only way to maintain Ford's lead was to continue to innovate and push the art of the possible, including achieving greater fuel economy and increased performance through ultralight bodies. The team also knew that to be successful the company would need product engineers, material engineers, and manufacturing engineers to be seamlessly integrated right from the start of the project. This long-term learning process required large-scale innovation along the entire value stream, including design, materials, coatings, forming, joining, and logistics. The team faced many challenges, the majority of which are proprietary. But we will share several:

- **Formability.** The material properties of aluminum make it inherently far more difficult to form into the complex shapes required for a truck body. The Ford team took a three-pronged approach to this challenge:

  1. Ford product, materials, and manufacturing engineers worked directly with material suppliers to match or develop specific material properties to both the vehicle performance requirements and the formability challenges of critical parts.

2. Product engineers worked with manufacturing engineers to modify part design where required in order to accommodate particularly difficult forming conditions.

3. Manufacturing engineers modified tools and process and also allowed significantly more time for experimentation and tool tryout right from the start of the program for critical parts. They identified high-risk parts early in the program and built a longer experimentation period into the cost and development timing plans.

- **Cost.** Aluminum is generally more expensive than steel, and just passing that cost on to customers would diminish the overall value proposition and threaten sales leadership. Product, materials, and manufacturing engineers worked through each part together to maximize efficient use of the material. The stamping of large parts is a material-inefficient process, with as much as 30 percent of an individual blank (starting piece of material) trimmed off and sent down the scrap shoot after forming for difficult parts. The team modified designs, processes, and blank shapes, and also formed smaller parts within the scrap areas of larger parts wherever possible to significantly improve yield. Ford also worked with material suppliers to design the most efficient material recycling value stream possible.

The resulting pickup was more than 700 pounds lighter than its predecessor, and it was lauded for its "towing and hauling capacities, top-notch fuel economy estimates, impressive tech features, and room to seat up to six with ease."[10] It also earned a five-star safety rating and Top Safety Pick award from the Insurance Institute for Highway Safety,[11] and it was *Motor Trend's* "Truck of the Year"[12] and *Consumer Reports'* best full-size pickup truck,as well as "green truck" of the year.[13] This game-changing product would never have been possible without an enterprise-wide approach to product development, including an incredible level of manufacturing and materials innovation, which started at the very beginning of the program. In the end, the F-Series cruised to 41 consecutive years as the bestselling truck as well as the bestselling vehicle in North America.

Dearborn Tool and Die   As we have said, process engineering and tool and equipment manufacturing are critical to the creation of physical products. Yet many companies we encounter continue to treat "tool release" as the time to throw the product drawing over the wall and hope for the best. They do not recognize it as the potential competitive advantage it truly is. This was definitely one of the problems the Ford team faced in the beginning of its transformation.

One thing that was clear when Terry Henning became plant manager at Ford's Dearborn Tool and Die (DT&D) facility was that it was not competitive. What was less clear was exactly what represented best-in-class performance in tool and die manufacture. This was particularly problematic for an automaker, whose ability to create high-quality tools, dies, and fixtures is integral to new product development. Henning knew this, and so did Henry Ford. The once-beautiful, 420,000-square-foot facility was designed by Albert Kahn and built by the company's founder to be the most technologically advanced tool facility in the world. But years of neglect and complacency had reduced it to a slow and expensive operation and the tooling source with which engineers least wanted to work. Henning, a long-time stamping manager and tool and die maker himself, was determined to change this. He partnered with John Davis, Ford's stamping engineering manager, and together they mapped a path forward.

In order to find out exactly where DT&D stood, Henning, B&SE Asia Pacific tooling manager Jesse Jou, stamping engineering supervisor Eric Frevik, Jim, and purchasing counterparts decided to study toolmaking capability around the globe. They visited tool shops in the United States, Germany, Japan, Korea, Taiwan, China, and Thailand. They also deeply studied the actual tool development work back in Dearborn, engaging directly with the shop-floor team who understood the process best. From this work, the stamping engineering and toolmaking team developed a "gap chart" that identified the performance gaps the company was facing at each stage of the shop-floor process and with die development. For each of these gaps, the team utilized A3s to develop countermeasures. Some gaps were technological, many were process-related, but some were caused by a lack of alignment and integration between engineering and DT&D. Because of DT&D's poor reputation, it had become largely isolated from Ford's body engineering team and not well integrated into the development system, resulting in poor communication and little understanding of each other's processes or challenges.

Weekly stand-ups were held at DT&D, and Davis's stamping engineers along with Henning's toolmakers collectively reviewed each set of tools and resulting parts. They worked at the gemba, assessed progress, and developed an agreed-to plan to move forward. Henning's powerful if somewhat unlikely partner in this process was Joe Sammut, the integration chief for the B&SE team. He was a longtime body engineer and engineering leader, and his team was responsible for delivering product programs from beginning to end for the B&SE function. Although initially a bit resistant, Sammut was quick to see the value of the integrated organization, was crucial in engaging engineers and communicating directly to program chief engineers, and helped to build teamwork and maintain accountability on both sides. The leadership that Sammut and Henning provided was key to integrating B&SE efforts and delivering ever-better results to Ford's program teams.

To improve the toolmaking coordination and communication process, Henning agreed with stamping engineering to collocate a number of tool designers and process engineers at DT&D so that they could more quickly respond to issues and learn firsthand the problems the toolmakers faced. These process engineers and toolmakers also worked together on improvement initiatives that reached into both DT&D and engineering.

In addition to joining some of the weekly stand-ups, Jim visited the site for more "formal" reviews once each quarter. As Henning and the team reviewed their progress to plan on each visit, he saw performance, energy, and enthusiasm grow. The UAW leadership, while initially skeptical, became true partners in the work and joined in the visits as well. Soon these visits became a highlight on Jim's schedule. About a year and a half into the journey, Jim decided to bring a friend to one of the reviews. The energy and excitement level was off the charts when Mulally walked into the plant. The team shared the incredible accomplishments with the CEO as he walked the plant floor, shaking hands, hugging, asking questions, and thanking the team members for their work. There was no stopping them now.

The results are impressive: from 2004 to 2010, DT&D cut lead time by about half in full support of GPDS requirements, reduced labor and overhead costs by the same amount, and improved tool and die as well as first-part-to-gauge quality by about 80 percent. The contribution to Ford's product and process development capability of this work is massive. But since many tools are made outside Ford at suppliers, to get full benefit the improvements would have to be spread to those dies as well.

Once DT&D had mastered the process, Henning and his team shared openly with suppliers—sometimes one at a time, but also through larger-scale, more formal events that integrated the engineering department, DT&D, purchasing, supplier quality, and a large number of suppliers, in which both methods and expectations were shared. At the first of these events, the supplier quality director started her talk by saying, "First, I would like to congratulate the Dearborn Tool and Die team. I have to say that a couple of years ago I would not have thought this possible."

Henning and his team continue to host benchmarking visits at DT&D to this day. After the word got out, not only suppliers, but other automakers and companies from many other industries visited to learn about the DT&D world-class processes and technologies. Many often overlook the real secret behind the transformation—the people!

Simultaneous Engineering at Toyota Toyota has leveraged its manufacturing excellence as a competitive advantage for decades. You would be hard-pressed to find a manufacturing leader in any industry that does not know about the power of the Toyota Production System. But what may be less well known is that Toyota's excellence in manufacturing begins way upstream in the development process through production engineering.

Toyota's Production Engineering Center in Motomachi, Japan, has been the source of countless innovations in manufacturing technologies and methods that have gone on to change the industry. Whether it is the most flexible assembly lines in the industry, the shortest paint lines, or one-by-one fascia (bumper) manufacturing with zero inventory between molding and painting, the hard work and expertise of this team has kept Toyota the leader in manufacturing performance. But this group is also just as critical in achieving Toyoda's goal of "ever better cars." Toyota is about producing *and* finding solutions, as in creating great products *and* improving lean manufacturing, or creating great products *and* being environmentally responsible.

Think about a great football quarterback throwing balls to receivers who frequently drop them. A great product engineer cannot deliver great products if engineers in manufacturing drop the ball. We have been talking about simultaneous engineering for over 40 years. Yet simultaneous engineering depends on two parties—product engineers and process engineers. Unfortunately, too many companies outsource the core expertise of production engineering and create a huge gap between product and process. Leveraging manufacturing innovation and extraordinary capability into development—and mutually reinforcing each—is a key to product excellence. We think the next two examples provide some insight into this organizational characteristic:

- **Improving ride and handling.** Toyota dramatically improved vehicle ride and handling characteristics through TNGA. Increasing body stiffness improves ride and handling, so Toyota set an objective of increasing stiffness anywhere from 30 to 60 percent, depending on the car model. One way to reach this goal is to increase the number of spot welds on the body. However, this can significantly increase cycle times and/or drive costly investment in additional welding equipment. In many companies, this conflict would result in cross-functional battles, compromised product and process performance, and far less value delivered to the customer.

  Toyota product development and process engineers worked *together* to improve product geometry and develop laser screw welding (LSW) technology that requires less than half the cycle time of conventional spot welding and less than half the plant-floor space, yet still delivers the required body stiffness. No doubling of equipment or floor space needed. Nothing less would have been acceptable. LSW also has the added benefit of being far more flexible than traditional spot welding, applicable to various new products and multiple material types. This has contributed to major reductions in the time and cost to launch new vehicles.

- **Weight reduction.** Another product priority for Toyota is to reduce weight to increase fuel efficiency. One way to accomplish this is to engineer parts out of high-strength, lightweight materials of a thinner gauge that replace heavier multiple-part subassemblies. However, some of these materials have to be superheated prior to forming, which traditionally required very large, dedicated gas ovens that heat steel blanks in large batches, plus an added operation to remove oxidation caused by the heating process. This might be an acceptable compromise for many companies, but working in batches and adding operations in TPS is a nonstarter.

  Once again, Toyota product development and process engineers collaborated to tailor blanks and create a joule heating process that heats blanks one at a time, in 5 to 10 seconds—and with no added operations required. Some companies improve products and then pass new, added costs to customers; the LPPD system embedded at Toyota enables the company to deliver lighter, safer vehicles at even *lower costs* than the earlier designs could.

Evolution of Manufacturing Know-How in Product Development

The level of manufacturing integration that occurs within Toyota and other LPPD companies is unheard of at many firms. In fact, some companies struggle to visualize what it would even look like in their environment. One way to grasp this and move toward such integration—if a bit contrived—is to think about manufacturing's role in product and process development as evolving through four stages of maturity.

Stage 1: Survival In this stage, manufacturing is in survival mode as new products seem to be inflicted on the function. Symptoms of this stage typically include more complaining than actual improvement action. Rework, heroics, redesign on the fly, and short tempers reign. Launch problems are not so much a matter of "if" but "when." Product engineers don't engage until "too late" and get stuck in launch mode, which then delays their start on other new programs and launches, which leads to a product development death spiral. Products often have significant quality issues both in the plant and in the field. Elon Musk's "production hell" at Tesla seems to be an example of this. All the frustrations and a sense that "there must be a better way" motivate manufacturing to move to Stage 2.

Stage 2: Manufacturing Feasibility Assessments Manufacturing managers want to improve the situation but are unsure how. They move manufacturing people upstream to influence product design, but their engineers have no real framework with which to engage. When asked for input, they typically offer only thumbnail, anecdotal assessments. These "feasibility assessments" change as the physical product begins to emerge, which results in lots of late changes, rework, and frustration on both sides. There is more activity than true value created, but it's a start. And this work often raises the visibility of problems to senior management. The end result is often an organizational imperative to "design for manufacturing."

Stage 3: Design for Manufacturing Manufacturing now has a seat at the table, and the organization starts to create and use tools like design for manufacturability (DFM) standards, process failure mode and effects analysis, and lots of metrics and scorecards. The organization establishes advanced manufacturing teams who may even collocate with product engineers. While they do make progress, the focus tends to be on the manufacturing department's feasibility rejection of any product attribute that challenges current manufacturing capability. Engineers sometimes behave as if DFM is an end in itself. The company may have reduced launch and manufacturing issues, but integration problems still prevent the sort of game-changing products that are crucial to growth. Companies also have neglected the role of suppliers in product development, and new types of development and launch issues begin to emerge and are incorrectly characterized as "part of the development process." Some companies stop at this stage, but a select few persevere to create a true partnership and profitable value streams.

Stage 4: Design-Manufacturing Collaboration In this stage, a true partnership has been forged between manufacturing and product development, with aligned objectives that focus on delivering both great products *and* value-stream excellence. Manufacturing has established a robust manufacturing development system that is fully integrated and drives process and product development. It provides the critical infrastructure, a common language, a process that enables JIT input, the right skill sets, clear roles and responsibilities, and powerful tools, and it drives collaboration.

There is still stress and even conflict, but it is a creative tension born of professionals stretching the organization's capability. The result is not only great, innovative products, but also manufacturing processes and capabilities that serve as lasting and powerful competitive advantages. Suppliers, too, are valuable partners and capture both product and process knowledge as a foundation of continuous improvement. A system based on collaboration and organizational focus delivers maximum value to the customer, creates a powerful competitive advantage, and provides the foundation for an actual lean enterprise.

The Extended Enterprise—Suppliers in Product Development

Much has been written about the role of suppliers in product development, including in our earlier book. The short version is that the customer will not forgive you even if you blame a poor design on a supplier. Every part of what you sell is your responsibility and has to meet the same standards of quality, appearance, and function. Therefore, suppliers need to be integrated into the development process. That being said, all supplied parts are not created equal. Some suppliers provide readily available commodities, and fairness and due diligence around quality, cost, and delivery are often sufficient in managing these relationships. But for the rest of your suppliers—those that create parts and subsystems integral to your products' value propositions—something more is needed. These suppliers are partners in your product and should be treated as such. Each is a core part of your team—a fellow "wolf," as it were—with the same expectation for respect and mutual performance as any other team member. Your success is inextricably linked.

Ford historically struggled with supplier relationships, perpetually landing among the lowest-scoring companies on the annual automotive supplier survey that identified the worst and best automakers with which to work. Then in 2007, it happened. Ford came in dead last. And perhaps not surprisingly, Ford's suppliers had become absolutely dreadful to work with as well. Quality issues, late deliveries, and surprise costs were just business as usual.

As the members of the Ford leadership team began to study the problem in detail, they realized that any improvement in supplier relationships had to start with their own team. It was apparent that the Ford organization was not as aligned internally as it needed to be when it came to working with suppliers. Confusing or even contradicting directions to suppliers were clearly adding to the problems in these relationships and had to be addressed.

The leadership teams of the engineering and purchasing departments came together to work out an organizational countermeasure in the form of matched pairs. Matched pairs brought together leaders in each organization based on the subsystems for which they were responsible. For example, in Jim's organization the leader for global body structures engineering worked directly with the leader for global steel, aluminum, and stamping procurement; the leader for global lamp engineering worked with the global leader for lighting procurement, etc. Jim was matched with Susan DeSandre, who was the global director for all body exterior commodities and materials worldwide. DeSandre and her team brought the commercial acumen and deep knowledge of the supplier companies and their capabilities to bear in jointly developing both short- and long-term strategies for each of the subsystems and supplier companies. It did not take long for a partnership to form between the pairs that eventually extended to key suppliers.

Short-term strategies were especially important during the Great Recession, when the commercial viability of a number of suppliers was in doubt and the two groups needed to act seamlessly and quickly to head off potential disasters. This short-term work also included the "normal" day-to-day business of attaining program cost targets, managing supplier performance, and achieving annual cost-savings requirements for each pair's area of responsibility. Through the matched-pair system, the pair partners were now able to speak with a single, aligned voice and leverage both commercial and technical solutions in a way they had not in the past. This short-term, joint work was largely managed through weekly matched-pair meetings, jointly chaired by DeSandre and Jim. In addition, the two also met regularly in one-to-one meetings as well as special "one-off" meetings with specific supplier companies and the appropriate subsystem matched-pair team. The weekly meetings were attended by all subsystem matched pairs and sometimes by supplier representatives for increased directness and transparency.

Long-term strategies were also developed by the matched-pair teams based on the technical and commercial requirements of their subsystems. These strategies were largely embodied in five-year commodity business plans. The plans attempted to anticipate important changes in product performance characteristics, such as weight reduction for better fuel economy or improved lighting performance, and laid out a strategy to meet those requirements technically, commercially, and logistically for their subsystem across products and around the world. These integrated plans proved a powerful planning and alignment tool for the purchasing team, engineering, and suppliers, which were often an integral part of their development. The plans were approved through the matched-pair leadership chain to ensure cross-subsystem coordination and were updated on an ongoing basis.

Matched-pair teams also made a point to visit several suppliers each year. These two-day visits (one day commercial and one day technical) were a great way to build stronger relationships, address issues, improve communication, and share new technologies and plans for the future.

As an example, one benefit of improved supplier relations was seen in the new technologies applied to Fusion B pillar development (center pillar between doors). This subsystem is very important to body performance, integrity, and safety, and is typically made from multiple stamped, high-strength steel parts that are welded together. Ford learned from a supplier about advances being developed in hydroforming technology (the process of using high-pressure fluids for forming) that could potentially allow the process to be far more accurate and work with highly engineered, high-strength steels. Ford product and process engineers worked directly with the supplier to mature the technology and adapt product and assembly process design to accommodate it. The result was a much lighter, stronger subassembly with fewer parts and lower costs than previous versions.

The Ford team was very careful not to strain these improved relationships by asking suppliers to do anything that Ford was not willing or able to do. One example of this was the Dearborn Tool and Die story, where Ford reduced cost and lead time and improved the quality of its own toolmaking before asking suppliers to do it. Ford then openly shared its improvement journey and methods with suppliers. Another example of this philosophy was Ford's aluminum design, forming, and assembly expertise. Ford invested years in developing this capability internally before working with suppliers to help them grow these same skills.

The result of working more closely and collaboratively with suppliers was not only stronger performance in the annual supplier survey (in 2010, Ford was the highest-ranked U.S. automaker) but also far better supplier performance and an incredible bond between the engineering and purchasing teams. Working on these and other high-performance teams were very fulfilling for those involved. Consider Jim's reflection on being part of high-performance teams in the boxed insert.

JIM: ON BEING A MEMBER OF A HIGH-PERFORMING TEAM

By far, the thing I miss most since "retiring" and joining the largely solitary world of writing and coaching is being part of a high-performance team. As with many things in life, we often only truly appreciate something when it is gone. As impactful as my team experiences are to me, they are, nonetheless, difficult to describe. And I am sure that with the passing of time, my memories are likely a bit rosier than was the actual experience. So please take my enthusiasm with some healthy skepticism.

I was part of several memorable teams. While the challenges faced by each team were quite different, they shared some characteristics. I have also spoken to a number of people inside and outside of Ford who have had very similar experiences, with similar characteristics.

- **Taking on a challenge.** My experience and those of the people I spoke with typically started with a difficult challenge, which rallied some of the team and culled others. People who did not want to be part of the effort self-selected out in one way or another. The challenge stirs a general recognition that we are not going to accomplish this without working together. It creates pressure that brings people together with some urgency to accomplish a difficult and important objective.

  How leadership frames the challenge also is key. Mulally never sugarcoated our situation, but neither did he ever suggest we might not be successful: "It's going to feel so good coming out the other side!" The challenge does not have to be saving the company or large-scale growth. It could be changing the way work gets done in your industry by applying lean or creating a game-changing product.

- **Creating a larger context.** Most people want to be part of something special, something that matters. People often have a limited vantage point in the organization and are unable to see the big picture amid their day-to-day difficulties. Leadership paints this large picture, showing how everyone's contribution creates a much bigger thing and demonstrating how each contribution is important.

  There is an old story about the different perspectives of three stonecutters: The first one says, "I have to work in the hot sun all day long, working with these heavy, filthy stones; my hands have become callused, and my back aches, and no one even cares." The second stonecutter says, "Well, things may not be perfect, but I focus on doing the best job of cutting stones I can despite the conditions. I keep my tools sharp, I practice my craft, and I am focused on cutting the best stones possible." The third stonecutter looks up and says, "I'm building a cathedral."

- **Peer-to-peer accountability.** Leadership's role is important in creating the right context in the early days, but over time there is a subtle shift in the emotional focus of team members. Leadership still matters, but members become much more concerned with not letting each other down and work hard to keep up their end. You never want to let your teammates down. This cycle continues to build, raising the performance bar for the entire team, often above a level that a single leader would likely ever hope the team could achieve.

- **Trust.** As peer-to-peer accountability grows and members continue to contribute at higher levels, mutual professional respect evolves into trust. Members have earned each other's trust over time by their performance. No one feels like they have to check up on anyone. They are confident in their teammates. They are learning together and share what they know without hesitation or fear. This trust, which can be fragile, is a significant competitive advantage while it lasts.

- **Expanding the "art of the possible."** An interesting thing happens as the team members continue to work together in a trustful way. They build confidence (not arrogance, although it can certainly turn into that if allowed). There becomes a thoughtful understanding that the team is far more capable than previously believed. The team stretches and challenges itself, and members take pride in what they have accomplished together, create more excitement, and build even stronger connections among one another. Leadership plays an important role in keeping this from turning into overconfidence by elevating their focus—raising the bar. This is delicate work because you certainly don't want to be the one to "break" this confidence. Truly knowing and reading the team is important.

- **Humor.** This characteristic may strike some as odd, and I don't know that it is a condition of success. But the great teams I have been a part of and those with whom I talked had an "insider's sense of humor" that kept people going through long days and the many setbacks they encountered. The jokes were often self-effacing and based on their current situation. The humor acted as a release. It helped to provide some much-needed perspective at times. But most of all, sharing those jokes meant you belonged.

- **A bond.** The team members really care about each other. I honestly don't know if this is the result of their facing adversity together or if it is what enabled them; perhaps a bit of both. In any case, team members care about each other on a personal level, and there is an unmistakable bond that is created. It is a bond that endures. I found this out in the process of talking to people about this book. It had been several years since I had spoken to some, but it was as if no time had passed at all. It is the wolf-pack bond that is implied in the Kipling quote that started this chapter.

- **So why share this?** The reason Jeff and I decided that I should share this admittedly subjective experience is in an attempt to communicate why it is important to work hard at building a high-performance team. Not only does it lead to better performance outcomes, but it is also a tremendous personal experience. Why in the world would you not want to be part of something so great? And why would you not want to experience it with others? A desire and, ideally, ability to develop high-performance teams is a powerful recruitment and retention tool. Pay, benefits, and personal growth opportunities have to be competitive, but all else being equal, most people will choose to be a part of a high-performance team.

LOOKING AHEAD

While the allure of the latest technology is tempting and can often contribute to your improvement efforts, it is your team and the way the team members work together more than anything else that will determine your success in product and process development. Your development team should include everyone necessary to contribute to creating a new value stream, and the continual development of each member should be a priority for leadership at all levels.

In the next chapter, we will talk about leadership and the role of leaders in high-performance product development organizations.

Your Reflection

Creating a Vision

In some ways this chapter is the core of the book—developing high-performance teams and team members. The vision for developing and supporting high-performance teams described here includes:

- A mutual commitment between the organization that supports, recognizes, and rewards individuals and the individuals who commit to doing the best possible work for the organization and its customers

- A clearly defined, deliberate culture for high performance that is consistently reinforced by leadership at all levels

- People who are hired based not only on technical credentials but also on fit with the desired culture
- A process of developing people from the time they enter the company and extending over their careers, with the right mix of professional training and learning at the gemba with a coach
- Ongoing performance feedback in the shortest practical intervals, with constructive guidance on how to improve
- Leaders with the skills to engage individuals to become a high-performing team
- An environment in which people are continually challenged with the next big opportunity to satisfy and excite customers
- A supportive organizational structure that strikes a balance between deep development of functional expertise and multifunctional focus on customers
- Downstream functions that are responsible for building and delivering the product or service that become fully engaged as part of the team up front in the development process
- An engaged enterprise including all key internal functions and external suppliers of critical components and systems which are enrolled as part of one team

How does this model of building high-performance teams and team members fit what you think is needed for the products and services offered by your company? How would you revise the vision to better fit your company's situation?

Your Current Condition

How good is your organization at developing talent and building high-performance teams?

1. How much time and effort goes into building high-performing teams and developing the organizational and technical skills of all team members in your organization? How much of a priority is it at all levels of leadership?

2. Is your product and process development work truly an enterprise activity? How might you engage more effectively across your extended enterprise?

3. How do you personally feel about being part of your team? Could it be better? What can you do about it?

Taking Action

1. Form an empowered, cross-functional team with representation from functions across the product development value stream.

2. As a team, reflect on your current state of developing people and teams. What would a better, future state look like? How would it function differently from what currently happens?

3. Take actions based on this work, and reflect on what worked and why, as well as where challenges remain—both in addressing the organizational gaps and in progressing as a high-performance team.

5
Leading Development

There are no bad teams, just bad leaders.
> —Jocko Willink and Leif Babin,
> U.S. Navy SEAL Officers
> in Task Force Bruiser

Why Leadership Matters in Development

Great leadership is an indispensable ingredient of successful teams in all walks of life. High-performance teams (Chapter 4) do not just happen. They are developed and continually nurtured by excellent leaders. This is certainly true in product and process development, where problems are a daily reality, leaders face hundreds of time-critical decisions, and the efforts of talented people from wildly diverse backgrounds must be integrated in order to move the team forward toward the creation of something new to the world.

Effective leaders put all the LPPD puzzle pieces together and create a whole greater than the sum of its parts. All the principles and practices in this book are just nice things to talk about or visualize until leaders bring them to life through the actual work of smart, motivated, and well-trained people. As you will see in this chapter, leaders are necessary at all organizational levels and play various roles in development. But their unifying task is to focus the efforts of highly skilled people from across the enterprise on creating exceptional new value for the customer and a better future for all stakeholders. What translates LPPD principles and concepts into actual behavior is exceptional leadership.

Writing a book that gives advice is incredibly humbling, and telling people how to lead is presumptuous and not our intent. Rather, our goal is to share our experiences with the defining characteristics of the great leaders we have known and make the point that such leaders can and should be developed. Like all our readers, we have had experience with mediocre leaders, but we have also had wonderful experiences with great leaders.

The difference between ineffective and effective leadership was shown in sharp contrast during Ford's turnaround. The leadership difference between those who created the crisis and CEO Alan Mulally and his team that followed was night and day. Great leaders help to turn groups of ordinary people into high-performance teams, while poor leaders destroy great potential.

Great Leadership Starts with Humility

Leadership skills can be learned. No, strike that. Leadership skills *must* be learned. While some people seem to have greater natural gifts for leadership, there is no replacement for the learning gained from the real-world challenges of leading teams of people under the watchful eye of a mentor—trying things, failing, getting feedback, adjusting, and trying again. There is definitely a PDCA cycle of leadership.

Although Jim had been in leadership roles for well over a decade before joining Ford, his most valuable lessons took place during the tumultuous Ford turnaround. He was very fortunate to have extraordinary mentors who "who walked the talk" and did not hesitate to provide useful and direct feedback. Those valuable lessons started with a simple, handwritten note he received through intracompany mail one afternoon. Mulally had just left Boeing to join Ford as its president and CEO during a difficult and pivotal time in Ford's history. Mulally's unpretentious note, suggesting they meet, was the beginning of a seven-year relationship, during which Jim learned many things, like the importance of providing people with context, the value of always working on *a better plan*, and the magic of truly working together as a team. But none of these lessons were more important than seeing firsthand how Mulally approached his leadership role in the company, day in and day out. He had authentic humility and deep respect and affection for others. It was never about him—always about Ford. This never changed, whether in the darkest depths of Ford's corporate crisis or later as the company became ever more successful and Mulally grew into a rock star CEO. His people-first approach allowed Mulally to connect with people in a powerful way and enabled him to lead Ford through one of the most dramatic turnarounds in business history.

After working for Mulally awhile, it occurred to Jim that he had seen this approach before. He remembered many years ago when he first began to train, walking through the doors of the East West Brazilian Jiu Jitsu (BJJ) center and encountering the sign "Leave Your Ego at the Door" emblazoned above the training area. He knew that, like Mulally, Jim found that the best BJJ fighters were often the humblest.

Sam Sheridan, author of the insightful book *A Fighter's Heart*, had apparently received the same message when he interviewed some of the best fighters in the world: Time and again during interviews, he heard that "humility was the most important attribute for a great fighter."[1] To some extent it is the nature of BJJ that keeps a fighter humble. Just as for any skill, there are basic routines that need to be learned as a foundation. But unlike many martial arts practiced in the gym and in simulated competition, BJJ is based on real-world rolling or sparring with opponents. There is no ambiguity and no rationalization—"You got tapped [forced to submit]; deal with it." It crushes illusions and forces the critical self-examination required for improvement. But the most important reason great fighters put their ego aside is because ego inhibits progress. They work harder than anyone else, always look for gaps in their game, and constantly push their limits. A big ego makes you afraid to push, to try new things, to open up, to grow. Ego makes you complacent and fat, and it makes you afraid to take a risk. You are stuck.

But don't ever make the mistake of confusing humility with weakness. The best fighters have an inner fierceness and focus that belies their calm appearance; they have a no-excuses drive to do whatever it takes. Likewise, taking in Alan Mulally's easy smile and sincere "honor to serve" attitude, the casual observer could be forgiven for missing the stoic resolve, incredible work ethic, and laser-focused drive that have made Mulally one of the most successful leaders in U.S. business history.

Many years of experience have taught us that leadership, like BJJ, can be learned and that your capabilities can be constantly improved. But like most difficult and tacit skills, you can only learn leadership by doing, and constant learning is based on experience. Your efforts will be helped along considerably by working with outstanding mentors to guide you on your journey—people who have actually done it before.

Leadership Characteristics

We did not set out to develop the next great leadership model; there are already plenty of those. And what follows is not proposed as "the" leadership principles. These are simply an assortment of observations that come from many years of working with and studying people who have been very successful in leading others. In our experience these leadership characteristics are common to those leading a team that needs to accomplish something challenging, something, perhaps, that has never done before.

It's About the Team

In 1983, legendary Michigan football coach Bo Schembechler told his Wolverines in an emotionally charged speech, "No man is more important than the team, no coach is more important than the team. The team, the team, the team!" And while most development work takes place far from the football field, the message is no less important. The essence of leadership is building the capability and performance of your team. Your team comes first. If you forget this, or if team members or leaders put themselves above the team, you are in serious trouble.

In product and process development, you are trying to bring together people of diverse backgrounds and skill sets to achieve a common and usually difficult goal. It's the leader's job to create a compelling, inclusive vision of what's possible with everyone's contribution—and to build a team where members check their egos at the door.

Building One Aligned and Focused Team

Many companies apply "one" to their company name to imply that they want some things in common across the company and everyone in the company to share that view—one core set of values, one core set of beliefs, and one common direction. However, few companies seem to actually accomplish it.

Toyota may be unusual in having more or less a common culture from its founding. While this was not documented until 2001 as the "Toyota Way," it goes back almost a century to when Toyota was a loom company. The two pillars of the Toyota Way are "respect for people" and "continuous improvement," and the expectation is that members all have common company goals linked to the annual business plan, or *hoshin*, of the company. Respect for people, customers, team members, and communities is core to lean leadership, and caring about people is essential in creating sustainable high-performance teams. In our research for this book, we found that highly successful leaders embody this philosophy.

What has helped to maintain Toyota's culture is consistent leadership at the top of the company, mostly Toyoda family members. Few companies have that kindred luxury, so instead leaders elsewhere often find themselves in positions where they have to knit together a divided company to get unity of direction. In our experience, one of the best at doing this is Mulally.

Prior to joining Ford as president and CEO and shepherding the product-led turnaround, Mulally had a long history of successfully leading diverse and highly skilled product-focused teams under the most challenging conditions. He led the highly technical development of the Boeing 757 and 767 flight management systems, guided thousands of people around the world in the complete development of the 777, and later served as CEO of Boeing Commercial Airplanes, integrating Boeing's purchase of McDonnell Douglas and Rockwell defense, space, and information assets into the largest aerospace company in the world. In our interviews with Mulally for this book, he said that throughout his career, "I used the same working-together principles and practices."

Historically at both Boeing and Ford, these team-centered principles were weak or missing. Mulally brought them to life working to achieve the goal of "an exciting, viable, profitably growing company for the benefit of all the stakeholders—the customers, the employees, the suppliers, the investors, the unions, and the communities in which we operate around the world. Profitable growth for all equals revenue times margins. And the only way you can profitably grow in a sustainable way is working as a focused team to make products and service that people want and they value."

For Mulally, effective leadership is putting people first and being accountable for creating an environment where everyone can flourish and work as a single, aligned team. These values came through vividly in our interview with him, and we believe the best way to share his outlook is in his own words:

People first. That's code for "I love you as a human being." That's the purpose of life, to love and be loved, including everybody. I've always respected people. I wanted to help them find meaning in what they're doing. I want to listen to them. I want to appreciate their work. I want to recognize their work. I want to include them. What you're seeing, that's me, and that's what the working-together principles and practices are about, both the process and the expected leadership behaviors.

I love you. I really love people. The way I grew up . . . I didn't have a lot. But we had a lot of love in our family. Every day my mom would say, "Now, remember what your purpose in life is; it's to love and be loved, in that order. Also, to serve is to live, and it's nice to be important, but it's much more important to be nice." This was my foundation.

Some people would say to me, "Well, Alan . . . I see these working-together principles and practices and your working-together management system, and it sounds like you want us to remove fear and intimidation from our management toolbox?" And I always answer, "Yes." Then we talk about why. This is a very competitive world, and everybody has access to talented people. It is all about skilled and motivated people working together to create an exciting, viable, sustainable, growing organization, profit or nonprofit.

In order for leaders to create environments where skilled and motivated people can bring their skills, work together in a safe environment as well as a smart environment, to make the best products and services in the world, and improve their efficiency every year, we need their hearts and minds.

We have all seen employee surveys where less than half of the people in an organization feel good about being part of the company. That means that the majority of employees that are going to work every day are going for a salary, and not to build a cathedral. I look at all that data, and I'll know that the competitive advantage to do great things for as many people as possible around the world is going to be based on these working-together principles and practices.

We know that these principles and practices have worked for a lot of years, a lot of years. We know they have worked for a lot of years to bring people together to do important stuff. I know that I'm honored to get a chance to hold ourselves responsible and accountable for operating this way.

I know that people are going to move from the dark—Grendel's mother and the swamps, Grendel's extended family[2]—into the light. Once you move into the light and you realize how warm it is and how effective it is, people working together, you'll never go back.

People first, everyone is included, compelling vision, comprehensive strategy, relentless implementation plan, clear performance goals, one plan.

We had a strikingly similar response in our conversations with Tyler Schilling, founder and CEO of the hugely successful Schilling Robotics. The company is not only commercially successful, but a truly great place to work. We heard it from every employee with whom we spoke and sensed it in all our interactions with them. Schilling shared his thoughts about leadership and people:

Our history is that I started the business in 1985, and then sold it to a multinational company called GEC Alsthom in 1992. [I] then decided after 11 years that we should take the company back and take another run at it, and this time we shouldn't do this as an on-the-job training exercise. I wanted to hire some people that had experience at more mature, developed organizations, and we hired some really capable folks.

It's interesting because they had a lot of the important experience, but a lot of them also brought with them something I didn't want, which was a ruthlessness with regard to people.

In fact, the biggest mistake I used to make in the hiring process was when I saw a résumé where the experience looked perfect and the individual's career history was an exact match for what we wanted; it caused what I think of as a soft-skills blindness. Then, when we get them into the organization, they were toxic in terms of what you look for in a leader.

I just want to add one other nuance about a leader's being obsessive about arriving at the destination. There is really the balance you're trying to strike. But it's not succeeding at any cost, especially when it comes to human wreckage in your wake. That's not a durable circumstance. Behaving poorly with respect to people is probably the worst thing that a leader can do, because all you have to do is do it to one person and virtually the entire organization has you figured out at that point. Getting to the destination and leaving human wreckage behind you is not success in my opinion.

I actually have a secret in this space. On my to-do list is to file a patent for this. It works in every situation with regard to the way people think about you. It goes like this: What is the best way to make someone think you care about them? It's to actually care about them.

It works in all aspects, where you're interested in what somebody thinks. The other dimension that I think is critically important is to be respectful. Einstein is quoted as saying that he treats the janitor the same way he treats the president of the university.

I think the clearest currency to let someone know about your respect for them is to be generous with your time. . . . When they say, "Tyler, do you have a moment?" the answer has to be, "Yes," unless you're being wheeled into surgery.

Own It

One of Jim's favorite books on leadership is *Extreme Ownership*,[3] by ex-U.S. Navy SEAL officers Jocko Willink and Leif Babin, not only because the leadership lessons have emerged from some of the most difficult and challenging environments imaginable, but because it reinforces a basic leadership truth: as a leader, it's always your fault. This revelation should fire you up, not bring you down. It means that leadership matters—that you can make a difference. And that the ability to make a difference is completely under your control. It's not your boss's fault, it's not your company's fault, and it definitely is not the fault of the "C players that you're stuck with."

There are a number of great stories in *Extreme Ownership*, but one that stands out comes from SEAL junior officer training at Basic Underwater Demolition and SEAL Training (BUD/S). This is possibly the toughest military training on the planet and especially difficult for those who wish to lead the elite SEAL warriors. According to Willink and Babin, junior officers serve as leaders of seven-man boat crews who, among other things, are challenged to paddle their large rubber boats out into the Pacific Ocean surf and race each other down the Coronado coastline.

During "hell week," the teams work with little rest and no sleep, under the constant harassment of SEAL instructors, while their huge, awkward boats continue to flip in the rough surf, requiring the teams to scramble back aboard and continue the race. During one particular training evolution, boat team II won nearly every race. The team pushed hard, worked in unison, and executed as a team. There was one other boat that stood out as well, but for very different reasons. Boat IV constantly was found in the rear of the pack. Instead of working together, this boat crew argued, blamed each other, and fell further behind. The young leader of the poorly performing team IV received a great deal of unwanted attention from the SEAL instructors, "Yet he seemed indifferent, as though fate had dealt him a poor hand: a team of underperformers who, no matter how hard he tried, simply could not get the job done." The instructors decided to swap boat crew leaders between II and IV. The boat IV team, with its new leader, won the very next race, barely beating out boat II. Boat IV then went on to win the majority of the races of that evolution. By swapping leaders everything changed for boat IV—gone was the blaming, the fighting, and the losing. What do Willink and Babin have to say about this miraculous turnaround? "It was a glaring, undeniable example of one of the most fundamental and important truths of *Extreme Ownership*: there are no bad teams, only bad leaders."

Make a Call—Find a Way

There is an incredibly tense scene in the movie *Master and Commander* in which the grizzled crew of an 1805 British warship stares at an uncertain young naval officer, awaiting his command. The seconds creep by as the crew begins to grumble, until finally the young officer's colleague whispers emphatically, "For God's sake, make a decision!" Things did not turn out well in the movie for the indecisive officer,[4] and while this example is a bit extreme, it does make two critical points:

- It is not easy to be a leader.
- There are times when a leader has to make a tough decision.

You don't have to be perfect; you don't have to have all the answers. Sometimes you are going to be wrong. We all are at one time or another. But that does not absolve you of the responsibility for finding a way forward for the team. That's what leaders do. Absolutely engage your team; seek input from others; do your homework, build consensus if you can, but make the call. If you don't, people will soon be looking for leadership elsewhere. In the next section we will share the story of a chief engineer who demonstrated the courage of his well-thought-out convictions and made the right call for his program.

Leading the 747   Joe Sutter humbly claims he was asked to lead the development of the Boeing 747 and change the world of commercial aviation "because I was in the right place at the right time."[5] Sutter had innumerable problems to solve and incredibly difficult decisions to make in the creation of what many people thought was an impossible product.

One of the first challenges Sutter faced involved the fuselage architecture of this mammoth plane. The assumption going in was that it would be a narrow, two-story airplane. But with billions of dollars at stake and hundreds of engineers chomping at the bit to get started, Sutter continued to study the problem. The more he looked at it, the more it made sense to make a wide-body aircraft. When he approached Boeing senior leadership with this idea, he was told that Juan Trippe, the autocratic leader of Pan Am, Boeing's largest customer by far, was set on a narrow, two-story product and would accept nothing else. Boeing knew from previous dealings with Trippe that it was a very bad idea to cross him. But Sutter stuck to his guns and went to Pan Am headquarters to meet with Trippe and his engineering team. After a very difficult meeting, Sutter was given the okay to build a scale model of the wide-body version. After walking through the model, Pan Am engineers and Trippe agreed that it was the right way to go and said so. From that point on, it was truly Sutter's program. Because he studied the situation, made a call, and found a way forward, he was recognized as the real leader of the program from then on.

But just because he was recognized as the leader did not mean that Sutter would go unchallenged for the rest of the program. Another major challenge came from inside the company.

Boeing was going through difficult financial times, and Sutter was directed by his boss to cut 1,000 engineers from the program. Sutter asked, "How many weeks can we slide the schedule?" "None" was the answer. At that point, he had about 4,500 people on the program, 2,700 of whom were engineers. He went back to his team and asked each of his area leads to look at what reductions they could make. As he expected, they all returned with the same answer—zero.

Sutter had several meetings with his boss to explain that he could not make the cuts and still deliver the program, but he was ignored. Sutter was "invited" to a meeting with the company chairman and figured, "Well, I guess today is as good as any day to get fired." The chairman strode briskly into the room, announcing that he was already late to catch a flight. Sutter began his presentation, but instead of showing how he would cut 1,000 engineers, he demonstrated how he actually needed 800 more to hold the deadline. His boss blurted out, "You're not going to get more engineers!" Sutter responded, "I know, but I wanted you to know why we are working so much overtime." The room fell silent. Then the chairman abruptly stood up and walked out of the room. Next, one by one, the other executives departed. Sutter figured it was curtains for him. But after two weeks of not hearing anything, he thought, "No news is good news," and he continued to lead a successful program. He never got fired.

Emotional Resilience

Newsflash: Things are going to go wrong. You are going to screw up, and so is your team. Bad stuff is going to happen that is out of your control, including some questionable senior management decisions. It's guaranteed. The only question is, how are you going to deal with it?

Difficult times are not new in history for any leader trying to accomplish something major under pressure. More than 2,000 years ago, the Greek Stoic philosopher Epictetus said, "It's not what happens to you, but how you react that matters." We love the term *grit* to describe this personal characteristic. Grit is the ability to persist through the toughest obstacles (internal and external) and drive to accomplish your goal. It is a no-excuses approach to achieving an objective, and it may be more important to success than talent.

Often it can be a matter of framing the situation. How you characterize a difficult situation can have a major impact on how you react to it: Is it an opportunity to learn and grow, or is it the end of the world? It's up to you. But when you are in a position of leadership, how you react and the decision you make impacts the whole team. People take their cue from the leader. Confidence and resilience are contagious, and so is their absence.

Through the most difficult times in U.S. automotive history, Mulally maintained his composure and kept the company focused on delivering the plan—the most exciting cars in the industry. The engineering of these products was not in his direct control, but he made the commitment. He was investing in the future—not retreating, shrinking the organization, or demanding across-the-board cost reductions. While the press was putting the finishing touches on Ford's obituary, he remained calm, confident, and available. He never sugarcoated the situation, but neither did he over-react to it. He believed in his vision, and it was contagious.

Toward the end of January 2009, shortly after Mulally had famously declined a government bailout, Ford posted a $14.8 billion loss. To make matters even worse, the bankruptcy of Lehman Brothers had disintegrated $900 million of Ford liquidity, and several other banks critical to Ford were hanging on by a thread. This forced Ford to call on its revolving credit line while it still existed in order to continue operations. This was it, the last financial trick in the bag, and everyone knew it.

Mulally and his team took a collective deep breath and scrutinized the data. There was a bit of good news hiding there: Ford's market share had grown, which supported its product focus, and the cash burn rate was steadily declining as a result of rigorous, product development improvement initiatives. The conclusion was to stick to the plan. In fact, accelerate it.

Consequently, on a conference call with analysts and reporters announc-ing the staggering 2008 loss, Mulally said, "Ford has sufficient liquidity to make it through this global downturn and maintain our current product plans without the need for government bridge loans."[6]

At one of Jim's all-hands meetings at Ford, Mulally relayed a story from that tense period. A member of Mulally's staff had walked into his office, first thing in the morning, to find him squeezing a small foam ball. "Oh no," she exclaimed. "If you're nervous, it must really be time to worry." Mulally laughed and said, "No. I just tweaked my wrist playing tennis last night."

Both inside and outside the organization, people take their cues from the leader. The leader's resilience provides stability for the team—people depend on it, especially during difficult times.

Authenticity

We can all grow, evolve, and improve, and we should. But it steals way too much energy to try to be someone you are not. The pretense typically can't be kept up, and people will figure it out sooner or later anyway. And when they do, the mutual trust so important to that relationship becomes just that much more elusive. We think leaders are better off to maintain an honest and open relationship with their team. Do what you say, admit your mistakes, and lead the best way you know how. Another lesson from Mulally's time at Ford might help.

In an industry where many senior executives prided themselves on their expensive, custom-tailored suits and sported exclusive watches or purses, you can imagine the reaction to Mulally showing up in a blue blazer and gray pants. His use of words like *cool* and *neat* likely did not improve early impressions among his peers.[7] And initially his habit of hugging, drawing smiling airplanes, or putting your name in a heart was admittedly a bit disconcerting. It was kind of difficult to determine if he was for real.

But over time his approach to leadership not only proved to be authentic; it was absolutely infectious. His behavior demonstrated the same transparency and love for people that he expected from everyone on his leadership team. And many of those leaders grew from the experience.

So, was Mulally all smiling jumbo jets? Of course not. He also possessed a remarkable level of determination and drive to achieve, and it came out in many ways. He would ask leaders for "a better plan" or suggest that some would "flourish elsewhere." His "tough love" sometimes seemed like an understatement given his intensity. But his approach was, we believe, a sincere and honest expression of his energy, enthusiasm, and priorities. It was who he was, it had worked for him through many years, and he was not about to change for the auto exec crowd. And his team loved him for it.

Schilling sees it the same way when he is recruiting new leaders: "They feel authentic to you. That's a really important trait. The technical stuff can be taught, but the aspects of things that people must learn in their childhood. . . . oftentimes only a portion of those can be taught."

Personal Health Management

This may be an underappreciated aspect of leadership. It might not even occur to those who have not been through a difficult transformation. But leading a team through a difficult program or organizational transformation requires a great deal of personal energy. Part of managing your energy is taking care of your health. Getting enough sleep, no matter the time zone; eating well; and making time to exercise are fundamental to delivering your best as a leader.

Living an integrated life in which you can express your personal values through your work and have some balance in your personal life is healthy for you and those around you. Pausing to reflect on how you are spending your time and energy represents who you are and where you want to go. And finally, engaging in work that you are passionate about, work that matters, will actually energize instead of drain you. That is also why a good fit is so important between the individual and the organization.

Leadership Roles in Product Development

While there are similarities in the work of leaders at every level, their specific contributions depend on their roles in the organization. In this section we will focus on how senior leaders create an environment to increase their teams' chances for success; the efficacy of functional centers of excellence in delivering competitive advantage; and the unique role of the chief engineer.

Senior Leaders

Senior leaders, especially CEOs, have wide-ranging responsibilities, and a complete discussion of their role is well beyond the scope of this book. We will limit our comments to addressing their role in new product creation. That being said, we believe that new product development should be a top priority for any CEO. As Mulally said, "The work of the CEO is holding yourself and the team accountable for a viable plan to profitably grow the organization based on products and services people want, value, and will pay for, and improving your quality and your efficiency every year forever."

Create a Context for Success   In any moderate-sized organization, senior leaders typically do not directly add value in product development. They are not designing things. But senior leaders have great influence on the organizational context. We propose that senior leaders contribute to great product creation in three fundamental ways:

- Creating a culture for success
- Developing and deploying an organizational strategy

- Establishing an operating system to power the organization forward toward its goals

Create Culture   Senior leaders have a dramatic impact on culture. They directly affect organizational culture both by the behaviors they demonstrate and tolerate and by the people they choose to be part of their leadership team. All eyes are on them, and whether they realize it or not, they set the tone for and influence what the organization is going to be about.

Akio Toyoda's call for the Toyota organization to create "ever better cars" establishes product development as the No. 1 priority for the organization. It rallies the entire organization around delivering ever-greater value to customers through the products Toyota creates, and it clearly establishes the guiding priority for the company.

Toyoda is walking the talk and leading by example. He races cars. He often shows up at dealerships and helps repair cars. And when there has been a weak point in the company, he takes direct leadership, such as leading a new Lexus business unit and leading a new electric car division when Toyota, a bit belatedly, realized how rapidly the electric car market was growing. His modeling of the desired culture brought Toyota's far-flung organization together in a powerful way. During the research for this book, no matter where in the world we went or what department we encountered, we saw Toyota people contributing to ever-better products. Then we saw the results appearing in the very dramatic way that new vehicles were launched on the TNGA platform.

Provide Strategic Direction   Senior leaders create and communicate the strategy and key objectives for the organization. Hoshin kanri and Mulally's business plan review process are both proven methods to deploy and execute a company's strategy. Product should be a major component of this strategy. It either guides or establishes the organization's product portfolio, cycle plan, and product execution strategy. Senior leaders are the front line of defense against stagnation. They must keep the organization focused moving forward.

To do this, senior leaders need to be able to put the pieces together to help all those in their organization see the big picture and how they can contribute. Schilling is constantly monitoring the environment at Schilling Robotics, thinking about the long-term implications of what he sees and their impact on product decisions:

I work really hard to connect the dots, to go through the "If this happened, then this one or two outcomes are likely, this could happen, and then that could happen." It's thinking about the consequences as deeply as you can. I've had experiences in my career when some innocuous thing that happened three months ago has now matured to a nearly fatal set of circumstances. Some people describe success as thinking as many moves in the future as possible.

That's what I really liked about the set-based design approach. I've experienced far too many times in my career that people will fall in love with a concept early and then spend the rest of its development with the concept on life support, trying to salvage a bad idea.

Schilling also finds that today's instantaneous communication and access to information creates an ultra-noisy environment that can become deafening, and thus can prevent executives from identifying potentially fatal outcomes that are a mile away but rapidly approaching. When they finally break through the noise, it's too late. An overbooked CEO with a full calendar further contributes to such noise, and "that just terrifies me."

Establish an Effective Operating System   Senior leaders can't just continually raise the bar. They must also establish and constantly improve the operating system that enables their organizations to be successful. This is the framework in which the organization must do its work. (We will talk more specifically about the role of the operating system later in the chapter.) It's the integrated set of management and work patterns that guides the organization toward its objectives in order to accomplish its mission. It is an execution system that makes the strategy a reality.

An operating system creates a cadence of regularly occurring management activities instead of episodic management interventions. A good operating system enables leaders by providing a framework and routine for engagement, understanding, and execution. Schilling said, "Helping the company find a direction is an important piece. But maybe even more important is fueling the will to actually arrive at the destination. In my estimation, what you really need to put all your energy and all of your obsession around is reaching the destination. . . . Actually, arriving is what separates the winners from the losers, not that they magically picked 'the correct destination.'" It is senior leadership's responsibility to create an operating system that helps the organization reach the destination and be most successful.

Centers of Functional Excellence

Our friend Scott Tobin, director of Lincoln product development at Ford, used to say that "functional engineering directors labored below deck in the engine room." While they may not receive the level of public recognition that a CEO or chief engineer does, they get the core value-added work done. Whether leading software engineering, electrical engineering, manufacturing engineering, or some other discipline, these leaders are responsible for creating centers of excellence (CoEs) that become a source of competitive advantage in the creation of great products for the enterprise.

If the CE is responsible for determining "what" the product needs to be, it is the functional leaders who determine "how" to achieve the objective within their specialty. They provide critical guidance to the CE within their areas of expertise and should have the power to say no to the CE if it is in the best interest of the product. While most LPPD writing has focused on the importance of the CE, each CoE leader has a critical role to play in the success of your company's products. In a successful product matrix organization, functional CoE leaders are responsible for three things:

- **Achieving functional excellence.** CoE leaders contribute to the organization by building a team that is the very best at what it does. To do this, these leaders must be the ultimate learning organization—extracting, creating, and applying knowledge across all product programs. They learn from internal product programs as well as from the outside environment, and they are able to turn that learning into demonstrated capability that shows up in products. They pursue the state of the art within their discipline, thoroughly understand competitor capability, and continually challenge "the art of the possible" for the sake of creating ever-greater value for their customers through the products to which they contribute.

  This responsibility extends the length of their value stream and includes working with suppliers within their discipline. CoE leaders are responsible for developing, applying, and constantly improving standards for their area. They are also accountable for developing the long-term strategy for their area of responsibility to help ensure that the enterprise remains fully competitive within that functional capability. When Ford executives made the bold decision to build an all-aluminum F-Series truck, it was the decades of functional learning in how to design, stamp, and assemble aluminum bodies that made this a reality.

- **Developing exceptional engineers.** CoE leaders are responsible for hiring and developing engineers and specialists within their area of expertise. Your people are the key to creating a sustainable competitive advantage, and this is where it begins. The CoE leaders are responsible for the growth and career paths of the majority of the people who do the hands-on development work on new products. We have already talked about the importance as well as some methods of people development. It is not always a matter of hiring talent, but rather hiring for fit and growing talent. Managing talent at the functional level is a critical and fundamental responsibility of the CoE leadership team. As we saw in Chapter 4, senior leaders at Toyota actually teach courses in their area of specialty for junior engineers.

- **Making product programs successful.** The first two areas of responsibility only matter to the degree that they make products better and product programs more successful. The customers do not care if you are the best at any particular discipline or how good your engineers are, except if it means providing them with a better solution to their problem. CoE leaders work with the CE to develop the "how" part of the concept paper, they assign the appropriate resources to support program content, and they deliver on quality, attribute performance, cost, and schedule commitments in order to make the program a success. While there is almost always creative tension between CoE and program leadership, it is a conflict of ideas, not people, and it is focused on making the product better.

The Chief Engineer—Leading the Creation of New Value for Customers

The chief engineer has received the lion's share of attention in LPPD literature, including our last book,[8] and rightly so. He or she is the person who is ultimately responsible for the success of the product—*every* aspect of the product. And with very few people who report directly to the CE, it is a true test of leadership ability. Jim's old Ford colleague Hau Tai Tang, who at the time of this writing is the EVP of product development and purchasing for Ford, calls it "the ultimate stand-and-deliver job."

Depending on program scale, CEs typically lead a small group that includes a lead for finance, marketing, and each of the major CoEs, as well as a program manager who is responsible for managing the development program. They may also have an assistant chief engineer on their team, who could be responsible for regionalization on a global program or some other critical product attribute, such as a new technology. It is the CE's vision, passion, and energy that drive the entire program forward. While a CE can certainly escalate issues if required, all those we spoke with at Ford and Toyota said that they would consider the need to escalate a problem a personal failure. To do that would undermine their leadership—and probably mean that either an idea was not good enough or they did not do a good enough job explaining it. It's on them—no excuses.

Despite the attention we and others have given to the CE role, many companies are hesitant to try it. Some realistically observe that they have not developed people who are capable of being successful in that role. Others have an established system that relies on program managers, who focus on cost and timing and fear out-of-control costs should a CE dream up new lavish product features that cause delays and run over budget. Some even object to the name. They don't believe that anyone called "engineer" can possibly lead all aspects of a product program, and prefer technical leads who report to business-minded program managers.

These are all legitimate concerns in organizations that have not developed the unique leaders who have the right blend of deep customer understanding, systems engineering capability, and business sense. Toyota started the automotive business with the role of CE. The company recruited from the aerospace industry where CEs were standard practice. It is clearly harder to incorporate this role for companies that have not spent the decades Toyota has in growing people for it. Yet we have seen companies that did not start out with these special leaders persevere, and they worked both to develop qualified people for the position and to create an environment in which they can be successful. In each and every case, we witnessed step-function improvements over their previous development-by-committee approach. With the endless reviews, constant oversight, and focus on compromise, maybe nothing really stupid will happen without a CE—but neither is anything truly brilliant likely to occur. Developing CEs is challenging but worth the effort. So how does an organization that does not have this role select and develop people for such an important position?

Selecting CE Candidates   Based on our discussions with successful chief engineers and senior leaders of organizations who have invested in this as a new role, we have accumulated a set of broad criteria to consider as you select potential candidates for such a role:

- **Passion.** They have a burning desire to lead the creation of great products. Passion was the universal attribute identified by just about everyone with whom we spoke. In fact, several CEs said that passion was the single most important characteristic for a successful chief and that lack of passion was an automatic disqualifier. Ford's Pericak said he could determine this most important trait within a few minutes of meeting someone. Toyota's Akihiro Wada, former executive vice president responsible for engineering and product development, went a step further, saying, "You can tell whether an individual is ready to be a Chief Engineer by looking at their face."[9] This passion will carry the CE through many difficulties.

- **Learner.** CEs are fast and effective learners. It is very likely that they will not know everything they need to know going into the project. Consequently, the ability to learn as they go is important.

- **Big-picture thinker.** They have the ability to put the pieces together. Good ones can "connect the dots" to see the whole. They understand how all the pieces fit together to create value. This enables good trade-off decisions.

- **Communicator.** They are excellent and inclusive communicators. The ability to share their vision and effectively communicate to a diverse team of specialists is fundamental to their success.

- **Technical understanding.** They possess a strong technical acumen. They do not have to be a technical wunderkind or super-engineer, but they should have sufficient mastery to understand the product or process they are developing.

- **Player.** They understand the company's informal systems. They just know how to get things done.

- **Resolute.** They possess an especially high level of grit. They are tenacious and not easily deterred in the completion of their mission. We are not saying achieve objectives at all costs, but being a CE is a tough job and the fainthearted need not apply.

Developing CEs Developing CEs is not easy. We have found that a process that puts candidates in increasingly challenging and cross-functional leadership roles can be very effective.

For example, at Ford a CE candidate would spend sufficient time in a functional organization to develop proficiency and might then become that function's single point of contact for a specific program. In that role (called an "integration manager" at Ford), the candidate would need to integrate the various subsystems within a given function and represent it to the overall product team. In body and stamping engineering, integration managers were responsible for the vehicle program's subsystems, such as body structures, mechanisms, trim, lighting, glass, and stamping. An advancing candidate then might take on a program manager role, working directly for the CE, coordinating the work of all the functional groups, and being responsible for project delivery. The program manager is a key member of the CE's team and gains a deeper understanding of how the program is run. Finally, a candidate could take on a role as the assistant CE, which is focused on a specific aspect of product delivery (e.g., leading the regionalization of a product for a given country or region). This is also the typical career path for a Toyota CE.

We know of no guaranteed methods for developing CEs, and many people will self-select out as they progress through these roles. However, we see this process as a necessary investment in what might be the most important leadership role in product and process development. Toyota also has a chief production engineer role for developing processes and launching new products. Like the CE role, the job is very difficult and definitely not for everyone. Our recommendations are aimed at improving your chances for success. But the success of the position is not only up to the individuals and their preparation. Often overlooked is creating the right environmental context for success.

Creating the Context for Success Even the best CEs can be defeated by an ineffective operating system or dysfunctional culture. The CE represents the customer, and his or her success should be the goal of the entire organization. Please consider this carefully: This does not mean rolling over and saying yes to the CE on every matter. Neither does it mean always pushing all decisions to that role. What it does mean is doing everything you can to make the CE and his or her program a success and sharing fully in that responsibility.

The organizational focus needs to be on making the horizontal value streams—the product programs and therefore the CE—successful. This priority should be reflected in your operating system and your leadership behaviors throughout the organization. This was made quite clear during the Ford transformation. A poor-performing CE was never an excuse for an unsuccessful product. Not all CEs were superstars, especially in the early days. Some truly struggled with the role. Sometimes these struggles led to indecision and changing priorities that threatened to impact a function's ability to deliver. Yet all knew that these issues would eventually be addressed and were never an excuse for not delivering on functional commitments to the program. Because in the end, the focus was on the customer and the creation of great products and services that deliver value to that customer.

Here are five suggestions to help create a supportive environment for CEs:

- Allow CEs to focus on their products and do not overburden them with major people-development responsibilities. That is the responsibility of the functional leaders. However, always solicit their input on the people that contribute to their program.
- Establish your most important team metrics based on product success.
- Build "CE-centric" tools and methods into your development process. The concept paper, kickoff meetings, and CE reviews are examples.
- Create CE-centric senior leader forums within your operating system to promote a product-first focus.
- Groom some of your best people for the CE role and provide appropriate recognition.

Extending the CE Leadership Model   "The chief engineer's reward for a successful product is that he gets to do it again" is something we heard often at Toyota in our earlier research, and it makes a great deal of sense. Leading a product's development through multiple generations can lead to deep and profound knowledge of who the product's customer is and how the product delivers very specific value to that customer. This provides the CE with powerful insights that can result in class-leading products. Toyota has certainly used this strategy to great effect over the years.

But consider an additional perspective. The CE also can be an exceptional developmental role for prospective senior leaders: CEs are responsible for every aspect of the product (design, engineering, manufacturing, finance, marketing, etc.). This unique perspective is difficult to get in other roles. The role also requires that they lead specialists in these functions, who almost certainly know more about their individual specialty than the CEs do, which encourages them to be collaborative and focus on a team objective. It is a true test of leadership.

Pericak, who led the very successful 2015 Mustang development, went on to lead the Ford Performance business, responsible for Ford's specialty products (GT40, Mustang Shelby Cobra, Focus ST, and Raptor, as well as Ford racing teams, aftermarket products, and clothing). He is essentially running a very large, global business. He believes the skills he developed as a CE are 100 percent transferable to his new role. "As long as you don't think you're the smartest guy in the room, you will be just fine," he advised. "People want someone with a vision and focus, with tenacity, and someone who will make a decision. They want a leader who knows how to get the best out of all the experience and ability in the team."

Mulally started out as an aerospace engineer, led the development of the cockpit and flight management systems on the Boeing 757 and 767, and was eventually the CE for development of the 777. Those experiences helped him save Boeing Commercial after the 9/11 disaster as well as orchestrate Ford's historic turnaround. He said, "I used the same principles of skilled, motivated teams, and the working-together principles and practices" for each of those leadership challenges. "Designing is creating something out of nothing that enhances people's lives and has value; balancing hundreds of objectives and doing that on a timetable; delivering a commitment; employing hundreds of thousands of people; and doing it by working together. That is the essence, whether they're small programs or projects or whether they're big ones, whether it's being the CEO of commercial airplanes or CEO of Ford, in my mind it is program product management."

We are not advocating that the CE role become merely a step on the career path to "greater things." In fact, many excellent CEs are a better fit for and by far prefer to stay in that role. Kelly Johnson, the famed aeronautical and systems engineer at Lockheed, reportedly turned down promotion from CE to vice president multiple times because he feared being too far removed from his passion; he eventually acquiesced.[10] We also caution companies about promoting CEs too soon. Our point is that the characteristics that make people successful in the CE role and the skills they develop while in that role can also make them successful in more senior leadership positions.

Creating a Management System (LB x OS = MS)

Research that looked at the management practices and performance of 12,000 firms across 34 different countries reveals that management and operational excellence are a competitive advantage: "If you look at the data, it becomes clear that core management practices can't be taken for granted. . . . Firms with strong managerial processes perform significantly better on high-level metrics such as productivity, profitability, growth, and longevity. In addition, the differences in the quality of these processes—and in performance—persist over time, suggesting that competent management is not easy to replicate." The authors behind the research further note, "Achieving managerial competence takes effort, though: It requires sizable investments in people and processes throughout good times and bad. These investments, we argue, represent a major barrier to imitation."[11] We agree. Time and again we have seen companies that struggle to create an effective management system pay the price in their performance.

Although the term *management system* is used in different ways, we believe a management system is the product of two elements: leadership behaviors and an operating system (LB × OS = MS). If either multiplying factor is weak, then the resulting product is weakened. Leadership behaviors and your operating system are interdependent. There is no operating system you can possibly devise that can compensate for incompetent leadership, and of course, as W. Edwards Deming said, "A bad [operating] system will beat a good person every time." A strong management system requires you to strengthen both elements. We have talked a great deal so far about leadership behaviors in this book. And while they are crucial to success, they are only part of the story. Leaders energize and bring life to a management system, and an effective operating system can focus and magnify leadership effectiveness just as a poor one can diminish it. So, what is an operating system?

Operating System and Its Characteristics

An operating system is made up of the tools, processes, standard work, cadenced activities, and other mechanisms that enable the work to get done. If a leader is the craftsperson, then the operating system is his or her collection of tools. But a good operating system is far more than the sum of its parts.

An effective operating system moves an organization toward its objectives in order to accomplish its mission. It creates a cadence of regularly occurring management activities instead of episodic management interventions. It is a single, integrated system, not a hodgepodge of departmental plans that do not hang together. It is transparent, has multilevels, and cascades throughout the organization. It establishes objectives, allocates resources, and provides clear, aligned roles and responsibilities in order to deliver the plan. It provides the structure that enables (or inhibits) people to do their work. It knits together and drives critical value-creating activities, such as strategy deployment, continuous improvement, new product delivery, people development and working environment, manufacturing, and supply chain. Finally, the operating system provides its own performance feedback on how you are doing.

An effective operating system helps brings strategy to life. It synchronizes critical activities, enables the organization to respond quickly to a changing environment, and allows plans and teams to move together. And when executed with discipline and coupled with effective leadership behaviors, it provides a tremendous competitive advantage for any organization.

An operating system should accomplish six basic things:

- Deploy your organizational strategy, align your organization, and allocate resources to ensure success.

- Drive the creation of new value through products and services that your customers truly value.

- Support daily operations, providing support for the basic work of the organization.

- Develop people and create a great work environment. This should be designed such that it provides a competitive advantage for years to come.

- Provide ongoing system-performance feedback and enable continuous improvement. The system should have a built-in improvement and course-correction capability.

- Create a framework for manager standard work. This framework should provide a disciplined cadence of management activities (daily, weekly, monthly, quarterly) that organizes leaders' work and enhances their effectiveness.

A System to Create Focus

Companies often talk about how their latest initiative will create greater "organizational synergy"; however, the result is often nearer to "organizational antagonism," where the performance of the whole does not equal anything near the sum of talent of its individuals. Well-intentioned leaders add new initiatives in the hope of tapping into unused human potential, but they then find themselves facing greater entropy because of the increased chaos that the initiative creates in the system.[12]

This was certainly the case when Mulally arrived at Ford in 2006. As described at the beginning of the book, in "Ford's Historical Turnaround," there was no shortage of initiatives to improve organizational performance. There were programs to design for manufacturing, programs to bring in the voice of the customer, programs to integrate suppliers, and on and on. Programs were simply layered one on another, all competing for precious time and resources. Unfortunately these chaotic initiatives served primarily to create organizational drag, squandered resources, and cynical people. So, what was the problem? In large part, it was a lack of both organizational focus and a common operating system to align the company.

And we don't believe lack of organizational focus to be an unusual problem. Stanford professor Jeff Pfeffer explains, "Companies have managed to convince themselves that, since what gets measured is what gets done, the more they measure, the more stuff will get done." He shared a conversation he had with a woman who works for a large oil company who had 105 metrics for which she was responsible. How many did she actually pay attention to? Her answer was zero. It was just too overwhelming. And this behavior has led Professor Pfeffer to what he calls his "Otis Redding Theory of Measurement," which is named for Redding's song "Sitting on the Dock of the Bay." In the song, Redding sings, "I can't do what ten people tell me to do, so I guess I'll remain the same."[13] When faced with too much, people will inevitably do too little or nothing.

We believe that the focus created by Alan's working-together management system and the focus it created was one of the most important elements of Ford's turnaround. With its disciplined cadence, it clarified priorities and focused initiatives, leveraging their interdependencies toward a common set of goals. And perhaps most importantly, it enrolled everyone in the effort.

A System to Highlight Abnormalities for Quick Response

While an operating system provides higher-level portfolio planning, prioritization, and resource allocation, it must also create mechanisms and practices that provide team members with an ability to distinguish abnormal from normal conditions, to communicate abnormal conditions effectively, and to respond to these conditions consistently and effectively.

Distinguish Abnormal from Normal   Solving problems, mitigating risk, and closing knowledge gaps are a fundamental part of development work, so much so that developers often have difficulty distinguishing normal from abnormal situations. Consequently, development teams must have a method for understanding where they are relative to a performance standard. Are they where they need to be at a given point in the project to have a high likelihood of success?

Engineers often don't surface problems "early" because they are not completely sure when "early" is. They have no model with which to compare. We don't advocate embedding hundreds of requirements in your project management standards; in fact, too many requirements (if they are read at all) usually detract from a developer's ability to distinguish the truly critical criteria. We recommend scalable guidelines that provide developers with acceptable risk profiles over time (i.e., the acceptable number of open issues at each milestone, along with corresponding severity levels); cadenced knowledge-gap closure (i.e., the acceptable percentage of product design completion at each gate); and a focus on synchronized solution convergence across functions (i.e., time-bound input-output requirements across functions). Milestone quality requirements, such as attribute (cost, quality, performance), achievement glide paths, and issue/knowledge-gap closure charts are all useful.

Effectively Communicate Abnormal Conditions   Once you have established critical criteria, you have to have a way to make abnormal conditions visible to critical participants in the development system. In lean manufacturing this is accomplished with *andon*. It is the warning— e.g., flashing light, sound—that calls a team's attention to an issue on production. Think of this step as creating a development andon system. Obeya visual management and associated "dashboard strategies" that contain the vital few indicators are a few of the most powerful ways to accomplish this. Daily or weekly reviews of these key indicators provide team members the opportunity to "pull the andon" and request help. And while milestone quality requirements are important, the best obeya management systems focus on "leading indicators" prior to major milestones. If you wait until the milestone, you are likely to impact a larger portion of the program, since milestones also serve as key integration points. The idea is to identify a potential issue early enough that it can be resolved prior to affecting the entire program.

It is, of course, not enough to make abnormal conditions visible, just like it is not enough to just detect a land mine; you have to defuse or avoid it. Most engineers hesitate to raise problems because they have no realistic expectation that they will get the support they need to deal with them. Just imagine if there were no response to andon on a production line. How long do you think people would continue to pull the cord?

Respond Consistently and Effectively   Perhaps the most important part of that management system is a response to the andon that actually feels like help to the team. This does not include increasing report-outs to management. Rather, it should focus on the development team and making the team successful.

When teams need help—when they themselves admit they need help or when it's obvious—one response is to link their awareness of abnormal conditions to the cadence of recurring events within the operating system; these events are designed to respond to such conditions and provide rapid support. For example, regular cross-functional leadership reviews on cost, quality, or technical issues present opportunities for the teams to escalate issues that are beyond their scope of control. A tightly synchronized operating system should provide your development teams with the best possible chance of success, especially when problems arise.

Obeya Management System   Throughout this book, we have talked a great deal about the obeya management system for effective program management. While it was originally developed for the delivery of product and process programs, we have seen it used successfully in a number of other applications. Obeya meetings act as "superchargers" to align participants, build team momentum and confidence, and continually move the program forward. In between events, the obeya area serves as a central hub where subgroups gather to share information and study the progress of other areas.

The obeya system extends leadership effectiveness and provides a forum in which to demonstrate best leadership behaviors. The obeya management system creates a disciplined cadence and a high level of transparency for the entire team, which leads to much greater inclusiveness and collaboration, improved problem solving, and faster and better decision making. Because of this, the system has not only proved effective for product and process development teams; it has also proved effective as a senior or functional management enabler and as a continuous improvement center, and as well, it provides support for specific task force–type efforts. We have created, used, and helped other companies adopt this powerful system in a wide variety of industries, including healthcare, automotive, consumer electronics, heavy equipment, robotics services, aerospace, and others. Perhaps it is a system you might consider?

The Issue of Fit

It is worth repeating: in order to reap the benefits of an effective management system, it is important that the operating system and leadership behaviors be aligned and consistent. For example, the operating system elements of obeya and A3 are exceptionally effective in promoting transparency, problem solving, and collaboration. But if leaders "do not want to hear problems," attack people who surface issues, or don't actually use the tools or collaborate with their colleagues, the tools will be worthless. If you install an operating system that includes annual strategy deployment and a cadenced review process to promote focus, but leaders continually chase after the next shiny object, what's the use? Well, you get it. Both your operating system and leadership capability should be continually and intentionally nurtured and evolved such that they are mutually reinforcing and always improving.

LOOKING FORWARD

Great leadership matters, and it does not happen by accident. Teams with effective leaders do better whether it is a seven-person boat crew or a corporation made up of hundreds of thousands. It is not easy to be a good leader. Organizations and individuals need to invest significant effort and resources into intentionally nurturing characteristics and developing skills. Leadership behaviors coupled with an effective operating system can create a powerful management system that consistently moves the organization toward its objectives. For a product development organization, the objective is, ultimately, great products.

Leaders do not work in a vacuum. Another way to visualize the role of leaders is to consider the context in which they operate. The leaders sell a vision that is aligned with the strategic direction of the company. Their vision is only as good as the strategy established by more senior leaders. The leaders of a development project depend on all the functional organizations to deliver highly trained people who are highly customer focused. They work within an established system of roles and responsibilities and the operating system we have discussed here. They can contribute to a learning culture, but the culture needs to be established as a context for each individual development program.

In the next chapter, we will focus on building a learning culture. What do we mean by a learning culture? How do we create a supportive environment for learning? How do we develop people who have the skills and mindset to continually learn?

Your Reflection

Creating a Vision

We have identified from our experience key characteristics of highly effective leaders. They:

- Are humble
- Walk the talk
- Give unpretentious and constructive feedback
- Put other people and the team first
- Build a single aligned team
- Have respect for every person
- Are persistent and determined to achieve every objective
- Have emotional resilience
- Are authentic
- Are physically and mentally healthy
- Have clear roles and responsibilities, including the chief engineer's role
- Create a context for success
- Create and sustain a management operating system

We could go on and list dozens more characteristics, but so can our readers. How would you revise these characteristics of effective leaders to better fit your company's situation?

Your Current Condition

1. Who is ultimately responsible for the success of your new products? What are you doing to ensure that your organization rallies around that person to achieve highly successful products?

2. How do you clarify the leader's roles and responsibilities in the development of new products and services?

3. How much time and effort are you putting into identifying and developing your leaders? Is it sufficient?

4. To what degree do your leaders epitomize the desired characteristics of effective leaders? (Rate strengths on each one.)

5. How is your current operating system performing? How might it be improved? Where are gaps? Does it function seamlessly with leadership behaviors to create a powerful management system?

Taking Action

1. Select a subset of the most important leaders in product-process development in your organization. Assess these leaders against the vision you developed for highly effective leaders, and identify gaps for each individual.

2. What actions can be taken and support offered to close the gaps? For example, does your operating system lack the review structure and cadence to keep leaders routinely engaged and aware of issues? Are you providing sufficient mentoring and other training in order to intentionally develop and continually improve leadership capability? Are some of the leaders in the wrong position?

6

Creating and Applying Knowledge as a Learning Organization

Learning is not compulsory . . . neither is survival.
—W. EDWARDS DEMING

Learning Challenges

It seems we have been talking about learning organizations for a long time now. Back in the mid-1980s, Dr. W. Edwards Deming urged American companies to improve their ability to learn in order to keep pace with Japanese firms, such as Toyota, which were beginning to dominate their industries. In 1990, Peter Senge's seminal book *The Fifth Discipline* introduced us to the incredible potential of becoming a true "learning organization."[1] Harvard's Chris Argyris went into even more detail in his excellent book *On Organizational Learning*, distinquishing between single-loop learning focused only on correcting deviations from an established direction, and double-loop learning that continually questions the direction.[2] In 1995, Ikujiro Nonaka concluded that the "one source of lasting competitive advantage is knowledge."[3] Takahiro Fujimoto wrote that information creation and transmission, through rapid learning cycles, is the key driver of Toyota's product development and production systems.[4] In our last book we detailed how Toyota leverages its powerful learning network to continuously improve new product quality. And countless other books and scholarly articles have identified the ability to create and apply knowledge as central to an organization's success.

Yet despite a high level of awareness and an increasingly dynamic environment, where new information is being generated at a staggering rate, most organizations we encounter have not gotten much further than creating knowledge-storage tools—a book, a database, or a wiki. In a few cases, they may have even established a reflection event at the end of a program. Nevertheless, we continue to hear the same concerns and see companies that, despite repeated efforts, have not realized anywhere near the benefit they had hoped to achieve.

In 1999, Robert Cole observed that the Japanese advantage through the 1980s was principally because of their capacity for organizational learning, whereas in the West we were better at individual learning.[5] He describes organizational learning as the process of turning individual learning into organizational routines—standards that sit above any particular individual: "The process by which we transmit and evolve organizational routines is organizational learning. We, of course, can learn good and bad things. We want, however, to define organizational learning in terms of identifying and creating best-practice work routines, standardizing these practices, diffusing them (i.e., actualizing them) throughout the organization, and then renewing the process."

Creating and applying new knowledge is the crux of product and process development excellence. It is the essence of creating new value. To become a high-performance product development organization essentially means to become effective learners. Many companies recognize this, and we are often asked about some tool or new technology that can help them to become more proficient in this area. There certainly are some tools, such as A3s, that can be helpful; however, in our experience, the struggles that most companies encounter are rarely caused by a lack of tools or technologies, but rather are rooted in more fundamental organizational issues. We have found four fairly common organizational roadblocks to effective learning:

- **There is a fear of openly sharing information.** This is the No. 1 inhibitor to becoming a learning organization. The effects of fear are multidimensional and crush learning in many ways. First, leaders with big egos are typically afraid to promote an authentic culture of inquiry for fear they will be found to be wrong, thus, somehow, bruising their ego and diminishing their authority. Second, fear for job security will cause people to hoard their knowledge. Knowledge becomes power and a way to protect a position or employment. Third, people in fear-ridden organizations spend most of their time in self-protection mode and will rarely open up about mistakes—a potent source of learning. Fear creates stress and anxiety, known to inhibit learning. Further, if these conditions are experienced over long periods of time, it can even lead to learned helplessness among employees. And really, who would want to work in such a hostile environment anyway? It sounds like the very definition of workplace hell. Consequently, the brightest and most capable people are likely to leave, further diminishing the organization's ability to learn.

- **Learning is not truly valued.** Although leaders of an organization may talk about the importance of learning, their actions frequently say, "Just deliver results now," and everyone knows it. Taking the time to learn is pushed to the back burner. There are many symptoms: Reflection events are irregular and attendance spotty. Knowledge repositories and standards are rarely used or even referenced by leaders. Time for learning and experimentation is not allocated. Knowledge-enhancing tools like checklists or A3s become check-the-box exercises. New ideas are rarely given a chance, and real experiments are all but nonexistent.

  There can be lots of reasons for these conditions. Perhaps the company is profitable and is happy to just keep plodding along. Perhaps the leaders cannot understand the value of taking the time to learn, a vague and uncertain activity compared with actions that deliver tangible results now. Perhaps they are afraid to invest in learning amid the pressure for immediate results. Whatever the case, these companies often become so stuck that they are incapable of learning and responding even to imminent threats.

- **Companies confuse talking with doing.** In a wonderful book two Stanford professors, Jeffrey Pfeffer and Robert Sutton, explain *The Knowing-Doing Gap*.[6] The gap comes when managers think that presenting, discussing, or even deciding is the same as actually doing something. So dialogue replaces action, choosing a path becomes the same as traveling it, and PowerPoint presentations usurp real change. What's worse, Pfeffer reports in a *Fast Company* article that talking can actually become more valued than doing: "Being critical is interpreted as a sign of intelligence. The fastest way for me to seem smart is to cut you down. So you come up with an idea, and I come up with a thousand reasons why that idea won't work. Now everyone sees you as dumb and me as smart—and we've created an environment where no one wants to come up with ideas."[7]

- **Learning is not seamlessly integrated into "the real work" of the organization.** This, of course, can be a result of not valuing learning, but it also can be caused by not knowing how to learn. Organizations need to actively pursue learning, explore ways to learn, and build these into their work every day. It is a skill, and like any other skill, it gets better with practice. Organizations have to learn to leverage everyday activities to promote learning and improvement. The countless problems that crop up in projects, design reviews, testing, and many other elements of development work provide rich opportunities for learning, and yet companies often fail to harness the potential of these activities.

We believe that a learning organization has a set of key features that are integral to learning, storing, and sharing critical information, shown in Table 6.1. We initially began thinking about it conceptually as an equation. Mathematically this may not make sense, but if we think of it as an equation, it is more like a product term than additive. In other words, if a company has any of these factors at zero, then it is not an effective learning organization.

Table 6.1 Learning Organization = Culture × Occasions × Scientific Thinking × Gatekeepers × Communication

Culture	Supportive culture for learning
Occasions	Opportunities for learning (e.g., design reviews, reflection, obeya)
Scientific thinking	People have developed the habit of scientific systems thinking
Gatekeepers	Technical gatekeepers of the knowledge base
Communication	Crisp, clear communication for collaboration and knowledge transfer

Supportive Culture for Learning

What is a learning culture? It can be a bit difficult to describe. Peter Senge defined a learning organization as one in which learning and capacity expand and results are continually achieved. We think a learning culture is a bit like art in that you know it when you see it—or better yet, experience it. You can feel it at Toyota, you notice it when you talk to people from Schilling Robotics, and you could sense it at Ford during the Mulally days. It is a fragile thing, and it does not happen by accident. It requires constant effort and "a constancy of purpose," to quote Deming once again. Where we have seen a learning culture, we've also noted some shared, important characteristics.

Leaders as Learners

It starts with leaders who are committed to driving fear out of the organization. We noted how Mulally required leaders to remove fear from their toolbox. That is just the start. Creating a learning culture requires that leaders lead by example, display an active intellectual curiosity, and personally work to learn and grow. Only then can they expect the same from others.

Kelly Johnson, the iconic head of the famous Lockheed Skunk Works, was a great learning leader. Ben Rich, Johnson's lead engineering manager and eventual replacement, and coauthor Leo Janos describe the dynamic and hard-driving culture of experimentation and learning that led to unprecedented levels of scientific and product breakthroughs in their amazing book *Skunk Works*.[8] Johnson insisted on a hands-on environment where engineers were located "within a stone's throw" of the physical work—an environment where ideas were tested, experimentation expected, and the art of the possible expanded on a regular basis. By all reports, Johnson had high expectations and little patience for engineers who did not "know their stuff"; however, he had even higher standards for himself and knew that learning was the key to delivering path-breaking products.

Johnson's passion for learning seems to have begun during his time as an engineering student at the University of Michigan and continued into his early days as an aeronautical engineer, when he spent vacations working out every single problem in *Aircraft Propeller Design*[9] and *Differential and*

Integral Calculus[10] so as not to lose his engineering edge.[11] He later took up flying experimental aircraft to better understand the challenges that pilots were facing and the performance of his products firsthand. He also regularly attended evening classes at Cal Tech, and later he personally set up seminars at Lockheed through Cal Tech for his engineers and managers.

Problems, Problems, and More Problems

For many real-world practitioners, it can be hard to appreciate the "joy of problems" promoted by some in the lean community. In fact, problems usually cause them an initial reaction that is the opposite of joy—if for no other reason than that they always seemed to occur at the worst possible times. Jim for one is quite sure that the problems he has experienced in product development programs have taken years off his life. That being said, problems, big and small, are an integral part of product development, and ignoring them, or, even worse, criticizing those who surface them, will make the situation much, much worse and over time have an insidious effect on organizational culture. It will create a cult of silence and sarcasm. Development leaders must get comfortable with problems and see them as a target rich opportunity for learning and improvement.

Alan Mulally often referred to them as "gems," and he insisted that Ford leaders actively mine them as opportunities for breakthroughs. And since problems are a fundamental part of product development (and business in general), it only makes sense that the better you get at learning from them, the better you get at development. So instead of ignoring or hiding them, seize them; attack them.

First, you have to create an environment where it's okay to recognize and raise problems, where it is not career-limiting to be the bearer of bad news. Mulally would say, "You may have a problem, but you are not the problem," and recognize that it is leadership's role to react with real and useful help in solving the problem—not just demands for ever more report-outs.

True learning organizations develop and employ powerful problem-solving protocols that enable them to both effectively solve and learn from problems that they inevitably face. Later in this chapter, we will talk more about how companies use A3s, design reviews, and other mechanisms to constantly improve this capability. But it all starts with establishing a culture of experimentation.

A Culture of Experimentation

One of the best countermeasures to conquer the "knowing-doing gap" is to develop a culture that thrives on experimentation, an organization where there is a bias for active learning at the gemba. Instead of endless conference room presentations and pointless arguments, you ask, "How can we understand this better? What simple experiment might we do right now to prove or disprove what we are thinking?" Imagine a culture where it's not just okay to fail, but one in which failure is considered a fundamental part of how we move forward as an organization.

By all reports, Thomas Edison's lab in Menlo Park, New Jersey, was a place like this, where ideas were constantly tested and boundaries pushed. It was a place where things blew up (both figuratively and actually) and failure was just part of the deal. It was also a place that generated an astounding number of technological breakthroughs. Menlo Innovations is also such a place. Just as it was for its namesake, experimenting is part of Menlo's DNA. In interviews for this book, Rich Sheridan, author of *Joy Inc.*[12] and cofounder and CEO of Menlo, told us, "If we are not trying new things, we aren't learning. If we are not learning, we are falling behind."

Sheridan says that to get people to try new things, you have to "pump fear out of the room and make it okay to make mistakes—to fail." It's something that the people at Menlo work at continually. "As professionals, we'd prefer not to make any mistakes at all. However, being human means that we will." This is especially true if you really experiment and stretch your capability. "At Menlo, we "accept that we will make mistakes, make them quickly, adjust based on what we have learned, and move on."

Build Learning into the Work

In the best learning cultures, the learning is so prevalent as to be inconspicuous. Rather than being made up of major bolt-on events, learning is integrated into the way the work is done every day. It is thought of as "what we do," not "something else we have to do." People openly share information, transparency is the norm, and the learning is designed in.

Learning is central to almost everything Toyota does. Whether it is in accomplishing day-to-day tasks, partnering with General Motors on NUMMI, or developing and building the Mirai to understand fuel cells, Toyota exemplifies a company in which learning is seamlessly integrated into its work.

In our last book, we talked about Toyota's incredible learning network and its impact on its product development capability. Whether it's work during the study (kentou) phase, structured problem solving, supplier technology demonstration events, checklists or a know-how database, reflection (hansei) events, or program manager conferences, learning is central to development at Toyota. And based on our recent research, this network is stronger than ever. In previous chapters, we shared numerous examples of how Toyota builds people development into the way everyone works every day. The company also seizes on every opportunity it can to build in learning.

Opportunities for Learning

Creative problem solving and innovation are incredibly important to product development capability, and in pursuit of these goals, companies often resort to extraordinary, special strategies and facilitated off-site events. While we do not necessarily oppose such events, there is a far more organic, seamless, and effective way to cultivate creativity and collaboration in your organization. And it is likely a practice that you are already doing and one that will help to create an ongoing development cadence and act as a powerful cultural transformation lever. We are talking about design reviews.

Design Reviews

Design reviews are an oft-overlooked, even maligned opportunity for real-time learning and innovation. But we are not talking about what passes for design reviews in many companies: using poor cousins of a status review, "wire-brushing" anyone who identifies issues, grilling engineers for design release dates and tool starts, and putting on a pre-milestone dog and pony show that serves primarily to give senior management a much desired—but usually false—sense of security. Most engineers' primary objective during these types of design reviews is to "get offstage" with minimal negative exposure and never violate the tacit agreement that if you don't pick on my project, I won't pick on yours.

Effective design reviews can be the heartbeat of your development project and a critical part of your overall development operating system. They provide a common link for distributed teams and are a primary mechanism for learning and doing, at program speed. Generally, we think in terms of two broad categories of design reviews:

- A *cadenced review* is used to raise and resolve technical issues in a timely manner. It provides a consistent, recurring forum with required cross-functional participants to work on the inevitable technical challenges that come with development, thus preventing the waste of engineers chasing down much-needed help.
- A *system-focused review* is scheduled in support of key integration events. It typically involves representatives from the entire development team, who focus on interfaces and interdependencies. This type of review is scheduled such that sufficient time is allowed for postreview work without disrupting the program.

Either type of design review should be challenging, rigorous, and, above all, alive and energizing. It should raise performance expectations for both the product and the team with the aim of making both better. This is not a check-the-box event; far from it. It is a demanding crucible of ideas— testing, challenging, and improving—that generates both heat and light.

Effective design reviews are not a PowerPoint show. Participants should bring only those materials they are already using in development, such as early prototypes, test data, simulation results, or CAD, with perhaps a one-page problem statement. The events themselves should be held at the gemba whenever possible—this creates a powerful dynamic in which problems are not an anomaly and real-time learning is the objective.

As discussed in Chapter 4, design reviews also should be a tremendous opportunity for people development and cultural change. They are an opportunity for leadership to evaluate both design solutions and the thinking behind them by asking probing questions and actively coaching in real time. More importantly, they are an opportunity for leadership to demonstrate the behaviors they expect from their teams, such as collaboration, experimentation, rigor, detail, and ultimate ownership. The environment is not punitive; in fact, there may be far more pressure on leadership because they have to be on their toes to quickly see opportunities for constructive probing and feedback. It is about stretching the team members and self-pressurizing to achieve more together than they ever could separately.

Although initially uncomfortable, your team will begin to thrive on these events, relishing the opportunity to engage and grow as engineers and leaders as long as leaders remember to ask tough questions, challenge ideas, and always support their people. This is not a place for individual performance reviews or finger-pointing. It is about working as a team to constantly improve in order to deliver ever-greater value to your customer.

Here are a few points you may wish to consider as you think about your next design review:

1. Actively manage the agenda and scheduling. Make sure all the right people are there for the right discussions (including subject matter experts)—and not present when they don't need to be (wasteful). Also be sure to allow sufficient time for in-depth dialogue on topics.

2. Be prepared—this applies to all participants, especially leaders. Send out critical information in advance whenever possible. Presenters should have a clear problem statement, show work to date, and explore alternative solutions (A3s can be useful for this). This is not a place to just dump a problem on the team for feedback.

3. Hold the review at the gemba whenever possible. Make sure the actual product, critical data, and CAD are available.

4. Ask probing, meaningful questions. Leaders should not play "stump the chump" to show how smart they are or just provide answers. If you choose the former, people will shut down; if you take the latter approach, you will soon find yourself owning a lot of problems.

5. Encourage robust and candid dialogue—ask the tough questions. Creative tension is an important part of creating great products. But never, ever allow attacks on people. Think about interfaces and interdependencies and where the program is in the development process.

6. Remember to "do the experiment." It's not a debate club. Ask how you can simply and effectively test a hypothesis.

7. Capture and apply knowledge. These are your learning cycles and your opportunity to enforce, update, and create standards through learning. Be sure to fully leverage existing knowledge and capture new information.

8. Make design reviews a foundational part of your overall development operating system. In larger organizations, an integrated network of design reviews may be appropriate. And participation is not optional.

9. Set high expectations for both the product and the participants. But set even higher expectations for yourself.

Leadership Learning Cycles

While engineers are busy designing, testing, learning, and capturing knowledge, their leaders should be doing the same thing. Leaders need to monitor internal progress to the plan and continually scan the external environment for changes that may impact the organization. They need to exchange this information with each other and make adjustments accordingly. These learning cycles should take place throughout the organization and be tightly linked. We will share two mechanisms for creating effective leadership learning cycles.

Obeya Learning   The obeya is the drumbeat of learning and a central hub of a program. The obeya is where people constantly update their information or get an update from the information provided by others. The walls of the obeya are filled with visual information on the current status to objective for the most critical information from the concept paper. Schedules, customer feedback, results of experiments, storyboards, attribute performance glide paths, critical tests, the latest drawings or prototypes, and other information are available to any team member at any time.

Regular meetings in the obeya are similar to design reviews, but they occur more frequently—weekly or even daily for some organizations. At each meeting, the program team reviews the overall design program, area by area, and shares updates, issues, and newly identified risks. Everyone is engaged, and everyone learns from each other, although detailed work is generally not done in the obeya meeting. Updates by each function are usually brief, focusing on areas that do not meet standards—mainly red items. Issues are assigned to an individual to resolve, often with a cross-functional team, with results reported back in future obeya meetings.

This forum for learning also helps to demonstrate the essence of an effective operating system. Because of the level of transparency, breadth of participation, and tight cadence of the learning cycle, the effect can increase asymptotically. And if you learn to utilize milestones or some other mechanism as built-in reflection events, you can create an opportunity for what Argyris called double-loop learning. Single-loop learning is like a thermostat. A standard is set and then adjustments are made to bring the process back to standard. In double-loop learning, you regularly question the standard before making it the goal for adjustment. For example, is this design going to satisfy the customer? Are we confident this is the correct tolerance? Have we missed something in the plan?

Unfortunately, some companies take a very limited approach to their visual management system. They recognize the power of getting the team together each week, but only use the obeya to manage a program's status to schedule. While this is better than hiding information on someone's computer, it misses the tremendous opportunity to learn together by including all the program deliverables. Entering the obeya space should be an immersive experience—all the latest and most important project information should be available. This is not nearly as overwhelming as it may sound at first. Remember, you should be dealing with the critical few program elements that are most important, and responsibility is shared among different team members, who provide different bits of critical information. One of the roles of the obeya is to differentiate the important information from the white noise that surrounds every program. In fact, this is one of the first things the team should learn from the obeya—what is truly important about this program.

Business Plan Review as Rapid Learning Cycles   This can be thought of as an obeya for leadership, and in fact, it may warrant its own visual planning room. The cycles should start with the most senior leader in the company. Mulally's business plan review (BPR) at Ford enabled senior leaders from each functional group and geographical organization to come together weekly and share changes in their progress to plan as well as changes in their particular external environment. If any of those changes was deemed sufficiently serious or required a deeper dive to better understand, it was directed to a special attention review (SAR), where a subset of the leadership, those particularly knowledgeable or impacted by the change, would spend additional time on the issue. The SAR teams would then report back to the larger group in the BPR as required.

The level of simplicity in reporting, transparency, and the weekly cadence of the BPR allowed the leadership team to create highly effective rapid learning cycles in minimal time. The BPR created a natural PDCA cadence and framework for the leadership team. This practice then flowed throughout the entire organization through the senior leaders, extending to all levels. By constantly learning together and adjusting as required, they were able to steer the organization through some of the most turbulent times in modern business history.

Developing People to Think and Act Scientifically and Systemically

Individual learning capability is key to organizational learning, and learning to think scientifically can enhance an individual's learning capability. It may seem strange to even mention the need to teach engineers to think scientifically. Isn't that a given, with all their training in science and innovation? Not necessarily.

By improving their scientific thinking skills, engineers and developers address inherent weaknesses in two ways and, thus, will improve their performance:

- Development engineers are often more focused on what they are designing than the work processes they use for development. Some feel that they do not need any structure. They are engineers and will just figure it out as they go. Scientific thinking about the way they do work provides structure to their process.

- Even though they are quite scientific in many aspects of development—analyzing stresses and strains, calculating, testing prototypes, and thinking creatively about alternatives, there are other instances where they tend to jump to conclusions before thinking deeply, for example, in the stage of understanding customers. Scientific thinking can be applied to the range of their activities.

Scientific thinking in lean is perhaps best represented by PDCA. Let's first consider a common but poor way of thinking about PDCA and then contrast that with a more scientific approach.

There seems to be a natural human tendency—to which engineers are not immune—to assume the world is an orderly, predictable place that we control. This is not simply wishful thinking; it is related to our evolutionary heritage where survivors were those who could win every day against hostile animals, weather, and other people. Survival was a matter of reading and reacting, not deeply analyzing and thinking. Humans had to be hyperalert, but they also had to go with their instincts about the right thing to do at any moment. This was a period that demanded fast thinking and acting and results in what we call "reactive PDCA" (Figure 6.1):

1. **Plan** the solution and implementation. This is mainly a matter of reacting quickly to the problem at hand based on your current knowledge and skills.

2. **Do** means implementation. Make it happen as quickly and efficiently as possible.

3. **Check** means confirm the results. Did we win? Is the animal dead?

4. **Act** means control. Be sure the situation is in control and wrapped up so we are ready for the next crisis.

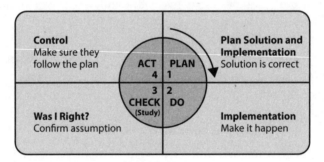

Figure 6.1   Reactive PDCA with assumed certainty.
(*Source: Modified from Mike Rother,* Toyota Kata Culture, *NY: McGraw-Hill, 2017*)

Reactive PDCA is applied in many circumstances where we assume we know what to do and how—assumed certainty. If we are right, we win. If we are wrong, oh well. Those who are right the most often may become the leaders. In poorly organized product development programs, particularly where the front end is rushed, we end up fixing bad assumptions and firefighting under pressure; many people are quite good at it and emerge as heroes.

But what happens when we are in uncharted territory and take some time for a more systematic approach? If we start with a scientific approach in the front end, including deeply understanding the customer, we are less likely to find ourselves behind schedule and in crisis mode. In this case we can follow the true intent of what we call "reflective PDCA" (Figure 6.2):

1. **Plan.** Make a specific prediction of what will happen as a result of a decision. This becomes a hypothesis, and we also plan how we will test the hypothesis.

2. **Do.** Carry out the experiment to test the hypothesis.

3. **Check.** What actually happened? Get the facts.

4. **Act.** Evaluate what happened, why, and what we learned.

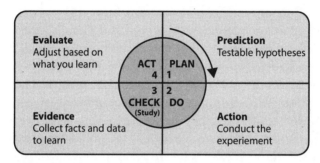

Figure 6.2   Reflective PDCA with assumed uncertainty: a scientific approach.
(*Source: Modified from Mike Rother,* Toyota Kata Culture, *NY: McGraw-Hill, 2017*)

One PDCA cycle will lead to some knowledge and some questions, which then often leads naturally to the next PDCA loop. The more rapidly we can execute a PDCA cycle, the faster we learn and the faster we get to the desired result. This is one reason Toyota likes rapid prototyping so much. A lot of the discussion of prototyping in Chapter 1 was about rapid iteration and learning by using the least complex prototype possible for the question at hand.

Reflective PDCA can be applied to the development of the product and process, beginning with understanding the customer and formulating requirements. It can also be applied to the development process itself. "What did we learn from that? How might we carry out this next step? What are alternative methods? What should we experiment with next?"

Unfortunately there is often a gap between what we need and what comes naturally to us. Reactive PDCA often feels more natural because of our genetic heritage, yet we need a more reflective approach. To close this gap people need to be taught the less comfortable reflective way of thinking and acting. At Toyota this is a critical role of leadership. In 2001, Toyota for the first time published "The Toyota Way," an internal document that describes a training program for all executives. Soon thereafter, Toyota released "Toyota Business Practices" (TBP), which is the concrete method for putting the Toyota Way into action. TBP is an eight-step problem-solving process that is formally coached over a five- to eight-month period. It follows PDCA, heavily emphasizing the front-end planning.[13]

There is a very explicit role for leadership in the TBP teaching processes. Leaders must learn first, doing a TBP project with a coach. Then they must coach their direct reports, who similarly do TBP projects. The initial introduction of TBP was cascaded from the very top of Toyota, layer by layer, as leaders were first coached and then became the coaches. The vision is a leadership culture based more on teaching than telling. At all levels, leaders are mentors, every day teaching others the scientific thinking way. When "students" assume they know, the teacher intervenes with a question: "How do you know that is true? Have you confirmed that assumption?"

Mike Rother has worked to systematize the process of making reflective PDCA a habit through kata. Kata are small routines that we can practice toward the purpose of developing a complex skill. Ideally, the routines are practiced every day by a "learner" with a "coach," who provides corrective feedback so that we develop new, habitual ways of thinking and acting (Figure 6.3).

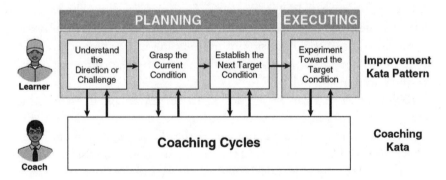

Figure 6.3 The practice routines of the improvement kata and the coaching kata are starter drills for developing a scientific way of thinking.
(*Source: Mike Rother,* Toyota Kata Culture, *NY: McGraw Hill, 2017*)

The improvement kata is designed specifically to start the learner down the path of scientific thinking:

1. It starts with a model or pattern of practical scientific thinking, which occurs in four steps: understand a broad organizational challenge, grasp the current condition linked to the challenge, establish a target condition that helps to address the challenge, and experiment toward the target condition.

2. Practice routines have been developed for beginners as they learn each step. These are called *starter kata.*

3. There is a complementary coaching kata, which helps beginning coaches practice sensing how the learner is thinking and giving effective corrective feedback in daily interactions, called *coaching cycles.*

4. The learner and coach repeat the cycle daily, with the learner iteratively pursuing the target condition or, if reached, developing and pursuing the next target condition. Like reflective PDCA, there is incremental but meaningful improvement.[14]

Kata has been well documented, and its growing application provides evidence that scientific thinking and acting can be taught, not simply as a concept, but as a new set of habits to replace the often bad habits of reactive PDCA. Just like a complex skill, music, sports, art, and even fighting, we need to learn through deliberate practice every day. We also need a coach to check what we are doing and provide feedback. Few people are good at self-feedback, particularly when trying to change a well-worn habit. The coach—maybe your boss—has to learn to teach rather than tell, by asking questions instead of providing answers.

Technical Gatekeepers of the Knowledge Base

The accumulation and application of deep, specialized technical knowledge is an important aspect of successful product and process development for many organizations. There are many powerful technologies available to assist in organizing this knowledge in an easily accessible way. But it requires more than sophisticated technology; it also requires experts to validate and help apply this knowledge. In this way, know-how databases and technical gatekeepers combine to become a competitive advantage.

Know-How Databases

For years we heard about Toyota's engineering checklists and how important they were in product development. These were pencil-and-paper
checklists, stored in three-ring binders. They were organized by functional specialty or parts of the car—plastic bumpers, stamped body parts,
glass, heating and cooling system, etc. They included information that
ranged from technical details, such as part characteristics that create stress
on stamping dies and can lead to defects, to administrative minutiae,
such as properly filling out a "title" box and dating a drawing. As engineers worked, they checked off each issue on the checklist that they had
addressed. Addressing an issue does not always mean compliance with a
standard; it could mean, "I am deviating from the standard, and I have an
appropriately tested countermeasure."

Toyota engineers were very diligent in using the checklists for each
design. They would go through the notebook and check off and sign their
name when they addressed each item. Their supervisor would then sign
off that he or she had confirmed that the checklist item was appropriately
addressed. Some readers may recognize the similarity to pilot preflight
checklists that made a huge difference in airline safety.

After writing about checklists, we were often asked whether it was
necessary to use pencil and paper rather than a computer database.
Eventually even Toyota began migrating to a computerized "know-how
database." The information was largely the same, with the addition of
CAD data, various digital photographs, 3D scans, and technical information extracted from a variety of sources. Like the pencil-and-paper
predecessor, the know-how database allowed the engineers to check off
an item as they addressed it and their supervisor to confirm satisfactory
completion of each item. Thus, it was a digital representation of the manual process with a few enhancements.

Troy Design and Manufacturing (TDM), a medium-sized tool
and engineering firm, decided to adapt the know-how database idea
to a process engineering application shortly after learning about it. A
cross-functional engineering team, led by Bill Anglin, Steve Guido, and
Steve Mortens, captured and codified successful stamping tool designs
and made the information available to engineers by category of part.
These "digital templates," along with 3D scans, tryout notes, and checklist requirements, became a foundation that served as a head start for

new tool designs for parts (grouped by stamping category). The project was so successful that Ned Oliver and Tim Jagoda led a similar effort in the company's fixture and build area, which also featured reconfigurable components. Together these efforts reduced cost and lead time and increased first-time quality dramatically.

Other companies have also launched significant knowledge-capture-and-application efforts employing increasingly sophisticated technologies. Many were eager to share their accomplishments and the truly impressive capabilities of their computer systems. There was one problem: these companies often struggled to get engineers to put information into the database or use the tool to its full potential. A bit of discussion with company representatives revealed that engineers thought of the tool as an IT solution rather than an engineering tool. In fact, it was often assigned to the IT department, resulting in programmers begging and pleading with engineers to provide them with technical information to load into the database. This big misunderstanding was a big problem.

As we reflected on this, we realized that these companies were getting the knowledge-capture-and-application process backward. Knowledge gets generated in the course of doing engineering work. It originates with people, and then it is people who have to decide what to capture, what to load into the computer, and what to take seriously and use in a design. What the companies were missing were the people—the key role of subject matter experts and gatekeepers of the knowledge database as we saw at Toyota and TDM.

The Role of Technical Gatekeepers

When Charlie Baker was a young product development engineer at General Motors, he read *The Machine That Changed the World.*[15] It had a major impact on how he thought about his work, and he became very interested in what Japanese auto companies were doing in product development. He decided he needed to learn about lean product development so he could share it with the world. He wrote a letter to an executive at Honda of America and was shocked when he was asked to come to Honda for a meeting. It turned out to be a job interview. He was hired, became the first American large program leader (chief engineer) for a full model change, and eventually became the first American VP of product engineering for Honda North America.

When Baker left Honda for his new job at Johnson Controls (JCI), he was eager to find out the company's current state. What he found were huge gaps between the success factors he experienced at Honda and what he observed at JCI.[16] Among the glaring differences was the role of deep expertise.

At Honda he was considered an apprentice learning the engineering trade. The master teachers were mostly in Japan. And as chief engineer, first of the Acura CL, then the Acura MDS, then the Honda Pilot, and then the Honda Accord, he had to go before these subject matter experts in design reviews focused on where function meets manufacturability. These were not relaxed gatherings to celebrate his success. For each specialty—body, chassis, electrical, powertrain, exterior, interior—there was an expert who had dedicated his career to building expertise in that discipline. These were nerve-racking reviews, as the experts could see each and every weakness in his design simply by looking at prints. As Charlie explained to us:

> Usually a somewhat junior person created and presented the design, supported by their direct supervisor. The development team (me, my direct staff) gave input on acceptability and appropriateness from a customer and value standpoint, including weighing in on requirements, timing and cost. The technical experts weighed in on risk and how to optimize (tradeoff curves), appropriate solution sets, requirements, timing and cost. People did get out of their swim lanes and venture opinions, and there was passionate debate. The key was to walk out with a consensus of a way forward, or at least a clear plan.

Honda, Ford, and Toyota all have this level of expertise, people who are able to dissect and validate information for the knowledge database. Nothing gets into or out of the database without the approval of the technical gatekeeper for that area. No one from IT has to cajole anyone into adding knowledge to the database. The database is used as more than a checklist. There is a good deal of active discussion, as Charlie points out:

> Not all knowledge was "check the box"—some was centered around discussion of how a basic principle needed to be applied across a variety of situations. Judgement and discussion was required. I heard an example attributed to Toyota regarding a checklist for squeaks

and rattles—many traditional companies would be all about volumes of data defining clearances of 0.1 mm. Toyota's approach was to say that squeaks needed to be prevented by 1) guaranteeing clearance (discussion of what does this mean in a particular example), 2) guaranteeing NO clearance, and no relative movement (again, discussion), or 3) materials that do not generate noise with relative movement (still more discussion). This is the essence of Lean design checklists—the WHY not just the what.

At JCI there were no such roles. Among the many changes Baker introduced was to create the role of subject matter technical expert (SMTE), and to his delight people with this level of expertise already existed in JCI: "JCI (and most companies) had legitimate technical experts, but these folks were typically squandered by just applying them to one project as a project engineer (even though they typically were given challenging projects). My biggest innovation was defining the role of a SMTE as belonging to no project, but responsible for all projects for a technical specialty. Once you do this, and rotate PDCA, you can mature rapidly. Without it you will never mature, in my experience."

Crisp, Clear Communication for Collaboration and Knowledge Transfer

Product development is frequently a pressure-packed, time-constrained environment in which complex issues must be quickly addressed and analyzed and decided by cross-functional teams who may communicate in very different ways. Three unique methods—A3s, trade-off curves, and reflection events—help to tackle such challenges with clarity and efficiency.

A3 Collaboration

In our previous book we wrote about Toyota's four types of A3s and their use in the Toyota product development system. Since then, there has been a great deal written about A3s, including our favorite book about the process of using the A3 as a people development tool, John Shook's *Managing to Learn*;[17] we have still not seen a more effective tool for collaborative problem solving, communication, and learning if practiced with the A3 spirit of inquiry and continuous improvement.

Named for the international-sized paper (11 inches by 17 inches), A3 reports are a way of structuring and sharing information that aids teams in practicing scientific thinking collaboratively. In his book, Shook defines A3s as "a visual manifestation of a problem-solving thought process involving continual dialogue between the owner of the issue and others in the organization. It is a foundational management process that encourages learning through the scientific method." And the A3 has proven very effective in product development. Benefits of using A3 as a tool for learning and collaboration include:

- **Promotes collaboration.** Many engineers have a tendency to solve problems on their own. This is partially what brought them to engineering in the first place—they are good problem solvers. This practice is further reinforced during their college training. Unfortunately, the real-world product development environment is far more complex and interdependent than engineering classes. Problem solving in isolation can lead to suboptimized and poorly communicated solutions. As Jim Womack likes to say, "you can't A3 alone." Developing A3s is a team sport and requires engineers to seek out and engage people from other perspectives and work together on a solution. Leaders and mentors should ask whether all critical participants have been considered when reviewing A3s.

- **Slows down your thinking.** Sir Arthur Conan Doyle's master sleuth, Sherlock Holmes, once said, "There is nothing more deceptive than an obvious fact." Humans are conclusion jumpers by nature. We think we know, that the facts are obvious, and it is very tempting to go into solution mode before really understanding. Further exacerbating this tendency is the tremendous amount of pressure on people during a product development program, the pressure to deliver cost, quality, and attribute performance. And on top of all this is the pressure of time— you are always on the clock. Deadlines must be met, and in the heat of the action, people do not always take the necessary time to fully think through the problem definition, causes, possible countermeasures, and how to quickly test the countermeasures.

    In his landmark book *Thinking, Fast and Slow*,[18] Nobel Prize winner Daniel Kahneman proposes two fictitious characters residing in our brain that control the way we think: System 1 is an automatic, low-effort system, and System 2 is a slower, more effortful system. He effectively demonstrates that we too often make mistakes because we are too quick to accept information from System 1 without sufficiently analyzing it. In fact, he postulates that the brain is naturally "lazy" and looks for shortcuts. He characterizes these errors as a number of specific biases, such as overconfidence in what "we know," which are flaws in our thinking. He suggests that you can combat these biases by first slowing down and recognizing that you may fall prey to one of these biases. System 2 is the slower, more systematic approach to analyzing information and drawing out useful propositions to be tested. He says that organizations can improve their effectiveness by imposing orderly procedures that routinely frame the problem, collect the necessary data, apply checklists, and reflect and review. Organizations also should continually look to improve on each of these steps.

One "trick" to check the quality of your A3, recommended by Lean Enterprise Institute coaches Eric Ethington and Tracey Richardson, is to read your A3 backward. A3s combined with checklists and used in a design review can benefit from this approach.

- **Improves communication accuracy.** One of the major challenges in product development is the many functional disciplines involved: finance, engineering, design, marketing, and manufacturing have not only different perspectives—different ways that they view the world—but also different and largely specialized languages. This can make problem solving and even communicating difficult. Because an A3 requires you to boil problems down to their essential elements to fit on a single page, it encourages the use of graphs and figures to minimize text usage and space. This helps to eliminate excess jargon and encourages plain, straightforward language. An A3 also requires you to solve a problem together, thus encouraging direct, face-to-face communication where questions can be asked and clarifications made.

- **Becomes a repository for knowledge.** The knowledge generated by the A3 process is a potentially invaluable asset for your organization. Consequently, it should be protected and leveraged just as any other asset would. The A3 contains not only the solution implemented by the team, but also the specific problem it sought to resolve, and it may include countermeasures tried that did not work.

By organizing A3s and making them available, you create a tremendous knowledge resource for developers and a possible competitive advantage. We saw that Toyota had organized A3s from various manufacturing engineers into binders, organized them by topic, and made them available to all employees. In addition, it was the responsibility of each engineer who developed an A3 to think about who might benefit from the information and e-mail it to those people. Engineers also circulate "white papers" widely. This brings to mind lengthy reports, but at Toyota white papers are A3 stories that share some technical knowledge.

For product development engineers, especially those who work in distributed engineering environments, A3s can be made available digitally. Even though it is often valuable to create A3s by hand, with the introduction of optical character recognition technology you can now simply take a picture of your finished A3 and it becomes fully searchable from anywhere in the world. Of course, this still requires a governance process and an owner, just as any effective system of standards does. Ford utilized the engineering quality group within each discipline in this role, assessing the worthiness of an A3 for the standards database. Alternatively, given the exponential growth of data in modern product development, you could, as Mary Morgan suggests, invest in an information science specialist to organize and serve as the steward for this information.[19] This is a small investment considering what is at stake. In any case, if you only leverage the A3 for the initial problem, you are missing at least half the benefit.

- **Improves the productivity of design reviews.** While A3s are useful in many different situations, they can be especially effective in design reviews. As discussed, they promote scientific thinking and facilitate collaboration. In addition, A3s require engineers to develop a succinct problem statement, describe the current situation supported by data, outline specific potential countermeasures (experiments), and provide a time-bound action plan. And the single-page format forces people to reduce problems to their essential elements, which makes design review discussions much more productive. An A3 also serves as a record of the agreed plan, and it can be stored and recalled after the specific problem is resolved. We don't advocate doing an A3 for every item on your design review agenda. However, if you have a challenging problem that involves multiple disciplines, an important decision that requires understanding a trade-off, a recurring issue that you have not been able to kill, or a relatively new phenomenon you need to better understand, an A3 can be an excellent aid in your review.

Trade-Off Curves

In the book *Lean Product and Process Development*[20] by Al Ward and Durward Sobeck, the authors advise, "If I could teach you only one lean tool, tradeoff curves would be it." Trade-off curves are a powerful method to display many types of information. As Ward used to say, they turn data into reusable knowledge. Very often the best way to represent the underlying physics or chemistry of a design and to understand both relative and ultimate performance is with trade-off curves.

Trade-off curves were introduced in the first article Ward and associates wrote about Toyota's product development system: "The Second Toyota Paradox: How Delaying Decisions Can Make Better Cars Faster."[21] Their work introduced the concept of set-based concurrent engineering. The title gave the impression that the purpose was to keep multiple design possibilities open for as long as possible, which, in fact, was only one possibility. There were a number of other ways that Toyota used set-based thinking. One was through trade-off curves that represented the set of possible solutions.

For the article the authors interviewed Toyota engineers and suppliers in Japan. Trade-off curves came up frequently. One curiosity was the large number of prototypes built by Toyota suppliers compared with that of their American counterparts. One supplier of exhaust systems in Japan clarified this for us. It was not making lots of prototypes of the same design, but rather single prototypes of a variety of different designs. It bench-tested these and represented these in trade-off curves. The supplier showed us an example of the trade-off between the buildup of back pressure in the muffler and noise-reduction capability. The supplier said, "The Chief Engineer wants to see the tradeoffs so he can make the final decision."

At Honda, Charlie Baker also learned about the power of trade-off curves and brought these to JCI: "When I went to JCI one big issue was simply not really understanding root cause, or overcomplicating root cause with a great deal of extraneous information. I challenged the organization to find a problem that required more than 1 tradeoff curve to solve. I did lose, but it took 3 months (and hundreds of problems) before there was legitimately a problem requiring more than one tradeoff curve."

Reflecting to Learn from Experience

The ancient Greek philosopher Socrates is quoted as saying, "The unexamined life is not worth living." We are not sure we would say that the unexamined product development program is not worth doing, but if you don't intentionally learn from your development programs, you are missing a huge opportunity to improve both your products and your development performance.

In our previous book,[22] we shared the details of Toyota's hansei, or reflection, events, as well as the similar practice of after-action reviews (AARs) created by the U.S. Army. Both organizations have used these events as part of a greater learning system to significant competitive advantage, and since then, many other organizations have added this practice to their repertoire. We also identified the major impediments to effective reflection events as well as key characteristics of successful reviews. We will not repeat that information here, but it is worth sharing a few additional insights we have gained in the years since *The Toyota Product Development System* was written.

Build It into the Work

Waiting until the end of the project is one of the most common failure modes we see in organizations that attempt reflection as a learning mechanism. By waiting until the very end, far too much information can be lost, participants move on, and memories get increasingly fuzzy over time.

It is not easy. Learning from the past is indeed very challenging. In the book *The Black Swan*,[23] Nassim Taleb describes how our continual attempts to make sense of the world result in flawed stories of the past that end up impacting our view of the world. In *Thinking, Fast and Slow*,[24] Kahneman also reminds us just how difficult it is to learn from the past due to the built-in System 1 biases (fast thinking). For example, they cause us to "focus on a few striking events that happened rather than on the countless events that failed to happen," thus attributing too much credit or blame to those events. Another important factor that affects our judgment of the past, according to Kahneman, is "hindsight bias." Hindsight bias, or outcome bias, causes us to judge the past more or less favorably based on whether or not the project was successful. In the case of an unsuccessful venture, many of the things we did might have been very good and worth sharing, and the failure of the project may have been unrelated to these good practices. It is important to be aware of these biases and call them out when you reflect on an event.

One other way to help combat the difficulties of learning from the past is to hold your events more frequently. Build mini-reflection points into the development process. For example, you can add a reflection component to your milestone reviews or perhaps even add a few minutes to reflect at the end of each obeya meeting. In this way, information is more available in memory and less subject to the impacts of time. Also, by reflecting more often, you will get better because of the extra practice. It will feel more natural—teams are more likely to be open. And finally, the accumulative information from each mini-event feeds the final reflection event, making it much more effective.

Caterpillar is an example of one company that has learned the benefit of regularly scheduled reflection events to accelerate learning and continuously improve its development programs. Caterpillar had been practicing LPPD for over a decade. In the early stages they were primarily focused on value-stream mapping and obeya to accelerate an unusual number of PD programs dealing with new emissions standards. As they advanced their maturity, they realized they were not doing a good job of the C and A parts of PDCA. They decided to hold formal reflection events to capture learning and build on that learning. They started with a pilot for a group designing "medium wheel loaders." Initially the MWL team stayed primarily true to the formal hansei and the associated questions as described in our previous book.

Early on, the members of the team uncovered a number of design challenges that required them to invest a significant amount of time to get to the root cause. It turned out that formal reflection events were of great value to deepen learning and make better decisions.

As the team members gained experience, they developed a "decision A3" story as a way to clarify their thinking, circulate the document to get broad input, and document their thought process, considerations, and justifications to inform similar decisions in the future. Capturing knowledge "real time" with these decision A3s has proved a key enabler to the effectiveness of future reflections because it creates "bread crumbs" for the teams to follow to help them understand why specific decisions were

made. Adding formal reflection events and the decision A3 has been transformational for teams at Caterpillar.

Toyota holds major several-day reflection events at the end of each development program. The participants in each program group are brought into
a room where they write down their reflections on flip charts. Functional
specialists are assigned to share important lessons learned with relevant
parties, and the program manager shares in a global program management
meeting. But this major reflection event is actually a culmination of many
smaller reflections throughout the development process.

Both Toyota's hansei events and the Army's AARs work with relatively
simple questions; for example:

- What did we set out to do?
- What actually happened?
- What is the gap?
- Why did the gap occur?

For anyone who has actually attempted this, you know answering these
questions is more difficult than it at first appears. This is especially true if
you lack supporting data, evidence of what actually took place, or a record
of what you were trying to do. But if you created a concept paper and used
an obeya, you will have all kinds of data.

Your concept paper should state very clearly what you were trying to do.
The attribute achievement glide paths, marked-up schedules, and many
other artifacts in the obeya provide a rich history of planned program
performance versus actual results. In fact, many advanced lean organizations hold their reflection events in the obeya. If you used A3s to resolve
issues along the way, you will have excellent reference documents for both
what and why you took the actions that you took. And if you held mini-
reflection events at milestones, you will have the reports that were generated from those events. By utilizing these documents, along with open,
honest, no-blame dialogue, you should be able to piece together the history of the program and provide a foundation to discuss opportunities to
improve your future products and development performance. Effective
reflection events can help to accelerate your learning and spread knowledge across your organization.

Wrap Up

Our point in writing this chapter is quite straightforward: organizational learning is no longer optional. Companies that do not improve their ability to learn, to evolve, and to improve will not succeed in product development. We have suggested a number of ways to build learning into the way you do your work. However, ultimately, learning is a choice. It needs to be an organizational priority that starts with leadership.

LOOKING FORWARD

The pursuit of product perfection can have a transformational impact on both your product and your organization. In Chapter 7 we focus on the end game of great products and services. What makes a great product? How do you measure a product's effectiveness? And how do you develop the team mindset to view development as a craft with product excellence as the goal?

Your Reflection

Creating a Vision

Becoming a learning organization can seem a bit abstract. It is easier to understand becoming a learning individual. Yet a collection of individuals who learn independently is not a learning organization. There need to be ways to share, store, and reuse knowledge. We have described some of the key characteristics of a learning organization:

- Individual learning is codified as standards and shared and used.
- The culture supports openly sharing learning, even from mistakes.
- Occasions for learning are designed into the design process (e.g., design reviews, reflection, obeya meetings).
- People develop the habit of scientific systems thinking through daily practice with coaching.
- Technical gatekeepers have deep mastery of their craft and are the formal guardians of the knowledge base.

- Communication is crisp, clear, and succinct to encourage collaboration and knowledge transfer (e.g., through A3 reports).

Does this vision fit what you think is needed in your company to become a learning organization? How would you revise this vision to better fit your company's situation?

Your Current Condition

1. Evaluate your overall organization against the characteristics of a learning organization.
2. What organizational constraints are inhibiting learning in your company?
3. Are you getting the most out of your design reviews? How can you improve them?
4. Do you learn from the problems you experience? Do you seem to be experiencing the same issues repeatedly?
5. Do you use an obeya? Is your obeya the hub of your programs? Is it a center for immersive learning?
6. Are you teaching your people to think scientifically on an ongoing basis through actual improvement projects with a qualified coach?

Taking Action

1. Create a learning strategy A3 and enlist cross-functional support in developing it.
2. Clearly identify in the A3 why learning systems need to be developed (background), the current learning condition in product development, and the gap between your current capabilities and what you hope to achieve.
3. Develop some experimental countermeasures aimed at closing that gap, capture and share learning from the experiments, and reflect on what occurred.

7

The Pursuit of
Product Perfection

*Perfection is not attainable. But if we chase perfection,
we can catch excellence.*

—VINCE LOMBARDI

The pursuit of perfection has captured the human imagination for thousands of years. It is a driving force of our better selves. From the beginning of recorded history, we have debated what it is and how we can achieve it. We like Aristotle's view in that it is not a target level of achievement, but rather a way of being: "We are what we repeatedly do. Excellence, then, is not an act but a habit." This mentality still separates exceptional organizations and individuals from "wannabes" today.

In *Lean Thinking*, James Womack and Dan Jones wrote that the "pursuit of perfection" is a fundamental tenet of lean thinking and the foundation of continuous improvement.[1] This is, indeed, powerful advice for product and process developers and the implicit goal of the processes, tools, and methods described throughout this book.

In this chapter, we will discuss several important characteristics of excellent products, and we will share some examples of practices used by successful product companies to consistently deliver them. First and foremost, excellent products and services create value for their customers; they solve their customers' problems in innovative and delightful ways. But they don't stop there: the very best products—differentiated by beautiful design and superb craftsmanship—are reliable, sustainable, and efficiently engineered to achieve an elegant solution. In short, they deliver a total experience unmatched by competitors.

The first step in developing the capability to deliver exceptional products and services is to fully engage your organization in the endeavor. To create an environment where excellence is expected, it's your people that make the difference.

A Passion for Excellence

We believe that "catching excellence" is less about genius than it is relentless hard work in the pursuit of something that seems always to be just a little out of reach. It requires being personally invested in your work, which is, unfortunately, a rarity in our daily experiences. In fact, our day-to-day experiences tend to be a bit more like that described in Robert Pirsig's wonderful classic, *Zen and the Art of Motorcycle Maintenance*.[2] In the central character's pursuit of truth, one of the issues he grapples with is the existential meaning of "quality" in our lives. He begins this journey in a motorcycle repair shop. After three separate engine overhauls, the narrator arrives at the repair shop to pick up his bike, and when the valve covers need to once again be removed, he observes:

> . . . the kid came with an open-end adjustable wrench, set wrong, and swiftly rounded both of the sheet-aluminum tappet covers, ruining both of them. "I hope we've got some of those in stock," he said. I nodded. He brought out a hammer and a cold chisel and started to pound them loose. The chisel punched through the aluminum cover and I could see he was pounding the chisel right into the engine head. On the next blow he missed the chisel completely and struck the head with the hammer, breaking off a portion of two of the cooling fins. "Just stop," I said politely, feeling this was a bad dream.

Pirsig's rider finally pulls his grease-covered bike out onto the road only to discover that the shop had neglected to fully bolt the engine back into the frame. He wonders:

Why did they butcher it so? . . . They sat down to do a job and they performed like chimpanzees. Nothing personal in it. . . . The biggest clue seemed to be their expressions. They were hard to explain. Good-natured, friendly, easygoing—and uninvolved. They were like spectators. You had the feeling they had just wandered in there themselves and someone had handed them a wrench. There was no identification with the job. No saying, "I'm a mechanic." At 5 P.M. or whenever their eight hours were in, you knew they would cut it off and not have another thought about their work. They were already trying not to have any thoughts about their work on the job.

Pirsig's story gives us a very human take on the pursuit of excellence. The pursuit must start with people who truly care about their work. We have seen people in all walks of life and types of work become energized and excited about their work. Leaders must enroll their teams with a clear and compelling vision of the purpose of the work, and then lead by example. Leaders listen, as well as teach. Team members are treated as important rather than a pair of hands and understand how their contribution matters to doing something important.

Companies that fail to create conditions that truly engage people often end up with "check-the-box" or "tool-centric" quality efforts. For them, quality belongs to the quality group, which tries to enforce the company's standards. As Tom Peters and Robert Waterman said in the landmark book *In Search of Excellence*,[3] "Without exception, the dominance and coherence of culture proved to be an essential quality of the excellent companies." Exceptional companies engage their employees and give them a chance to both achieve their potential and be part of something bigger than themselves. Your culture is the basis for creating product excellence.

So how do you create a culture of great products? Largely by applying the same hiring, people development, and leadership practices we discussed in Chapters 4 and 5. High-performance teams with excellent leaders tend to produce exceptional outcomes. And true leadership is especially important in the pursuit of product excellence. It's easy to talk the quality talk, but how do leaders actually behave? Where do they spend their time? What expectations do they set? How do they engage team members?

In the early days of the Ford turnaround, the body and stamping team worked extremely hard to improve exterior body quality. The team had benchmarked the best in the world and set its targets at or above those levels. But it became clear that not all managers were committed to the effort. In the middle of a particularly intense exchange over part quality requirements at a product review, a frustrated longtime Ford manager blurted out, "We will not sell one more damn car because of sharper radii or tighter margins!" Not only did that not turn out to be true (exterior body fit and finish was one of the most noted characteristics of the new products), but more importantly, it wasn't the point. The point was to create an environment where excellence is expected. When you create this environment, excellence permeates everywhere. It is the leader's responsibility to create that environment, especially at the most difficult times. You can't pick and choose where you want excellence and where you will be satisfied with mediocrity.

This focus on delivering excellence has, perhaps, an unexpected side benefit—its impact on the people engaged in it. We agree with Richard Sennett, the Centennial Professor of Sociology at the London School of Economics, that there is an innate desire in most people to do a job well for its own sake.[4] This is the spirit of craftsmanship. It is universal, and it connects people to their work in a very personal way by conferring pride and giving meaning to their work. Consequently, the achievement of mastery in one's work brings an internal joy only possible by accomplishing something incredibly difficult—and personal. To be sure, this arduous journey has a lasting impact on those who choose to follow this path. Yet as lean thinkers, value creation and the pursuit of perfection are, after all, what we are all about. The spirit of craftsmanship is a key component of creating something of lasting value.

Customer-Defined Value

According to Womack and Jones, the first principle of lean thinking is to understand and deliver customer-defined value. It is also the foundation for product excellence. If your product does not solve your customer's problem or provide your customer's desired experience, he or she is unlikely to consider it excellent. In Chapter 1 we discussed the roles that the chief engineer, immersion, "High-Tech Anthropologists," hackathons, rapid experimentation, and the concept paper play in understanding and aligning the organization around how to deliver maximum customer value. But adding value to customers is worth further discussion and is core to any product excellence discussion.

We also want to emphasize that to be successful, the focus on creating exceptional customer value needs to go well beyond the actions of an individual product team. It must permeate the entire organization. When explaining the "close-to-the-customer" theme, Peters and Waterman write, "The good news from the excellent companies is the extent to which, and the intensity with which, the customer intrudes into every nook and cranny of the business—sales, manufacturing, research accounting."[5]

Toyota has a very simple and challenging way of thinking about customer satisfaction: "If even one customer has a defective product, that represents 100% of our products to that customer," and "The product is both the vehicle the customer buys and their overall experience including dealer and service experience." (See Figure 7.1.)

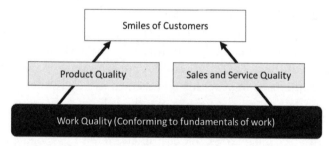

Figure 7.1   Toyota's model of customer-defined value.
(*Source: http://www.toyota-global.com/sustainability/society/quality/*)

Toyota traces its customer-first philosophy to the innovative thinking of Sakichi Toyoda many years ago. This philosophy was further embodied in Kiichiro Toyoda's spirit of continuous improvement. This led to Toyota's culture that focuses particular attention on quality that the customer will experience and on continuous kaizen achieved through genchi genbutsu (on-site, hands-on experience). This may help explain why Toyota's chief engineers spend so much time observing how customers use their cars in their own natural settings.

Not only does a passion for customers help to keep customers happy; the reverse is also true. People get excited about delighting customers. It is an excitement you rarely see when parading out PowerPoint presentations of costs, benefits, and anticipated profits for the company. Focusing on the customer will increase the drive of the team members and make them even more customer centered. And by focusing more deeply on how your product creates value for your customer, your people will better understand how they can each contribute directly to your mission.

Customer-Driven Design

Great design strikes an emotional chord, whether it is a car, a smartphone, an appliance, or a shaver. In his enlightening book *The Design of Everyday Things*,[6] Donald Norman, cognitive scientist, usability engineer, and professor emeritus at the University of California, San Diego, demonstrates that "design is really an act of communication, which means having a deep understanding of the person with whom the designer is communicating." This then is the essence of a lean approach to design.

It is easy to get so bogged down in operational efficiency and execution excellence that we miss the forest for the trees. Customers are not buying great execution. They are buying a great product. The auto industry got a wake-up call when Elon Musk introduced the Tesla Model S to the world. Every aspect of the design, from exterior appearance to speed to the clean digital user interface, was exciting and seemed to surpass the competition. When looking beyond the vehicle, it's clear that Tesla's execution was a far cry from auto industry standards—financial loss, late delivery with poor quality (see Chapter 8). Yet customers were so passionate about the product, they rushed to buy the Model S and signed up in droves to place an order for the Model 3. We are not saying that execution does not matter—it does. And Tesla's poor execution may yet be its undoing. However, the product has clearly connected with customers in a very special way.

Apple's Commitment to Design

Steve Jobs was obsessed with the look and feel of Apple products. Apple's design chief, Jony Ive, is equally obsessed with beauty, with feel, and with every millisecond of the user experience. Jobs deeply understood the value of an emotional connection with customers and bet right that people would pay a premium for design excellence in their products. The bet has clearly paid off.

Beginning with Jobs's return to Apple in 1997, design has dramatically differentiated the company from its competitors. It was the key ingredient in the products that propelled Apple from death's door to arguably the most successful company of our time. Jobs's biographer, Walter Isaacson, wrote that Jobs was passionate to the point of obsession about design, insisting that his computers look perfect inside and out: "Distinctive design—clean and friendly and fun—would become the hallmark of Apple products under Jobs. In an era not known for great industrial designers, Jobs' partnerships with Hartmut Esslinger in the 1980s and then with Jony Ive starting in 1997 created an engineering and design aesthetic that set Apple apart from other technology companies and ultimately helped make it the most valuable company in the world."[7]

By now it is well known that Jobs valued simplicity in design above all else. In 1977, Apple's first brochure boasted "Simplicity is the ultimate sophistication." According to Jobs, "It takes a lot of hard work to make something simple, to truly understand the underlying challenges and come up with elegant solutions."[8] When many manufacturers were heaping on features and hoping to add customer value, Apple's approach was a breath of fresh air for consumers, and the company has been amply rewarded.

Jim was fortunate to meet with Ive during his discussions with Apple, and he was impressed by Ive's humility, absolute commitment to creating great products, and deep knowledge not only of design but of engineering, materials, and manufacturing.

Like the leaders described earlier in this book, Ive clearly recognizes and appreciates the many contributions required to create great products. He consistently refers to what "we" did rather than what "I" did. He seems to treasure the teamwork that is so crucial to creating Apple's iconic products, and his team mentality extends well beyond his direct design team to broader groups across Apple and its suppliers. Says Ive, "More than ever I am aware that what we have achieved with design is massively reliant on the commitment of lots of different teams to solve the same problems."[9]

In Ive's view, a new product must be new and different in ways that matter to the customer: "Most of our competitors are interested in doing something different, or want to appear new—I think those are completely wrong goals. A product has to be genuinely better. This requires real discipline, and that's what drives us—a sincere, genuine appetite to create something that is better."[10]

Ive's depth and breadth of knowledge extends to materials and manufacturing. It's clear he thinks of design as so much more than ideation and styling. He wants to understand as much as he can about materials and manufacturing so that he and his team can continue to push the boundaries in design. And he is willing to go to extraordinary lengths. Apple's drive to apply Gorilla Glass is well known, as is the story of machining products out of a single block of aluminum. Ive also famously once led his team to visit with traditional samurai sword makers to better understand their materials and the principles of their craft.[11]

Akio Toyoda's Passion for Design Excellence

In January 2016, Akio Toyoda took the stage at the Detroit International Auto Show and addressed the standing-room-only crowd. He wanted attendees to know he was listening to the Lexus customer, and he agreed that Lexus design had become boring. He went on to state that he "never wanted to see 'Lexus' and 'boring' in the same sentence again." And with that he unveiled the LC500, one of the boldest designs of a production car ever. But Toyoda did not stop there. All across the Toyota lineup, from the subcompact SUV crossover C-HR to the new Toyota Camry, vehicles showed bold, edgy designs. Toyoda, a race car driver who loves cars, clearly heard Toyota customers loud and clear—no more boring cars! Without giving up anything from its original value proposition, Toyota is now intent on leveraging design to increase its connection with the customer. While exciting design has never been one of Toyota's strengths, it is clear that its current CEO recognizes its potential for creating customer value and is determined to improve.

Working to strengthen customer connection through design continues at Lexus. In our discussion with Yoshihiro Sawa, president of Lexus and managing officer of Toyota, he talked passionately about the importance of design and building a strong connection with the next generation of creatives around the world. Lexus identifies and supports artists and other creative types from around the world. Through stories and key design words, like *seamless, zero gravity, elegance, incisive simplicity, bleeding edge*, it shares the spirit of Lexus with them. Then the designers—who may be from Europe, Japan, or the United States—create their vision of the Lexus worldview within their particular medium. In some cases, artists may go on to work directly with Lexus studios on designing a next-generation vehicle. Lexus is also the first automaker to sponsor major design competitions in places like Milan so that it can both support young artists and work closely with and learn from attendees of these events to strengthen its aesthetic connection with the next generation of luxury vehicle buyers.

Ford's Engineering-Enabled Design

Exciting "kinetic" design was a major part of the Ford revitalization, and it proved a powerful differentiator of Ford products. Mustang, Fusion, and Focus designs set them apart in their categories and started an industry trend. However, while kinetic design was edgy and exciting, it was also quite challenging from both an engineering and manufacturing perspective. And this was particularly problematic at Ford, where for far too long engineering—both product and production—acted as an inhibitor of great design, protecting the manufacturing operations from edgy designs that would cause problems for the plants. This practice may have killed some of Ford's best designs.

The body and stamping engineering (B&SE) team set out to change that. The team wanted to become the enabler of great design—so it worked closely with its colleagues in the design studio and the manufacturing plants to figure out how to deliver great designs without gumming up the works in the plants. Delivering products with an exacting degree of design fidelity and precision became B&SE's new mission. The engineering team worked upstream with the design studio, and designers went downstream to work directly with engineers and toolmakers. For several of the designers, it was the first time they had been in an assembly plant or tool shop, and it had a significant impact on how they thought about their craft going forward. The result was a series of breakthrough products with some of the most exciting designs in Ford's history. It also was the impetus for a new way of thinking about excellence in manufacturing, as a competitive advantage in developing great products.

Craftsmanship

Jim's passion for craftsmanship likely started with the 1992 Lexus commercial, in which the camera zoomed in on a tiny ball bearing rolling effortlessly down the precise margins of the exterior body panels of the ES300. Or possibly, his passion may have started earlier when he worked as a journeyman model maker, under the watchful eye of highly skilled and demanding craftsmen while they built tools and hand-fabricated and welded precision vehicle bodies. In either case, he began to notice that there was a sharp contrast between well-made, crafted products and poorly made ones, and an even greater distinction between the people who made them. He immediately and instinctively knew which one he wanted to make and to be. Thus began Jim's multidecade-long obsession with craftsmanship and the human spirit behind it.

To be clear, what we are not talking about is some pseudo-magical, romantic craftsmanship of a bygone era, but a vibrant creative force, those who create unique and lasting value in products and drive the development of truly exceptional people across all walks of life right now. In his book *The Craftsman,* Sennett describes the relationship between making and thinking. He explains, "The carpenter, lab technician, and conductor are all craftsmen because they are dedicated to good work for its own sake," and notes that "craftsmanship names an enduring, basic human impulse, the desire to do a job well for its own sake."[12] This is a powerful human impulse, which is all too often ignored in today's organizations. It is an organic, fulfilling way to work whose nature is captured in the wonderful book *Shop Class as Soulcraft.*[13] However, it is not limited to people working solo, as suggested by its author Matthew Crawford—it can be, and is, alive and well in a handful of organizations.

Crafting Distinctive Products

So what is craftsmanship in new products and services? In our view it is nothing less than the visual, tactile, and audible characteristics of a product that drive your customers' perceptions of quality. Excellence in craftsmanship enhances the total customer experience and creates unique value. You can recognize craftsmanship in products and services by their simple elegance and seamless fit. They embody the elimination of the superfluous and the precise execution of the essential. It is that certain something about a product that says "well made" and actually draws you to it. Like the simple elegance and fit and finish of an Apple device enclosure, an Audi car interior, or a church pew from the Katrina Furniture Project[14] (made from hurricane debris), it elicits a deep and emotional appreciation. Great craftsmanship is not just for traditional hard goods either. As we discussed in earlier chapters, we see this in Menlo Innovation's creative and deeply researched user interfaces, the precision movements of a surgeon who has mastered her craft, and even Marcelo Garcia's exacting Brazilian jiujitsu, all of which leave the observer wide-eyed.

This response to precisely crafted products is also apparent in the "now I get it" reaction that Jim has seen so many times from overworked and previously skeptical engineers—after seeing for the first time the physical result of hard work combined with craftsmanship standards. Far from magical, the process of creating truly exceptional products is the outcome of rigorous and objective performance standards for both people and products. It requires incredible attention to a thousand details, an obsession with excellence, and, especially, the seamless collaboration of design, engineering, and manufacturing to produce something of exceptional value.

Creating Crafted Bodies at Ford

The people on the Ford B&SE leadership team started their craftsmanship journey in earnest with a team trip to the Detroit International Auto Show. What they saw there was more than a little troubling. While Ford vehicles matched their North American competitors, they were far behind the best companies from Europe and Japan. Specifically, Audi and Lexus were more than just a little better—they were setting a new standard for exterior craftsmanship. The difference in perceived quality of the products was so striking that it served as a powerful call to action.

When they returned, the B&SE folks put together a plan, consisting of five key elements, to significantly strengthen existing craftsmanship enablers and add others: improved craftsmanship standards, a biweekly global craftsmanship forum, a craftsmanship plan built into every product through the product development process, an increased emphasis on functional build, and strengthened audit events and updated auditor training.

Improved Craftsmanship Standards   The B&SE team benchmarked the very best vehicles in the world and cherry-picked the best performers in each category. In nearly every case the team set standards at or above those levels. The team members met with Ford's design studio to align on their objectives and prioritize implementation based on specific design themes. The metal standards included "best-in-world" (BIW) requirements for margins, radii, surfaces, flushness, and gaps, while other standards addressed invisible mechanisms, handle stroke, hidden fasteners, and even door-closing sound. The team created an easy-to-use knowledge repository that included detailed pictures of BIW examples as well as acceptable and unacceptable levels of execution for each standard, with each level assigned a numeric value.

The new standards created many technical challenges, and the cross-functional team worked through the solutions before implementing new standards—but no one backed off the new objectives. In each case the team members worked to understand the physical enablers that would allow them to deliver, and only then would they approve the standard. For example, several suppliers initially balked at sharper radii on front and rear fascia (bumpers) due to a risk of poor paint adherence. Ford engineers were dispatched to work directly with the suppliers to resolve the issues. Cross-functional teams successfully addressed formability issues, tolerance stack-ups, and attach strategies, and they keep updated standards as they made improvements.

Creating a Craftsmanship Forum With all these challenges the members of the team quickly realized that they needed a cadenced event where craftsmanship experts, designers, engineers, and manufacturing leaders from around the world could come together and collaborate to improve new product craftsmanship. They organized a biweekly, global craftsmanship forum for this purpose.

The craftsmanship forum enabled the cross-functional, global group to review and debate new standards and initiate experiments. It also allowed people to track the progress of individual programs to the craftsmanship objectives. This periodic monitoring gave the program teams a place to escalate and resolve issues as well as capture and share lessons learned across programs.

Building Craftsmanship into the Development Process To be consistently successful, craftsmanship could not be an afterthought or just a "bolt-on" part of the process. It needed to become a central and fully integrated part of the overall development process. To accomplish this, the team established specific, progressive craftsmanship events throughout the development process.

Craftsmanship events started at the very beginning of a program, when the cross-functional team reviewed the outgoing Ford model against its competition and set targets for the new model. Events were used to work through design and manufacturing issues digitally, identifying tolerance stack-ups and formability issues, which could then be resolved in design reviews or the craftsmanship forum, long before physical tools or parts were created. Walk-around events took place first in the styling studio and continued through prototype, functional, and early production builds. Craftsmanship requirements, especially dimensional control, became another important part of the compatibility before completion (CbC) practices at Ford.

Functional Build   One of the key methods for enabling the craftsmanship effort was functional build. Originally developed and practiced by Toyota and Mazda, functional build is a fundamentally different philosophy about how to assemble hundreds of metal parts into complex vehicle bodies during the development process.

The problem with stamped metal parts is that it can be difficult to accurately predict what the part will look like until you try stamping it. This is particularly true with the many specialized alloys often employed to reduce weight and increase strength. This can result in a need to regrind the die and through trial and error get closer to the specifications of the body engineers. The traditional approach assumed the body engineer must be right, and the money was spent on grinding and rework of each part with the belief that "perfect parts build perfect bodies." Consequently, toolmakers would invest enormous amounts of time, money, and effort into making individual parts precisely meet the engineers' specifications, ironically to find they still had major problems with how the parts fit together into the resulting auto body. This led to expensive and time-consuming rework loops, as nearly finished tools had to be changed to resolve build issues often extending into or beyond production launch of the vehicle. The traditional approach also reduced the opportunity for system-level optimization and drove functional chimney behavior—people focused their energy on demonstrating that their individual part was right, and any fit and finish problem must be someone else's fault.

Functional build is a complete reversal of the traditional philosophy. It assumes that there will always be some work to be done in fine tuning in order to optimize the overall body system. It takes a collaborative, systems approach between design and manufacturing and is an excellent example of compatibility before completion in action (see Chapter 2). Early in the tool and die making process, individual parts that achieve a minimally viable level of dimensional accuracy are screwed together in special fixtures. The fixtures enable a cross-functional team of designers, body engineers, production engineers, and plant engineers to study the body to evaluate the body fit and finish as a complete system. Individual part changes are made based on what is best for the *overall* body craftsmanship, which is, of course, what the customer sees. When team members have a choice, they can correct dies that are easiest to change. Through this iterative-learning process evolves a body that meets all the criteria and delivers intended styling. This process not only results in improved body craftsmanship; it also dramatically reduces die development cost and timing.

To implement the fundamentally different functional-build approach to body development, the Ford team turned to Troy Design and Manufacturing (TDM) to facilitate the actual builds. TDM, a wholly owned subsidiary of Ford, already managed much of the digital dimensional portion of the CbC process, and it also had the capability to create the specialized fixtures and provide the skilled technicians required for a successful functional-build process. Additionally, TDM served as a sort of neutral third-party host for the many functional representatives involved in the process.

While exceptional Ford engineers were critical to establishing this important practice, it is doubtful that functional build and its significant benefits would have been possible without the hard work of John Lowery, Ned Oliver, and the rest of the TDM team.

Craftsmanship Audits Ford already had craftsmanship audits and knowledgeable specialists for reviewing and scoring products. However, Ford needed to update the auditing standards, significantly strengthen the voice of the auditors by partnering them with the developers, and provide updated training. The auditors were a very small group, and the team was much better able to leverage their know-how by teaming with the engineers in the craftsmanship cross-functional activities. The team also strengthened the impact of the audits by reviewing them in the craftsmanship forum.

Just the Beginning What we have shared was just the start of Ford's craftsmanship journey. Once a strong foundation was laid, the Ford team continued to improve on all elements of the plan and expanded it to include tactile requirements for things like door handles and technical audio requirements for door-closing sound ("a jury of our ears"). The objective was simple but challenging: provide the customer with a much-improved overall experience with Ford products. Through these efforts Ford was able to surpass most competitors, including Japanese competitors, and began to rival BIW performers. The change in the perceived quality of Ford products was profound, and the feedback from customers was extremely positive.

Reliability

By "reliability," we mean that the product should perform as expected under defined conditions and for a defined period of time, and in doing so, it should meet customers' expectations for safety, dependability, and durability. It is in some sense the most fundamental of quality expectations. It is a major part of what quality evangelist Joseph Juran described as "fit for use," and what Noriaki Kano, a customer-satisfaction guru, referred to as the "must-be" dimension of his two-dimensional Kano model of quality. Both of these icons have written broadly and profoundly on these topics, and we refer you to their books as well as those of W. Edwards Deming for a detailed, technical discussion of reliability. In this section, we only intend to share a few proven practices for reliability from our set of lean companies.

Toyota Reliability

The headline in the *Detroit Free Press* for October 19, 2017, came as no surprise to students of the auto industry: "Consumer Reports: Toyota Tops for Reliability—and Cadillac Is Last." In fact, according to the article, Toyota and Lexus were ranked No. 1 and No 2, respectively, for the fifth consecutive year of the survey.[15] This is hardly new news; in 2007, Thomas Stewart and Anand Raman wrote, "For almost 15 years J.D. Powers and other research firms have consistently rated Toyota and its luxury line, Lexus, among the top automotive brands in terms of reliability, initial quality, and long-term reliability."[16] In fact, according to a look back at *Consumer Reports* car reliability surveys, Toyota products led or were among the most reliable since the 1970s.[17]

Toyota has built an exceptional lasting culture of quality and reliability throughout its enterprise, from its emphasis on andon to signal abnormal conditions, to its focus on creating a company of problem solvers, to the Five Whys investigative methodology and disciplined use of A3s. Less known is the enormous impact of product and process design on reliability. Many of the tools and practices already described in this book also contributed to the company's incredible success. However, there are two design-quality practices that deserve further attention. And as with nearly every practice in this book, these can be adapted for use with processes or services.

Proactive Problem Prevention at Toyota   Toyota's formidable learning capability (described in our previous book[18] and in Chapter 6 of this one) has enabled the company to capture, share, and apply knowledge effectively throughout its global organization. The application of this knowledge in the design and development process is one of the keys to the unmatched levels of reliability and robustness that characterize the company's products. By utilizing this knowledge to determine the likelihood that a new design will experience a field failure or other quality issue based on previous and well-understood problems, Toyota has been able to design proven countermeasures into the new components and subsystems. This system was eventually formalized as *mizenboushi* and was first shared outside Toyota by Tatsuhiko Yoshimura, a retired Toyota quality executive and professor at Kyushu University. As we have come to expect from Toyota the system is a disciplined approach to the basics rather than a new plug-in computer algorithm.

Yoshimura authored the book *Toyota Styled Mizenboushi Method— GD3 Preventative Measures—How to Prevent a Problem Before It Occurs.*[19] As suggested by the book's title, the methodology consists of three phases that start with the initials "GD"—good design, good discussion, and good dissection—and that are used to minimize or eliminate the likelihood for potential product problems:[20]

1. **Good design** emphasizes creating a robust design by reusing proven components and characteristics of previously successful designs as part of a set-based process wherever possible. Furthermore, developers should minimize the number of changes in any single part and proactively manage any disruptive influence of new technologies or materials. Finally, product features are designed in a way that will make the presence of budding problems visible as soon as possible. You can think of the way a smoke detector chirps when the battery is low.

2. **Good discussion** of the designs should be cross-functional and focus on new parts, features, interfaces, or other changes to previ-

ous designs or their intended use. Yoshimura teaches not to trivialize changes—as we are often prone to do—but to fully understand all risks associated with those changes and to begin this process as early as possible. He developed a tool for this purpose called design review based on failure mode (DRBFM) that is similar to failure mode and effects analysis (FMEA); however, Yoshimura's tool focuses on areas of design or interface change and associated risk management, and thus it is potentially more efficient than FMEA while being as effective as a complete FMEA. This efficiency is welcome given that meticulously evaluating and documenting every possible failure mode combined with shorter development lead times can sometimes drive engineers to shortcut the process. DRBFM can be effectively combined with other design review improvements, discussed in Chapter 6.

3. **Good dissection** is a methodology for analyzing test results, which starts with a detailed review of any signs of unacceptable or inconsistent performance during testing. Parts from the completed test are "dissected" and closely studied for any signs of wear or degradation that might signal a potential weakness in the design. This practice is an important part of the genchi genbutsu product development discussed earlier in this book. Yoshimura introduced a tool—design review based on test results—to enable this process, document results and observations, and enable a robust discussion of potential issues, which is led by the validation (test) engineer with a cross-functional group to determine what, if any, corrective actions should be taken.

We can anticipate some readers' reactions to this intense emphasis on reliability—innovation will suffer and products will become boring. Toyota indeed has had this reputation. On the other hand, the philosophy of Toyota is more about understanding how the product delivers value to a specific customer and focusing innovation there instead of innovation for its own sake. The first Lexus model discussed in this book and in Liker's *The Toyota Way* was an example where the chief engineer used his understanding of the customer to develop breakthrough areas where he would achieve "this yet that" and exceed all competition. Every Toyota chief engineer develops targeted areas for breakthrough innovation and then for the rest of the vehicles relies on proven design in order to minimize unnecessary risk to create features that will likely not be valued by the customer.

Program-Level Prevention at Toyota While it is important to understand how mizenboushi works at the individual engineering-section level, it is crucial to understand how all this good work manifested itself at the program level. So we asked Randy Stephens, Toyota's chief engineer (CE) for the 2018 Avalon and the person responsible for overall product quality, how all the individual engineering problem-prevention work was brought together at the program level.

Stephens explained that there are between three and four cadenced design-quality reviews that take place a few weeks prior to major milestones. At those reviews, each of the various engineering groups reviews its documentation with the CE. These reviews may take place at the car, at the build site, or with specific parts, depending on the topics to be covered. It may require a couple of weeks for the CE to get through all the data generated from the reviews. The CE is required to sign off that the vehicle is at the appropriate level of quality relative to each milestone in the project. The final review is just before launch, and then it requires a sign-off on quality as well as safety as part of the "hand-over" to production.

G3 Applied to Processes Mark Dolsen, Eric Legary, and Murray Phillips have described the application of mizenboushi G3 methodology to several high-volume production processes at TRQSS Inc., a supplier of automotive seat-belt systems to Toyota. In an interesting IEOM paper, the authors present case studies of how TRQSS leveraged the mizenboushi framework and focused on changes in the production process as a result of volume fluctuation, product changeover, production rate change, new suppliers, operators, or materials, and other variations. They also report how the G3 framework for processes was creatively combined with Mike Rother's kata method to drive kaizen activities.[21]

Testing to Failure to Understand Limits In our previous research, we found that Toyota did significantly more testing to failure than did its competitors, which were more likely than Toyota to test to specifications (i.e., "pass-fail" testing) and approve prototypes based on meeting a predetermined threshold. While testing to specification is a common practice across many industries and completely appropriate for some applications, you don't really learn anything when the component or subsystem passes the test, except that it can meet a certain threshold. In testing to failure, tests are not stopped until there is failure, which is then investigated for root cause.

At Toyota, testing to failure is often referred to as *ijiwaru* testing. *Ijiwaru* is a Japanese word that roughly translated means "a cross-tempered or ill-natured person," terminology that absolutely captures the spirit of the testing. The test is as onerous and difficult as possible and pushes components and subsystems past their limits in order to identify and deeply understand failure modes. After a failure, Toyota engineers are better able to employ their problem-solving skills and tools to develop potential countermeasures.

Ijiwaru testing is not practiced on every component every time. As we mentioned in the prototyping section of Chapter 1, the scope of testing depends on what the team needs to learn on a specific part at a specific time. This practice also produces a significant amount of new knowledge to feed Toyota's potent organizational learning capability. One of the ways to capture and preserve that knowledge is through trade-off curves.

New Model-Quality Matrices at Ford Once you have successfully resolved an issue, it's important to share the countermeasure across products where appropriate. It's also nice to not have to solve the same issue again. One simple tool that was helpful at Ford for this purpose was the quality matrix.

The quality matrix was simply a linked Excel spreadsheet that captured and organized current model-quality countermeasures by subsystem. Among other information, it contained the affected parts, the problem, the countermeasure, and the lead person to contact with questions for each issue. Relevant entries were tracked as red (not currently in the plan—requires action), yellow (in the plan, not executed), or green (implemented and complete) on new model programs to ensure that these countermeasures or a more efficient version was incorporated into the new designs. The matrices also helped to ensure that sufficient funding was available for the new program to incorporate these solutions.

Sustainable Design

Given what we understand about the relationship between the products we create and our fragile environment, as well as the finite nature of our precious natural resources, any discussion of product excellence must include design for sustainability. By sustainable design we are referring to the entire value stream—not just the product—and this broader definition presents a much more difficult challenge. LPPD's "designing value streams" approach to development enables designers to think through all potential environmental implications of their products or processes. Jim Womack recently reminded us of this in an excellent post on *Planet Lean*.[22] For example, Womack tells us that according to Argonne National Laboratory's Greenhouse Gases, Regulated Emissions, and Energy Use in Transportation (GREET) model, a battery electric vehicle will produce about half the emissions per mile than a comparable internal combustion engine. But that is only part of the story. This number assumes that the electricity is generated conventionally. The total emissions, of course, can vary significantly if the electricity is generated by coal versus solar methods. But there is another important yet sometimes overlooked part of the equation, and that is the resources consumed and emissions created in the development and production of the product. The best way to impact both the design and value stream of our products is early in development. This is where "lean-and-green" thinking in design and development can create significant value.

The Toyota Production System has long been the global benchmark for creating maximum value while consuming minimum resources in manufacturing and logistics, and that capability starts in the development process. Toyota also has been a leader in the auto industry for sustainable products and practices. It introduced the first hybrid to the industry in 1997, currently produces the third bestselling electric vehicle (Prius Prime),[23] and leads the way in hydrogen-powered vehicles with the Mirai. The reuse of hybrid batteries for power storage in Toyota plants and other operational practices have earned 12 consecutive Environment Protection Agency Energy Star Partner of the Year Awards.

In Chapter 4 we shared how Toyota product and production engineers not only worked to create a more sustainable product by lowering vehicle weight and consequently improving fuel economy, but also worked together to create a manufacturing value stream for the required hot-stamped parts that was far more sustainable than that used by competitors. Consequently, Toyota serves as a model of how to get started in lean-and-green thinking for design and development, but we believe there is still much more that can be done.

Companies can make a good start by setting specific targets for each program and by adding "sustainable value-stream" checks to their manufacturability and other checks to the development process through CbC work. Track it and post it in your obeya like any other important attribute. As you will recall, one of the ways that the Ford B&SE team did this was by setting and tracking targets that significantly reduced stamping material waste and creating an efficient material recycling process. Environmental sustainability must be a part of how companies think about efficient design.

Efficient Design—Achieving the Elegant Solution

Understanding how your product will create unique value for your customer, as discussed in Chapter 1, is just the beginning of the design process. There are often many ways to deliver that value. A design can be created without regard to waste (i.e., just throw the kitchen sink at the problem) or optimized to be efficient with respect to almost any number of attributes or characteristics. One way to think about it is to characterize some product attributes as detracting from customer value, such as excess weight, cost, or complexity (waste), and to identify others as adding to customer value, such as enhanced performance, safety, or capability. The goal, of course, is to minimize the former while maximizing the latter. Two basic approaches to design efficiency can be utilized simultaneously: a time-based or cadenced, cross-program approach and a within-program approach.

- **Annual cross-program efficiency improvements.** These improvements are often made in support of an annual hoshin, or strategy deployment process, and/or are the result of accumulated best practices from numerous individual projects. In other words, improvements from one program become the baseline for the next program. There are a number of mechanisms to enable this approach, e.g., a strong strategy deployment process, commodity business plans, an active system of standards, and supporting knowledge repositories. Achieving these targets will definitely test your organizational learning muscles a bit. Standard bill of process, first-pick material lists, common fasteners, and standard architectures are examples of enablers, among many, that work particularly well.

- **Program-centered efficiency improvements.** These are specific efficiency targets established in order to maximize the value of an individual product for a specific customer. For example, a Mustang customer may value excellence in ride and handling more than an Explorer customer, who instead may value "go-anywhere" ruggedness. These and many other preferences will have specific implications for design-efficiency decisions that are made during development. The role of the CE and up-front work (e.g., front loading and the kentou, or study, phase) are crucial here. Individual programs should set specific part-by-part targets for critical attributes, both negative and positive, and develop a plan to achieve them. A deep understanding of customer value and a good concept paper will serve as your Rosetta stone for this work, and *monozukuri* (making things of value) will be one of your most powerful up-front tools.

Minimizing the Impact of Negative Attributes

Achieving excellence in product and process design is more than just hitting a set of product performance targets. Almost any company can accomplish a realistic design task if it just throws enough money, complexity, and weight at it. Excellence in design is about achieving elegant solutions to difficult problems. Likewise, lean product and process development aims to deliver maximum value with minimum waste. What's more, we have often seen the most innovative design solutions emerge in the face of intelligently applied constraints. The constraints, when applied thoughtfully, can act as a forcing function to improve the overall product and value stream and help to deliver optimum value to the customer.

Managing Cost in Development   Design waste comes in many forms—weight, complexity, part count, etc. However, cost is often a good surrogate for most types of waste. The first thing to understand is that your customer pays for everything, and your best chance to increase value and reduce cost is during development. Consequently, the total cost of your product has a major impact on the actual value you deliver. We believe that cost is like any other product attribute: it must be understood and trade-offs must be managed throughout the development process. Cost also has important implications for resource utilization and environmental sustainability.

We are definitely not saying that cheaper is always better. It is not. What we are saying is that it is important to fully understand your costs, know how to deliver maximum performance levels for the lowest possible cost, and deliberately decide on your cost-performance trade-offs. There are a number of cost categories, each with its own set of implications. While they may vary somewhat across industries, costs are typically grouped into development cost, investment cost, variable or unit cost, and ongoing cost or cost of ownership (see Table 7.1).

Table 7.1 Cost Categories

Cost Category	Example	Methods to Reduce Cost
Development cost	Engineering hours, prototypes, and testing	Standard architecture, part reuse, development process optimization, lean testing and prototype facility work, engineering change reduction, and targeted prototyping
Investment cost	Dies, tools, and facilities	Tool and manufacturing process standardization, such as standard bill of process or PDPD, work with suppliers on trade-offs, and improvement of tool-creating capability
Variable or unit cost	Cost to make the product (e.g., labor, materials, components)	Design for manufacturing, optimized material utilization, common materials and fasteners, part reuse, weight and complexity reduction, and supplier cost-reduction contributions
Ongoing cost or cost of ownership	Installation, maintenance, and servicing costs	Design for installation and serviceability as part of the CbC process and robust designs through the use of problem prevention (mizenboushi) and testing to failure (ijiwaru)

Actively Managing Objectives and Trade-Offs The tools and methods we have discussed throughout this book can contribute to reducing waste and increasing the value-creation characteristics of your products. But they only work if you *actively* work to reduce waste and increase the efficiency of your designs. At Ford, Jim and his team learned to manage cost just like any other attribute, and created simple summary documents to demonstrate waste (all costs, weight, or complexity) against value-creating characteristics (e.g., safety, torsional stiffness, and craftsmanship) and set targets. They actively managed these relationships on glide paths posted in the obeya. They also worked closely with their matched-pair partners and suppliers to address design, process, and commercial aspects of the targets throughout the process.

One very powerful example of utilizing LPPD tools and methods to achieve a dramatically more efficient product design occurred not in the auto industry, but in the challenging industry of subsea oil and gas technology.

Efficient Product Design with Subsea 2.0

One of the most dramatic stories of the application of LPPD principles to achieve both a more efficient design and a revolutionary new way of doing business was at TechnipFMC. TechnipFMC is a global leader in energy technologies, complex engineered systems, and services in the subsea oil and gas industry. Among other things, the London-headquartered company designs and builds subsea production systems that control and commingle fluids on the seafloor at depths of up to 9,842 feet; the deepest a human has dived is nearly 2,300 feet, a world record held by French company Compagnie Maritime d'Expertises.[24] So in some ways these systems would be easier to install, operate, and service if they were in space.

The production systems consist of enormous components, including "Christmas trees," manifolds, valves, and connectors spread out over a 30-square-kilometer area on the seafloor (see Figures 7.2a and 7.2b). They must withstand crushing pressures and incredible temperatures; resist corrosion, sand, and debris; and be operated remotely with virtually no maintenance for 25 years. And they can absolutely never, ever leak—all while controlling 10,000 barrels of oil per well per day at 1,000 psi and at temperatures higher than 100°F.

Oil and gas are finite resources, and as more easily tapped reservoirs are depleted, oil companies are forced to move to ever more challenging environments. Oil still provides a significant amount of the world's energy needs,[25] and according to Couto, the percentage of that oil coming from the subsea is predicted to steadily increase.

The oil and gas industry faced an environment of increasingly difficult engineering challenges and ever-escalating costs. Paulo Couto, VP of global subsea technology and engineering and based in TechnipFMC's Brazil Technical Center in Rio de Janeiro, and his colleagues knew this pattern could not last. They had to find another way of meeting these formidable challenges other than just throwing money at them. This thinking was confirmed when oil prices plummeted from $100 per barrel to about $50.

Couto was aware that the company's manufacturing operations had made some significant improvements with lean methods, so he started his search there. However, two things were quickly apparent: (1) the improvements in manufacturing, while impressive, would never get the company anywhere near where it needed to be, and (2) the specific methods and

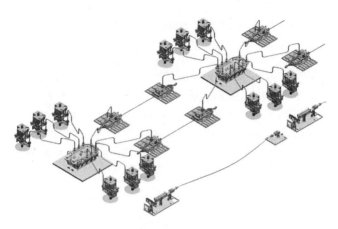

Figure 7.2a   Seafloor production system example

Figure 7.2b   Individual Christmas tree

techniques in manufacturing would not help the company in engineering and development. So he looked further and got acquainted with lean product and process development, and he quickly tasked the members of his team to learn everything they could about it.

Senior management also was challenging the technology and engineering team to lead a companywide change in its approach to the business. So, while the team in Brazil continued to learn more about and experiment with LPPD, Couto reached out to his counterparts in other parts of the world: David MacFarland, Mike Tierney, and Andy Houk, engineering leaders in Houston, Scotland, and California, respectively. Alan Labes was tagged as the first-ever chief engineer in the company, and he led the development of Subsea 2.0, a product targeted to transform not only a company but an entire industry. Setting targets for the project was simple: half the size, half the part count, half the weight, and half the cost, which would make it the foundation of a completely new way of doing business. But there was nothing simple about achieving this challenge.

The technology and engineering team employed many LPPD tools and methods. Most prominent in developing the Subsea 2.0 were the CE, concept paper, obeya management system, set-based concurrent engineering, and trade-off curves:

- **Chief engineer.** In addition to Labes's role as overall program CE, a CE was assigned for each major subsystem. This approach had mixed results because the technology and engineering team had not had time to create an environment or context for the role's success, and subsequently there was pushback from some internal "experts" who did not understand what the team was trying to do, nor the roles and the responsibilities. Interaction with the manufacturing and marketing teams also needed to be improved. However, leadership set clear expectations for Labes and supported him and the subsystem CEs throughout the project. The technology and engineering team later declared the CE experiment was a major success and did not think the project would have been possible without it. Having full accountability for project success and a product-focused mindset was crucially important to the success of the CE.

- **Concept paper.** Labes started with a concept paper to clarify and align around the vision for this project. He found that the first benefit was that it helped him work through his own thinking on the project, identifying holes in his logic and conflicts in his vision. He used it to better understand and communicate the urgency of the current-state situation for the company—to provide the "why." In addition to the vision and current state, it established targets, set up the global schedule, and assigned specific design work to the various engineering centers around the world. The concept paper also helped to connect with manufacturing, which would need to change its processes dramatically for the team to hit its targets. The document also initiated some difficult-but-needed discussions across the entire team, set the scope and functional requirements, and acted as a contract. This enabled Labes to move forward without last-minute, top-down changes; it created a true north for the team against which to measure its performance; and it virtually eliminated late "deviation requests" from the team.

- **Obeya.** The team needed a level of transparency, collaboration, and fast decision making that had not seemed possible in the past, and team members agreed to visit Herman Miller in Holland, Michigan. It was an epiphany. Not only did they see the use of the obeya system in action, but they learned about how to use milestones more effectively. The members returned to Brazil fired up about employing what they learned in Michigan. The obeya system completely revolutionized the way that the team worked together. TechnipFMC also established the obeya system in the other engineering centers. According to Labes:

> When creating a new system from scratch, the tradeoffs involved in architectural decisions at the system, subsystem, and component level need to be tested extremely fast so the full spectrum of possibilities is covered. The obeya system enables not only that, but also enables a deep and common understanding for all the team members of the most valuable characteristics of the system and what their work must deliver to support it. The obeya management system improved the process dramatically—especially due to the novel nature of the project, and the many unknowns the team had to deal with and lessons that had to be learned during the development process.

- **Set-based concurrent engineering (SBCE) and trade-off curves.** These practices, used in conjunction with targeted, rapid prototyping, enabled the team to look at many alternatives and understand the impact of the various alternatives. With this approach, the people on the team could identify which technologies the company should invest in and what the total system would look like in various configurations. Labes and Couto describe the process:

> The process started with the CEs locking in boundaries, constraints, and variables, such as material strengths, torsion, and other mechanical properties (such as friction, tolerances, and product architecture). Then CEs conducted brainstorm sessions with cross-functional teams in order to generate different design

ideas. The team then established a de-selection process where the concepts were ranked and the concepts that were proven not to work or were ranked very low were quickly eliminated, until a manageable number of concepts were left. This process continued, gradually adding more engineering effort to the remaining concepts for each subsequent de-selection round, so knowledge about the concepts was being developed and the team continually evolved their thinking. During the process, it was not unusual that a new concept was created out of cross-pollination between existing concepts.

Once the set of options was reduced to three to five, the team started to assess in detail how each concept would react to a change in one of the variables mentioned above. This was an intense process, as every option had to be computer-simulated and/or physically prototyped and its design adjusted accordingly. Out of this process, the team saw that some concepts were more sensitive to one variable than others, and they also identified which design changes would deliver the biggest benefit as well as at what point an improvement in performance would no longer deliver any value to the design. This knowledge was captured in tradeoff-curve charts that could visually communicate how each concept would have its overall design efficiency affected by the full range of the variables. The team was amazed at how well the curves communicated a complex set of technical relationships. In fact, one CE, John Calder, commented that "tradeoff curves were a simple, elegant and powerful representation of a tremendous amount of work—similar to Einstein's $E = MC^2$.

This was not a short sprint. It was a long and arduous process. And the team had no idea what the outcome would be when they started [the] Subsea 2.0 program, composed of multiple complex development projects going on simultaneously. SBCE and tradeoff curves were central to the team's ability to develop a disruptive system because they would not be able to do so had they not been able to fully explore the design space with these methods. The long cycles in fine tuning the design after they went to testing [provided] a reassurance that no matter how confident you are on the design, it's not [until] fully tested that victory can be claimed and all knowledge is captured.

The team achieved the objectives of half the weight, half the size, and half the part count, and did so at a dramatically lower price point; see Figures 7.3*a* and 7.3*b* for size and complexity comparisons. And it delivered the project on time, at cost, and at a projected lead-time reduction of one-third on future orders. And best of all . . . the teams love working this way! And now TechnipFMC is working to spread this design philosophy and approach around the global company.

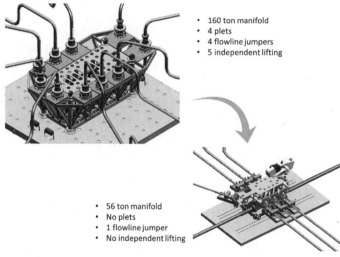

- 160 ton manifold
- 4 plets
- 4 flowline jumpers
- 5 independent lifting

- 56 ton manifold
- No plets
- 1 flowline jumper
- No independent lifting

Figure 7.3a   Manifold construction comparison

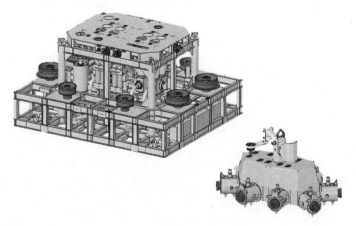

Figure 7.3b   Conventional subsea manifold versus Subsea 2.0 manifold—same functionality, half the size and weight

But there is more. Not only did the team hit its targets on time, but it created a significant competitive advantage and a new development operating system for the company. And investors and analysts have noticed. Couto presented the breakthrough product and new methodology to an outside group of analysts, and the result was an upgrade of the company stock from "hold" to "buy" and an immediate 3 percent jump in the stock price. Byron Pope, managing director of Tudor, Pickering, Holt & Co., wrote just one of many glowing reports:

> Seeing is (fully) believing, and we very much like what we saw (and heard) at the Analyst Day. We were treated to what was a rather compelling TechnipFMC Analyst Day in which the company illustrated how its radical rethinking of how to best help its E&P customers improve their offshore/deepwater project economics has resulted in both improved form and functionality of the company's subsea systems offering (FTI's "Subsea 2.0"), a harbinger of an eventual renaissance in subsea projects being sanctioned in 2018+. The essence of Subsea 2.0 and why it is the proverbial game changer? . . . try 50%+ reductions in the size, weight and number of parts associated with key subsea production systems elements (trees, manifolds, etc.). It is these sorts of innovations which heighten our confidence. Lightbulb moment of confirmation was during our rotation through the company's Innovation & Technology Showroom (which, by the way, was our up-close . . . but no cameras allowed . . . looksee at some of the key hardware elements of Subsea 2.0) when it came to light that TechnipFMC's leadership challenged the organization to think differently well before the most recent oilfield service industry downturn began in earnest.[26]

The TechnipFMC team had, indeed, designed the future. Couto describes the TechnipFMC experience with LPPD this way:

> LPPD was key to enabling the disruptive change we were looking for. And it is much more than love at first sight; in this case, the more we learn, the stronger the passion. We simply cannot imagine how we would work without it now.

LOOKING FORWARD

Your product—whether physical product, software, or a service—embodies the value you create for your customer. The best companies in any industry, such as TechnipFMC, are driven to understand that value, and they continually improve on its delivery in a constant pursuit of excellence. Companies that do not chase perfection will soon find themselves irrelevant.

The roots of our LPPD model and the one leveraged by TechnipFMC are firmly embedded in Toyota. In the next chapter, we will examine how Toyota has long been designing the future of the auto industry through product and process development and how it continues to do so today.

Your Reflection

Creating a Vision

If you develop the people, the supporting infrastructure, and the lean processes described in the first six principles, you are well on your way to very good products, delivered on time, within budget. To go the extra mile to product excellence takes another step, and it is all in the people through creating a culture of excellence. This chapter focused on the pursuit of product perfection—an elusive pursuit, but the secret to the next level of excellence. It is hard to measure, it is hard to prescribe through specific methodologies or actions, yet you know it when you see it. We argued that what is needed to achieve product excellence includes:

- A passion for excellence in the hearts and minds of all your people
- A spirit of craftsmanship that taps into the internal joy of accomplishing something incredible, and incredibly difficult, that delivers an unparalleled experience to your customer
- An emotional connection with customers
- Best-in-world requirements for measurable product and service features
- Methods and a forum for evaluating and sharing craftsmanship
- Measures of world-class reliability
- Proactive problem prevention
- Fanatical use of all the best quality methods

- Sustainable design
- An obsession with efficient design to deliver the highest possible value

Does this vision fit what you think is needed in your company? How would you revise this vision to better fit your company's situation?

Your Current Condition

1. Are your people engaged in creating product excellence? What have you done to create an environment to promote product excellence? What more can you do?

2. Are you using design to differentiate your product and make a stronger connection with your customer?

3. Is craftsmanship enhancing your customers' experiences with your product and communicating "well made"? How can it be improved?

4. Is the reliability of your product or service a competitive advantage? What actions have you taken to improve its performance?

5. How are you managing the efficiency of your designs and driving waste out of your product and your value stream? What actions can you take to improve?

Taking Action

1. Assemble several cross-functional, multilevel groups of people to identify any possible impediments to creating a culture of excellence in your organization. Consider and prioritize possible countermeasures.

2. Organize a cross-function product teardown event to compare your products with those of your best competitors. Look outside your industry, if necessary. Get input from design, product engineering, manufacturing, and suppliers. Capture opportunities for improvement based on the above categories. Develop and prioritize possible countermeasures to improve.

8

Designing the Future by Linking Strategy to Execution

A Toyota-Tesla Comparison

There is nothing that can't be done. If you can't make something, it's because you haven't tried hard enough.

—SAKICHI TOYODA

Navigating into the Future of Transport

Which automakers will survive for coming generations, becoming the Ford or Mercedes-Benz of the twenty-first century? Which automakers will become extinct like Studebaker or Packard? The future of transport is now rapidly unfolding, with strategic lines being drawn—disruptive technologies on one side and experience and operational excellence on the other. But things are not always as they appear, and there are many lessons to be learned—in the auto industry and for other businesses—as this industrial drama plays out.

This industry transformation provides a great case study for looking at the relationship between strategy, product development, and operational excellence. Strategy provides direction for all product development efforts. What gets many excited is the image of the maverick entrepreneur who takes on an established industry and wins, like David versus Goliath. Is a bold, disruptive strategy for a newcomer to the industry enough to overcome weak execution of the novice? Do the LPPD principles in this book apply in a rapidly changing world of disruptive technologies? As we pointed out in the beginning of this book, we believe the answer is a matter of short-term versus long-term perspective. In the short term the right breakthrough technology can win. But long-term sustainable competitive advantage comes from linking well-thought-out strategy to developing and delivering exceptional products.

The main disruptive force threatening the traditional auto industry is computer technology in both the product and the processes. Self-driving electric vehicles, ride-hailing through websites, and even totally automated factories are thought to be as big a shift in the future of transport as the transformation from the horse and buggy to the car. Tesla has been one of the most visible icons in this charge to the future. With CEO Elon Musk's vision of autonomous vehicles powered by batteries from Tesla's Gigafactory, with batteries recharged through Tesla's solar technology, Tesla is seen by many as the great disruptor—the Amazon or Uber of the vehicle production world. Stunts like launching a Tesla Roadster into space help embolden the image. But it is a long, and apparently bumpy, road from start-up to automotive powerhouse.

Automotive engineering firm Munro & Associates Inc. tore down a Tesla Model 3 to basic components and found many quality issues: It took two hands to get the door open. Body panels were far out of specification, leading to a very bad fit and finish. Great product, but poor execution has been the calling card of Tesla. Studying the tear-down, CEO Sandy Munro noted, "If we look over here I can barely get my fingernail in. . . . And then we look over here, I can almost put my thumb in. This is, this is very unusual; the stackups, the tolerance stackups on this car are just like nothing we've ever seen before. Not since, like I say, the '70s or something. I don't, I don't understand how it got to this point.'"[1]

Tesla made a huge impact on the world by introducing the Model S. The all-electric car excited early adopters and was viewed by industry analysts as a disruptive product design. By July 2017, Elon Musk's electric personality and the early success of the Model S skyrocketed Tesla's stock price to one of the highest market caps in the industry, exceeding that of Ford and chasing General Motors. The next big leap forward was the lower-priced, but still expensive, Model 3 for mass production. By February 2018, Tesla had missed many promised delivery dates for the Model 3. Production delay followed production delay, and a very low volume of cars was being built "by hand" because the production line was not working. Then Tesla's Gigafactory, which made batteries, also experienced production delays because of supplied parts problems and became a bottleneck for Model 3 production.

Craig Trudell of Bloomberg News described three major promises that Elon Musk made and Tesla had failed to deliver on:[2]

Cruising Coast-to-Coast on Autopilot
Musk said in October 2016 that the company planned to do a Los Angeles-to-New York trip "without the need for a single touch" of the steering wheel by the end of last year [2016] to demonstrate the capabilities of Autopilot. Tesla has promised the driver-assistance system will eventually be capable of full autonomy.

That didn't pan out. In February, Musk said Tesla would attempt the trip in another three to six months.

Failure to Launch (on Time)
Each of the new vehicles Tesla has rolled out over the years has been behind schedule. Its first car, the Roadster, arrived about nine months late in March 2008. The Model S was introduced about six months after Musk's target in June 2012, and the Model X was tardy by about two years when it hit the market in September 2015.

The Model 3 also landed later than was suggested by Musk's famous "master plan" posted on Tesla's blog in August 2006. He said back then that an affordable model costing roughly half the price of the $89,000 Roadster would be Tesla's second model.

The CEO handed over the first keys to customers for the Model 3—which starts at $35,000 but is initially being delivered at higher prices—in July [2017].

Off-Putting Output
[Musk] told analysts in May 2016 that Tesla was aiming to produce 100,000 to 200,000 of the [Model 3] sedans in the second half of 2017. . . . In May 2017, the company projected it would make 5,000

a week by the end of the year. It's since pushed that goalpost back to sometime within the next three months.

One would at least expect that with high levels of automation Tesla would need less labor than traditional automakers. Yet, one journalist reported: "The plant has 'a workforce that's twice the size of what it's required to build the car,' said one former high-level employee. With more than 10,000 factory employees making about 100,000 cars last year, Tesla's Fremont facility makes about 10 vehicles per employee at a factory that never made fewer than 26 vehicles per employee (and made as many as 74 vehicles per employee) when it was a joint venture between General Motors and Toyota."[3] And this was before Tesla reported in May that they would need to hire more workers to produce the Model X and 5,000 vehicles per week.[4]

Each month Tesla's losses got worse. *AutoWeek* reported in November 2017 that Tesla was burning through $8,000 per minute, spending $1 billion per quarter,[5] and had sold 50,000 cars for all of 2017 (equivalent to a single, low-volume model for major automakers). Nonetheless, in early 2018 investors continued to line up to buy Tesla stock; customers continued to hand money to Tesla to reserve slots for its Model 3, which they might not receive until 2019; and companies gave money in advance to reserve Tesla's electric super-heavy-duty trucks that were still in the concept stage. By June of 2018 Tesla erected a tent to quickly install another assembly line and managed to get up to 5000 vehicles in a week.

Tesla's reality appears to fly in the face of our advice, which is to design in quality, precisely execute, design for manufacturing, and design out every possible penny of cost. We also argue that LPPD requires effective communication and coordination across the enterprise, including with outside suppliers. Working with outside suppliers also has been a weak point in the start-up of Tesla. It has been reported by CNBC that "Tesla is struggling to manage and fix a significant volume of flawed or damaged parts from its suppliers, sending some to local machine shops for rework, according to several current and former Tesla engineers. The company said it also makes adjustments to the design of some parts after receiving them from suppliers."[6] One of the biggest bottlenecks for Model 3 production was from an internal supplier, the battery Gigafactory. "Tesla says there isn't any single problem slowing production down now. Instead, the heavy reliance on automation and new production methods have created a galaxy of smaller problems that must be addressed individually."[7]

Arguably Tesla is going through growing pains as a start-up entering a new technical arena, and the automaker will figure it out. Though 15 years in business does not seem like a startup. Some argue that electric vehicles will have so few parts and be so simple to build that anyone can do it, especially if 3D printing becomes viable for car bodies. This raises an interesting question: Does a bold vision about disruptive technology trump efficient execution and cost? Is most of the auto industry in the dark ages to be supplanted by more forward-looking automotive start-ups like Tesla, Waymo, and Uber? Will traditional automakers go the way of the buggy whip?

Corporate strategy guru Michael Porter warned in a classic 1996 *Harvard Business Review* article that "operational effectiveness is not strategy."[8] He also warned that Japanese companies could be on their way to a downward spiral: "The dangers of Japanese-style competition are now becoming easier to recognize. In the 1980s, with rivals operating far from the productivity frontier, it seemed possible to win on both cost and quality indefinitely. . . . But as the gap in operational effectiveness narrows, Japanese companies are increasingly caught in a trap of their own making. If they are to escape the mutually destructive battles now ravaging their performance, Japanese companies will have to learn strategy."

As we write this more than 20 years after Porter predicted the need for Japanese automakers to learn strategy, there certainly have been large struggles in Japan auto. Nissan was on the verge of bankruptcy before being taken over by Renault. Mazda, Subaru, Suzuki, and Mitsubishi all had to be taken over. Honda is more diversified and relatively healthy, and Toyota is still going strong. While Porter believed a carefully crafted strategy should lead the way, he did not suggest throwing out operational effectiveness. In fact, he advised companies to marry strategy and operational effectiveness. The key is to have a unique offering and a unique set of activities aligned with the strategy to deliver a competitive advantage. We believe that's been the history of Toyota and fits the way Toyota is approaching the future.

Has Toyota Been a Disruptor?

Toyota's history of industry disruption started with the introduction of high-quality, fuel-efficient, low-cost cars in the 1970s that completely changed customers' expectations and rocked the auto establishment, forcing dramatic change on the entire industry. As established European and American auto companies tried to figure out how Toyota did this, they discovered the Toyota Production System, which Toyota had been perfecting since World War II. The tools of TPS were easy to copy, but the underlying drive and philosophy were not easy to imitate. Then Toyota ventured into the luxury market, creating a new brand, Lexus. The story of the development of the first Lexus, introduced in 1989, is one of breaking industry norms and achieving aerodynamics with attractive styling, power with high fuel economy and low noise and vibration, and a next level of quality at an industry-leading cost.[9] Toyota disrupted the status quo of the European luxury set and raised the bar such that it became the leading luxury brand by sales in three years and nearly eclipsed North American luxury brands. Then in 1997, long before most in the auto industry were thinking about designing for environmental sustainability, the first gas-electric hybrid—Prius—rolled out of Toyota. In Prius, Toyota designed a product that created demand where none had previously existed and forced the rest of the industry to follow its lead. Most recently, with the introduction of the Mirai for a "hydrogen-powered society" and the solid-state battery technology research that powers it, Toyota continues to push the boundaries of conventional thinking through its approach to learning and new product and process development.[10]

We do think Toyota has learned a great deal more about stepping outside the box and adopting bold strategies since Akio Toyoda became president, as evidenced by industry-leading spending on autonomous and connected vehicle technology. On the software side alone, Toyota has invested billions just to develop the artificial intelligence software for driverless cars and seeks to become the global leader—doing it its way in-house. Still, looking at Toyota's vehicle lineup in 2018, one can legitimately question whether it is on the road to leadership, or even keeping up, when it comes to future mobility. Toyota's motto is "Underpromise, overdeliver." You will not likely hear Toyota boasting about its advanced connected mobility, but we suspect that the billions of dollars invested and Toyota's history of getting a lot for its R&D money will keep the company at the forefront.

According to Musk, the future of automotive is clear, and there is only one solution: self-driving, electric vehicles of all sizes and shapes using renewable energy, with ride-hailing so you can get where you want when you want without owning and operating your own car. The old gas-guzzling engines with their complex web of emissions controls are dinosaurs of the past. Electric vehicles greatly simplify the design and production of powertrains and lower barriers to entry into the auto industry—one reason so many high-tech companies claim they will build electric cars.

We agree, as does the entire industry, that the traditional transportation industry is heading for major disruption leading to environmentally friendly, self-driving cars, using renewable energy, with new business models. Self-driving vehicles are on the road as we write this and will continue to come online, and continue to get outsized attention in the media. The strategy question for each competitor is, How can we plan the transition to this new world and gain a competitive advantage? One of the first questions that have to be answered to begin the strategic planning process is when? Companies have to forecast the future and predict when this new generation of vehicles will dominate the market. This is a long-term forecast, which means it is bound to be wrong. Yet some best guesses have to be made. We believe, as does Toyota, that the vision of sales dominated by self-driving, electrified vehicles will take decades to achieve, not years. Here is why:

1. **Change is rarely simple, linear, and predictable.** The dot-com bubble and its spectacular crash are now legend. The internet went live in 1991 with ATT and NCR. The bubble grew rapidly between 1995 and 2000 and burst in 2001, with bubble company bankruptcies and a loss of value of up to 70 or 80 percent. Looking back at 2002, we could say the internet was a big myth and those who predicted the internet would change everything—and brick-and-mortar stores would cease to exist—were deluded. Yet here we are now, and the internet has changed everything, and there are major threats to brick-and-mortar stores. It just took a lot longer than we expected, by about two decades, and it still is far from the extreme visions of the internet prophets.

2. **Acceptance of new technology takes time.** There are always early adopters, but the large mass of people will not change habits easily. It will take time to accept self-driving, ride-hailing vehicles as the norm. We have spoken to many people who are giddy over the idea of taking out their smartphone and signaling for a nearby robot car that drives them wherever they want to go. Those same people say things like, "But I would not trust that robot car to drive 70 miles per hour with one of my children in it."

Fear of the unknown is natural. The media struck fear into ordinary citizens when they claimed Toyota vehicles were being taken over by their computers and accelerating uncontrollably, even though this was a myth.[11] Each crash of a self-driving vehicle leads to intense media scrutiny and investigation.[12] It will take time to overcome fear of computer drivers gone awry. Most analysts predict the starting point will be limited to autonomous vehicles in defined roadways in urban areas specially equipped for that type of vehicle. And ride-hailing is a type of public transportation, and the United States, in particular, has never strongly embraced public transportation because its citizens highly value independence and control. We like our vehicles parked by our residence for use when we want, and many people love their vehicles as a source of identity. This may well change, but it will not come fast or easy.

3. **Ordinary citizens will not easily surrender their gas-powered vehicles.** Various automakers have made commitments to abandon pure gas-powered vehicles and sell only electrified vehicles by certain dates, such as 2030. Let's assume that happens. So in 2025 gas-powered vehicles will still be sold. It seems likely people will want to use their existing vehicles for some time, at least for 10 years. This keeps gas-powered vehicles on the road until, say, 2035, and probably beyond. And automakers will, in fact, continue to sell gas or gas-electric hybrids beyond 2025 as long as there is demand someplace in the world.

4. **Electrification means more than pure battery-powered vehicles.** Many automakers have made commitments to stop selling gas-only vehicles by some date. Toyota committed to offering an electrified version of all models in its line up by "around 2025." But the company forecasts that pure electric vehicles will still be a minority, mostly focused on shorter travel distances within urban centers. Mainly, Toyota expects it will be selling gas-electric hybrids and plug-in hybrids by 2025. And it predicts that longer term there will be a growing demand for electric vehicles within urban centers and hydrogen fuel cells for longer distances and for bigger, heavier vehicles that would otherwise require very expensive banks of batteries.[13] More on this later.

The Center for Automotive Research (CAR) agrees with our prognosis. It predicted in early 2018 that "electrification [and] autonomy won't gain widespread adoption for decades."[14] After doing a study of industry experts that attempts to forecast the future, CAR expects that "Level 4 and Level 5 self-driving vehicles will account for less than 4 percent of new-vehicle sales by 2030, although that number will increase steadily to roughly 55 percent by 2040." The research center predicts that alternative powertrains, including both battery-powered electric vehicles and fuel cell vehicles, will make up 8 percent of the market by 2030. That means that 92 percent will be gas-powered and hybrids. That is still a lot of electric vehicles by 2030 and self-driving vehicles by 2040, but hardly the instant industry disruption that many industry analysts are expecting. And major auto companies prepared to abandon gas-powered or hybrid powertrains in the next 10 years would be in serious trouble according to this forecast. It is just a forecast . . . but it certainly makes you think. This may help explain why Toyota in 2018 announced that it had developed the world's most thermally efficient 2.0-liter gas engine, reducing emissions by at least 18 percent.[15] Why bother if gas engines are history? The answer is that Toyota believes it will be selling gas engines as the only power source or parts of hybrids for enough years to justify the investment and what the company learns will help it with new electrified vehicles.

Comparing Tesla's and Toyota's Strategic Visions and Operations Philosophies

Strategy as Direction

The truth is, we do not know the future. What we believe is that the way of thinking in Toyota is a strong model for flexibly navigating an undoubtedly rocky road into the future. Toyota's strategic vision and approach to getting there is in stark contrast to that of Musk, and the differences between the two are informative. We make this comparison not to hold up Toyota as a model and Tesla as a cautionary tale, but rather because the differences illustrate competing strategic operational philosophies that are increasingly common—the big bang disrupter based on a new idea against the current industry leader that has consistently delivered value taking measured steps into the future. Both could have identical long-term views of the destination (in this case they do in the abstract, but not in the specifics), but we are interested in the path to get there. Let's consider each company's approach.

Tesla's Disrupter Vision

Our simplified sketch of Musk's vision for Tesla (Figure 8.1) focuses on vehicles (Tesla also manufactures batteries, solar panels, and stand-alone power systems). In the current condition, Tesla has shown us some of its breakthrough all-electric products in the Model S, Model X, and Model 3, along with a prototype of a super-heavy-duty truck. They all include "Autopilot," though at the time of this writing, this would be considered level 2 (out of five levels) and the driver still must be in control. We did not distinguish between medium-term and long-term goals because we could not discern a difference. The singular vision is high-performance electric vehicles combined with complete autonomous driving capability.

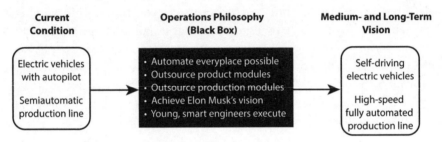

Figure 8.1   Tesla's big bang strategic vision

Porter taught us that a key part of strategy is the unique activities that will support it. Musk seems to recognize this. In fact, he claimed that the real vision is not the vehicle, but how he will build the cars in highly automated manufacturing facilities far faster than could be done in conventional assembly plants. As he explained in an earnings call to stockholders on February 7, 2018: "The competitive strength of Tesla long-term is not going to be the car: It's going to be the factory. We are going to productize the factory. . . . The Model T wasn't the product. It was the River Rouge. We will have a great product. But the factory is going to be the product that has the long-term sustained competitive advantage."[16]

In a recent conversation about this topic, John Shook clarified the history of the River Rouge and Toyota's contribution:

> Henry Ford figured out much of this (the principles of flow) just a little over a century ago. But, that was a simple case, where achieving high speed production (very much as Elon now seeks) was relatively

straightforward. The products were all simple and, more importantly, they were all the same. As soon as complexity was added (in the form of types of products and options as well as more complex technology like electronics), Henry's simple system broke down. What worked great as an initial attempt in Highland Park proved a disaster when he tried to scale it even more at the Rouge, adding complexity that the system wasn't capable of handling. Half a century later, Toyota came along and figured out the next essential part of the equation, how to achieve the speed, but also the built-in quality, with the complexity of mixed model production.

Will Tesla repeat Henry Ford's mishaps in trying to scale up rapidly toward the idealistic vision of the River Rouge complex? In early 2018 it appears Tesla's Achilles' heel is its ability to design for and execute in manufacturing.[17] Yet that is precisely how the company wants to compete against traditional automakers with many decades of manufacturing experience. Musk explained, "The most fundamental difference is thinking about the factory really as a product, as a quite vertically integrated product." Added chief technical officer J. B. Straubel, "It's treating it as more of an engineering and a technical problem as well." Musk envisions the most automated vehicle plants in the world where material delivery, manufacture, and assembly are done without human intervention and his production lines will be far faster than the conventional manual assembly lines that he mocks: "Grandma with a walker can exceed the speed of the fastest production line."[18]

We like Straubel's idea of thinking of future production systems as a design problem, but we would view it through the lens of LPPD. Recall the principle of front-loading the design process and using set-based concurrent engineering. It seems that Tesla is falling into the trap of jumping into an all-or-nothing solution, skipping any serious analysis or attempt to explore the solution space. Electric cars are good, and hydrogen fuel cells are bad. Automated factories are good, and factories with manual work are old school. When thinking about the design requirements for the future factory, there is a fundamental design question. Is this purely a technical design problem, as Straubel suggests, or is it a sociotechnical design problem? Who will be controlling the daily operation of the automation? Who will be responding to problems and how? Who will be improving the technology? We would submit it is people, and the need for motivated, engaged, and capable people will if anything be even greater in a complex, automated environment.

Steven St. Angelo is senior managing officer and CEO of the Toyota Latin America and Caribbean region. He recalls his younger days as an engineer at General Motors when CEO Roger Smith made a similar bold statement in the 1980s. Ironically, it was about the same time that Smith agreed to a joint venture with Toyota that would become NUMMI—at that time the most productive plant in North America, and there was not a lot of automation. While NUMMI prospered, Smith was spending billions of dollars on a joint venture with robotics manufacturer Fanuc, purchasing Electronic Data Systems, and investing toward his vision of completely automated factories with lights turned out and no people. As St. Angelo recalls: "He [Smith] also tried to automate out of GM's problems. It was a disaster. I have many patents for automation, and I learned that if you can't do a process manually . . . you will not be able to do it with a robot. Also, all automation works in a lab environment, however, when you add the ingredient of variation it's a new ball game."

Tesla's super-automated production line depends on hiring large numbers of bright young engineers who have not worked together, giving them a top-down vision of the desired product and process characteristics, and demanding they engineer and build it. It also depends on a good deal of purchased product subsystems and turnkey production lines from inside and outside vendors. Speaking about Tesla's Gigafactory for batteries, Musk called the experience to date "production hell," but assured investors in an earnings call that help is on the way in the form of German automation companies that will deliver perfect systems that can simply be plugged in and played to perfection: "We expect the new automated lines to arrive next month in March, and then it's already—it's been—it's working in Germany. So, that's got to be disassembled, brought over to the Gigafactory, and re-assembled and then brought into operation at the Gigafactory. It's not a question of whether it works or not. It's just a question of disassembly, transport, and reassembly."[19]

It is ironic that Tesla took over the factory formerly occupied by NUMMI, an icon of the Toyota Production System. In the early stages of Tesla production, Toyota sent top people to help. Yet so much of Tesla's vision of manufacturing is completely contrary to TPS: Spend large amounts of capital to automate everything possible. Rely on hiring many engineers to make it work rather than carefully developing talent from within. Repair in quality rather than designing and building in quality. Aim for an ultrafast assembly line instead of building to the rate of customer demand (takt). Note that the idea of people continuously improving does not seem to appear in the Tesla playbook. It seems like a vision born of the machine paradigm, not a living system paradigm. It is also interesting that in the Gigafactory's "production hell," Elon Musk developed some appreciation of the value of people in crisis management: "It has to some degree renewed my faith in humanity that the rapid evolution of progress and the ability of people to adapt rapidly is quite remarkable."

As week after week went by and Tesla repeatedly missed production targets for the Model 3, Elon Musk spent more time in the factory, even sleeping in a conference room. He claimed being close to the action allowed him to see problems quickly and then go and help to solve them. Perhaps this intense experience on the shop floor awoke some new thoughts, because suddenly Musk was talking about how the company had used too much automation and too many robots and the value of people was unappreciated. He said the company needed more people and fewer robots.[20] When interviewed for *CBS This Morning*, Musk was asked about the reasons for what he called the "production hell" that Tesla was going through. He explained that the company got "complacent about some of the things that we thought were our core technology. We put too much technology into the Model 3 all at once. This should have been staged."[21] He also admitted that the concept of a complex set of conveyors that automatically delivered parts to the point of use was not a great idea. "We had this crazy complicated network of conveyor belts. And it was not working. So we got rid of the whole thing." He certainly sounds like a man who is beginning to discover the importance of the principles of LPPD that we have talked about in this book.

We don't know if Tesla will ultimately struggle as a business or succeed lavishly. The vision and approach of Tesla, however, is interesting because we see it so often. Obviously, Musk has wowed many investors who are betting with their wallets on him. The image is that of a strong individual entrepreneur with a bold disruptive vision who is willing to take risks and persist until his vision is achieved. After all, that is how Microsoft, Apple, Amazon, Google, Facebook, and (name your wildly successful software start-up) did it. And that was how Musk's PayPal did it. The "how" is less important than the charisma of the leader who has the right big idea at the right time.

This seems to be the American dream of how we reach for the future: start-up firms led by visionary individual leaders with the next disruptive idea who make billions as their company grows, then the company grows to be a large bureaucracy that loses its innovative edge and ends up defending existing products until the next disruptive innovation puts the stodgy old firm out of business, and so on. This is survival of the fittest, and the fittest are perceived to be the brilliant individual visionaries who can outthink all their established competitors. With a vision, execution will follow. Toyota's approach to working toward a vision is about 180 degrees different.

Toyota's Balanced Vision

Toyota has not been the leader in vocalizing a commitment to pure electric vehicles. Instead its strategy has been parallel development of a range of types of electrification. Toyota began developing electrified vehicles decades before Tesla was formed, and it pioneered mass production with the Prius in 1997. More recently, it has been making huge investments in big data and artificial intelligence to move toward autonomous vehicles. More than $1.5 billion was spent on R&D for autonomous vehicles through the Toyota Research Institute in the United States launched in 2015, and in 2018 Toyota announced another $2.8 billion to start up Toyota Research Institute–Advanced Development in Tokyo. Toyota is working to apply TPS principles to accelerate the millions of lines of computer code needed for driverless vehicles. According to Toyota Executive Vice President Shigeki Tomoyama, "If we want to make the most of Toyota's strength in creating new business models, it's going to require applying TPS. We want to show people inside and outside the company that TPS is still central to Toyota.[22] Toyota has not rejected autonomous electric vehicles and has committed to putting highly automated cars on highways by 2020. Toyota simply sees a more extended transition period where hybrid and plug-in hybrid sales will grow, followed later by a combination of electric and hydrogen-powered vehicles. But Toyota is moving toward the vision incrementally based on its two core principles: respect for people and continuous improvement (Figure 8.2).

Medium-Term and Long-Term Challenges Toyota firmly believes that human-induced climate change is real. The company states on its website that "extreme weather phenomena around the world are wreaking havoc

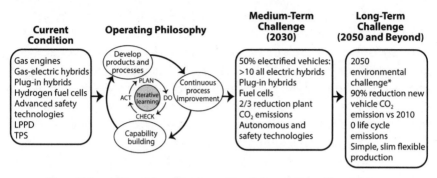

*New vehicle zero CO_2 emissions, life cycle zero CO_2 emissinos, plant zero CO_2 emissions, minimum water usage, 100% recycling, future society in harmony with nature

Figure 8.2 Toyota's strategic vision and operating philosophy

on society, attesting to the reality of global warming. If further measures are not taken to reduce emissions of greenhouse gases, it is estimated that average global temperatures could rise between 3.7 and 4.8°C by 2100 compared with pre-industrial levels."

Thus Toyota laid out its "Toyota Environmental Challenge 2050."[23] A "vision" is a long-term ideal that may not be achievable. A "challenge" is a measurable goal that Toyota is committed to achieving. It starts with zero CO_2 emissions over the life cycle of the vehicle, but Toyota wants to go beyond that: "To go beyond zero environmental impact and achieve a net positive impact, Toyota has set itself six challenges. All these challenges, whether in climate change or resource and water recycling, are beset with difficulties, however we are committed to continuing toward the year 2050 with steady initiatives in order to realize sustainable development together with society."[24]

Toyota defined six challenges that focus on new vehicle zero CO_2 emissions, zero life cycle (total value chain) CO_2 emissions, zero plant CO_2 emissions, minimum water usage with no contamination, zero landfill use, and environmental conservation. Not satisfied with no harm to the environment, Toyota wants to have a net positive impact on the environment.

For new vehicles, the very long-term vision is to get to 100 percent electrification through a combination of electric vehicles, hydrogen-powered vehicles, and some hybrids. Toyota is committed to contributing not only to hydrogen vehicles, but more broadly to a hydrogen society.

The 2050 challenge is to reduce overall CO_2 emissions by 90 percent of the 2010 levels. Toyota's 2030 challenge is that half of its vehicles will be electrified (about 5.5 million vehicles). It intends to offer electrified versions of all vehicles by 2025, which means predominately hybrids. This is different from Tesla's vision of 100 percent all-electric cars. Toyota's challenge by early 2020s is to have at least 10 all-electric vehicles on the market, as well as to grow sales of hydrogen fuel cell (FC) vehicles, but the company expects the large majority of the 5.5 million vehicles to be hybrids and plug-in hybrids. In other words, as CAR predicts, Toyota does not see gas as a power source disappearing by 2030. Mitsumasa Yamagata, chief engineer in Toyota Power Train Product Planning, forecasts that 90 percent of all vehicles in 2030 will still use some form of gas engine and explained: "Developing the most fuel-efficient powertrains using petrol engines and hybrid systems will be the best way to have an impact (on reducing emissions), and we remain committed to this. . . . At the same time we will be able to use the technology developed for the powertrains in EVs and FCVs."[25]

In the near term Toyota views most technologies for autonomous vehicles as safety technology to assist the driver. As of 2017, most vehicles have advanced safety equipment included in the base model (similar to several other automakers' vehicles). Toyota Safety Sense includes a pre-collision system that alerts the driver and applies the brakes to avoid a frontal collision, provides lane departure detection with steering assistant, has automatic high beams, features dynamic radar cruise control, and has pedestrian detection. This gives Toyota mass production experience with these technologies as the market evolves toward self-driving vehicles.

An important area of strategy setting is strategic portfolio management. Any established company has a range of products, some designed for near-term demand and others in R&D for the long term. The current cash cows generate funding to support long-term R&D. Some organizational theorists have argued that the most successful firms are "ambidextrous," with some parts of the organization focused on incremental improvement in the current product lineup and other parts focused on long-term technology development.[26] One study found that successful firms allocate on average 70 percent of their innovation funds to incremental innovation (short term), 20 percent to adjacent innovation (medium term), and 10 percent to radical or breakthrough initiatives (long term). Google is an example of one firm that works toward the 70-20-10 balance. Firms with this portfolio balance realized a price-earnings premium of 10 to 20 percent.[27]

Of course, Toyota as a highly successful, mature automaker is in a very different position from Tesla. Start-ups like Tesla do not have the luxury of using mature cash-cow products to fund advanced products. They must raise outside capital based on promises of disrupting the industry. In this sense Musk has been doing a masterful job. Perhaps the need to get investors excited is the motivation to paint a picture of breakthrough innovation surpassing all competitors in electric vehicles and automated manufacturing. Toyota's years of megaprofits (about $20 billion in fiscal 2017) and deep coffers of cash allowed it to spend $9.3 billion on R&D in 2017, the eleventh largest budget in the world. Tesla in that same period spent about one-tenth of that, which is still high for Tesla's revenue level.

Toyota's Operating Philosophy   To us, Tesla's operating philosophy appears a bit simplistic—automate, automate, automate. As a design approach, this is leaping to conclusions about the one best way. Toyota's philosophy is far more nuanced and has been refined for many years. In fact, Toyota's basic principles of operation have not changed since the Toyota Production System was created by Taiichi Ohno and his associates over six decades ago. It is still to have standard, stable operations that support just-in-time production to surface problems, build in quality, and continuously improve. That is as true in product development as it is in manufacturing. Short, rapid feedback loops are the engine that drives plan-do-check-act (PDCA), which fuels constant organizational learning by humans. Try something; see what happens; learn!

In Toyota assembly plants the vision has also been very consistent. The goal is not to build cars fast, nor to automate wherever possible. Rather the goal is to build only at the rate of customer demand; to achieve safety, high quality, flexibility in mix (eight models on the same line), and flexibility in volume (to make money at 70 percent of full capacity); and to reduce total cost through smooth and seamless operations and low capital costs. Flexibility in mix is important to level the schedule, creating stability in the health of each plant (heijunka). Since sales will fluctuate differently for different models, for example, passenger cars compared with sport utility vehicles, if they are both made on the same production line, that variability in demand will tend to level out. Large fluctuations in individual models will average out to smaller fluctuations. And if the plant can adjust to volume changes, down to 70 percent of full capacity, it can withstand even large drops in sales across all models. This is key to a commitment Toyota makes—respect for people. Respect for people begins with job security for team members in the plant and includes job security for supplier plants and for the local economy of communities where Toyota does business. People are not simply an incidental expense in Toyota, but rather at the center of its value system.

Toyota's product and process development system grew in parallel with TPS and, as we have explained in this book, is also centered on highly developed people spending many years deeply understanding their technical area and learning to meet breakthrough design challenges through teamwork. There have been refinements in methods, such as the obeya, and it wasn't until decades into maturation that Toyota first published its philosophy in "The Toyota Way 2001." Unlike Tesla, which is banking on technology to leapfrog all automotive competitors, Toyota banks on people continuously improving and places the highest value on respecting people.

People at the center of operations also can be traced at least as far back as Ohno and TPS. Technology serves people; people do not serve technology. Highly automated systems have to be carefully designed, trialed, and then maintained by people who own the work processes in factories. Lights-out factories assume that the automated systems need no maintenance or can self-maintain—bad assumption. Active PDCA is even more important in automated systems to identify and solve problems because the automation is not as capable as people in adapting to out-of-standard conditions. The out-of-standard conditions must be virtually eliminated for automation to work smoothly.

Self-maintain also does not assume self-improve: kaizen should not stop when you automate production. Toyota also believes in eliminating waste from automated lines through people studying and improving the lines as they are in operation. Mitsuru Kawai, Toyota's most senior expert on TPS, explains about automated machining and forging lines: "Materials will be flowing while changing shape at the speed we can sell the product. All else is waste. With automated lines, rookie team members think 'you push a red button and a part comes out.' Team members need to learn TPS to kaizen automated processes. They need to understand the gemba and learn to see waste even inside the process."

Toyota's principles of production equipment are "simple, slim, and flexible." Toyota is a learning organization with a long memory. In 1989, Toyota launched the Lexus LS400 with the most advanced automation in the company at its Tahara, Japan, plant, including robots in assembly doing jobs normally done by people. Sales were below expectations, and the plant was underutilized. Toyota's reflection was that the high capital costs were fixed and could not be adjusted to match demand. Toyota prides itself on only building to actual demand, and when demand is down, the company wants the flexibility to reduce costs to remain profitable. This is possible with people. While Toyota provides long-term job security for its regular team members, it uses a variable workforce of agency personnel who can be released in a sales downturn. It also plans overtime, which can be eliminated. In the Great Recession Toyota cut management pay and limited production team members to 35 paid hours a week. Toyota can always find useful things to do with team members not needed for production, but robots simply sit idle. Since the Tahara experience, Toyota reduced automation in some areas rather than accelerated it.

The Tesla-Toyota contrast extends to material conveyance: Musk cites "a very sophisticated automated parts conveyance system" in Fremont that is "probably the most sophisticated in the world."[28] Go to any Toyota plant in the world, and you will see some people driving electric tuggers pulling large parts (e.g., plastic bumpers) or small containers of parts on carts delivered frequently to the line. You will see even more parts delivered by automatic guided vehicles (AGVs), with sequenced kits arriving for each car. The kits—carts on wheels—travel along the assembly line with the assembly team members and contain exactly the parts needed for that car. When Toyota has used automated conveyance and long conveyors, it often was inflexible, hard to kaizen, and led to excessive inventory. The Toyota-built AGV is simple, slim, and flexible and can be repositioned as necessary.

John Shook shed further light on the importance of people in the complex logistical system of automotive that apparently became a logistical nightmare for Tesla:

> The tools required to run a great factory aren't merely math and engineering, but psychology and sociology. Social psychology and neuroscience. Organizational development and system dynamics— with "system" referring to not only the technical side, which Elon and team will figure out, but also the much more complex social side. The social side is difficult in its own right—add the technical complexity of orchestrating the operational execution and timing involved in gathering and assembling thousands of parts that arrive at exactly the right place at the right time in perfect (down to the minute) precision for thousands of humans to choreograph themselves to the precise (down to the second) rhythm and you've got a social-technical challenge of epic proportions.[29]

When Toyota developed a vision for the twenty-first century, it did not rush into it with one grand leap, but rather worked iteratively, starting with the first Prius hybrid. Iterative learning is at the heart of kaizen. Rapid learning cycles through PDCA allow Toyota to steadily advance toward breakthrough challenges in an orderly way with built-in quality. We can think of each generation of the Prius as a large PDCA loop, and Toyota has gone through more of these learning loops than any other automaker.

Let's consider how Toyota's long-term product development strategy and operational philosophy have been working in practice, starting with the Prius.

Prius: Starting to Prepare for the Twenty-First Century

The 1980s started a golden age for Toyota, reaching 2.5 million units sold annually in 1990, the peak of a bubble economy. When sales and profits are at a high, Toyota leaders get nervous. How long will it last? Will we grow complacent as a company? Are we prepared for a downturn? It's time for executives to manufacture a good old-fashioned crisis. True to form, in 1990 Toyota Chairman Eiji Toyoda threw down the gauntlet by asking two biting questions of the board of directors: "Should we continue building cars as we have been doing?" and "Can we really survive in the twenty-first century with the type of R&D we are doing now?" These two challenges would lead to the development of the Prius and launch Toyota ahead of its competition into the twenty-first century.

The story of the development of the first Prius has been told before,[30] including in Jeff's *The Toyota Way*. We provide a summary of the key milestones in Table 8.1. Clearly the hybrid was a great success, with cumulative sales of over 6 million Priuses (including all versions) and over 11 million of all hybrid vehicles by January 2018. Beneath the sales numbers we found three overarching lessons to be learned from the Prius success story: long-term strategic vision, incremental learning to develop core capabilities, and surprising benefits of an incremental approach to a breakthrough vision.

Table 8.1   Prius Development

Year	Milestone
1990	Japanese bubble economy peak; Eiji Toyoda proclaims need for cars for the twenty-first century
September 1993	G21 Business revolution team formed
November 1993	Uchiyamada named as G21 chief engineer
January 1994	Concept development team formed
June 1995	G21 becomes official project with people, budget, timing
December 1997	First Prius sold in Japan
2000	Prius goes global
2003	Second-generation Prius launched
2008	1 million Priuses sold
2009	Third-generation Prius launched
2010	2 million Priuses sold
2012	Bestselling car in Japan four consecutive years Bestselling car in California
2013	3 million Priuses sold
2015	Fourth-generation Prius launched
January 2017	Prius is 6.1 million of 10 million hybrids sold by Toyota worldwide

Volume sales are cumulative.

Twenty-First-Century Vision in the Twentieth Century

Chairman Toyoda's challenge started what would become the Prius success story, and the response was typical Toyota. In September 1993, a high-level business revolution team called G21 (cars for the twenty-first century) was formed, made up of some of the most senior executives in the company. Toyota does not delegate something of such strategic importance to middle managers. It starts with senior leaders who are expected to dig in; deeply understand market trends, societal trends, and technology trends; and develop the initial concept. In this case the team was led by Yoshiro Kimbara, executive vice president of R&D, who then selected 20 members of the working group from various parts of R&D.

Kimbara's R&D working group identified two key characteristics that defined the Prius through the entire development process:

- Environmentally friendly
- Small-sized car with a large cabin

On the surface the second characteristic appears contradictory. A small car does not have a large, spacious cabin. But in the spirit of the Toyota Way, a challenge often appears at first glance to be impossible, or at least improbable. The spacious feeling of Prius, with its great legroom in the rear seat, makes it attractive, even to taxi drivers, and would become one of its defining characteristics.

At Toyota, words in a report or PowerPoint are seldom satisfactory to propose a major program. The report-out to the board of directors would normally include building a concept vehicle that board members could drive. The G21 group wanted to build something, but with only months to work, the group settled for presenting a half-scale concept drawing with a high-level list of specifications, such as a 50 percent improvement in fuel economy.

The focus on an environmentally friendly vehicle fit with what would later be formalized as Toyota's long-term vision for the entire company. In 1996, President Hiroshi Okuda presented the 2005 global vision, which focused on "harmonious growth," including the need to facilitate harmony among the global environment, the world economy, and industries, local communities, and stakeholders. This was followed by objectives from President Fujio Cho, who in 2002 introduced Global Vision 2010 under the theme "Innovation into the Future," with four subthemes: "Kindness to the Earth," "Comfort of Life," "Excitement for the World," and "Respect for All People." Long-term thinking to invest toward a strategic future vision is common practice in Toyota.

Iterative Learning to Create Building Blocks for Long-Term Success

In July 1994, Takeshi Uchiyamada, who would later be referred to as "father of the Prius," was named as the head of a project team that would build on the conceptual work of the G21 group to develop an actual concept vehicle and as a result of this work, he would later be named CE of the Prius development team. From almost every perspective he was an odd choice for CE. Nobody was more surprised than Uchiyamada. He had spent his career in the research labs and in vehicle testing, not in product development. He had never been prepared to be a CE, and it was not a career goal.

But looking deeper, it was clear why he was selected: He repeatedly met difficult challenges through hard work and perseverance. He was the son of a former Toyota CE and understood the demands of the role. He led the only effort since the company founding to redesign the product development organization from the ground up. He knew people across all R&D departments. He was an exceptional leader. Because of his knowledge of the organization and the need to decide where to place Prius in the organizational structure, he had been part of the original G21 group. He understood how crucial this project was for the future of the company. Finally, Toyota wanted not only a car for the twenty-first century, but a new way of developing cars. Uchiyamada did not have preconceptions of how the job should be done, since he had no experience doing it.

Uchiyamada agreed to accept the position despite serious reservations. He did take a different approach and influenced the product development process in ways that are still seen today. He recalled this experience in an interview with Jeff in 2002:

> In the traditional way, in the planning phase, the CE comes up with the concept, discusses this with the design groups and planning groups and formulates a concrete plan as a result of joint discussion with those groups. With the Prius, I assembled a team of specialists from the various design and evaluation groups right from the beginning, and they sat right next to me. These were real experts who sat with me, and we formulated ideas in real time as a team. Joining that group were not only the design engineering managers, but the production engineering managers as well so they could have discussions together. We met in a big room, now called "obeya." To have coordination of those discussions, there were also CAD terminals put into our Prius room. And previously, the way was to use hard copies in meetings, but with the Prius we used the internet and the computer for the first time.

Uchiyamada further described the many decisions, challenges, and achievements in bringing the Prius to market.[31] He knew that the Prius was a more complex program than most. It would involve brand-new technology and, ultimately, some new manufacturing facilities to make batteries and switching circuits. He asked for three years of development time but got only two.

Despite all these pressures, Uchiyamada made the critical decision to develop in-house all the core technologies that would make up the Prius—electric motors, heavy-duty batteries, multiple switching circuits to change between DC and AC, computer systems to optimize the use of the gas engine and electric motor, and braking systems to convert mechanical energy to electrical energy stored in the battery. Knowledge of these technologies was available outside Toyota to subcontract, but instead these were all developed in-house. The reasoning was that if these truly were core technologies for the future of automotive, Toyota should have this expertise. Toyota is comfortable working with suppliers, which are treated as close partners codeveloping vehicles. But Toyota wants to have all the core competence in-house to develop vehicles so it can lead engineering when needed and supervise outside engineering.

Toyota was successful in technology development, with the exception of the battery technology, which required a partner. Toyota set up a joint venture with Panasonic for the Prius's nickel-hydride batteries, taking a majority stake. Panasonic had decades of expertise in developing and making batteries, but never automotive batteries. Toyota and Panasonic worked together on the development of the products and manufacturing processes. Eventually Panasonic sold all but a small percentage of its stake in the automotive battery business to Toyota. Panasonic is back in the automotive battery business working with Tesla. It is also partnering with Toyota to learn how to make solid-state batteries to lead a breakthrough in the industry.[32] Toyota is optimistic that solid-state lithium-ion batteries will have the capacity to go farther distances, with faster charging and at lower cost compared with today's lithium-ion batteries.

The first Prius came out on schedule through heroic efforts. The battery was overheating, and the car was shutting down, even in the latest stages of testing. In fact, it happened when the Toyota president came to try out a preproduction version. The battery was put into the trunk to deal with the overheating problem.

When the first Prius came out in December 1997, it was buggy by Toyota standards. One engineer involved at the time said it was more like an advanced prototype than a production vehicle. Many reviewers were not excited by the way it looked. But it exceeded sales targets and was loved by the early adopters. It became an icon for environmentally friendly cars. Owners formed clubs. They experimented with new computer chips to boost fuel economy. It was almost like a beta test with enthusiastic customers helping design the next generation.

The second generation was a huge advance in styling and function. It got the Prius up to 1 million vehicles sold and was the model that established the Prius as a success. The third generation was even more refined. Toyota reached 3 million sold. By the fourth generation, hybrids were accepted as normal vehicles. They worked seamlessly. Customers filled the tank at gas stations, with smaller amounts of gas since the tank was smaller, and saved money on gas, which was particularly important in Japan and European countries where gas is expensive. By 2017 the Prius was being hailed as one of the most important cars since the Model T.[33]

Toyota has added hybrid versions of most of its vehicles. The goal was to get the cost down so that the price difference between the hybrid and gas version was negligible. The 2018 Camry hybrid model cost customers about an extra $1,000 compared with the all-gas Camry. Toyota has sold over 11 million hybrids globally, far more than any other company. Over 6 million of these were Priuses (including all versions). Pure electric vehicle sales were still a small percentage of vehicles sold, though creeping up. In 2017, out of the 17 million vehicles that were sold in the United States, 200,000 (about .1 percent) were electric cars, including the plug-in Prius.[34]

A public perception, encouraged by the press, was that a new generation of all-electric vehicles, like those of Tesla, would rapidly dominate the industry. This seems very unrealistic. By 2017, Toyota was being admonished by the press for being late to the game of electric cars, trailing companies like Tesla, GM, and Nissan. One journalist wrote: "After being an industry leader in hybrids in the early 2000s, Toyota has almost entirely missed out on the electric vehicle revolution. There's a short-range electric Prius on the market, but Toyota doesn't have anything like the range of a Tesla Model S or GM's Chevy Bolt."[35]

Toyota historically has been a conservative company, but it also can be viewed as a very pragmatic company. As discussed regarding strategy, Toyota executives believe that the "revolution" in automotive technologies will take more time than many think and that the dominant technologies are yet to be determined. Some people will be willing to find an electric charging station, pay the extra cost of a large expensive battery or set of batteries, and be patient about the recharging time. But most will want to continue stopping at a gas station and filling the tank in minutes. Hybrids allow for this. Plug-in hybrids allow for a larger electric range while still going to the gas station to fuel up in the way we have become accustomed. Hydrogen fuel cells also have the potential benefit of rapid refilling, with relatively small batteries, when and if the infrastructure for refilling is developed.

Toyota has chosen an incremental approach to learning the new technologies of the future and introducing these technologies into mass-produced vehicles. With its technology capability and rapid product-process development systems, it can pivot quickly, shifting focus to electric vehicles, hydrogen fuel cell vehicles, or whatever else the market demands.

Benefits of an Incremental Approach to Breakthrough Programs

It was clear that Eiji Toyoda had a bold vision for Toyota, even at a time when it was not necessary for sales or profitability, and very early compared with most companies. He wanted Toyota to prepare for the twenty-first century in the twentieth century. This led to Herculean efforts to bring the first mass-produced hybrid vehicle to market. It ultimately led to large sales and profit numbers, but that is not all:

- **Learning by experimenting.** Toyota established its internal capability in developing and building many of the core technologies needed for the twenty-first century—high-performance batteries, electric motors, computer optimization algorithms, switching circuits, etc. It learned incrementally while other companies, like General Motors, made a big leap into electric cars. As a result, Toyota had four generations of Priuses on which to experiment with these technologies and learn step by step.

- **Leading in high-performance battery design and production.** Toyota's foray into this field has evolved (with Panasonic) into possibly being in the lead in commercializing a breakthrough in solid-state lithium-ion batteries. According to Professor Ryoji Kanno of the Tokyo Institute of Technology, the new batteries can store nearly twice the energy compared with batteries with liquid electrolyte, be less flammable by design, and be less sensitive to temperature. "Today's electric cars suffer from shortened range in cold or hot weather. Researchers at the Idaho National Laboratory found that electric vehicles had their range cut by a fourth during winters in Chicago."[36]

- **Redesigning the development process.** Computer communication use and the obeya have revolutionized Toyota's development process, and the company owes much to the first Prius development team.

- **Having the flexibility to quickly adapt.** The rapid, incremental approach to Prius was bold by any standards. The vision was bold. Toyota was selling large numbers of environmentally friendly cars while most of its competitors were studying them in the laboratory. While Uchiyamada initially believed all-electric cars would be too expensive because of the pace of battery development, he later learned that the technology for batteries was proceeding faster than he expected. Since Toyota had explored and developed multiple alternatives, it is well positioned to adapt to unexpected developments like these. The path of parallel development of alternatives is fundamentally pragmatic, rather than dogmatic, which leads to choosing a path based on limited knowledge. The hybrid itself—embracing the best of different technologies rather than insisting on one perfect solution—is an embodiment of this philosophy.

- **Steadily innovating.** Toyota is investing billions of dollars in hydrogen fuel cell vehicles, advanced battery technology, and technologies for self-driving vehicles (e.g., artificial intelligence, advanced sensor systems, and big data capabilities). Toyota is not always in the news as a major disruptor, but it is building incredible capability, mostly in-house and increasingly with external partnerships.

- **Evolving the company ecosystem.** One interesting analysis, written by a contributor to *Forbes,* compares the "ecosystem" of the Toyota Prius with that of Tesla's electric vehicles. The ecosystem is all the various industrial sectors and entities that influence the business. In automotive, an important part of the infrastructure consists of what happens after the sale of the vehicle, including the sale of parts, vehicle repairs, used car sales, scrap, and recycling. Most of the profits are made in this aftermarket. The Prius was designed in such a way that it barely impacted Toyota's existing ecosystem. On the other hand, Tesla decided to create its own dealer network, and the way the vehicle is designed and the business is set up will disrupt almost every part of the ecosystem. The author of the *Forbes* article does not take a position on whether this will be terribly harmful to Tesla's business, but concludes: "Toyota's—profitable—experiment [the Prius] increased social-commercial value

for most members of the ecosystem—worldwide—without asking any part of the system to lose value or pay high costs . . . Tesla is asking large parts of the ecosystem to change what they are doing, and this might not create positive value for many of them. That's all we need to know right now—to understand that Tesla's 'production hell' may expand to many parts of the after-sales chain as they scale."[37]

Toyota's decades of experience with hybrid technologies, which also happen to be core technologies for both electric and FC vehicles, will serve it well going forward. While Uchiyamada believes that electric cars will have an important place in the future—even more quickly than he originally thought since battery technology is developing more quickly—he also believes there is an important role for hydrogen-powered vehicles, which are also a type of hybrid.

Hydrogen: Paving the Way Forward

One of Toyota's parallel paths is the development of hydrogen fuel cells and hydrogen vehicles. Musk has called these "fool cells." Toyota believes hydrogen is the most environmentally friendly power source for the future, but recognizes it will take decades to develop the necessary infrastructure for filling stations. Nonetheless, it is plowing ahead, building on all current capabilities, and has spent over $1 billion developing the Mirai initially as a low-volume production model. Toyota is not alone. Also on the market around the same time are the Honda Clarity and the Hyundai ix35 FCEV.

It is interesting that the Mirai is a hybrid, building on the Prius, with the gas engine replaced by a fuel cell. This is necessary because hydrogen takes up a lot of space, and as a stand-alone hydrogen vehicle, the car would seem like it was only designed to carry hydrogen. Thus the Mirai and future hydrogen offerings are likely to combine electric and hydrogen technologies. Let's consider the strategic value of the Mirai and how it was developed.

Mirai Means "Future" in Japanese

Mirai may be the ultimate example of long-term strategic thinking, as well as a major risk most often associated with entrepreneurial companies, not mature megagiants. While proliferation of hydrogen-powered vehicles remains a question for the future, fuel cells themselves are not new technology. They have been used for decades and gained prominence in the U.S. space program in the 1950s. Research on fuel cells at Toyota actually began in 1992, and the first operating FC vehicle was "launched" in 2002—a Highlander research vehicle. Toyota conducted many experiments, collected tons of data, and made many improvements before revealing an FC concept car at the Tokyo Motor Show in 2013.

The Mirai was eventually introduced in the United States at the Los Angeles Auto Show in 2014. By the end of 2017, Toyota sold about 4,000 Mirais. It has an ambitious target of selling 30,000 of these vehicles by 2020, hardly enough to justify the more than $1 billion spent. But like the first Prius, the first Mirai is not intended to be a volume leader or money-maker. In fact, while on pace with planned sales, it is made in Japan on its own very small, manual assembly line and designed for very low volume. The point of the Mirai, which means "future," is to lead the way.

There is a chicken-and-egg problem for FC vehicles. There is virtually no infrastructure for refilling hydrogen vehicles anyplace. Until there are enough sales of FC vehicles to justify the infrastructure, energy companies will not invest. But there will not be a lot of sales of hydrogen FC vehicles until there is a fueling infrastructure. So Toyota decided to lead the way. Get something out there in very targeted places—Japan and California. Invest in filling stations. Learn and begin to educate the public.

From the beginning the Mirai team knew that it was working on a product that would not receive broad acceptance for many years or even decades. Yoshikazu Tanaka, the Mirai CE, told us in an interview in Japan: "Hydrogen is something we never expected to suddenly spread. Hydrogen use will not suddenly start just because of this car. We were thinking very long term. In fact, we often used the phrase 100 years from now to provide the team with the right image. We wanted to be the ones who are pioneers in starting this movement toward a hydrogen-based society."

Designing Mirai

Mirai development began in earnest around 2008 during the Great Recession. Despite significant financial constraints, Toyota senior leadership decided to continue to invest in the future, much like what we saw CEO Alan Mulally doing at Ford.

Far more than developing just another electric car, the team was taking on something that had never been done before, and consequently, both the product and process development challenges of this program were formidable and a true test of Toyota's capability.

One of the most difficult challenges on the design side is how to make the FC technology far more compact, while simultaneously coaxing high-power output. The current Mirai FC has more than 2.2 times the power density of the 2008 version, but even the much more compact version requires 370 cells of 1.34-mm thickness that must be assembled to create the stack for the Mirai.

Design of the cells was difficult enough, but manufacturing them efficiently and with consistently high quality for potential high volume has been an even greater challenge. Of course, Toyota decided to do the manufacturing itself. Toyota's design team and production engineering team have worked very closely throughout the development process. The 3D fine-mesh film is made by a Toyota subsidiary, Toyota Auto Body, which also played a pivotal role in development and the success of ongoing production. Assembling the FC system and vehicle requires an extreme level of precision and built-in quality.

To be successful the Mirai must have more to offer than just its power source. Tanaka fully realized this: "The Mirai, just by having a fuel cell, will not be enough to be successful in the market. It must be attractive, fun to drive, and above all safe." Since the Mirai motor does not vibrate like an internal combustion engine, Toyota fixed the motor rigidly to the cross plate without need for rubber dampening mounts. It also employed increased carbon fiber in vehicle components and added braces. Together these changes increased torsional stiffness by 60 percent and dramatically improved ride and handling. We had the chance to drive one on the test track in Toyota City—we can confirm it is fun to drive!

Since it was a new application of this technology, the team had to establish standards for safety and reliability. Tanaka told the team to "design and build a car that you would rely on to put your family members in." The team members crashed cars at high speeds and consistently found them to be safer than vehicles with internal combustion engines. They subjected the car to intense reliability testing in the most difficult conditions to be sure that the vehicle not only would be safe, but would continue to perform at a high level. They also had to work with numerous regional and global authorities to be sure that the end product complied with all regulations.

Hydrogen-Powered Society and Infrastructure

If FC vehicles have any chance of viability, Toyota knows it must both create a reliable and available infrastructure for hydrogen delivery and increase critical mass of use cases. This adds an additional level of complexity, not to mention difficulty, to the development task. Developing a product ecosystem is becoming more common, but we have not seen one on this scale before. Toyota is approaching this with the same methodical, small steps leading to a large result that it does with most product and process development.

Massive infrastructure investment will be required to make FC vehicles a viable transportation choice for large numbers of people. Safely making and delivering hydrogen on any kind of global scale is a seemingly impossible challenge. It is clearly far more than Toyota could ever do on its own. So it has begun to reach out and form partnerships with various government agencies as well as other companies, including competitors. For example, Toyota is leading a group of 11 Japanese companies that includes Nissan and Honda in a collaborative agreement to build 160 hydrogen stations in Japan, which are expected to serve 40,000 in-use FC vehicles by fiscal 2020. Toyota also is openly sharing its know-how with the Japanese government in an effort to create further infrastructure, and it has opened all its hydrogen FC patents to competitors to encourage further development. Toyota also is partnering with Royal Dutch Shell to build seven hydrogen refueling stations in California, getting the state closer to its goal of having 100 commercial stations operating by 2024.[38] In December 2017, Toyota even announced an investment to build one of the world's biggest FC power plants in California, to power homes and buildings, coupled with a hydrogen fueling station. Biowaste will be used to create the hydrogen.[39]

Cars alone will not support the massive infrastructure investment required to make hydrogen readily and safely available to the public. Consequently, Toyota is developing FC-powered buses and envisions at least 100 FC buses crisscrossing Tokyo by 2020. Toyota also has been working to gain support with numerous government agencies, especially in Japan, where efforts have begun to nurture the emerging hydrogen-powered society:

- Japanese Prime Minister Abe has become a vocal proponent of fuel cells, especially since Japan has shuttered most of its nuclear power plants since the Fukushima disaster. And many large facilities, including hospitals and large buildings in Japan and the United States, already have hydrogen FC generators, most often used as backup power sources.

- The Japanese government plans 1.4 million "ene-farm" installations for home FC power by 2020 and 5.3 million by 2030.[40]

- Tokyo aims to significantly invest in a "hydrogen society" by 2020. This will be advertised during the 2020 Olympics, hosted in Tokyo and with Toyota as a key partner.

- A number of hydrogen-based pilots are being conducted on public transportation in places including London, China, and South Korea. H2 ferries have been running in Norway, and other H2 oceangoing vessels are being developed.

- Toyota co-chairs (with Air Liquide) the Hydrogen Council. Formed with only 13 member companies in 2017, it continues to grow with 39 companies as of March 2018.

The Challenge Continues

Toyota is seldom satisfied with its current level of performance; continuous improvement is a foundational element of the Toyota Way. So the Mirai story is far from over. For one thing, the company recognizes that the cost of an FC vehicle remains far too high to be competitive, and without a significant cost reduction, Toyota is unlikely to make the next step beyond the few thousand initial sales. Consequently, Toyota has committed to slash the costs of the zero-emissions components by more than half by 2020 and further reduce costs by another 25 percent by 2025—in total, nearly a two-thirds cost-reduction challenge.

Even though Mirai has the longest range and highest efficiency rating of any FC vehicle—and definitely more range than any battery electric vehicle currently on the road—Toyota has challenged all involved to dramatically increase the range of Mirai. As part of this effort, Toyota has developed and unveiled a concept FC vehicle that has double the range of the current Mirai (increased to 620 miles). Although still a concept vehicle, it demonstrates the art of the possible and Toyota's willingness to continually embrace difficult challenges and push the limits of current understanding in order to create ever-better cars.

As Tanaka explained to us: "We know we are just one small stone in the big sea. There is no guarantee of success, but if you do not do anything, if you do not take a first step, then nothing will happen."

As the Nobel Prize–winning physicist Niels Bohr once said, "Prediction is very difficult, especially if it's about the future." Likewise, we can't possibly know the future of mobility. Musk and his followers may well hit a home run by jumping into all-electric vehicles. However, Toyota's approach of exploring and developing multiple alternatives is certainly the safer and perhaps the smarter way forward. In the worst case of hydrogen failing to become a major fuel source for vehicles, Toyota will have learned an incredible amount in both design and manufacturing that can and will be applied across the company to help it further refine its product and process development system and continue to design the future of the industry. It is well equipped to shift all its eggs into the electric vehicle basket if that is what the market demands.

LOOKING FORWARD

In this chapter we illustrated how a long-term vision and a near-term strategy provide direction to the development of products and processes. We agree with Porter that operational excellence is not a strategy, and its power comes from the direction of a well-thought-out strategy for products and services. Toyota does not eschew strategy or breakthrough innovation in favor of efficient operations and incremental kaizen. Rather, it breaks those distinctions down. Remember the yin and yang discussed in Chapter 3. Strategy versus execution is arguably mostly a Western and mostly an abstract distinction. Toyota puts the two in a blender and integrates them, using whatever approach seems to work, for both the immediate and longer term.

We contrasted Toyota's and Tesla's visions, strategies, and operations philosophies to make a point. Toyota's vision is far more developed and nuanced than Tesla's. Tesla is putting all its eggs in one product basket—all-electric vehicles—and a manufacturing vision centered only on automation that purports to be twenty-first-century advanced manufacturing. Toyota, on the other hand, has people at the center of its design and production process and has developed both the product and process competencies and the quick response time to pursue multiple paths and respond to the future market as it evolves. For its hydrogen FC vehicle, as with many of its disruptive innovations in the auto industry, Toyota is there at the beginning, defining the product and the processes to create it.

Your product and process development may not be as future-forward as Toyota's nor your innovations as disruptive. Nonetheless, much of what occurs at Toyota on a grand scale can happen within your organization, as we will explain in Chapter 9.

Your Reflection

Creating a Vision

This chapter contrasted the approaches of Toyota and Tesla to designing their future to illustrate the close connection between strategy and operational excellence. LPPD is an approach to delivering exceptional value to customers, but it starts with the question for the enterprise: What is our unique value proposition to our customers? Michael Porter, one of the gurus of strategy, believes great strategy will trump operational excellence. He argues that a value proposition that says we will imitate our competitors, but do it cheaper, will lead to companies cannibalizing each other's technology and methods, decreasing profit margins for all. Firms need something that sets them apart beyond operational excellence. He also argues it is important to have unique operational capabilities that deliver on the strategy—so they go hand in hand.

We argued in this chapter that Toyota's approach that takes a long-term vision with iterative learning by rapidly developing generations of products to learn from—for example, the Prius hybrid technology—and combines it with the delivery mechanism for speed, quality, and reliability has been a winning formula for the company. And it seems likely to be a source of sustainable competitive advantage well into the future. By contrast, Tesla's bold but narrow vision primarily coming out of one individual entrepreneur, Elon Musk, will need to be combined with a distinctive set of activities to become a serious disruptor. Musk seems to realize that and is betting on the most computerized factories in the business to separate Tesla from the competition. People do not seem to have a central place in his vision. So far Tesla has not proved capable of consistently delivering on its vision, though it is a very young company.

It is difficult to develop a general vision of strategy since strategy needs to be very specific to each business. We can say that great firms:

1. Develop and continually adjust a well-crafted strategy that sets them apart from the competition
2. Pursue the strategy with focus and passion for the long term, without dropping it when times get tough
3. Connect the vision to a set of distinctive activities that they deliver on with excellence

Your Current Condition

1. Toyota's vision is to be the leader in the future of mobility. It has a specific strategy for the future of mobility going out to 2050. What is your company's vision and strategy, and how far out does it go?
2. Toyota has been relentless in the pursuit of its long-term visions, not wavering even through multiple recessions and crises. How steady has your organization been in sticking to its vision in the face of crises?
3. Toyota's progression of innovative vehicles—Lexus, Prius, Mirai—reveals a culture that strives for innovation and a distaste for complacency. Does your company push the boundaries of its field in product and process development?
4. Toyota has a very distinctive set of activities to deliver value to customers, one that is being copied around the world called "lean management." It has stuck to its core operations strategy and has constantly improved since its founding. What are the distinctive activities of your firm that link to the strategy?
5. Has your company ever developed a product or process that your customers and competitors would describe as disruptive? Why or why not?
6. How closely aligned are your strategy and your development capability?
7. Are you waiting for the big bang? Do you have an incremental approach to rapidly learning your way into the next generation of technologies? Best of all, are you combining these strategies with exceptional execution to lead the way in your industry?

Taking Action

1. Assemble a small, cross-functional team to answer two questions: "Where is it even remotely possible to be disruptive in our industry today?" "What is our strategy for becoming an industry leader?"

2. Based on the answers to those questions, decide how you will experiment with low-cost, low-risk trials to gauge market interest and to determine what knowledge you must acquire or develop to proceed.

3. Define a vision for a set of distinctive activities to deliver on the strategy.

9

Designing Your Future

Transforming Your Product and Process Development Capability

A vision is not just a picture of what could be; it is an appeal to our better selves, a call to become something more.

      —Rosabeth Moss Kanter, in Blagg and Young,
       "What Makes a Good Leader," *Alumni Stories*

Building on Change Management Basics

Since our first book together, we have learned a great deal about implementing LPPD by working with many different companies in a variety of industries. Enthusiastic to share what we have learned, we, nonetheless, faced a conundrum. We began by trying to envision a product development–

oriented change management model to add to the many already published. Each time we tried to lay out a standard process for transformation, we could see its glaring weaknesses. Each model suggested a far more
orderly step-by-step process than we have ever experienced. While there
are a few tools we routinely use, each company, and each situation, is
different. There are probably as many ways to improve your development
capability as there are engineers' definitions of "done." Consequently, we
do not offer a "five easy steps to better development" template.

If you want to get some powerful, general advice on managing organizational change, you cannot go too far wrong with John Kotter's *Leading
Change*,[1] or Rosabeth Moss Kanter's *The Change Masters*,[2] or Noel Tichy
and Mary Anne Devanna's *The Transformational Leader*,[3] or Robert
Quinn's *Deep Change*.[4]

So rather than developing yet another general model of change management, we will share stories about LPPD transformation from companies
with which we have worked. We will then draw lessons from these cases
that are more specific to the LPPD journey than we see in the existing
models of managing change. Next, we will share an emerging collaborative learning model of product-led change that approaches organizational
transformation as a design problem. Finally, we will highlight the importance of thinking about change from a combination of political, cultural,
and psychological perspectives. But first we will address one important
element of change often overlooked: the level of the organization from
which the change is being led.

Starting Level of Leadership Engagement

"A major enterprise transformation is best led from the top" is the equivalent of Newton's laws of motion in physics. All the evidence supports it,
and many models assume it. This was the case with the Ford story we shared
throughout this book. Unfortunately, what happened at Ford is likely the
exception rather than the rule. Most companies will not have a CEO and
senior team sufficiently knowledgeable and engaged to lead an LPPD transformation. And few will be in a crisis with a CEO who sees a product-led
transformation as the only path to success. In the majority of companies,
the transformation work will start at lower levels of the organization.

The organizational level at which the LPPD work is initiated will have
a significant impact on both your approach and scope of impact. Change

efforts that begin at lower levels of the organization are not likely to have the cross-functional impact of one started at a higher level. However, that does not mean you can't make a significant positive impact that can lead to greater opportunities, as you will see in various examples in this chapter.

Top Management Down

It is particularly important when introducing LPPD to have dedicated senior executives leading the charge, because (1) it is inherently cross-functional, and this is the best way to engage leadership across all organizational functions, and (2) new product development should be directly linked to the strategy of the firm, and the most senior executives should be setting the direction and ensuring the commitment and support for the programs as they develop.

In this case the motivation and initial leadership for a transformation starts with the CEO and executive team, who understand what LPPD is and incorporate it into their strategic plans. Then they actively lead the transformation. We illustrate this in Figure 9.1.

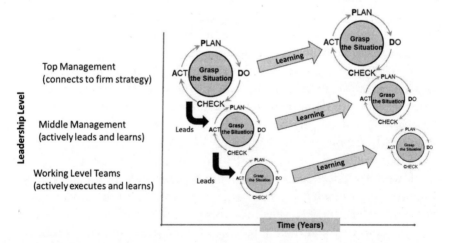

Figure 9.1   The ideal state of top-led, enterprisewide transformation to LPPD

When Toyota introduces a new program to strengthen management, it always uses the same approach. Start at the top by training senior executives who are expected to lead the way in their part of the organization. For example, when Toyota introduced "The Toyota Way 2001," the company developed an initial training program followed by projects. The first students were vice presidents, who then became coaches for their direct reports, cascading the concepts down through the organization hierarchy. This was soon followed up with "Toyota Business Practices" to strengthen problem solving, again taught from the top down. Each leader was responsible for leading a major project to achieve breakthrough objectives. The leader had a coach assigned to lead them through the process, and the projects were complex enough to typically take eight months. These leaders reported out to a board of examiners, and they were usually being sent back to do some rework. When they passed, they became the teachers for their subordinates and part of their board of examiners, and so on down the organization.

As we said, the Ford transformation is also an example of a top-down case. Unfortunately, in our experience this does not happen often. While a senior leader may support the transformation of a company's product development system and authorize the program, he or she very often delegates responsibility to middle management.

Another aspect of the Ford case that is unusual is the life-threatening crisis the company faced to motivate the change. And company executives often bring up a lack of urgency for change as a major impediment to their own company's progress. We hear this often enough that we were interested in what Mulally thought about the role of the crisis in motivating Ford's response. So we asked him about the difference in leading Ford and Boeing through crisis compared with leading them post-crisis. His reaction was interesting and quite definitive: "Transforming a troubled company and managing post-crisis is exactly the same thing," Mulally vehemently responded.

"What about the level of intensity after the crisis?" we asked.

"I would argue that maintaining the right level of intensity is an important part of what separates great companies from the others. Look, at Ford we didn't say, 'Hey, let's use this powerful management system to save the company and then jettison it as soon as we are making money.' No, we said, 'We are going to deal with our current reality of a $17 billion loss, and we are going to come up with a plan by working together to not only save the company, but to create a profitable growing and thriving company."

Throughout his tenure at Ford, Mulally employed his working-together management system to drive "profitable growth for all."

From Middle Management, Up and Across

It is much more common to find one or more engineering managers in an organization who love the idea of LPPD and become dedicated students. In a small to medium-sized organization, this may be the VP of product development. In a larger organization, this may be the head of a business unit or functional department. Even in an organization that has weak senior executive support, these individual leaders can still accomplish a great deal within their domain. Our advice is to focus on what you can influence, do the best job possible, and get visible results. These results are the best possible advertisement for the effectiveness of LPPD. And of course, create opportunities to share these results—both up and across the organization. While starting at middle management may not be optimal, a number of companies we have worked with have started there and gone on to have a much broader influence across the company.

One such company is Solar Turbines, which we introduced in Chapter 2 and discuss further in the next section of this chapter. It is a medium-sized company that got LPPD going with the passionate leadership of one director and a program leader and went on to influence all of Solar Turbines. We illustrate this in Figure 9.2.

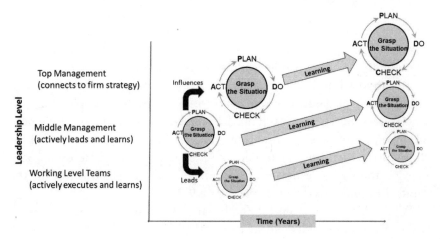

Figure 9.2 Middle management leads LPPD transformation within span of control.

From Working Level Up

A bottom-up approach might seem ideal to some. Empowerment has become a management buzzword. Toyota often draws its organization chart upside down—with team members at the top. But introducing lean development at the working level is by far the most difficult path to success.

Lean development is, by its nature, an enterprise transformation. It cannot thrive in one engineering department. Senior management generally determines which new products will be worked on, and these management leaders are also the ones to allocate resources. Sales is also involved and often calls the shots on the product characteristics it believes the customers desire. Manufacturing too has its own objectives—which usually start with today's production—not supporting engineering in product launches. How can those on the front line change any of this? Simple. They cannot.

But all is not lost if this is your situation. While it will require hard work and a great deal of persistence, starting at this level can still be successful by taking a page out of the Toyota Production System Support Center (TSSC) playbook. TSSC is a nonprofit company set up by Toyota to work with organizations in any industry to implement TPS principles in their operations.[5] One of the practices TSSC employs is to start with a model line.

The idea behind the model line is to go deep in one area, starting with a very challenging goal, working step by step through PDCA in the direction of the goal over a long period of time—in this case one or more years of effort. Many of the core elements of LPPD within the team's span of control are introduced so that the company has a live demonstration of the system, including people leading continuous improvement.

The model line is for teaching. It is for developing internal change agents and management zealots, who will keep spreading deployment. In this process the TSSC consultant does not design anything or implement anything, but challenges, questions, and teaches only what is needed for those inside the company to take the next step. At the same time TSSC engages the senior leaders and encourages them to get involved in the model line and learn from it. See Figure 9.3.

While this is a long and difficult path to follow, it can be successful. TSSC has had considerable success with this approach because while it may focus its efforts at the working level, it actually engages all three levels

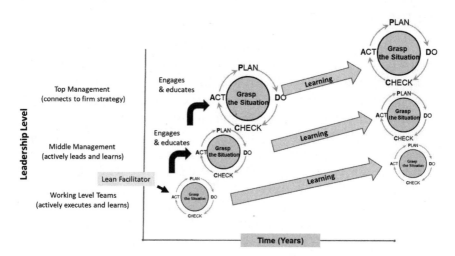

Figure 9.3 Lean facilitator leads LPPD project at working level.

of the organization. TSSC will not take on a client unless senior leadership makes a strong commitment. In the model line process they actively engage both senior management and middle management over that area. Not all managers or consultants have the power to choose their clients and require senior management commitment. Often the manager must do their best to lead the change in their own area, and it is a very challenging path. It is possible to be successful, and it may need some years to wait for a new senior executive who supports LPPD to take over. Even if it does not spread deeply beyond your department, you will learn important skills you can take to your next job.

LPPD Transformation Examples

We have already described LPPD activities at a number of companies outside Toyota: Ford, Herman Miller, GE, Caterpillar, Schilling Robotics, Solar Turbines, and Technip FMC. In this section we will focus primarily on the early days of the LPPD initiative and the different approaches used in turbine development, clinical processes in healthcare, aerospace, and construction to further illustrate the diversity of lean transformations. Each used a somewhat different approach to transformation, and each had a considerable degree of success.

The Solar Turbines Story

We have mentioned Solar Turbines, part of Caterpillar, several times in this book. Jeff and our colleague John Drogosz have worked with Solar for many years, and Jim has engaged with its senior executive team on occasion. We believe that Solar is one of the best examples of a middle management-led change as well one of the longest sustained efforts we have seen.[6]

Solar Turbines Incorporated is an example of a medium-sized organization that has supported LPPD with middle management-led programs and has continued to progress for over a decade. We described its more recent use of LPPD for execution excellence in Chapter 2, when the company had a pretty mature level of understanding.

Before being introduced to LPPD, the company already had a strong culture of teamwork and meeting facilitation.

In connection with Caterpillar's focus on implementing lean, Solar Turbines had seen considerable success with lean manufacturing in its manufacturing and assembly operations. Could lean apply to development programs to more effectively meet cost and timing goals? The organization became increasing interested in Lean development and took the opportunity to work with Jeff to get started.

By focusing on overall corporate leadership and leading with the values of a chief engineer (CE), one of the first pilot programs focused on uprating an existing turbine.

There was an urgent priority visible to the board. Solar Turbines historically used its innovative capability to deliver best-in-class product performance, but one product line had experienced significant challenges. Bringing an uprate to market fast was paramount to maintaining the company's market position. The problem was that this cycle took two years or more to accomplish. Sales indicated that this would not support requirements and in fact promised customers a faster turnaround. There was urgency to satisfy customers and bring the new product to market faster.

Jeff facilitated a three-day product development value-stream mapping (PDVSM) workshop in May 2008 to get the program started. There were over 20 people in the room from all functions, including the supplier of castings, which was critical to prototype development. The group, while large, worked well together throughout the process.

The group had never done PDVSM before. They first walked the gemba visiting each department (many seeing other departments for the first time) and then enthusiastically dove into detailing the current state in three subgroups for the front, middle, and back end of the development process. The mapping was organized by horizontal swim lanes, each representing a function, and time to launch was shown across the top (Figure 9.4). Each step in the process was represented by a Post-it Note. People were not shy about exposing problems. What they saw was how all the functions impacted each other's work, but it was not pretty. The current state was a clear waterfall model, starting both with advanced engineers who handed off the work to prototype engineers, and with purchasing, which bought the components and handed off the work to production preparation. The process was relatively clean and simple in the concept stage, but it got increasingly complex as it moved to other departments that had to rework earlier decisions. By the time the process got to production engineering, all swim lanes were filled with so many Post-its they could barely fit on the paper. It was all chaos, confusion, and firefighting by this point. Clearly there were opportunities.

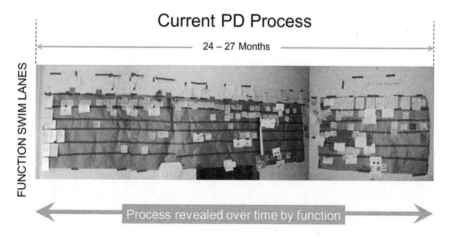

Figure 9.4   Solar current-state map: power generator uprate program

They then worked as one large group to develop a future-state map of the process that would meet the aggressive timeline sales had promised to customers. It was the team's vision for how they wanted the program to proceed (Figure 9.5). There were many innovative ideas, but some of the biggest changes focused on key problem areas exposed in the current-state map:

- **Front-end loading.** In the current state, senior management and marketing and sales authorized a program, a team was assembled under a program manager, and engineering began developing a concept to meet the development project goals with little involvement from other functions. As the detailed engineering proceeded, it was common to get directives from above for major changes in the design—what management referred to as "scope creep." This led to many rework cycles.

  In the future state, the program manager was to act more like a chief engineer and develop a concept paper. The reasoning was that a well-reasoned concept paper, agreed to by the executive board, would limit late changes to requirements. In addition, from the very start, the CE also would assemble a cross-functional team, including purchasing, tool design, packaging, testing, sales and marketing, and manufacturing, and use simultaneous engineering beginning in the concept stage.

- **Batching work.** A major current bottleneck in development programs was design and manufacturing of machine tooling. The current-state PDVSM revealed that tool orders would accumulate into large batches, which overwhelmed the capacity of the tooling design group.

  In the future state, the tool orders were to be released early and sequentially. This would allow the tool design group to single-piece flow the design and fabricate the tools through the process without the inherent waiting and bottleneck cycles created by batched work.

- **Early supplier involvement.** The current development process did not engage manufacturing and key suppliers in the design process. Often the first time these groups would be engaged was during the release of a detailed drawing. Any suggested improvements for cost and producibility improvements were typically left for the next project, since there was no time for rework.

  In the future state, members from manufacturing and key suppliers would be a part of the development team from the beginning. They would provide cost and producibility trade-offs to the design engineers while the layout and detail designs were being developed. Bringing these key inputs to the front of the design process would allow the inputs to be factored into the design. The process was described as having manufacturing and design engineering jointly at the drawing table, so process and design would be created at the same time. This cocreation process would lead to tremendous cost savings and quality improvements, while maintaining the design enhancements needed to meet customer expectations.

- **Rapid prototype testing.** Combustion processes are not entirely predictable, so there is always iterative testing and redesign in development. The current-state testing bays were a key bottleneck.

     The future-state map called for using lean concepts to redesign the test process, with the aim of achieving one-piece flow and using visual management to make visible the flow of tests to be conducted and their stage of completion.

Shared Cross-Functional Vision

15 – 16 Months

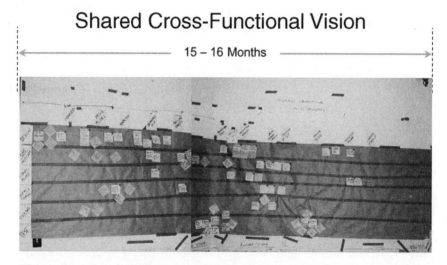

People coming to agreement to work in a new way

Figure 9.5   Solar future-state map: power generator uprate program

The team agreed that to put all of this into practice required weekly team meetings in an obeya (Figures 9.6). Once the meetings were started, the VSM shifted into the background. The highly committed team met or exceeded targets on schedule deadlines and cost, and the uprated turbine was a hit in the market. It was, however, not smooth sailing. The group was highly focused and dedicated and worked through many obstacles, including a several month setback.

Figure 9.6 Obeya for the power generator uprate program. The room was organized by disciplines: packaging, engineering, purchasing, manufacturing, casting supplier, etc.

In parallel to the turbine program, a second team was leading an LPPD pilot program to redesign a fuel injector, a key component in the combustion system. The team used the same PDVSM process and execution in an obeya. The fuel injector redesign team attained equally dramatic positive results, achieving cost and timing targets.

The success of these programs, after years of missing target after target, was exhilarating, and there was now a lot of support for LPPD. All new programs soon began with VSM workshops, facilitated internally, and obeya. Innovative ideas to control work-in-process inventory, connect processes, and continue to reduce lead time were emerging throughout product development. Further development was made in creating books of knowledge, standardizing designs, and extending lead-time reduction to maintenance in the field.

We would *like* to report that with the success of many development programs and improvement of many processes LPPD continued to evolve linearly like we showed in Figure 9.2. Unfortunately, the road forward was much more complicated than this diagram suggests. Consistent education needed to be provided throughout the organization on LPPD. Key advocates found that they need to keep championing lean to maintain progress and gains.

Leading from the middle was certainly a challenge, but progress continued. Key lean champions continued to sell the program horizontally and upward. A breakthrough occurred in 2016 when one of the original LPPD champions was given responsibility for all new development for one product family (gas compressors), as described in Chapter 2. In 2018, after 10 years, LPPD was still going strong in Solar Turbines.

Clinical Process as Product at Michigan Medicine

To the best of our knowledge, Michigan Medicine (formally the University of Michigan Health System) represents the first application of LPPD principles and methods to the development of clinical processes in a healthcare setting. While the members of the clinical design and innovation (CDI) team were initially resistant because they assumed a product design method could not work for them, they came to embrace the LPPD practices and successfully adapted them to their very unique environment. The key was to think of processes as products and subject them to the same intentional development rigor that we have been recommending for physical products. Although at the time of this writing, the transformation is still a work in progress, we believe that the Michigan Medicine experience can serve as a powerful model for healthcare improvement initiatives and demonstrates the efficacy of the LPPD model for service processes. As Dr. Marentette and Jim have begun to share the Michigan Medicine story with other healthcare organizations, it has generated a great deal of enthusiasm—so watch this space in the future because we believe there is much more to come. Our sincere thanks to our colleagues Dr. Larry Marentette, Paul Paliani, Matt Zayko, and the Michigan CDI team for their help with the following vignette.

About nine years into Jim's work at Ford, he was diagnosed with sarcoma and was treated at Michigan Medicine. This diagnosis, among other things, gave him a new appreciation for the challenges facing healthcare professionals and patients. During his cancer journey he met a number of amazing people, joined Michigan's patient-centered care initiative, and renewed acquaintances with some old friends. One old friend was Dr. Jack Billi, associate vice president for medical affairs and professor of internal medicine at Michigan Medicine, who, in addition to being an amazing physician and teacher, is also a longtime champion of lean in healthcare. Jack and Jim had spoken many times about the possible application of LPPD in healthcare. Billi shared the progress that Michigan Medicine had made with lean management methods. However, he was more than aware that there was still so much left to do and suspected that LPPD might be able to contribute. Jim was recovering from his treatment and took the opportunity to spend time at the gemba with Dr. Billi and his colleagues.

Billi introduced Jim to a number of people at Michigan Medicine including Dr. Steve Bernstein, the chief quality officer, who recommended they talk with Dr. Larry Marentette and Paul Paliani who were leading improvement efforts in the clinical design and innovation group. The CDI team had been successfully applying lean tools and methods to a number of clinical processes, such as implementing an enhanced recovery program to reduce readmissions for colorectal surgery patients and creating a new electrophysiology rapid follow-up clinic to reduce hospital admissions for patients. Marentette and Paliani shared that these early successes had led to higher expectations and a larger workload for them. To meet these new challenges efficiently, they would need to dramatically improve their own process. This discussion started a wonderful collaboration between the CDI team, the team's LPPD coach Matt Zayko, and Jim as they explored the application of LPPD principles to the creation of clinical processes.

Engaging Leadership   They started by organizing a steering team that consisted of senior leaders from both Michigan Medicine and the Lean Enterprise Institute (LEI) in order to provide ongoing support for the CDI team. The first step for the steering team was to gain a common understanding of LPPD and the concept of "process as product" in order to start the process of gaining support. Together they agreed to try the LPPD experiment and see if clinical processes could be treated as products. The steering team met quarterly to review progress, help resolve problems, and provide feedback for the team throughout the initiative. This was an important step for enrolling the superbusy senior leadership at Michigan Medicine in the process and also helped to motivate the CDI team.

Product Development Value-Stream Mapping—Making Work Visible
The CDI team was made up of talented and experienced lean coaches, engineers, and project managers who had utilized value-stream mapping

many times before; they had just never done it on the clinical process development process. So they agreed that Zayko and Paliani would facilitate a PDVSM workshop focused on how they created new clinical processes. They began with a recent head and neck surgery program and identified several areas ripe for improvement. Overall the program took six months longer than expected, and it only accomplished about half of what was originally envisioned. The VSM workshop highlighted a number of specific opportunities for improvement: (1) The CDI team experienced long delays in acquiring data and scheduling meetings with key stakeholders and process owners early in the program. (2) They did not fully align on goals and objectives for the program with key stakeholders and jumped into doing work too soon. (3) They lacked a way to identify and react to issues quickly. The good news was that through the workshop the team could "actually see both the work and the delays" (Figure 9.7).

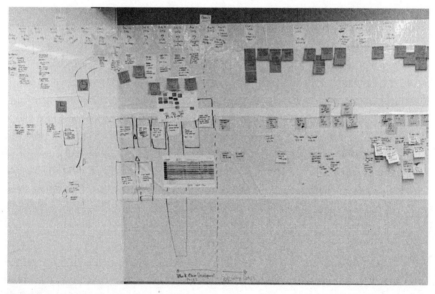

Figure 9.7   Current-state clinical design

The new understanding of the development process gained through PDVSM, the promise of LPPD tools and practices, and the opportunity to create a new future state energized the members of the CDI team (Figure 9.8). For their future state, they decided to lay out the development work by functional areas (swim lanes) and come up with an improved model

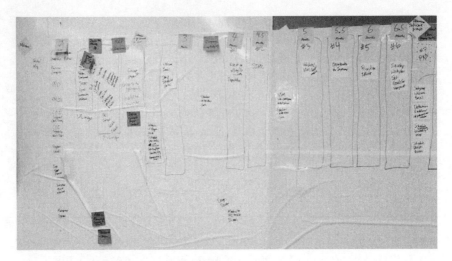

Figure 9.8   Future-state clinical design

for what engagement with clinical design should look like and how long a design program should take.

To move toward their future-state vision, the members of the CDI team agreed to try the following LPPD experiments: (1) Operate all programs utilizing a common obeya management system and effective milestones to improve collaboration, communication, learning, and project management effectiveness. (2) Front-load their process with a "study period" and increased stakeholder engagement, experimentation, and learning. (3) Create a concept paper through the work in the study period to better align the team and key stakeholders. (4) Incorporate design reviews and experimenting through targeted prototyping and deeper "cross-functional" engagement to improve problem solving and increase innovation.

You Can't Manage a Secret—Obeya   One of the first things to resonate with the CDI team was Mulally's quote that "you can't manage a secret." Schedules and other important information were generally squirreled away on project leader laptops, and each improvement pair operated independently. The team members badly needed greater transparency, increased cross-project learning, and improved collaboration to decrease lead time in order to successfully manage increased workload. Transparency could help them know if a program was ahead or behind schedule as well as allowing them to support the work their teams were doing in real time.

The team members worked with Zayko to build an obeya by creating program schedules for their current programs.

They met in the obeya weekly for four weeks and laid out the timelines for six programs. After realizing how much they liked "seeing" the work displayed this way, they developed program schedules for four more mature programs. This enabled them "to see" their entire workload. After finishing the program schedules, the team experimented with weekly stand-up meetings where the individual project managers reported out on their projects. The goal was to get through the 10 programs in 30 minutes, so they allocated 3 minutes to each program. The first few stand-ups took longer than the targeted 30 minutes. To improve on obeya effectiveness, they added a reflection after every other stand-up meeting in order to come up with ideas to help the process. They added rules, like assigning a facilitator, timekeeper, and scribe to keep the stand-up moving; they designated the first 2 minutes of each program as uninterrupted time and the last minute as question time. They also learned that it helped if each program focused on things that were red and commented on the "plan to green" instead of thinking about the stand-up as a time to resolve the issues. Finally, if a program needed help on an issue, they captured needs on a "things to do" sheet and, if required, a separate "andon" sheet to escalate those bigger issues.

After working with obeya for a while, the CDI team reviewed their progress with Jim, and a portion of the team visited LEI's headquarters in Cambridge, Massachusetts, and observed that LEI's obeya was much more than just the schedule—other critical information was posted. So the members of the team pulled together visual management elements for other aspects of their work, like the six steps of a process for CDI project intake, so that they could look ahead at new work. In addition, they set up a display to show the process for developing patient pathways and the status of pathways currently being created and also to show a summary of what data was being requested and provided for each program. Ultimately, the team decided that it was best to post and make visible in the obeya as many trackers and summary spreadsheets as possible.

The team reflected on the obeya (Figure 9.9): it was a much better process because people could "see" their work, and the weekly stand-ups were faster and more effective than their past, lengthy, sit-down meetings. Overall, the team was pleased with the obeya because it enabled far more transparency, and it also allowed for more inclusiveness, which increased collaboration both within the CDI team and with their clients.

Figure 9.9   Clinical design obeya

Milestones—Normal from Abnormal   In order to understand if projects were truly on schedule, the clinical design team created quality of event criteria (QEC) for each milestone. The team started with a clear purpose statement for each milestone and derived QEC from that. The team also created key indicators for early warning of milestones in jeopardy. This was done by breaking down the milestones into substeps and monitoring them along the way (lead versus lag indicators). When integrated into the obeya management reviews, this helped the team to better understand critical elements of the process and determine normal from abnormal conditions and respond accordingly. So far, between obeya management and improved use of milestones, all programs are on track, and none are shifting out the way they used to.

Study Period   Another problem the team members uncovered was that they were sometimes doing too much work on a project before they fully understood the current situation or had key stakeholders on board. To address this issue they reorganized their clinical design process into a study phase and an execution phase, consisting of six steps that correlated with medical terminology (Figure 9.10). The study phase allows the team to focus on achieving a deep understanding of the patient, of the process owner, of the environment, and of just how their process will create value.

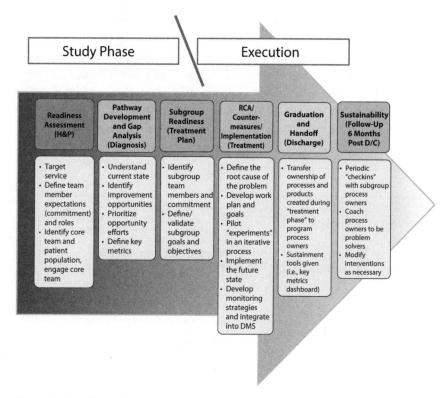

Figure 9.10   Clinical design process

They adopted the "Go slow to go fast" mantra. They used the readiness phase to find out what other healthcare organizations might be doing in similar situations; met with key leaders to get their support; significantly increased the number, duration, and quality of "go and sees" that they conducted before starting work; and pulled together a core group of people, many who normally do not talk to each other, to participate in the gap analysis work that allows them to zero in on the problems they want to tackle. They use the kickoff of the gap analysis work sessions to let all the stakeholders know that the team will be in a relationship with them for about a year and will go over the clinical design process.

The team members also visited Menlo Innovations and talked with the High-Tech Anthropologists to improve their observation and empathy skill sets and tools. They learned from GE Appliances' FirstBuild, as well as low-fidelity prototyping at Schilling Robotics as part of LEI's learning group of companies. Based on what they learned, they began to create their own low-fidelity prototypes (Figures 9.11*a* and 9.11*b*), which they tested with key stakeholders utilizing their newly acquired observation skills and methods. Examples of the early, targeted prototypes included pocket cards, patient care outlines, sketches of software interfaces, process flows, and many others. Using these simple prototypes enabled them to work closely with users and make important changes to the prototypes easily and quickly. The study period and the use of targeted prototypes have already led to key insights and helped to reduce the amount of rework normally experienced on clinical process design programs.

Icon	Meaning?	When used?	Hover Text
⚠	Primary Trigger is positive	After primary Trigger goes off, but before secondary screen has been completed	qSofa and SIRS scores, categories that Triggered. For example, "qSofa = 2, SIRS = 2. GCS, SBP, HR, RR"
❗	Clinical confirmation of sepsis alert	After positive Triage Screen or after positive secondary screen	Positive Sepsis Screen
✚	Patient being treated for sepsis	Provider accepts BPA or uses Sepsis Order Set	Patient being treated for sepsis
🔒	Primary Trigger is locked out	Provider chooses "no" to sepsis BPA	"Locked out of Primary Trigger"

Figure 9.11a   Clinical design low-fidelity prototype—track board

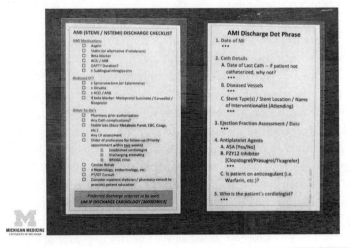

Figure 9.11b   Clinical design low-fidelity prototype—pocket card

Concept Paper   The most recent LPPD tool that the CDI team agreed to experiment with was the concept paper. Two project managers, Heidi McCoy and Andy Scott, began to create concept papers for their projects based on the work being done during the study period in order to improve their internal logic, to create a better project plan, and especially to align with all key stakeholders. Although it is early days, both Scott and McCoy believe that the concept paper is already making a significant positive impact on understanding, planning, and alignment, and they plan to use and evolve this tool in future projects.

Design Reviews   Cross-functional design reviews were held with subgroups. The subgroups were formed once the team members completed a study period and had a good understanding of the problem, key gaps, stakeholders, etc. Each subgroup focused on reviewing a specific element of the new clinical process.

The clinical design program used two types of design reviews: The first is an innovation design review performed by each subgroup team on a biweekly cadence—it includes all members of the subgroup. They work on root-cause analysis, develop countermeasures, create low-fidelity prototypes, and experiment (Figure 9.12). The second type consists of integration design reviews to look at how all the subgroups align and integrate their work, as well as the process launch. Both types of design reviews have helped in earlier problem identification, increased collaborative problem solving, and far greater potential for innovation in the design of clinical processes.

In Figure 9.12, five subgroups responsible for the upper-left hand box each have a specific task for which they are responsible—these come out of the study phase. These groups are actually making prototypes, and the integration design review (in the box below that) explains various prototypes and their uses. Prototypes are tested with patients, physicians, nurses, process owners, etc.

Although the members of the Michigan Medicine CDI team are less than a year into their journey, they and their stakeholders are excited about the results to date. These results have been noticed elsewhere in the Michigan healthcare system, and other groups have started to study what is going on in the CDI team with an eye toward spreading the practice.

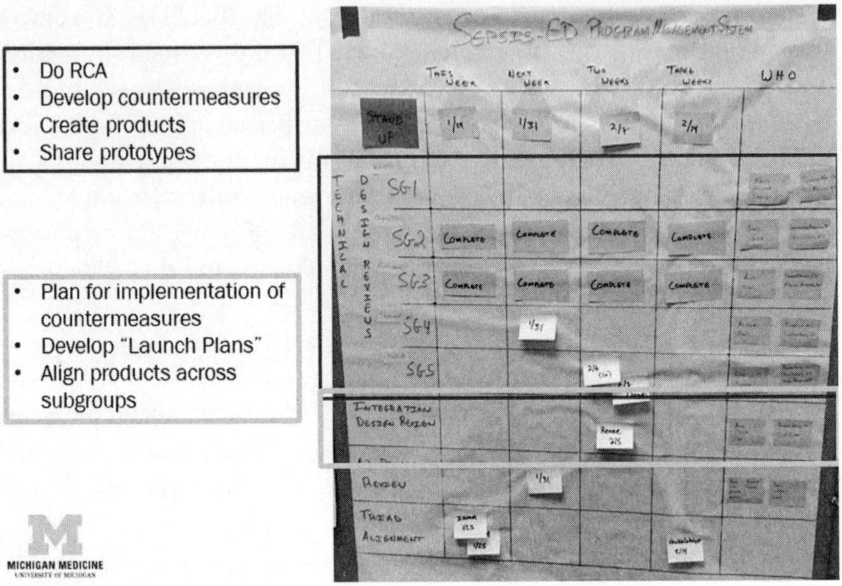

- Do RCA
- Develop countermeasures
- Create products
- Share prototypes

- Plan for implementation of countermeasures
- Develop "Launch Plans"
- Align products across subgroups

Figure 9.12   Design review experiments

Flying On-Time at Embraer

Embraer started its lean journey not only on the shop floor but throughout the entire company. Its enterprise transformation was led from the very top. The team's first quick wins, however, were experienced at the gemba on the shop floor. So they began their LPPD efforts by trying to apply the same tools and methods from manufacturing (kaizen blitzes) to development, but struggled to adapt it for the engineering context. What made the transformation eventually successful is that those involved persevered, got the knowledge they needed, worked hard, and continued to learn. One other success factor was that they imbedded an LPPD coach into each program team. This worked because they had developed very capable and respected coaches. We are most grateful to our colleague and friend John Drogosz for this vignette.[7]

Embraer is a Brazilian designer and manufacturer of executive jets, small commercial airliners, and defense aircraft, and it has annual revenues of about $6 billion. Embraer started its lean journey around 2007 and achieved significant success on the shop floor. Executives were forward thinking enough to realize the company would not achieve the full potential of a lean enterprise without engaging the product development organization. The total-company approach was termed the Embraer Enterprise Excellence Program (P3E). Initially they attempted to apply lean manufacturing tools and techniques in product development with limited success. And as you would expect, they had difficulty engaging the development community.

Embraer sent several of its best coaches to LPPD classes at the University of Michigan (U of M). These classes, developed by Jim based on his Toyota product development system research, introduced the participants to a powerful set of practices and tools for improving product development capability. It also introduced them to our colleague John Drogosz, who was their instructor at U of M and who supported their LPPD journey for the next five years. Embraer's LPPD implementation journey evolved through three phases: (1) kaizen events, (2) embedded coaches on pilot projects, and (3) value-stream management.

Kaizen Events   Embraer started its lean journey by conducting kaizen-type events in product development to address local issues, much as it had in manufacturing. Also called "rapid improvement workshops," the events were typically scheduled for five days. There is preparation, such as selecting project themes and identifying a team, and then the team analyzes the current condition, sets goals, and tries making changes as rapidly as possible. In a well-run event, by the end of the week the participants are exhausted and exhilarated. They present a final summary to senior managers and celebrate their successes. As time went on they learned that they could get the majority of the benefits in engineering with shorter events, sometimes as fast as one-day kaizen and usually three-day kaizen workshops. And whenever the project scope required, more than five days, although the team members were not scheduled full time, but rather brought in and out as needed.

The goal for Embraer was to get a product development transformation started—experience firsthand the benefits of LPPD to solve specific problems, learn some basic lean tools and techniques, and get excited enough to develop a broader vision. A kaizen promotion office (KPO) was formed to facilitate kaizen events and establish in-house capabilities. The KPO team did an initial assessment of the product development process and established guidelines and objectives for its work. The KPO team used these guidelines and objectives in conducting numerous kaizen events over the next year and was able to successfully demonstrate the potential of LPPD tools and methods to the product development community. But it soon became apparent that kaizen events alone would not deliver the full potential of LPPD. The team was ready for more.

Pilot Projects   While the kaizen events achieved localized performance benefits and created an enthusiastic LPPD following, the overall results on projects were still uneven and often not sustained. Short bursts of learning and activity can be energizing, but they also limit what the team can accomplish and experience. The KPO team decided to focus its resources by assigning one internal LPPD coach to each development team, with each team assigned to work on one major design project.

The coach was embedded within the team and worked with members to solve specific project challenges using LPPD tools and techniques. The coach was now more than a facilitator for improvement events—the coach was at the gemba and was part of the team throughout the development process. That meant that the coach could see firsthand the struggles of the project teams and provide just-in-time assistance. The coach was also able to form a stronger relationship with the project leadership and act as a true coach to help guide changes in the cultural behaviors. This approach drove far more effective results on the overall performance of projects and helped to better embed LPPD principles into the working project teams than the kaizen events had ever done in the past.

Value-Stream Management   As Embraer's LPPD journey continued, the company identified even broader challenges that could not be addressed either through a kaizen event approach or even at the individual project level. Senior leadership recognized that they needed to organize themselves along the lines in which they delivered value to their customers. They saw they needed to improve entire value streams and make key trade-off decisions across functions more holistically than in the past. Also, measuring "success" needed to be done across the enterprise rather than by function or department. As a result, the management restructured the organization along value streams and aligned the continuous improvement team accordingly. For managing each product development value stream, the role of a "manager of continuous improvement" was established to help create a transformation plan, guide the implementation, and measure the results.

Creating Flow, Decreasing Lead Time, and Delivering the Cargo Plane KC Program on Time   The KC program was one of the first programs to benefit fully from the LPPD work at Embraer. The KC program was the first multi-mission military transport aircraft developed by Embraer. In fact, it was the largest and most complex aircraft ever designed and manufactured in Embraer's history. In addition to significant technical challenges and the need for a rapid learning curve, the team also faced a very aggressive timeline.

The KC-390 engineering vice-president Waldir Goncalves developed a very comprehensive strategy for the LLPD implementation for his programs. As a supporter of the LLPD effort since its inception at Embraer, and thinking about product development as a socio-technical system, he methodically addressed all three pillars of this system in his strategy—people, process, and tools.

As a first step Waldir, with his leadership team, created the KC-390 product development team purpose. With the purpose defined and well communicated, all team members felt engaged and proud of what they were doing. In Waldir's opinion, this step, focusing on the human side of program management, was the most important to the program success.

As a second important step, in order to develop the KC-390 leveraging Embraer's best understanding of LPPD principles, Waldir brought Manoel Santos, one of the most experienced LPPD coaches, to be the KC-390 excellence plan manager. His responsibility was to structure the processes and manage the application of the LLPD tools to support the KC-390 team.

The third important step was the application of the obeya management system, which provided an effective way to monitor the progress of the program and provided a process for effective communication and alignment.

The team was organized into cross-functional module development teams, responsible for a particular subsystem of the product. Each team included product engineering, manufacturing engineering, quality, and supply chain. Based on what they learned in *The Toyota Product Development System*,[8] the module development teams managed their activities using a combination of visual management and other lean techniques to drive rapid learning cycles up front and precise execution during the development phase. Each project team ran their part of the program using their obeya.

The program-level team created low-fidelity prototype mock-ups of several parts of the aircraft, including the forward fuselage, to enable rapid learning cycles early in the project. The program team brought the customer's pilots and Embraer-experienced engineers to get their direct feedback on the design. Manufacturing was also able to provide more input than usual through targeted, cross-functional process development workshops (3Ps). One outcome of this work was a dramatic reduction in part count and manufacturing complexity. The team also similarly engaged several key suppliers to provide input and ensure that supplier designs could be better integrated into the overall KC design. The team also took advantage of new simulation technologies in their up-front work to prove concepts earlier and to get their virtual aircraft "flying" sooner than on any other program. Looking back, the team felt that the degree of collaboration and team problem solving was the best they had experienced since joining the company.

The E2 Program—Fastest Ever: On Schedule, On Budget, and Delivered Better Than Original Specifications The E2 commercial aircraft program is the latest project as of 2018 to apply LPPD principles at Embraer. This program began with the most aggressive timeline for any Embraer commercial program in its history, with a budget smaller than other similar airliner programs and a spec that would create the most competitive aircraft of its segment. The vision for the project was grand and challenging, including 75 percent all new systems compared to its previous generation and many new suppliers. It was a breakthrough new product introduction, not an incremental improvement over previous e-jets.

Right from the start, the leaders on the E2 program team, including its program director, Fernando Antonio Oliveira, met with their counterparts on the KC cargo plane program in order to glean all the lessons they could to apply on their E2 project.

As the foundation of its original spec, the program created a Customer Value Proposition that reflected its competitiveness and set the goals of the high-level requirements to be deployed and monitored throughout its development using specific tools as well as a physical and virtual obeya.

Given the extremely challenging timeline, budgets, and specifications for the E2, the team needed to look very closely at the overall value stream to identify any opportunities to further front-load learning and maximize their execution velocity. In addition to applying the lessons from the KC and other previous projects, the team conducted several value-stream mapping planning sessions and applied critical chain methods to help them optimize workflow at the program level. Kaizen workshops were conducted to further clarify the value proposition and how the project would be managed in the obeya. Risk and preventive management was key to performance and driven by the value proposition goals.

The team that was selected to execute the program was very experienced. Embraer has had the fastest product development programs among its direct competitors, which allowed its engineers to participate in more programs during the same period. For example, an Embraer engineer with 15 years of experience had the opportunity to learn through the development cycles of three to four previous programs, instead of only two as in other aircraft companies.

The team found several opportunities to increase their front loading of the program and close a number of critical knowledge gaps—the use of virtual tools coupled with low-fidelity mock-ups sped up their learning significantly. They also were able to reuse some of the knowledge gained from prior programs to reduce the learning curve.

The focus on simultaneous engineering was intense. Key suppliers were involved early and as true partners in the design. Front-end loading allowed the team to dramatically improve both design interfaces and the manufacturing feasibility of designs early in the program.

Embraer did significant work on design for assembly. It revamped the assembly line to make it a "hybrid line" that allowed the assembly of the new E2 while not impacting the E1 deliveries. It ran several "3P" workshops (production preparation process), which reduced the learning curve for the assembly operators and shortened production ramp-up time.

The first flight on May 23, 2016 (Figure 9.13), was the most comprehensive to date on an aircraft program and took place months ahead of its original schedule. Weight was on target and systems operation was flawless. After the team included retracting landing gear as well as flaps and performed additional tests, it climbed to its maximum altitude (41,000 feet) and accelerated to maximum speed (Mach 0.82), (a reported first in aerospace). The fly-by-wire system was engaged in normal mode during the flight. It landed 3 hours and 20 minutes after takeoff, the longest duration of a narrow body airliner first flight. The second flight was only two days later. After 50 days, it flawlessly crossed the Atlantic to be presented at the Farnborough Air Show in the United Kingdom.

Figure 9.13   Embraer E190-E2 first flight

According to Embraer executives, the overall performance was a first in aerospace. The airplane was very mature even at its first flight. That enabled them to conduct a simultaneous test campaign (both flying and static/fatigue testing) that led to a 25 percent improvement in the global effectiveness of the test campaign, allowing them to support the sales campaign with prototypes without jeopardizing the test and program schedules.

The final E2 program result, in an industry where one year or more delays and billion-dollar cost overruns are common: on-time delivery to the shortest timeline ever. It took 56 months from business plan approval to certification, instead of the typical market cycles of more than 90 months. The airplane was on budget, on time, and was actually better than the original specification requirements.

The E190-E2 was triple certified by the Brazilian Civil Aviation Agency (ANAC), the U.S. Federal Aviation Administration (FAA), and the European Aviation Safety Agency (EASA). According to Embraer "this was the first time an aircraft program as complex as the E2 received approval from the three major worldwide certification authorities simultaneously. Embraer CEO Paulo Cesar said, "Our development teams have once again excelled in their creativity, dedication, and competence. Not only all development targets were met, but several important ones like fuel burn, performance, noise, and maintenance costs came in better than originally specified."

A Building as Product: LPPD in Construction

Although LPPD practices may sometimes go by different names, such as "lean design," "lean project management," or "production preparation process (3P)," the basic principles and practices are the same. The construction industry has been experimenting with the basic principles and practices derived from LPPD for a decade or more. We will share a short story about the construction of a healthcare facility in Akron, Ohio. We think that this story illustrates that, as in other industries, the decisions you make during the development of a new building impact the future of everyone who works in or visits it and that LPPD principles and practices can have a significant positive impact. We believe that this is another area where there is a great deal more to be done.

Akron Children's Hospital Kay Jewelers Pavilion   Akron Children's Hospital is among a growing number of hospitals that are leveraging new construction to make dramatic improvements in their operating effectiveness. By front-loading the design process with input from users and key stakeholders, developers are able to conduct experiments, learn, and make improvements not possible once the facility is built. This example is based on the report "Building a Lean Hospital" from Catalysis (formerly ThedaCare Center for Healthcare Value).[9]

The seven-story, 370,000-square-foot facility—which houses a neonatal intensive care unit, emergency department, labor and delivery unit for high-risk newborns, and outpatient surgery center—broke ground in May 2013 and welcomed patients two years later. Catalysis reports that Akron Children's applied lean project management through all stages of the massive development: from real estate acquisition to contracting through design and construction. And when it was all done, the project beat the scheduled opening date by two months, was *$20 million under budget* ($60 million under traditional build estimates), and achieved the hospital's quality objectives.

Akron utilized three distinct design phases and focused on engaging the most important stakeholders early in the process. According to Catalysis, these phases were:

1. **Concept design.** Teams reviewed current conditions (volumes, flows, bottlenecks, etc.), envisioned characteristics of an improved state, and worked on general layouts with small-scale models and paper dolls.

2. **Functional design.** Using a 60,000-square-foot area, teams worked in *full-size* cardboard layouts and tested them for the seven healthcare flows (patients, family, staff, medications, equipment, supplies, and information). Teams were encouraged to repeatedly experiment—not to accept their initial efforts, but continue to improve.

3. **Detail design.** Teams mocked up their work areas to finalize details. Mock-ups consisted of cardboard rooms in which staff placed photos for the locations of wall outlets, light switches, devices, paper towel dispensers, and the like, and moved actual beds, furniture, and medical equipment around to test the setups. At this stage, design decisions were evaluated based on wants-versus-needs criteria.

Teams had approximately one month between each of the three design periods to build and test these prototypes. Architects and engineers studied the prototypes and offered guidance and ensured conformity to building codes and structural requirements.

In addition to engaging the right people in the early stages of design, Akron managed the entire project with concepts from integrated project delivery, starting with the contract, and incorporated lean tools such as visual management, A3 problem solving, and integrated team meetings throughout the project. The building was a hit with employees and customers.

What We Learned About Product-Led Transformation

Each case we have described had a unique experience, Yet, as we reflect on the various LPPD transformation efforts, there are some common themes in effective change management across the organizations.

When Top-Down Meets Bottom-Up, Power Is Unleashed

We, and many others, have emphasized the dynamic role of Mulally as a transformative leader at Ford. But as we saw in "Ford's Historical Turnaround" following the Introduction, it was the hard work by the body and stamping engineering team as well as many others on the front lines at Ford that actually made things happen. It was the combination of CEO leadership and relentless execution throughout the organization that led to Ford's success. The change resonated throughout the organization. Mulally did not come in to deploy LPPD; however, new products were central to his strategy. His leadership created "One Ford" with a common purpose and changed the culture of Ford to surface and solve problems, providing a context which supported the LPPD transformation and unleashed the team's capability. Combining the right leadership, knowledge, and capability creates a powerful force for product-led change.

Start with the Highest Level of Leader
Support You Can Garner, but No Higher

CEOs like Mulally, who are both results driven and people centric and have a passion for product excellence, are few and far between. Our colleague, former Toyota veteran Glenn Uminger, helped many suppliers learn TPS while inside Toyota and continues to do so as a retiree. He thinks about approaching change in organizations based on an embedded triangle model (Figure 9.14).

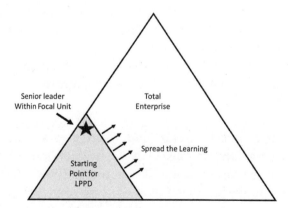

Figure 9.14   Embedded triangle model
(*Source: Glenn Uminger, former Toyota manager*)

Ideally, Uminger would from the start get strong commitment from the C-suite level—the whole triangle—but he realizes that often will not happen. So he identifies the highest level where he can get *real* commitment—a business unit, a department, a program (the focal triangle). That is where he focuses his attention. He aims for success and to get as much attention from higher-level leaders as possible. This forms the foundation for influencing up and sideways. The important thing is to enroll key leaders within that triangle by engaging them in an actual transformation that yields results important to the company. We saw this strategy in action at Solar Turbines. It worked there because the company had success with lean in manufacturing, there were key leaders within product development who were passionate about LPPD, and the results and the next steps were continually promoted.

Change Needs a Reason   Let's face it. Change is hard. And big change is really hard. Inertia is strong, and continuing with what we are doing is so much more comfortable. So we need a really good reason to change. The need was simple at Ford: change or go out of business. Toyota has been very good at creating a urgency even in the best of times when all seems to be going well, as when Eiji Toyoda stressed the need to prepare for the twenty-first century, which led to the Prius. Setting challenging goals for development teams can energize them, provided they also have effective leadership and the tools to succeed. The TechnipFMC case is an excellent example of this. Paulo Couto challenged his team with the Subsea 2.0 project, and the team responded with an industry-changing product. This was also apparent at Embraer, where increasingly aggressive goals were set for each aircraft program. The design teams were impassioned to beat the results of the last program even though the company as a whole was not in a financial crisis. Building your transformation around the challenge of creating breakthrough products can be an effective way to enroll your organization.

The Most Important Learning (and Change) Starts at the Gemba
None of the examples in this book focused on extensive classroom training for their transformation. While training was important in the Embraer story, it was just to get the basic knowledge that people needed to get started. We have seen far too many change management programs pull people out of their work in order to sit in large rooms and discuss

how they will change the way they work together when they get back to work. We have not seen these efforts go very far. All the cases we have described in this book started with real projects and with people learning by doing. Training was typically used only to teach something that would be immediately used. Coaches had enough experience to teach people at the gemba who were working on real programs with consequences, so abstract concepts quickly became real. We definitely agree with John Shook's philosophy of "acting your way to a new way of thinking" instead of "thinking your way to a new way of acting."

Rapid Learning Cycles Are Critical   Designing and building great products requires experimentation, learning, and improving. The members of the team work through rapid PDCA learning cycles as they converge on the best solution. These cycles are critical for learning in development. They are also required in product-led transformation. As we will discuss later in this chapter, an LPPD transformation can be seen as a design challenge, and many of the LPPD practices may be leveraged in a successful transformation. That includes rapid learning cycles. Just as in development, you will need to experiment, learn, and improve as you evolve your development system. None of the companies we worked with got it exactly right the first time. But they kept at it, they learned, and they improved. And equally as important, they made it their own. They adapted the principles and practices to fit their situation, their culture, by learning what was effective and what wasn't. They adapted what worked, rejected what did not, and added what was uniquely their own through PDCA learning cycles. It is a very necessary process.

Skeptics Are Best Converted by Positive Experiences and Can Become Your Strongest Advocates   In every case, we have worked with at least one skeptic who emerged as one of the strongest supporters. For example, at Embraer the K2 program manager did not believe LPPD could help until he personally experienced some benefits, and then he was on fire teaching LPPD principles without any push from the continuous improvement coach. The project Gemini manager at Schilling Robotics kept a secret schedule on his laptop because he did not believe the obeya management system would work. Engineers in particular seem to be trained for skepticism, or maybe it is a typical personality trait. They are technically oriented and used to the solutions being technical, like a better computer tool. All the soft stuff of lean management sounds like hocus-pocus to many of them. But they also have a tendency to learn quickly from experience. Show them it can work by putting them in a position to experience the benefits, and turn skeptics into converts. The most vocal skeptics often become the most vocal advocates.

Just Keep Showing Up "I have learned one thing," Woody Allen said. "Showing up is 80 percent of life. Sometimes it's easier to hide home in bed. I've done both." All the companies we have worked with have struggled at one point or another. Perhaps they got a good start, but then leadership was distracted by the next shiny object or just got busy with other things, and the lean transformation efforts languished. In some cases the companies were going great guns, and then there was a change from a supportive top leader to someone who did not believe in LPPD. In other cases, the company went through a financial downturn and cut LPPD resources. Or maybe an important experiment did not work out the way people thought it would, and pressure to demonstrate efficacy was building. In Chapter 5 we described "grit" and emotional resilience as important traits in successful leaders. These characteristics are equally important in successful transformations.

One trait the successful companies shared was persistence. They simply did not give up. Conditions changed, there was renewed support for their efforts, they reflected and relaunched the LPPD effort, and they were off and running again. Even at Toyota, reenergizing TPS and the Toyota Way never stops. Executive Vice President Shigeki Tomiyama announced an effort to apply the fundamentals of the TPS to new businesses like software development, ride-sharing, and robotics as Toyota moves into the future of mobility. Tomiyama explained, "If we want to make the most of Toyota's strength in creating new business models, it's going to require applying TPS. We want to show people inside and outside the company that TPS is still central to Toyota."[10]

LPPD Is a Long-Term Collaborative Learning Strategy, Not Discrete Projects or Events LPPD is not a kaizen event, nor is it a process reengineering initiative. There is a tendency to want to judge every activity, every program, by a cost-benefit analysis. Measurable benefits of product development improvement are rarely immediate and often not clear. Program teams are typically quick to appreciate the qualitative benefits of collaboration and the transparency of obeya management, and they are able to manage their programs more effectively using milestones. But the major benefits of LPPD will require several program cycles. Are products launching on time? Did we achieve our performance and cost targets? How did the product perform in the market? How profitable was the product? Another question: What would have happened without LPPD? Since most companies do not run experiments with "control" programs, we only have historical data from which to judge. We have reported many remarkable results experienced by companies in different industries by leveraging methods and tools from LPPD. But we believe that the most important results are far more difficult to quantify. Perhaps more important to long-term success than the cost-benefit of any one program are the answers to these questions: How much is the organization learning and growing? How much better will the next program be?

An Emerging Collaborative Model for Product-Led Transformation

When Jim first considered working with LEI after retiring from Ford, he was not crazy about the idea of consulting. He had not had the best experience with consultants in the past. Before Mulally joined Ford, the automaker had brought in several large consulting firms to help address difficulties being experienced by the company. It did not work out well. While some of their analysis may have been informative, the consultants were barely out of the door before Jim's team was telling him what a load of crap it was—all that time and money spent and nothing to show for it but a set of white binders.

As the Ford team talked about the experience, they concluded that while there may have been some good ideas in the consulting report, the consultants had not really enrolled the Ford team in the process. The Ford folks had not established any emotional or intellectual investment in the plan. And since they were the ones who had the most knowledge and experience—and would eventually have to execute the plan—this was a big problem.

Jim did decide to work with LEI in order to share what he had learned about LPPD, but he wanted to take a different approach than the one he had experienced. He and his LEI team had to create a model of support that fully engaged partner companies in the process. He felt it was critical that the companies develop sufficient emotional and intellectual equity in the plan to feel ownership, because in the end they were the ones that had to execute it. The LEI team and the companies had to become true partners in the work—learning on both sides: LEI learning about the clients' worlds and unique challenges; clients learning about LPPD methods and tools. In other words, the goal was to create a true learning partnership.

Developing a Learning Partnership Model

LEI was very receptive to this way of thinking. In fact, LEI had been successfully using a type of learning partner model with companies for many years. And Jim Womack (LEI founder) and John Shook (LEI CEO) completely agreed with Jim's views on coaching relationships. The challenge was to create something that could work in the unique and dynamic world of product and process development. The LEI team started by working with several companies that showed early interest in participating in this initiative to more deeply understand their challenges, concerns, and perspectives. The companies agreed to try some experiments.

Strategic A3 to Explore a Possible Partnership

A key to any successful partnership is that the partners commit to working together. It is a two-way street. The idea is not to put out an advertisement and accept whoever is willing to pay the fee. In fact, the LEI team does not accept every company who requests to join the group and have asked others to leave if they are not contributing sufficiently. Each relationship begins by walking and talking and spending time with a prospective partner company to better understand its specific situation and opportunities. This is an exploratory stage before either party makes any commitments. It involves learning at the gemba, talking to people across functions, looking at data or other artifacts, and working toward a common understanding of the problem to be solved. The LEI team shares the approach, provides information, and answers questions. The result of this visit is typically the assignment of a best-fit coach and the beginning of collaboration on a strategic A3 that develops and evolves over time. The important point is that both sides commit to working together to deliver on a plan they jointly own.

Organizational Transformation as a Design Problem

Once the foundation for a strong partnership was established, Jim wanted to establish a new, more effective methodology with which to approach the challenge of improving an organization's development capability. He determined that from an "LPPD perspective" an organizational transformation is essentially a design challenge. But instead of designing and building a new smartphone or airplane, your challenge is to design and create a better product and process development system. We believe this is a crucial insight into the nature of organizational transformation because, like a new product program, you are starting with so many unknowns in a complex and dynamic, human centric environment and your goal is to create something that delivers better value than any previous versions. Consequently you must start by deeply understanding your current situation, your customer, challenges and risks, and the key attributes of the new system you envision. From this "study" work, you carry out learning experiments to deepen your understanding, create and align around a plan, and execute to the plan, emphasizing transparency, cross-functional collaboration, and PDCA learning cycles.

Starting with a Challenge   As with the development of a new product, this work starts with a recognized performance gap, a problem to solve, or an opportunity to create a competitive advantage. This becomes your "why." But before you can begin to close the gap, you must first deeply understand the situation. This is the essence of the early assessment work and the beginning of the strategic A3 discussed earlier. It is also important to establish a steering team made up of senior leaders from the involved product or functional organizations. This group is responsible for leading the organization toward the challenge, providing guidance, breaking down barriers, and securing resources. The steering team is a great way to get senior leaders committed to the change. They have an active role, are expected to answer questions, and need to learn as their people learn.

Up-Front Study Period   After having a clearly defined challenge, any good product development process starts with understanding the customer and the current condition. We believe that the needs and context of the individual organization are much more important than strict compliance to any specific system. We do not believe in a one-size-fits-all, prescriptive approach to improving development capability. It is the responsibility of leadership and coaches to understand the needs and challenges of the organization before beginning implementation work. So dig in, take an unflinching look at the current situation right at the beginning. The LEI transformation model provides a useful set of questions as a starting point:

1. What problem are we trying to solve?
2. How will we understand and improve the work?
3. How will we develop our people?
4. How should we improve our management system?
5. What is our basic thinking, and what are our fundamental assumptions underlying this transformation?

There are a number of tools and methods to support this study period such as product development value-stream mapping workshops, performance data deep dives, diagonal slice interviews, skills and organizational health assessments, and many others. And don't stop inside your organization. The best chief engineers know their competitors and the context in which their product will operate. So read broadly, benchmark other organizations both inside and outside your industry, get a coach, join a learning group, go to conferences, whatever it takes to develop a thorough understanding of the situation.

The idea is to deeply understand your current situation as well as what is possible in order to develop potential countermeasures that will lead experiments and trials. Once the members of the on-site team have prioritized countermeasures (they are pushed to come up with more ideas than they can trial simultaneously), they create individual A3s for each of your proposed experiments and lay out plans to pilot them. As with early prototyping, you want these pilots to represent the minimum level of fidelity required to answer your questions quickly. You are trying to create rapid learning cycles to obtain knowledge that can be applied to your implementation phase. The outcome of this phase should be an implementation plan not totally dissimilar to a concept paper—a compelling vision, key system characteristics, objectives, an implementation plan, and responsible team members.

Concept Paper   Any time you embark on a new project with a cross-functional team, especially one of a transformational nature, there is significant opportunity for vague, even contradictory direction, misalignment, and serious misunderstanding that will eventually thwart even the best of intentions. Fortunately we have already discussed a countermeasure for this. As we discussed in Chapter 1, the concept paper is a powerful communication tool for transforming what you have learned during the study period into a compelling vision of your future state, identifying key attributes of the new system, including those that will be "fixed" (required) and "flexible" (teams may innovate), and creating a workable plan for delivering on those requirements. A concept paper can also serve as a crucial alignment and enrollment mechanism that is often missing from transformation efforts and provide a "true north" document that can be consulted and evolved by the group as required. The concept paper should both inform and inspire, and it should also provide the basis for execution.

A Few Key Tools for Execution   Utilize the obeya management system as an information and control center for deployment. As with a new product program the information from the concept paper should line the walls of the obeya. Key information from A3s, attribute glide paths, and schedule milestones are posted on the walls, an appropriate meeting cadence is set (at least weekly), and team members participate in stand-up reviews. The team identifies key milestones to provide a high-level schedule and to help determine normal from abnormal conditions. Teams also leverage design reviews to raise and resolve cross-functional "technical problems." The steering team should visit on some cadence to support the team with the goal of creating maximum transparency and collaboration (see Chapter 4).

Reflection and Learning   As the teams move through an evolution of this process, their pace of learning—learning gained from their own experiences and from learning partners in other companies—is remarkable. It is obviously important to capture this learning and apply it to their work both in real time and in the next evolution. If this becomes a one-time initiative, it is a failure. The point of this structured approach is to get started, not to finish. It should provide a solid foundation for a journey of continuous improvement that changes the way the whole organization thinks as an enterprise. This is how the organization develops a competitive advantage and achieves goals that in the past seemed impossible. Another advantage of this approach is that it gets people used to working in an LPPD system at the same time they are creating it.

Just Getting Started   Approaching an organizational transformation as a design problem is relatively new but has shown some encouraging results, many of which you have read about in this book. An LPPD approach provides a "fixed and flexible" framework for a product-led transformation that recognizes and addresses the people, process, and technological elements of a development system as well as their interdependencies. It strives for a deep understanding by learning and experimenting at the gemba and quickly testing countermeasures. It provides for a clearly articulated vision, plan, and relentless execution with transparency and collaboration. And it pursues perfection through learning and improving in PDCA cycles over time. However, as encouraging as early results may be, there is still far more to learn about the complex and messy business of organizational improvement, and that is our mission going forward.

And One More Thing

A Learning Community   Finally, another critical ingredient often missing from traditional consulting relationships is the opportunity to learn from other companies going through this same difficult work. Most companies keep their product development efforts under wraps. Conferences tend to focus on success stories, and companies rarely share shortcomings in such public forums. Consequently it can be very difficult to do much more than the highest-level learning—often not very helpful.

The LEI team decided to bring together a group of noncompeting companies, which all signed NDAs, with the goal of sharing their journey with one another on a regular cadence. In these events, companies share their latest experiments and share results, good or bad, and what they have learned from them. Events are held twice per year, and each company takes a turn hosting. These candid exchanges not only have led to greater learning on the part of the participants but have strengthened cross-company relationships—especially at the leadership level. And this in turn has enabled collaboration of companies in the time between learning events.

Political, Social, and Psychological Dimensions of Change

In many ways change is change and similar dynamics apply. As we mentioned at the beginning of this chapter there are many books written about managing the human side of change, and we did not want to reiterate all these models. But it is worth mentioning that managing a comprehensive enterprise transformation like LPPD requires an array of change management skills for managing the political, social, and psychological dimensions of change, and these three aspects are all intertwined. Let's briefly consider each.

The Organization as a Political System

Political systems focus on interests, power, and influence. We are used to thinking of politics in the government arena and the corporate arenas as bad. "Its all politics" means people are more concerned about manipulating the system for their personal interests than investing in what is good for the organization. The situation Mulally faced when he joined Ford was an example of bad politics that almost destroyed the company. But the way Mulally led Ford out of near bankruptcy was actually through politics. He effectively used the power of his formal authority as CEO as well as the influence of his leadership skills to work toward the mantra of "One Ford."

When we talk about getting commitment from the top of the organization we are talking politics. When we talk about getting commitment from the highest level possible and then growing influence outward from there we are talking politics. Without understanding and effectively leveraging politics major organizational change is unlikely.

The Organization as a Social System

It is difficult to discuss any type of serious change in an organization without discussing culture. "The people in this organization have been around for decades and are used to a culture of apathy." "There is no culture of disciplined execution here." "The culture is all about me, not we." These may be true statements, an accurate diagnosis of aspects of the culture, at least the most visible manifestations.

Edgar Schein, an organizational culture expert, asked us to look deeper.[11] To decipher culture you need to look below the surface of visible artifacts, and even beyond what people say, to basic underlying assumptions. The office layout is an artifact. An obeya is a different type of artifact. When people seem to focus on themselves it is a manifestation of something deeper in the culture. For example, an underlying belief at Ford before

Mulally was that admitting a problem means I become the problem and I get punished. A culture of fear manifested itself in many ways such as hiding problems and working to build walls against outside threats, which meant the outside departments that should be working collaboratively.

Mullaly's "working together management system" provided a vision of a new culture. But one thing tricky about culture is that new artifacts, new slogans, and even impassioned speeches do not penetrate to the basic beliefs of people. In other words the culture seems to change on the surface but does not change at the core. Actions definitely speak louder than words when it comes to culture. Part of that is the actions of key leaders, which need to be deliberate and very consistent with the beliefs and values of the new culture. But even more powerful are the actions of those the leader is trying to change. In other words, telling me that we will all be working together toward common goals is intriguing, showing me that you are serious about supporting teams working toward a higher goal is even more powerful, but engaging me in a situation where I am working as part of a team toward common goals is transformative.

The LPPD techniques and methods we have discussed throughout this book are designed to engage people in a collaborative effort with superordinate goals—becoming a great company by providing exceptional products and services to people. By making problems visible to cross-functional teams they have an opportunity to collaborate in overcoming the biggest obstacles to success. Repeated experience doing this is the only way we know to deeply change culture.

The Organization as a System of People with Individual Needs

We can't count high enough to recall the number of times we have been asked a question like: "But how will we answer the what's in it for me question?" The underlying cultural assumption is that people will only change if they see a concrete reward for working in the new way. They seem to take a "people are like Pavlov's dog" perspective. They need a juicy steak to motivate them to sit, or stand up, or fetch.

One simplistic view of motivation theory is that there are two types of motivation—extrinsic and intrinsic. Extrinsic answers the "whats in it for me" question by saying you will get this if you do that. The this could be money, or a promotion, or both. But it must be concrete and tangible.

We certainly have tendencies in this regard. And feeding our self-interest with goodies can be motivating—at least in the short term. But there is another side to humans—the intrinsic motivation that comes from working toward a calling and feeling ourselves make progress and grow. Self-efficacy is very important—our feeling we can make a difference and seeing the difference we make regularly, not occasionally.

There has been a lot of work on the subject of making jobs enriching so that doing the work has its own rewards.[12] In Daniel Pink's book *Drive*,[13] he summarizes research that shows that extrinsic motivation is useful for simple, repeatable work with clear results, like cutting wood in the same shape over and over, but intrinsic motivation is better for complex work that requires creativity and thought. Certainly we want development to be creative work, and the results of the work are separated by long periods of time from the actions.

Everything we have talked about in this book is designed to appeal to intrinsic motivation. Making work interesting, experiencing the joy of bonding with other people, and accomplishing something important for other people—making a difference. A simple method like obeya allows each participant to experience this regularly and get recognized for their work at least once a week. No more waiting for major milestone reviews months out where your contribution is insignificant in the myriad of issues quickly reviewed as green, yellow, or red.

IT IS A JOURNEY OF CREATING YOUR FUTURE

We cannot emphasize enough how profound the journey of LPPD can be for all involved.

After going through a few iterations of improvement, people say things like: "It was mind blowing." "It changed the way I look at what is possible in work and in my life." "I do not know how our organization could have survived without it." Our personal favorite: "Finally, coming to work was fun again."

Quite literally, product-process development is your future. You can do a lot of stuff and hope the future is bright, or you can take control and create your future. We recommend you do everything possible to take control.

Your Reflection

Creating a Vision

Managing change is complex and messy. We do not believe there is any standard sequence of steps to follow. Instead we used case examples of various organizations introducing LPPD to draw out some lessons learned—lessons that include:

- When top-down meets bottom-up, power is unleashed.
- Start with the highest level of leader support you can garner, but no higher.
- Change needs a reason.
- The most important learning (and change) starts at the gemba.
- Rapid learning cycles are critical.
- Skeptics are best converted by positive experiences and can become your strongest advocates.
- Just keep showing up.
- LPPD is a long-term collaborative learning strategy, not an initiative.
- There is a lot of benefit in a collaborative learning strategy across companies.
- Strategic A3s are a useful tool for planning and building consensus about your deployment strategy.
- There is growing evidence that a product-led organizational transformation can be viewed as a design problem using the principles and practices of LPPD.
- Value-stream mapping, obeya management systems, and "lean" design reviews are examples of powerful tools to get started in a way that is visible and delivers results.

How would you add to or revise these change management lessons learned based on your experience or what you got out of the cases described in this book?

Initial Planning

Rather than try to understand the current condition, in this case it seems more valuable to think about how you would get started. We suggest you reflect on the questions we use at LEI:

1. What problem are you trying to solve?

2. How will you understand and improve the work?

3. How will you develop people?

4. How should you improve your management system?

5. What is your basic thinking, and what are your fundamental assumptions underlying this transformation?

Taking Action

Get started. It's time to do something—to commit. Assemble a multifunctional team at the highest level possible and identify a program on which you can experiment with LPPD as we saw at Solar Turbine. This will allow you and your colleagues to see firsthand its benefits, solve real problems, learn some basic lean tools and techniques, and get excited *enough* to broaden LPPD. Consider all the change management lessons learned from this book and craft a rough plan for how to get started and what you will accomplish in the first year. It's your future we are talking about here. You have read about the great things other organizations are doing. Now it's your turn. *Get after it!*

Endnotes

Introduction

1. Joann Muller, "Musk Thinks Tesla Will School Toyota on Lean Manufacturing; Fixing Model 3 Launch Would Be a Start," *Forbes,* February 16, 2018.
2. Kim Clark and Takahiro Fujimoto, *Product Development Performance: Strategy, Organization, and Management in the World Auto Industry,* Cambridge, MA: Harvard Business School Press, 1991.

Ford's Historical Turnaround

1. Bryce G. Hoffman, *American Icon: Alan Mulally and the Fight to Save Ford Motor Company,* Crown Business, New York, 2012.
2. Bill Vlasic, "Choosing Its Own Path Ford Stayed Independent," *New York Times,* April 8, 2009.
3. Gerhard Geyer, *Ford Motor Company: The Greatest Corporate Turnaround in U.S. Business History,* Create Space Independent Publications, June 2011.
4. "The World's Most Admired Companies for 2017," *Fortune,* February 16, 2017.
5. Hoffman, *American Icon.*
6. *Ford Annual Reports.*
7. https://marketrealist.com/2016/03/fords-product-mix-reflected -gross-earnings-margins.
8. Gale Business Insights: Global.
9. http://shareholder.ford.com/stock-information/historical-stock -price.
10. https://malmc.org/documents/2014Presentations/LaborAffairs RoleinRestructuringFordMotorCo-MartinMulloy.pdf.
11. Michael Wayland, *Detroit News,* February 22, 2015.

12. Ibid.

13. http://www.fabricatingandmetalworking.com/2013/06/schuler
-incorporated-wins-2013-automotive-news-pace-award/.

Chapter 1

1. Leo Sun, "The 10 Biggest Tech Product Failures of the Past Decade,"
The Motley Fool, June 1, 2017.

2. Ibid.

3. Ibid.

4. Gail Sullivan, "Lululemon Still Suffering from Sheer Pants Debacle.
Founder in Warrior Pose," *Washington Post*, June 23, 2014.

5. Sam Becker, "15 Worst Product Failures and Flops from the Past 5
Years," *The Cheat Sheet*, December 7, 2017.

6. Jason Gilbert, "The 11 Biggest Tech Fails of 2012," *Huffington Post*,
December 27, 2012.

7. Becker, "15 Worst Product Failures and Flops from the Past 5 Years."

8. Steve Musal, "F-35 Program Remains Late and Over Budget, but
Doing Better: Pentagon," *Star-Telegram*, April 26, 2016, and Jared
Keller, "The Navy's New $13 Billion Aircraft Carrier Has Some
Serious Problems," *Task and Purpose*, Center for the National
Interest, February 18, 2018.

9. Clayton M. Christensen, Taddy Hall, Karen Dillon, and David
S. Duncan, "Know Your Customer's 'Jobs to Be Done,'" *Harvard
Business Review*, September 2016.

10. James. M. Morgan and Jeffrey K. Liker, *The Toyota Product
Development System,* Productivity Press, New York, 2006.

11. Bill Roberson, "Throttle Jockey: Harley Rolled Out New V-Twin
Engine, so We Asked Bill Davidson All About It," *The Manual*,
September 21, 2016.

12. Jim Morgan worked with Pericak at Ford and interviewed him for
this book.

13. Patrick Rall, "Ford Mustang Completes Shutout of Camaro, Wins
2015 Sales Title by $44k+," *Torque News*, January 5, 2016.

14. Chris Woodyard, "Ford Mustang vs. Chevrolet Camaro Leads the
Top 7 Auto Sales Battles," *USA Today*, January 4, 2018.

15. Kinsey Grant, "Ford Mustang Sales Are Plunging in America, but
Surprisingly Accelerating Hard Overseas," *The Street*, July 30, 2017.

16. Phoebe Wall Howard, "Top 10 Dream Cars," *Detroit Free Press*,
January 11, 2018.

17. Personal meetings with Richard Sheridan.
18. This is an interesting application of the set-based innovation principle (see Chapter 6 of *The Toyota Product Development System*).
19. Jeffrey K. Liker, *The Toyota Way: 14 Management Principles from the World's Greatest Manufacturer*, McGraw-Hill Education, New York, 2004.
20. Alan Ward, Jeffrey Liker, Durward Sobek, and John Cristiano, "The Second Toyota Paradox: How Delaying Decisions Can Make Better Cars Faster," *Sloan Management Review*, Spring 1995, pp. 43–61.
21. Mike Rother, *Toyota Kata*, McGraw-Hill, New York, 2009.
22. Eric Ries, *The Lean Startup*, Crown Business, New York, 2011.

Chapter 2

1. Herman Miller, hermanmiller.com.
2. Paul Adler, "Building Better Bureaucracies," *Academy of Management Perspectives*, 13, no. 4, 1999.

Chapter 3

1. Ford Motor Company, http://www.ford.com.
2. James M. Morgan and Jeffrey K. Liker, *The Toyota Product Development System*, Productivity Press, New York, 2006.
3. Personal interview with authors.
4. Personal interview in Toyota City.

Chapter 4

1. Ed Catmull, "How Pixar Fosters Collective Creativity," *Harvard Business Review*, September 2008.
2. Richard Sheridan, *Joy, Inc.*, Portfolio/Penguin, New York, 2013.
3. "The Toyota Way 2001," Toyota Motor Corp.
4. Keisuke Saka, *Karakuri: How to Make Mechanical Paper Models That Move*, St. Martin's Press, New York, 2010.
5. Much of this section first appeared in Jeffrey Liker and David Meier, *Toyota Talent*, McGraw-Hill Education, New York, 2007.
6. Alan M. Webber, "Why Can't We Get Anything Done," *Fast Company*, May 31, 2000.
7. Kelsey Gee, "Colleges That Prioritize Internships," *Wall Street Journal*, September 26, 2017.
8. Kiyoshi Suzaki, *The New Manufacturing Challenge*, Simon & Schuster, New York, 1987.

9. "Apple Awards Corning First Advanced Manufacturing Fund Investment," Apple Inc., May 12, 2017.
10. Brian McHugh, "Best Truck Brands for 2018," *U.S. News & World Report*, January 18, 2018.
11. Kelly Pleskot, "2018 Ford F-150 Earns IIHS Top Safety Pick Award," *Motor Trend*, October 20, 2017.
12. Brian Brantley, "Ford F-150 Is the 2018 Motor Trend Truck of the Year," *Motor Trend*, November 27, 2017.
13. Benjamin Zhang, "These Are the Best Cars, Trucks, and SUVs to Buy in 2018," *Business Insider*, February 23, 2018.

Chapter 5

1. Sam Sheridan, *A Fighter's Heart*, Grove Press, New York, 2008.
2. Grendel is a feared creature in *Beowulf*, an Old English poem believed to have been written around AD 1000.
3. Jocko Willink and Leif Babin, *Extreme Ownership*, St. Martin's Press, New York, 2015.
4. *Master and Commander*, directed by Peter Weir, Twentieth Century Fox, Miramax, Universal Pictures, and Samuel Goldwyn Films, 2003.
5. Joe Sutter and Jay Spencer, *747*, HarperCollins, New York, 2006.
6. Bryce G. Hoffman, *American Icon: Alan Mulally and the Fight to Save Ford Motor Company*, Crown Business, New York, 2012.
7. Ibid.
8. James. M. Morgan and Jeffrey K. Liker, *The Toyota Product Development System,* Productivity Press, New York, 2006.
9. Told to authors by John Shook, executive chairman of the Lean Enterprise Institute and former Toyota executive.
10. Clarence L. "Kelly" Johnson and Maggie Smith, *Kelly: More Than My Share of It All*, Smithsonian Institution Press, Washington, D.C., 1985.
11. Rafaella Sadun, Nicholas Bloom, and John Van Reenen, "Why Do We Undervalue Competent Management?," *Harvard Business Review*, October 2017.
12. Luis E. Romero, "The Ultimate Guide to Team Synergy," *Forbes*, December 1, 2015.
13. Alan M. Webber, "Why Can't We Get Anything Done," *Fast Company*, May 31, 2000.

Chapter 6

1. Peter Senge, *The Fifth Discipline*, Doubleday/Currency, New York, 1990.

2. Chris Argyris, *On Organizational Learning*, Blackwell Publishers, Malden, MA, 1992.

3. Ikujiro Nonaka, *The Knowledge-Creating Company*, Oxford University Press, New York, 1995.

4. Takahiro Fujimoto, *The Evolution of a Manufacturing System at Toyota*, Oxford University Press, New York, 1999.

5. Robert E. Cole, "Reflections on Learning in U.S. and Japanese Industry," in Jeffrey K. Liker, W. Mark Fruin, and Paul S. Adler, eds., *Remade in America: Transplanting and Transforming Japanese Production Systems*, Oxford University Press, New York, 1999, chap. 16.

6. Jeffrey Pfeffer and Robert Sutton, *The Knowing-Doing Gap*, Harvard Business School Press, Boston, 2000.

7. Jeffrey Pfeffer, "Why Can't We Get Anything Done?," *Fast Company*, May 31, 2000.

8. Ben Rich and Leo Janos, *Skunk Works*, Little, Brown, Boston, 1994.

9. Fred E. Weick, *Aircraft Propeller Design*, McGraw-Hill, New York, 1930.

10. Clyde E. Love, *Differential and Integral Calculus*, Macmillan, New York, 1947.

11. Clarence L. "Kelly" Johnson and Maggie Smith, *Kelly: More Than My Share of It All*, Smithsonian Institution Press, Washington, D.C., 1985.

12. Richard Sheridan, *Joy Inc.*, Portfolio/Penguin, New York, 2013.

13. This is explained in Jeffrey K. Liker and Gary L. Convis, *The Toyota Way to Lean Leadership*, McGraw-Hill, New York, 2011.

14. Mike Rother, *The Toyota Kata Practice Guide*, McGraw-Hill, New York, 2017.

15. James P. Womack, Daniel T. Jones, and Daniel Roos, *The Machine That Changed the World*, Rawson Associates, New York, 1990.

16. Chronicled in Jeffrey K. Liker and James K. Franz, "Transforming How Products Are Engineered at North American Auto Supplier (with Charlie Baker)," *The Toyota Way to Continuous Improvement*, McGraw-Hill, New York, 2011, chap. 11.

17. John Shook, *Managing to Learn*, Lean Enterprise Institute, Cambridge, MA, 2008.

18. Daniel Kahneman, *Thinking, Fast and Slow*, Farrar, Straus and Giroux, New York, 2013.
19. Mary Morgan, "Lean Thinking and Information Flow," *The Lean Post*, Lean Enterprise Institute, October 30, 2014.
20. Allen C. Ward and Durward K. Sobek III, *Lean Product and Process Development*, 2nd ed., Lean Enterprise Institute, Cambridge, MA, 2014.
21. A. Ward, J. K. Liker, D. Sobek, and J. Cristiano, "The Second Toyota Paradox: How Delaying Decisions Can Make Better Cars Faster," *Sloan Management Review*, Spring 1995.
22. James. M. Morgan and Jeffrey K. Liker, *The Toyota Product Development System*, Productivity Press, New York, 2006.
23. Nassim Taleb, *The Black Swan*, Random House, New York, 2007.
24. Kahneman, *Thinking, Fast and Slow*.

Chapter 7

1. James P. Womack and Daniel T. Jones, *Lean Thinking*, Simon & Schuster, New York, 1996.
2. Robert M. Pirsig, *Zen and the Art of Motorcycle Maintenance*, William Morrow and Company, New York, 1974.
3. Thomas J. Peters and Robert H. Waterman, *In Search of Excellence*, Warner Books, New York, 1982.
4. Richard Sennett, *The Craftsman*, Yale University Press, New Haven, CT, 2009.
5. Peters and Waterman, *In Search of Excellence*.
6. Donald A. Norman, *The Design of Everday Things*, Basic Books, New York, 1988.
7. Walter Isaacson, "How Steve Jobs' Love of Simplicity Fueled a Design Revolution," *Smithsonian*, September 2012.
8. Ibid.
9. "Jonathan Ive, Celebrating 25 Years of Design," Design Museum, 2007.
10. Jonathan Ive, *Innovation Excellence* post, which accompanied "Jonathon Ive, Celebrating 25 Years of Design."
11. Robert Waugh, "How Did a British Polytechnic Graduate Become the Design Genius Behind £200 Billion Apple?" *Daily Mail*, March 19, 2011.
12. Sennett, *The Craftsman*.

13. Matthew B. Crawford, *Shop Class as Soulcraft*, Penguin Press, New York, 2009.
14. katrinafurnitureproject.org.
15. Phoebe Wall Howard, "Consumer Reports: Toyota Tops for Reliability—and Cadillac Is Last," *Detroit Free Press*, October 19, 2017.
16. Thomas A. Stewart and Anand P. Raman, "Lesson's from Toyota's Long Drive," *Harvard Business Review*, July–August 2007.
17. "Consumer Reports' Reliability History: A Look Back at Our Survey Results over the Years," *Consumer Reports*, updated October 2017.
18. James. M. Morgan and Jeffrey K. Liker, *The Toyota Product Development System*, Productivity Press, New York, 2006.
19. Tatsuhiko Yoshimura, *Toyota Styled Mizenboushi Method—GD3 Preventative Measures—How to Prevent a Problem Before It Occurs*, JUSE Press Ltd., Tokyo, 2002.
20. Explanation of GD3 phases is based on Yoshimura, *Toyota Styled Mizenboushi Method*; a presentation by Yoshimura; discussions with Toyota; and James McLeish and William Haughey, "Introduction to Japanese Style Mizenboushi Methods for Preventing Problems Before They Occur," a white paper published by DfR Solutions.
21. Mark Dolsen, Eric Legary, and Murray Phillips, "Mizen Boushi in Mass Production," IEOM Society International, September 2016.
22. Jim Womack, "Jim Womack Drives the Toyota Mirai and Talks Lean and Green," *Planet Lean*, June 28, 2017.
23. Travis Hoium, "The 5 Best-Selling Electric Cars of 2017," The Motley Fool, Yahoo! Finance, December 30, 2017.
24. "COMEX Hyperbaric Experimental Centre," Comex SA, 2004.
25. "World Total Primary Energy Supply (TPES) by Fuel; 1973 and 2015 Fuel Shares of TPES," Key World Energy Statistics, International Energy Agency, September 2017.
26. Extracted from Tudor Pickering analyst report upgrading TechnipFMC stock, dated November 29, 2017.

Chapter 8

1. Jay Ramey, "Here's What a 'Teardown' Expert Has to Say About Tesla Model 3 Build Quality," *AutoWeek*, February 6, 2018.
2. Craig Trudell, "Musk's Spotty Predictions Muddle Tesla's Assurance on Cash," *Bloomberg News*, April 4, 2018.

3. Edward Niedermeyer, "Tesla Veterans Reveal Fires, Accidents, and Delays Inside Elon Musk's Company," *The Daily Beast*, June 5, 2018.
4. www.forbes.com/sites/joannmuller/2018/05/01/no-way-to-run-a-factory-teslas-hiring-binge-is-a-sign-of-trouble-not-progress/#58ebc6cf350d.
5. Jay Ramey, "Tesla Is Burning Through $8,000 a Minute as Model 3 Production Crawls Along, Report Says," *AutoWeek*, November 27, 2017.
6. https://www.cnbc.com/2018/04/13/tesla-sending-flawed-parts-from-suppliers-to-machine-shops-for-rework.html.
7. "Inside Tesla's Model 3 Factory," *Bloomberg Businessweek*, June 8, 2018.
8. Michael Porter, "What Is Strategy?," *Harvard Business Review*, November–December 1996.
9. Jeffrey K. Liker, *The Toyota Way: 14 Management Principles from the World's Greatest Manufacturer*, McGraw-Hill, New York, 2004.
10. For discussions of the development of the first Lexus and the first Prius, see Liker, *The Toyota Way*.
11. Csaba Csere, "It's All Your Fault: The DOT Renders Its Verdict on Toyota's Unintended-Acceleration Scare," *Car and Driver*, June 2011.
12. "Tesla in Fatal California Crash Was on Autopilot," BBC News, March 31, 2018, http://www.bbc.com/news/world-us-canada-43604440.
13. "Toyota to Halve Costs of Fuel Cell Cars' Core Components," *Nikkei Asian Review*, January 19, 2018.
14. Michael Martinez, "Electrification, Autonomy Won't Gain Widespread Adoption for Decades, CAR Study Says," *Automotive News*, February 21, 2018.
15. Jonathon Ramsey, "Toyota Creates World's Most Thermally Efficient 2.0 Liter Gas Engine," *Autoblog*, Yahoo! Finance, February 28, 2018.
16. Tesla (TSLA) Q4 2017 Results—Earnings Call Transcript, *Seeking Alpha*, February 7, 2018.
17. Joann Muller, "Musk Thinks Tesla Will School Toyota on Lean Manufacturing; Fixing Model 3 Launch Would Be a Start," *Forbes*, February 16, 2018.
18. Tesla (TSLA) Q4 2017 Results.
19. Ibid.

20. http://www.businessinsider.com/elon-musk-says-model-3 -production-using-to-many-robots-2018-4.
21. https://www.cbs.com/shows/cbs_this_morning/video/FMN4XL 5kYziyfOOgz_QcKARo7NWm0Gsf/tesla-ceo-elon-musk-offers -rare-look-inside-model-3-factory/.
22. https://www.bloomberg.com/news/articles/2018-02-04/toyota-s -way-changed-the-world-s-factories-now-comes-the-retool.
23. Toyota Environmental Challenge 2050, Toyota Motor Corporation.
24. Ibid.
25. Naomi Tajitsu, "Toyota Pursues Petrol but Sees Electric Potential in New Technology," Reuters, February 26, 2018.
26. Charles A. O Reilly III and Michael L. Tushman, "The Ambidextrous Organization," *Harvard Business Review*, April 2004.
27. Bansi Nagji and Geoff Tuff, "Managing Your Innovation Portfolio," *Harvard Business Review*, May 2012.
28. Tesla (TSLA) Q4 2017 Results.
29. Jeffrey Liker, "Tesla vs. TPS: Seeking the Soul in the New Machine," The Lean Post, Lean Enterprise Institute, March 2, 2018.
30. Hideshi Itazaki, *The Prius That Shook the World*, Nikkan Kogyo Shimbun, Ltd., Tokyo, 1999.
31. Many of the details of the development process of the first Prius come from Itazaki, *The Prius That Shook the World*.
32. Norihiko Shirouzu, "Toyota Scrambles to Ready Game-Changer EV Battery for Mass Market," Reuters, October 27, 2107.
33. http://www.businessinsider.com/toyota-prius-is-most-important -car-last-20-years-2017-12.
34. Jonathan M. Gitlin, "2017 Was the Best Year Ever for Electric Vehicle Sales in the US," ARS Technica, January 4, 2018.
35. Travis Hoium, "Will 2018 Be Toyota Motor Company's Best Year Yet?," *The Motley Fool*, January 23, 2018.
36. Sean McClain, "Toyota's Cure for Electric-Vehicle Range Anxiety: A Better Battery," *Wall Street Journal*, July 27, 2017.
37. Marty Anderson, "Tesla Cars Are Great—Their Ecosystem Strategy Not So Much," *Forbes*, January 27, 2018.
38. Craig Trudell, Yuki Hagiwara, and John Lippert, "Shell and Toyota Partner on California Refueling Stations," *Bloomberg*, February 2017.
39. Yuichico Kanematsu, "Toyota Seeks Fuel Cell Breakthrough with California Hydrogen Plant," *Nikkei Asian Review*, December 2, 2017.
40. "Japan Is at Odds with Elon Musk," *Bloomberg*, February 2017.

Chapter 9

1. John P. Kotter, *Leading Change*, Harvard Business School Press, Boston, 1996.
2. Rosabeth Moss Kanter, *The Change Masters: Innovation for Productivity in the American Corporation*, Simon & Schuster, New York, 1983.
3. Noel Tichy and Mary Anne Devanna, *The Transformational Leader*, Wiley, New York, 1986.
4. Robert E. Quinn, *Deep Change: Discovering the Leader Within*, Jossey-Bass, New York, 1996.
5. http://www.tssc.com.
6. This case was provided to us by our colleague and talented LPPD coach John Drogosz, who worked with Solar Turbines.
7. This case was provided to us by our colleague and talented LPPD coach John Drogosz, who worked with Embraer for five years.
8. James. M. Morgan and Jeffrey K. Liker, *The Toyota Product Development System*, Productivity Press, New York, 2006.
9. "Building a Lean Hospital," Catalysis, August 2016.
10. Kevin Buckland and Nao San, "Toyota's Way Changed the World's Factories. Now the Retool," *Bloomberg*, February 4, 2018.
11. Edgar Schein, *Organizational Culture and Leadership*, Wiley, 2016.
12. Frederick Herzberg, "One More Time: How Do You Motivate Employees?" *Harvard Business Review Classics*, July 14, 2008.
13. Daniel Pink, *Drive: The Surprising Truth About What Motivates Us*, Riverhead Books, 2001.

Index